YE SHALL RECEIVE POWER

E.G. WHITE

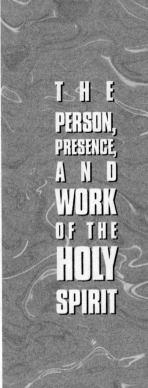

THE
PERSON,
PRESENCE,
A N D
WORK
OF THE
HOLY
SPIRIT

Devotional Readings From the Bible for 1996

YE SHALL RECEIVE POWER

E.G. WHITE

With Comments From the Writings of Ellen G. White

REVIEW AND HERALD® PUBLISHING ASSOCIATION
HAGERSTOWN, MD 21740

Bible texts credited to RSV are from the Revised Standard Version of the Bible, copyright © 1946, 1952, 1971, by the Division of Christian Education of the National Council of the Churches of Christ in the U.S.A. Used by permission.

Texts credited to RV are from the Revised Version, Oxford University Press, 1911.

This book was
Edited by Raymond H. Woolsey
Designed by Patricia S. Wegh
Cover design by Ron J. Pride
Typeset: 10/12 Janson

PRINTED IN U.S.A.

99 98 97 96 95   10 9 8 7 6 5 4 3 2 1

R&H Cataloging Service
White, Ellen Gould (Harmon) 1827-1915
    Ye shall receive power.

    1. Devotional calendars—Seventh-day Adventists.
2. Seventh-day Adventists—Prayer books—English.
I. Title.

                242.2

ISBN 0-8280-0972-4

ABOUT THE AUTHOR

Who was Ellen G. White, and why do millions consider her writings of special value and significance?

In brief, she was a woman of remarkable spiritual gifts who lived most of her life during the nineteenth century (1827-1915), yet through her writings and public ministry has made a revolutionary impact on millions of people around the world in the twentieth century.

During her lifetime she wrote more than 5,000 periodical articles and 26 books; but today, including compilations from her 55,000 pages of manuscript, more than 100 titles are available in English. From the information available, she may well be the most translated woman writer in the entire history of literature, and the most translated American author of either gender. Her writings cover a broad range of subjects, including education, health, prophecy, nutrition, cultural and ethno-linguistic issues, creationism, and the origin of life. Her life-changing masterpiece on successful Christian living, *Steps to Christ*, has been published in more than 135 languages.

Seventh-day Adventists believe that Mrs. White was more than a gifted writer; they believe she was appointed by God as a special messenger to draw the world's attention to the Holy Scriptures and help prepare people for Christ's second advent. From the time she was 17 years old until she died 70 years later, God gave her approximately 2,000 visions and dreams. The visions varied in length from less than a minute to nearly four hours. The knowledge and counsel received through these revelations she wrote out to be shared with others. Thus her special writings are accepted by Seventh-day Adventists as inspired, and their exceptional quality is recognized even by casual readers.

As stated in *Seventh-day Adventists Believe*, "the writings of Ellen White are not a substitute for Scripture. They cannot be placed on the same level. The Holy Scriptures stand alone, the unique standard by which her and all other writings must be judged and to which they must be subject" (p. 227). "Yet," as Ellen White herself noted, "the fact that God has revealed His will to men through His Word has not rendered needless the continued presence and guiding of the Holy Spirit. On the contrary, the Spirit was promised by our Saviour, to open the Word to His servants, to illuminate and apply its teachings" (*The Great Controversy*, p. VII).

This devotional book consists of choice selections from the writings of this remarkable woman who, meeting all the tests of a true prophet as set forth in the Holy Scriptures, helped found the Seventh-day Adventist Church.

CONTENTS

THE PROMISE OF THE SPIRIT

And I will pray the Father, and he shall give you another Comforter, that he may abide with you for ever. John 14:16.

When Christ gave His disciples the promise of the Spirit, He was nearing the close of His earthly ministry. He was standing in the shadow of the cross, with a full realization of the load of guilt that was to rest upon Him as the Sin Bearer. Before offering Himself as the sacrificial victim, He instructed His disciples regarding a most essential and complete gift which He was to bestow upon His followers—the gift that would bring within their reach the boundless resources of His grace.

"I will pray the Father," He said, "and he shall give you another Comforter, that he may abide with you for ever; even the Spirit of truth; whom the world cannot receive, because it seeth him not, neither knoweth him: but ye know him; for he dwelleth with you, and shall be in you" (John 14:16, 17). The Saviour was pointing forward to the time when the Holy Spirit should come to do a mighty work as His representative. The evil that had been accumulating for centuries was to be resisted by the divine power of the Holy Spirit. . . .

The promise of the Holy Spirit is not limited to any age or to any race. Christ declared that the divine influence of His Spirit was to be with His followers unto the end. From the day of Pentecost to the present time, the Comforter has been sent to all who have yielded themselves fully to the Lord and to His service. To all who have accepted Christ as a personal Saviour, the Holy Spirit has come as a counselor, sanctifier, guide, and witness. The more closely believers have walked with God, the more clearly and powerfully have they testified of their Redeemer's love and of His saving grace. The men and women who through long centuries of persecution and trial enjoyed a large measure of the presence of the Spirit in their lives have stood as signs and wonders in the world. Before angels and men they have revealed the transforming power of redeeming love.—*The Acts of the Apostles*, pp. 47-49.

THE COMFORTER

Howbeit when he, the Spirit of truth, is come, he will guide you into all truth: for he shall not speak of himself; but whatsoever he shall hear, that shall he speak: and he will shew you things to come. John 16:13.

How can we stand in the day of test if we do not understand the words of Christ? He said: "These things have I spoken unto you, being yet present with you. But the Comforter, which is the Holy Ghost, whom the Father will send in my name, he shall teach you all things, and bring all things to your remembrance, whatsoever I have said unto you" (John 14:25, 26). It is the Holy Spirit that is to bring to our remembrance the words of Christ. The theme Christ chose to dwell upon in His last discourse to His disciples was that of the office of the Holy Spirit. He opened before them a wide tract of truth. They were to receive His words by faith, and the Comforter, the Holy Spirit, was to bring all things to their remembrance.

The consolation given by Christ in this promise was found in the fact that the divine influence was to be with His followers to the end. But this promise is not accepted and believed by the people today, and therefore is not cherished by them, nor is its fulfillment seen in the experience of the church. The promise of the gift of the Spirit of God is left as a matter to be little considered by the church. It is not impressed upon the people, and the result is only that which might be expected—spiritual drought, spiritual darkness, spiritual declension and death. Minor matters occupy the mind and soul, but divine power which is necessary for the growth and prosperity of the church, which would, if possessed, bring all other blessings in its train, is lacking, although it is offered to us in infinite plentitude. Just as long as the church are satisfied with small things, they are disqualified to receive the great things of God. But why do we not hunger and thirst after the gift of the Holy Spirit, since it is the means whereby the heart may be kept pure? The Lord designs that divine power shall cooperate with human effort.

It is all-essential for the Christian to understand the meaning of the promise of the Holy Spirit just prior to the coming of our Lord Jesus the second time. Talk of it, pray for it, preach concerning it; for the Lord is more willing to give the Holy Spirit than parents are to give good gifts to their children.—*Review and Herald,* Nov. 15, 1892.

THE NATURE OF THE SPIRIT: A MYSTERY

Even the Spirit of truth; whom the world cannot receive, because it seeth him not, neither knoweth him: but ye know him; for he dwelleth with you, and shall be in you. John 14:17.

It is not essential for us to be able to define just what the Holy Spirit is. Christ tells us that the Spirit is the Comforter, "the Spirit of truth, which proceedeth from the Father." It is plainly declared regarding the Holy Spirit that, in His work of guiding men into all truth, "he shall not speak of himself" (John 15:26; 16:13).

The nature of the Holy Spirit is a mystery. Men cannot explain it, because the Lord has not revealed it to them. Men having fanciful views may bring together passages of Scripture and put a human construction on them, but the acceptance of these views will not strengthen the church. Regarding such mysteries, which are too deep for human understanding, silence is golden.

The office of the Holy Spirit is distinctly specified in the words of Christ: "When he is come, he will reprove the world of sin, and of righteousness, and of judgment" (John 16:8). It is the Holy Spirit that convicts of sin. If the sinner responds to the quickening influence of the Spirit, he will be brought to repentance and aroused to the importance of obeying the divine requirements.

To the repentant sinner, hungering and thirsting for righteousness, the Holy Spirit reveals the Lamb of God that taketh away the sin of the world. "He shall receive of mine, and shall shew it unto you," Christ said. "He shall teach you all things, and bring all things to your remembrance, whatsoever I have said unto you" (John 16:14; 14:26).

The Spirit is given as a regenerating agency, to make effectual the salvation wrought by the death of our Redeemer. The Spirit is constantly seeking to draw the attention of men to the great offering that was made on the cross of Calvary, to unfold to the world the love of God, and to open to the convicted soul the precious things of the Scriptures.—*The Acts of the Apostles*, pp. 51, 52.

THE SPIRIT: A WITNESS

The Spirit itself beareth witness with our spirit, that we are the children of God. Rom. 8:16.

If the Spirit beareth witness with our spirit that we are the children of God, what is the result? The believing soul comes into perfect submission to the will of God. The Majesty of heaven condescends to a holy, familiar intercourse with him who seeks God with the whole heart, and the child of God, through the abundant manifestation of His grace, is softened into a childlike dependence. You must commit your soul and body unto God with perfect trust in His power and willingness to bless you, helpless and unworthy as you are. "As many as received him, to them gave he power to become the sons of God, even to them that believe on his name" (John 1:12).

Do not become restlessly active, but zealous in faith, with one object, namely, to attract souls to Jesus Christ, the crucified Redeemer. It is not the logical sermon, the sermon to convince the intellect, that will do this work. The heart must be persuaded, and melted into tenderness. The will must be submitted to God's will, and the whole aspirations directed heavenward. You must feed upon the word of the living God. It must be brought into the practical life. It must take hold of and command the whole man. . . .

When Jesus is our abiding trust, our offering to God will be ourselves. Our dependence will be on the righteousness and intercession of Christ Jesus as our only hope. There is no confusion, no distrust, because by faith we see Jesus ordained of God for this very purpose, to make reconciliation for the sins of the world. He stands engaged by solemn covenant to mediate in behalf of all who come to God by Him, and to accomplish their salvation if they will only believe. The privilege is granted us to come boldly to the throne of grace, that we may obtain mercy, and find grace to help in every time of need.—*Manuscript Releases*, vol. 14, pp. 276, 277.

CHRIST'S REPRESENTATIVE

Nevertheless I tell you the truth; It is expedient for you that I go away: for if I go not away, the Comforter will not come unto you; but if I depart, I will send him unto you. John 16:7.

The Comforter is called "the Spirit of truth." His work is to define and maintain the truth. He first dwells in the heart as the Spirit of truth, and thus He becomes the Comforter. There is comfort and peace in the truth, but no real peace or comfort can be found in falsehood. It is through false theories and traditions that Satan gains his power over the mind. By directing men to false standards, he misshapes the character. Through the Scriptures the Holy Spirit speaks to the mind, and impresses truth upon the heart. Thus He exposes error, and expels it from the soul. It is by the Spirit of truth, working through the Word of God, that Christ subdues His chosen people to Himself.

In describing to His disciples the office work of the Holy Spirit, Jesus sought to inspire them with the joy and hope that inspired His own heart. He rejoiced because of the abundant help He had provided for His church. The Holy Spirit was the highest of all gifts that He could solicit from His Father for the exaltation of His people. The Spirit was to be given as a regenerating agent, and without this the sacrifice of Christ would have been of no avail. The power of evil had been strengthening for centuries, and the submission of men to this satanic captivity was amazing. Sin could be resisted and overcome only through the mighty agency of the third person of the Godhead, who would come with no modified energy, but in the fullness of divine power. It is the Spirit that makes effectual what has been wrought out by the world's Redeemer. It is by the Spirit that the heart is made pure. Through the Spirit the believer becomes a partaker of the divine nature. Christ has given His Spirit as a divine power to overcome all hereditary and cultivated tendencies to evil, and to impress His own character on His church.—*Review and Herald*, Nov. 19, 1908.

THE HEAVENLY DOVE

And John bare record, saying, I saw the Spirit descending from heaven like a dove, and it abode upon him. John 1:32.

Christ is our example in all things. In response to His prayer to His Father, heaven was opened, and the Spirit descended like a dove and abode upon Him. The Holy Spirit of God is to communicate with man, and to abide in the hearts of the obedient and faithful. Light and strength will come to those who earnestly seek it in order that they may have wisdom to resist Satan, and to overcome in times of temptation. We are to overcome even as Christ overcame.

Jesus opened His public mission with fervent prayer, and His example makes manifest the fact that prayer is necessary in order to lead a successful Christian life. He was constantly in communion with His Father, and His life presents to us a perfect pattern which we are to imitate. He appreciated the privilege of prayer, and His work showed the results of communion with God. Examining the record of His life, we find that upon all important occasions He retired to the grove, or to the solitude of the mountains, and offered earnest, persevering prayer to God. He frequently devoted the entire night to prayer just before He was called upon to work some mighty miracle. During these nightly seasons of prayer, after the labors of the day, He compassionately dismissed His disciples, that they might return to their homes for rest and sleep, while with strong crying and tears He poured forth earnest petitions to God in behalf of humanity.

Jesus was braced for duty and fortified for trial through the grace of God that came to Him in answer to prayer. We are dependent upon God for success in living the Christian life, and Christ's example opens before us the path by which we may come to a never-failing source of strength, from which we may draw grace and power to resist the enemy and to come off victorious. On the banks of Jordan Christ offered prayer as the representative of humanity, and the opening heaven and the voice of approval assures us that God accepts humanity through the merits of His Son.—*Signs of the Times*, July 24, 1893.

UNSEEN AS THE WIND

The wind blows where it wills, and you hear the sound of it, but you do not know whence it comes or whither it goes; so it is with every one who is born of the Spirit. John 3:8, RSV.

The wind is heard among the branches of the trees, rustling the leaves and flowers; yet it is invisible, and no man knows whence it comes or whither it goes. So with the work of the Holy Spirit upon the heart. [The Spirit] can no more be explained than can the movements of the wind. A person may not be able to tell the exact time or place, or to trace all the circumstances in the process of conversion; but this does not prove him to be unconverted.

By an agency as unseen as the wind, Christ is constantly working upon the heart. Little by little, perhaps unconsciously to the receiver, impressions are made that tend to draw the soul to Christ. These may be received through meditating upon Him, through reading the Scriptures, or through hearing the Word from the living preacher. Suddenly, as the Spirit comes with more direct appeal, the soul gladly surrenders itself to Jesus. By many this is called sudden conversion; but it is the result of long wooing by the Spirit of God—a patient, protracted process. While the wind is itself invisible, it produces effects that are seen and felt. So the work of the Spirit upon the soul will reveal itself in every act of Him who has felt its saving power. When the Spirit of God takes possession of the heart, He transforms the life. Sinful thoughts are put away, evil deeds are renounced; love, humility, and peace take the place of anger, envy, and strife. Joy takes the place of sadness, and the countenance reflects the light of heaven. No one sees the hand that lifts the burden, or beholds the light descend from the courts above. The blessing comes when by faith the soul surrenders itself to God. Then that power which no human eye can see creates a new being in the image of God.

It is impossible for finite minds to comprehend the work of redemption. Its mystery exceeds human knowledge; yet he who passes from death to life realizes that it is a divine reality. The beginning of redemption we may know here through a personal experience. Its results reach through the eternal ages.—*The Desire of Ages*, pp. 172, 173.

OIL IN YOUR VESSELS

They that were foolish took their lamps, and took no oil with them: but the wise took oil in their vessels with their lamps. Matt. 25:3, 4.

Many receive the truth readily, but they fail to assimilate truth, and its influence is not abiding. They are like the foolish virgins, who had no oil in their vessels with their lamps. Oil is a symbol of the Holy Spirit, which is brought into the soul through faith in Jesus Christ. Those who earnestly search the Scriptures with much prayer, who rely upon God with firm faith, who obey His commandments, will be among those who are represented as wise virgins. The teachings of the Word of God are not yea and nay, but yea and amen.

The requirement of the gospel is far-reaching. Says the apostle, "Whatsoever ye do in word or deed, do all in the name of the Lord Jesus, giving thanks to God and the Father by him" (Col. 3:17). "Whether therefore ye eat, or drink, or whatsoever ye do, do all to the glory of God" (1 Cor. 10:31). Practical piety will not be attained by giving the grand truths of the Bible a place in the outer courts of the heart. The religion of the Bible must be brought into the large and the little affairs of life. It must furnish the powerful motives and principles that will regulate the Christian's character and course of action. . . .

The oil so much needed by those who are represented as foolish virgins is not something to be put on the outside. They need to bring the truth into the sanctuary of the soul, that it may cleanse, refine, and sanctify. It is not theory that they need; it is the sacred teachings of the Bible, which are not uncertain, disconnected doctrines, but are living truths, that involve eternal interests that center in Christ. In Him is the complete system of divine truth. The salvation of the soul, through faith in Christ, is the ground and pillar of the truth.

Those who exercise true faith in Christ make it manifest by holiness of character, by obedience to the law of God. They realize that the truth as it is in Jesus reaches heaven, and compasses eternity. They understand that the Christian's character should represent the character of Christ, and be full of grace and truth. To them is imparted the oil of grace, which sustains a never-failing light. The Holy Spirit in the heart of the believer makes him complete in Christ.—*Review and Herald*, Sept. 17, 1895.

A Constant Flow of Oil

And I answered again, and said unto him, What be these two olive branches which through the two golden pipes empty the golden oil out of themselves? And he answered me and said, Knowest thou not what these be? And I said, No, my lord. Then said he, These are the two anointed ones, that stand by the Lord of the whole earth. Zech. 4:12-14.

The continual communication of the Holy Spirit to the church is represented by the prophet Zechariah under another figure, which contains a wonderful lesson of encouragement for us. The prophet says: "The angel that talked with me came again, and waked me, as a man that is wakened out of his sleep, and said unto me, What seest thou? And I said, I have looked, and behold a candlestick all of gold, with a bowl upon the top of it, and his seven lamps thereon, and seven pipes to the seven lamps, which are upon the top thereof: and two olive trees by it, one upon the right side of the bowl, and the other upon the left side thereof.

"So I answered and spake to the angel that talked with me, saying, What are these, my Lord? . . . Then he answered and spake unto me, saying, This is the word of the Lord unto Zerubbabel, saying, Not by might, nor by power, but by my Spirit, saith the Lord of hosts. . . . And I answered again, and said unto him, What be these two olive branches which through the two golden pipes empty the golden oil out of themselves? . . . Then said he, These are the two anointed ones, that stand by the Lord of the whole earth" (Zech. 4:1-14).

From the two olive trees, the golden oil was emptied through golden pipes into the bowl of the candlestick, and thence into the golden lamps that gave light to the sanctuary. So from the holy ones that stand in God's presence, His Spirit is imparted to human instrumentalities that are consecrated to His service. The mission of the two anointed ones is to communicate light and power to God's people. It is to receive blessing for us that they stand in God's presence. As the olive trees empty themselves into the golden pipes, so the heavenly messengers seek to communicate all that they receive from God. The whole heavenly treasure awaits our demand and reception; and as we receive the blessing, we in our turn are to impart it. Thus it is that the holy lamps are fed, and the church becomes a light-bearer in the world.—*Review and Herald*, Mar. 2, 1897.

LEAVEN IN OUR HEART

And again he said, Whereunto shall I liken the kingdom of God? It is like leaven, which a woman took and hid in three measures of meal, till the whole was leavened. Luke 13:20, 21.

This parable illustrates the penetrating and assimilating power of the gospel, which is to fashion the church after the divine similitude by working on the hearts of the individual members. As the leaven operates on the meal, so the Holy Spirit operates on the human heart, absorbing all its capabilities and powers, bringing soul, body, and spirit into conformity to Christ.

In the parable the woman placed the leaven in the meal. It was necessary to supply a want. By this God would teach us that, of himself, man does not possess the properties of salvation. He cannot transform himself by the exercise of his will. The truth must be received into the heart. Thus the divine leaven does its work. By its transforming, vitalizing power it produces a change in the heart. New thoughts, new feelings, new purposes are awakened. The mind is changed, the faculties are set to work. Man is not supplied with new faculties, but the faculties he has are sanctified. The conscience hitherto dead is aroused. But man cannot make this change himself. It can be made only by the Holy Spirit. All who would be saved, high or low, rich or poor, must submit to the working of this power.

This truth is presented in Christ's words to Nicodemus: "Verily, verily, I say unto thee, Except a man be born again, he cannot see the kingdom of God. . . . That which is born of the flesh is flesh; and that which is born of the Spirit is spirit. Marvel not that I said unto thee, Ye must be born again. The wind bloweth where it listeth, and thou hearest the sound thereof, but canst not tell whence it cometh, and whither it goeth: so is every one that is born of the Spirit" (John 3:3-8).

When our minds are controlled by the Spirit of God, we shall understand the lesson taught by the parable of the leaven. Those who open their hearts to receive the truth will realize that the Word of God is the great instrumentality in the transformation of character.—*Review and Herald*, July 25, 1899.

Living Water to Be Shared

But whosoever drinketh of the water that I shall give him shall never thirst; but the water that I shall give him shall be in him a well of water springing up into everlasting life. John 4:14.

As the plan of redemption begins and ends with a gift, so it is to be carried forward. The same spirit of sacrifice which purchased salvation for us will dwell in the hearts of all who become partakers of the heavenly gift. Says the apostle Peter: "As every man hath received the gift, even so minister the same one to another, as good stewards of the manifold grace of God" (1 Peter 4:10). Said Jesus to His disciples as He sent them forth, "Freely ye have received, freely give" (Matt. 10:8). In him who is fully in sympathy with Christ, there can be nothing selfish or exclusive. He who drinks of the living water will find that it is "in him a well of water springing up into everlasting life." The Spirit of Christ within him is like a spring welling up in the desert, flowing to refresh all, and making those who are ready to perish eager to drink of the water of life.

It was the same spirit of love and self-sacrifice which dwelt in Christ that impelled the apostle Paul to his manifold labors. "I am debtor," he says, "both to the Greeks, and to the barbarians; both to the wise, and to the unwise" (Rom. 1:14). "Unto me, who am less than the least of all saints, is this grace given, that I should preach among the Gentiles the unsearchable riches of Christ" (Eph. 3:8).

Our Lord designed that His church should reflect to the world the fullness and sufficiency that we find in Him. We are constantly receiving of God's bounty, and by imparting of the same we are to represent to the world the love and beneficence of Christ. While all heaven is astir, dispatching messengers to all parts of the earth to carry forward the work of redemption, the church of the living God are also to be co-laborers with Jesus Christ. We are members of His mystical body. He is the head, controlling all the members of the body. Jesus Himself, in His infinite mercy, is working on human hearts, effecting spiritual transformations so amazing that angels look on with astonishment and joy.—*Review and Herald*, Dec. 24, 1908.

LIFE-GIVING SAP

And it came to pass, that, while Apollos was at Corinth, Paul having passed through the upper coasts came to Ephesus: and finding certain disciples, he said unto them, Have ye received the Holy Ghost since ye believed? And they said unto him, We have not so much as heard whether there be any Holy Ghost. Acts 19:1, 2.

There are today many as ignorant of the Holy Spirit's work upon the heart as were those believers in Ephesus; yet no truth is more clearly taught in the Word of God. Prophets and apostles have dwelt upon this theme. Christ Himself calls our attention to the growth of the vegetable world as an illustration of the agency of His Spirit in sustaining spiritual life. The sap of the vine, ascending from the root, is diffused to the branches, sustaining growth and producing blossoms and fruit. So the life-giving power of the Holy Spirit, proceeding from the Saviour, pervades the soul, renews the motives and affections, and brings even the thoughts into obedience to the will of God, enabling the receiver to bear the precious fruit of holy deeds.

The Author of this spiritual life is unseen, and the exact method by which that life is imparted and sustained, it is beyond the power of human philosophy to explain. Yet the operations of the Spirit are always in harmony with the written Word. As in the natural, so in the spiritual world. The natural life is preserved moment by moment by divine power; yet it is not sustained by a direct miracle, but through the use of blessings placed within our reach. So the spiritual life is sustained by use of those means that Providence has supplied. If the follower of Christ would grow up "unto a perfect man, unto the measure of the stature of the fulness of Christ" (Eph. 4:13), he must eat of the bread of life and drink of the water of salvation. He must watch and pray and work, in all things giving heed to the instructions of God in His Word.—*The Acts of the Apostles*, pp. 284, 285.

THE "NEW WINE" OF THE KINGDOM

And no man putteth new wine into old bottles: else the new wine doth burst the bottles, and the wine is spilled, and the bottles will be marred: but new wine must be put into new bottles. Mark 2:22.

We need to be constantly filling the mind with Christ, and emptying it of selfishness and sin. When Christ came into the world, the leaders of the Jews were so permeated with Phariseeism that they could not receive His teachings. Jesus compared them to the shriveled wineskins which were not fit to receive the new wine from the vintage. He had to find new bottles into which to put the new wine of His kingdom. This was why He turned away from the Pharisees, and chose the lowly fishermen of Galilee.

Jesus was the greatest teacher the world ever knew, and He chose men whom He could educate, and who would take the words from His lips, and send them down along the line to our time. So, by His Spirit and His Word, He would educate you for His work. Just as surely as you empty your mind of vanity and frivolity, the vacuum will be supplied with that which God is waiting to give you—His Holy Spirit. Then out of the good treasure of the heart you will bring forth good things, rich gems of thought, and others will catch the words, and will begin to glorify God. Then you will not have the mind centered upon self. You will not be making a show of self; you will not be acting self; but your thoughts and affections will dwell upon Christ, and you will reflect upon others that which has shone upon you from the Sun of righteousness.

Christ has said: "If any man thirst, let him come unto me, and drink" (John 7:37). Have you exhausted the fountain? No; for it is inexhaustible. Just as soon as you feel your need, you may drink, and drink again. The fountain is always full. And when you have once drunk of that fountain, you will not be seeking to quench your thirst from the broken cisterns of this world; you will not be studying how you can find the most pleasure, amusement, fun, and frolic. No; because you have been drinking from the stream which makes glad the city of God. Then your joy will be full; for Christ will be in you, the hope of glory.— *Review and Herald*, Mar. 15, 1892.

A BURNING FIRE

Then I said, I will not make mention of him, nor speak any more in his name. But his word was in mine heart as a burning fire shut up in my bones, and I was weary with forbearing, and I could not stay. Jer. 20:9.

God will move upon men in humble positions to declare the message of present truth. Many such will be seen hastening hither and thither, constrained by the Spirit of God to give the light to those in darkness. The truth is as a fire in their bones, filling them with a burning desire to enlighten those who sit in darkness. Many, even among the educated, will proclaim the Word of the Lord. Children will be impelled by the Holy Spirit to go forth to declare the message of heaven. The Spirit will be poured out upon those who yield to His promptings. Casting off man's binding rules and cautious movements, they will join the army of the Lord.

In the future, men in the common walks of life will be impressed by the Spirit of the Lord to leave their ordinary employment and go forth to proclaim the last message of mercy. As rapidly as possible they are to be prepared for labor, that success may crown their efforts. They cooperate with heavenly agencies, for they are willing to spend and be spent in the service of the Master. No one is authorized to hinder these workers. They are to be bidden Godspeed as they go forth to fulfill the great commission. No taunting word is to be spoken of them as in the rough places of the earth they sow the gospel seed.

Life's best things—simplicity, honesty, truthfulness, purity, unsullied integrity—cannot be bought or sold; they are as free to the ignorant as to the educated, to the black man as to the white man, to the humble peasant as to the king upon his throne. Humble workers, who do not trust in their own strength, but who labor in simplicity, trusting always in God, will share in the joy of the Saviour. Their persevering prayers will bring souls to the cross. In cooperation with their self-sacrificing efforts Jesus will move upon hearts, working miracles in the conversion of souls. Men and women will be gathered into church fellowship. Meetinghouses will be built and schools established. The hearts of the workers will be filled with joy as they see the salvation of God.—*Testimonies*, vol. 7, pp. 26-28.

TONGUES OF FIRE

And there appeared unto them cloven tongues like as of fire, and it sat upon each of them. And they were all filled with the Holy Ghost, and began to speak with other tongues, as the Spirit gave them utterance. Acts 2:3, 4.

If you search the Scriptures with a meek and teachable spirit, your efforts will be richly rewarded. "The natural man receiveth not the things of the Spirit of God: for they are foolishness unto him: neither can he know them, because they are spiritually discerned" (1 Cor. 2:14). The Bible should be studied with prayer. We should pray as did David, "Open thou mine eyes, that I may behold wondrous things out of thy law" (Ps. 119:18). No man can have insight into the Word of God without the illumination of the Holy Spirit. If we will but come into the right position before God, His light will shine upon us in rich, clear rays.

This was the experience of the early disciples. The Scriptures declare that "when the day of Pentecost was fully come, they were all with one accord in one place. And suddenly there came a sound from heaven as a rushing mighty wind, and it filled all the house where they were sitting. And there appeared unto them cloven tongues like as of fire, and it sat upon each of them. And they were all filled with the Holy Ghost, and began to speak with other tongues, as the Spirit gave them utterance" (Acts 2:1-4). God is willing to give us a similar blessing, when we seek for it as earnestly.

The Lord did not lock the reservoir of heaven after pouring His Spirit upon the early disciples. We, also, may receive of the fullness of His blessing. Heaven is full of the treasures of His grace, and those who come to God in faith may claim all that He has promised. If we do not have His power, it is because of our spiritual lethargy, our indifference, our indolence. Let us come out of this formality and deadness.

There is a great work to be done for this time, and we do not half realize what the Lord is willing to do for His people. We talk about the first angel's message, and the second angel's message, and we think we have some understanding of the third angel's message; but we should not be satisfied with our present knowledge. Our petitions, mingled with faith and contrition, should go up to God, for an understanding of the mysteries that God would make known to His saints.—*Review and Herald*, June 4, 1889.

GIVER OF A NEW LIFE

Jesus answered, Verily, verily, I say unto thee, Except a man be born of water and of the Spirit, he cannot enter into the kingdom of God. John 3:5.

In order to serve God acceptably, we must be "born again." Our natural dispositions, which are in opposition to the Spirit of God, must be put away. We must be made new men and women in Christ Jesus. Our old, unrenewed lives must give place to a new life—a life full of love, of trust, of willing obedience. Think you that such a change is not necessary for entrance into the kingdom of God? Listen to the words of the Majesty of heaven: "Ye must be born again" (John 3:7). "Except ye be converted, and become as little children, ye shall not enter into the kingdom of heaven" (Matt. 18:3). Unless the change takes place, we cannot serve God aright. Our work will be defective; earthly plans will be brought in; strange fire, dishonoring to God, will be offered. Our lives will be unholy and unhappy, full of unrest and trouble.

The change of heart represented by the new birth can be brought about only by the effectual working of the Holy Spirit. He alone can cleanse us from all impurity. If He is allowed to mold and fashion our hearts, we shall be able to discern the character of the kingdom of God, and realize the necessity of the change which must be made before we can obtain entrance to this kingdom. Pride and self-love resist the Spirit of God; every natural inclination of the soul opposes the change from self-importance and pride to the meekness and lowliness of Christ. But if we would travel in the pathway to eternal life, we must not listen to the whispering of self. In humility and contrition we must beseech our heavenly Father, "Create in me a clean heart, O God; and renew a right spirit within me" (Ps. 51:10). As we receive divine light, and cooperate with the heavenly intelligences, we are "born again," freed from the defilement of sin by the power of Christ.

Christ came to our world because He saw that men had lost the image and nature of God. He saw that they had wandered far from the path of peace and purity, and that, if left to themselves, they would never find their way back. He came with a full and complete salvation, to change our stony hearts to hearts of flesh, to change our sinful natures into His similitude, that, by being partakers of the divine nature, we might be fitted for the heavenly courts.—*Youth's Instructor*, Sept. 9, 1897.

SHOWERS OF GRACE

Ask ye of the Lord rain in the time of the latter rain; so the Lord shall make bright clouds, and give them showers of rain, to every one grass in the field. Zech. 10:1.

In the East the former rain falls at the sowing time. It is necessary in order that the seed may germinate. Under the influence of the fertilizing showers, the tender shoot springs up. The latter rain, falling near the close of the season, ripens the grain, and prepares it for the sickle. The Lord employs these operations of nature to represent the work of the Holy Spirit. As the dew and the rain are given first to cause the seed to germinate, and then to ripen the harvest, so the Holy Spirit is given to carry forward, from one stage to another, the process of spiritual growth. The ripening of the grain represents the completion of the work of God's grace in the soul. By the power of the Holy Spirit the moral image of God is to be perfected in the character. We are to be wholly transformed into the likeness of Christ. . . .

Many have in a great measure failed to receive the former rain. They have not obtained all the benefits that God has thus provided for them. They expect that the lack will be supplied by the latter rain. When the richest abundance of grace shall be bestowed, they intend to open their hearts to receive it. They are making a terrible mistake. The work that God has begun in the human heart in giving His light and knowledge must be continually going forward. Every individual must realize his own necessity. The heart must be emptied of every defilement, and cleansed for the indwelling of the Spirit.

It was by the confession and forsaking of sin, by earnest prayer and consecration of themselves to God, that the early disciples prepared for the outpouring of the Holy Spirit on the day of Pentecost. The same work, only in greater degree, must be done now. Then the human agent had only to ask for the blessing, and wait for the Lord to perfect the work concerning him. It is God who began the work, and He will finish His work, making man complete in Jesus Christ. But there must be no neglect of the grace represented by the former rain. Only those who are living up to the light they have will receive greater light. Unless we are daily advancing in the exemplification of the active Christian virtues, we shall not recognize the manifestations of the Holy Spirit in the latter rain.—*Review and Herald*, Mar. 2, 1897.

THE SPIRIT HELPS US

Likewise the Spirit also helpeth our infirmities: for we know not what we should pray for as we ought: but the Spirit itself maketh intercession for us with groanings which cannot be uttered. Rom. 8:26.

The Holy Spirit indites all genuine prayer. I have learned to know that in all my intercessions the Spirit intercedes for me and for all saints; but His intercessions are according to the will of God, never contrary to His will. "The Spirit also helpeth our infirmities"; and the Spirit, being God, knoweth the mind of God; therefore in every prayer of ours for the sick, or for other needs, the will of God is to be regarded. "For what man knoweth the things of a man, save the spirit of man which is in him? even so the things of God knoweth no man, but the Spirit of God" (1 Cor. 2:11).

If we are taught of God, we shall pray in conformity to His revealed will, and in submission to His will which we know not. We are to make supplication according to the will of God, relying on the precious Word, and believing that Christ not only gave Himself for but to His disciples. The record declares, "He breathed on them, and saith unto them, Receive ye the Holy Ghost" (John 20:22).

Jesus is waiting to breathe upon all His disciples, and give them the inspiration of His sanctifying Spirit, and transfuse the vital influence from Himself to His people. He would have them understand that henceforth they cannot serve two masters. Their lives cannot be divided. Christ is to live in His human agents, and work through their faculties, and act through their capabilities. Their will must be submitted to His will, they must act with His Spirit that it may be no more they that live, but Christ that liveth in them. Jesus is seeking to impress upon them the thought that in giving His Holy Spirit He is giving to them the glory which the Father has given Him, that He and His people may be one in God. Our way and will must be in submission to God's will, knowing that it is holy, just, and good.—*Signs of the Times*, Oct. 3, 1892.

THE SPIRIT INTERCEDES FOR US

And he that searcheth the hearts knoweth what is the mind of the Spirit, because he maketh intercession for the saints according to the will of God. Rom. 8:27.

We have only one channel of approach to God. Our prayers can come to Him through one name only—that of the Lord Jesus our advocate. His Spirit must inspire our petitions. No strange fire was to be used in the censers that were waved before God in the sanctuary. So the Lord Himself must kindle in our hearts the burning desire, if our prayers are acceptable to Him. The Holy Spirit within must make intercessions for us, with groanings that cannot be uttered.

A deep sense of our need, and a great desire for the things for which we ask, must characterize our prayers, else they will not be heard. But we are not to become weary, and cease our petitions because the answer is not immediately received. "The kingdom of heaven suffereth violence, and the violent take it by force" (Matt. 11:12). The violence here meant is a holy earnestness, such as Jacob manifested. We need not try to work ourselves up into an intense feeling; but calmly, persistently, we are to press our petitions at the throne of grace. Our work is to humble our souls before God, confessing our sins, and in faith drawing nigh unto God. The Lord answered the prayer of Daniel, not that Daniel might glorify himself, but that the blessing might reflect glory to God. It is the design of God to reveal Himself in His providence and in His grace. The object of our prayers must be the glory of God, not the glorification of ourselves.

When we see ourselves weak, ignorant, and helpless, as we really are, we shall come before God as humble suppliants. It is ignorance of God and of Christ that makes any soul proud and self-righteous. The infallible indication that a man knows not God is found in the fact that he feels that in himself he is great or good. Pride of heart is always associated with ignorance of God. It is the light from God that discovers our darkness and destitution. When the divine glory was revealed to Daniel, he exclaimed, "My comeliness was turned in me into corruption, and I retained no strength" (Dan. 10:8).

The moment the humble seeker sees God as He is, that moment he will have the same view of himself that Daniel had. There will be no lifting up of the soul unto vanity, but a deep sense of the holiness of God and of the justice of His requirements.—*Review and Herald*, Feb. 9, 1897.

THE SPIRIT LEADS US TO BECOME GOD'S CHILDREN

For as many as are led by the Spirit of God, they are the sons of God. Rom. 8:14.

Christ took His stand among men as the Oracle of God. He spoke as one having authority, addressing Himself in strong terms to the people, and demanding implicit faith and obedience. We as a people have based our faith upon the principles set forth in His Word. We have pledged ourselves to bring heart and mind to obedience to the living Word, and to follow a "Thus saith the Lord."

All our present and future hopes depend upon our kinship with Christ and with God. The apostle Paul speaks strong words to confirm our faith in this respect. To those who are led by the Spirit of God, in whose hearts the grace of Christ is dwelling, he declares: "The Spirit itself beareth witness with our spirit, that we are the children of God: and if children, then heirs; heirs of God, and joint-heirs with Christ; if so be that we suffer with him, that we may be also glorified together" (Rom. 8:16, 17). "Ye have not received the spirit of bondage again to fear; but ye have received the Spirit of adoption, whereby we cry, Abba, Father" (verse 15).

We are called by Christ to come out from the world and to be separate. We are called to live holy lives, having our hearts continually drawn out to God, and having in our lives the Holy Spirit as an abiding presence. Every true believer in Christ will reveal that the grace of His love is in the heart. Where once there was estrangement from God, there will be revealed copartnership with Him; where once the carnal nature was manifest, there will be seen the attributes of the divine.

His people are to become workers of righteousness, constant seekers after God, constant workers of His will. This will make them complete in Christ. To angels and to men and to worlds unfallen they are to make it manifest that their lives are conforming to the will of God, that they are loyal adherents to the principles of His kingdom. The Holy Spirit, dwelling in their hearts by faith, will bring them into fellowship with Christ and with one another, and will yield in them the precious fruits of holiness.—*Review and Herald*, Aug. 19, 1909.

THE SPIRIT MOVES AMONG US

Hereby know we that we dwell in him, and he in us, because he hath given us of his Spirit. 1 John 4:13.

Though we cannot see the Spirit of God, we know that men who have been dead in trespasses and sins become convicted and converted under its operations. The thoughtless and wayward become serious. The hardened repent of their sins, and the faithless believe. The gambler, the drunkard, the licentious, become steady, sober, and pure. The rebellious and obstinate become meek and Christlike. When we see these changes in the character, we may be assured that the converting power of God has transformed the entire man. We saw not the Holy Spirit, but we saw the evidence of His work on the changed character of those who were hardened and obdurate sinners. As the wind moves in its force upon the lofty trees and brings them down, so the Holy Spirit can work upon human hearts, and no finite man can circumscribe the work of God.

The Spirit of God is manifested in different ways upon different men. One under the movings of this power will tremble before the Word of God. His convictions will be so deep that a hurricane and tumult of feeling seem to rage in his heart, and his whole being is prostrate under the convicting power of the truth. When the Lord speaks forgiveness to the repenting soul, he is full of ardor, full of love to God, full of earnestness and energy, and the life-giving Spirit which he has received cannot be repressed. Christ is in him, a well of water springing up into everlasting life. His feelings of love are as deep and ardent as was his distress and agony. His soul is like the fountain of the great deep broken up, and he pours forth his thanksgiving and praise, his gratitude and joy, until the heavenly harps are tuned to notes of rejoicing. He has a story to tell, but not in any precise, common, methodical way. He is a soul ransomed through the merits of Jesus Christ, and his whole being is thrilled with the realization of the salvation of God.—*Review and Herald*, May 5, 1896.

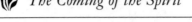

THE SPIRIT VISITS US

In whom ye also trusted, after that ye heard the word of truth, the gospel of your salvation: in whom also after that ye believed, ye were sealed with that holy Spirit of promise. Eph. 1:13.

Through the deep movings of the Spirit of God, I have had opened before me the character of the work of the visitation of the Spirit of God. I have had opened before me the danger in which souls would be placed who had been thus visited; for afterward, they would have to meet fiercer assaults of the enemy, who would press upon them his temptations to make of none effect the workings of the Spirit of God, and cause that the momentous truths presented and witnessed by the Holy Spirit should not purify and sanctify those who had received the light of heaven, and thus cause that Christ should not be glorified in them. The period of great spiritual light, if that light is not sacredly cherished and acted upon, will be turned into a time of corresponding spiritual darkness. The impression made by the Spirit of God, if men do not cherish the sacred impression, and occupy holy ground, will fade from the mind.

Those who would advance in spiritual knowledge must stand by the very fount of God, and drink again and again from the wells of salvation so graciously opened unto them. They must never leave the source of refreshment; but with hearts swelling with gratitude and love at the display of the goodness and compassion of God, they must be continually partakers of the living water. . . .

"But I said unto you, That ye also have seen me, and believe not" (John 6:36). This has been literally fulfilled in the cases of many; for the Lord gave them a deeper insight into truth, into His character of mercy and compassion and love; and yet after being thus enlightened, they have turned from Him in unbelief. They saw the deep movings of the Spirit of God; but when the insidious temptations of Satan came in, as they always will come after a season of revival, they did not resist unto blood, striving against sin; and those who might have stood on vantage ground, had they made a right use of the precious enlightenment that they had, were overcome by the enemy. They should have reflected the light that God gave to them upon the souls of others; they should have worked and acted in harmony with the sacred revealings of the Holy Spirit; and in not doing so, they suffered loss.—*Review and Herald*, Jan. 30, 1894.

THE SPIRIT SPEAKS TO US

But when the Comforter is come, whom I will send unto you from the Father, even the Spirit of truth, which proceedeth from the Father, he shall testify of me. John 15:26.

The Lord has condescended to give you an outpouring of His Holy Spirit. At the camp meetings, and in our various institutions, a great blessing has been showered upon you. You have been visited by the heavenly messengers of light and truth and power, and it should not be thought a strange thing that God should thus bless you. How does Christ subdue His chosen people to Himself? It is by the power of His Holy Spirit; for the Holy Spirit, through the Scriptures, speaks to the mind, and impresses truth upon the hearts of men.

Before His crucifixion, Christ promised that the Comforter should be sent to His disciples. He said: "It is expedient for you that I go away: for if I go not away, the Comforter will not come unto you; but if I depart, I will send him unto you. And when he is come, he will reprove the world of sin, and of righteousness, and of judgment" (John 16:7, 8). "When he, the Spirit of truth, is come, he will guide you into all truth: for he shall not speak of himself; but whatsoever he shall hear, that shall he speak: and he will shew you things to come. He shall glorify me: for he shall receive of mine, and shall shew it unto you" (verses 13, 14).

This promise of Christ has been made little enough of, and because of a dearth of the Spirit of God, the spirituality of the law and its eternal obligations have not been comprehended. Those who have professed to love Christ have not comprehended the relation which exists between them and God, and it is still but dimly outlined to their understanding. They but vaguely comprehend the amazing grace of God in giving His only begotten Son for the salvation of the world. They do not understand how far-reaching are the claims of the holy law, how intimately the precepts of the law are to be brought into practical life. They do not realize what a great privilege and necessity are prayer, repentance, and the doing of the words of Christ.

It is the office of the Holy Spirit to reveal to the mind the character of the consecration that God will accept. Through the agency of the Holy Spirit, the soul is enlightened, and the character is renewed, sanctified, and uplifted.—*Review and Herald*, Jan. 30, 1894.

THE SPIRIT ENLIGHTENS US

Then Jesus said unto them, Yet a little while is the light with you. Walk while ye have the light, lest darkness come upon you: for he that walketh in darkness knoweth not whither he goeth. John 12:35.

Jesus says, "Walk while ye have the light, lest darkness come upon you." Gather up every ray, pass not one by. Walk in the light. Practice every precept of truth presented to you. Live by every word that proceedeth out of the mouth of God, and you will then follow Jesus wherever He goeth. When the Lord presents evidence upon evidence and gives light upon light, why is it that souls hesitate to walk in the light? Why do men neglect to walk in light to a greater light?

The Lord does not refuse to give His Holy Spirit to them that ask Him. When conviction comes home to the conscience, why not listen, and heed the voice of the Spirit of God? By every hesitation and delay, we place ourselves where it is more and more difficult for us to accept the light of heaven, and at last it seems impossible to be impressed by admonitions and warnings. The sinner says, more and more easily, "Go thy way for this time; when I have a convenient season, I will call for thee" (Acts 24:25).

I know the danger of those who refuse to walk in the light as God gives it. They bring upon themselves the terrible crisis of being left to follow their own ways, to do after their own judgment. The conscience becomes less and less impressible. The voice of God seems to become more and more distant, and the wrongdoer is left to his own infatuation. In stubbornness he resists every appeal, despises all counsel and advice, and turns from every provision made for his salvation, and the voice of the messenger of God makes no impression upon his mind. The Spirit of God no longer exerts a restraining power over him, and the sentence is passed, "[He] is joined to idols, let him alone" (Hosea 4:17). Oh, how dark, how sullen, how obstinate, is his independence! It seems that the insensibility of death is upon his heart. This is the process through which the soul passes that rejects the working of the Holy Spirit.— *Review and Herald*, June 29, 1897.

THE SPIRIT CAN BE GRIEVED

And grieve not the holy Spirit of God, whereby ye are sealed unto the day of redemption. Eph. 4:30.

I would that all my brethren and sisters would remember that it is a serious thing to grieve the Holy Spirit; and He is grieved when the human agent seeks to work himself, and refuses to enter the service of the Lord because the cross is too heavy or the self-denial too great. The Holy Spirit seeks to abide in each soul. If He is welcomed as an honored guest, those who receive Him will be made complete in Christ; the good work begun will be finished; and holy thoughts, heavenly affections, and Christlike actions will take the place of impure thoughts, perverse sentiments, and rebellious acts.

The Holy Spirit is a divine teacher. If we will heed His lessons, we shall become wise unto salvation. But we need to guard well our hearts, for too often we forget the heavenly instruction we have received, and seek to act out the natural inclinations of our unconsecrated minds. Each one must fight his own battle against self. Heed the teachings of the Holy Spirit. If this is done, they will be repeated again and again until the impressions are as it were lead on the rock forever.

God has bought us, and He claims a throne in each heart. Our minds and bodies must be subordinated to Him; and the natural habits and appetites must be made subservient to the higher wants of the soul. But we can place no dependence upon ourselves in this work. We cannot with safety follow our own guidance. The Holy Spirit must renew and sanctify us. And in God's service there must be no halfway work. Those who profess to serve God and yet indulge their natural impulses will mislead other souls. Said Christ, "Thou shalt love the Lord thy God with all thy heart, and with all thy soul, and with all thy mind" (Matt. 22:37). "This do, and thou shalt live" (Luke 10:28).—*Manuscript Releases*, vol. 18, pp. 47, 48.

THE SPIRIT MAY DEPART

Of how much sorer punishment, suppose ye, shall he be thought worthy, who hath trodden under foot the Son of God, and hath counted the blood of the covenant, wherewith he was sanctified, an unholy thing, and hath done despite unto the Spirit of grace? Heb. 10:29.

Those who resist the Spirit of God, and provoke Him to depart, know not to what lengths Satan will lead them. When the Holy Spirit departs from the man, he will imperceptibly do those things which once he viewed, in a correct light, to be decided sin. Unless he heeds the warnings, he will wrap himself in a deception that, as in the case of Judas, will cause him to become a traitor and blind. He will follow step by step in the footsteps of Satan. Who, then, can strive with him to any purpose? Will the ministers plead with him and for him? All their words are as idle tales. Such souls have Satan as their chosen companion, to misconstrue the word spoken, and bring it to their understanding in a perverted light.

When the Spirit of God is grieved away, every appeal made through the Lord's servants is meaningless to them. They will misconstrue every word. They will laugh at and turn into ridicule the most solemn words of Scripture warnings, which, if they were not bewitched by satanic agencies, would make them tremble. Every appeal made to them is in vain. They will not hear reproof or counsel. They despise all the entreaties of the Spirit, and disobey the commandments of God which they once vindicated and exalted. Well may the words of the apostle come home to such souls, "Who hath bewitched you, that ye should not obey the truth?" (Gal. 3:1). They follow the counsel of their own heart until truth is no more truth to them. Barabbas is chosen, Christ is rejected.

It is essential to live by every word of God, else our old nature will constantly reassert itself. It is the Holy Spirit, the redeeming grace of truth in the soul, that makes the followers of Christ one with one another, and one with God. He alone can expel enmity, envy, and unbelief. He sanctifies the entire affections. He restores the willing, desirous soul from the power of Satan unto God. This is the power of grace. It is a divine power. Under its influence there is a change from the old habits, customs, and practices which, when cherished, separate the soul from God; and the work of sanctification goes on in the soul, constantly progressing and enlarging.—*Review and Herald*, Oct. 12, 1897.

THE SIN AGAINST THE SPIRIT

Wherefore I say unto you, All manner of sin and blasphemy shall be for-given unto men: but the blasphemy against the Holy Ghost shall not be for-given unto men. Matt. 12:31.

I will address these lines to those who have had light, those who have had privileges, those who have had warnings and entreaties, who have made no determined effort to yield themselves in full surren-der to God. I would warn you to fear lest you sin against the Holy Ghost, and be left to your own course, sunk in moral lethargy, and never obtain forgiveness. Why allow yourselves to be longer educated in the school of Satan, and pursue a course of action that will make repentance and reformation impossible? Why resist the overtures of mercy? Why say, "Let me alone," until God shall be compelled to give you your de-sire, since you will have it so?

Those who resist the Spirit of God think that they will repent at some future day, when they get ready to take a decided step toward re-formation; but repentance will then be beyond their power. According to the light and privileges given will be the darkness of those who refuse to walk in the light while they have the light.

No one need look upon the sin against the Holy Ghost as something mysterious and indefinable. The sin against the Holy Ghost is the sin of persistent refusal to respond to the invitation to repent. If you refuse to believe in Jesus Christ as your personal Saviour, you love darkness rather than light, you love the atmosphere that surrounded the first great apostate. You choose this atmosphere rather than the atmosphere that surrounds the Father and the Son, and God allows you to have your choice. But let no soul be discouraged by this presentation of the mat-ter. Let no one who is striving to do the will of the Master be cast down. Hope thou in God. The Lord Jesus has made it manifest that He re-gards you at an infinite estimation. He left His royal throne, He left His royal courts, He clothed His divinity with humanity, and died a shame-ful death upon the cross of Calvary, that you might be saved.—*Review and Herald*, June 29, 1897.

WILLFULLY REJECTING THE SPIRIT

And whosoever speaketh a word against the Son of man, it shall be forgiven him: but whosoever speaketh against the Holy Ghost, it shall not be forgiven him, neither in this world, neither in the world to come. Matt. 12:32.

It was just before this that Jesus had a second time performed the miracle of healing a man possessed, blind and dumb, and the Pharisees had reiterated the charge, "He casteth out devils through the prince of the devils" (Matt. 9:34). Christ told them plainly that in attributing the work of the Holy Spirit to Satan, they were cutting themselves off from the fountain of blessing. Those who had spoken against Jesus Himself, not discerning His divine character, might receive forgiveness; for through the Holy Spirit they might be brought to see their error and repent. Whatever the sin, if the soul repents and believes, the guilt is washed away in the blood of Christ; but he who rejects the work of the Holy Spirit is placing himself where repentance and faith cannot come to him.

It is by the Spirit that God works upon the heart; when men willfully reject the Spirit, and declare Him to be from Satan, they cut off the channel by which God can communicate with them. When the Spirit is finally rejected, there is no more that God can do for the soul. . . .

It is not God that blinds the eyes of men or hardens their hearts. He sends them light to correct their errors, and to lead them in safe paths; it is by the rejection of this light that the eyes are blinded and the heart hardened. Often the process is gradual, and almost imperceptible. Light comes to the soul through God's Word, through His servants, or by the direct agency of His Spirit; but when one ray of light is disregarded, there is a partial benumbing of the spiritual perceptions, and the second revealing of light is less clearly discerned. So the darkness increases, until it is night in the soul. Thus it had been with these Jewish leaders. They were convinced that a divine power attended Christ, but in order to resist the truth, they attributed the work of the Holy Spirit to Satan. In doing this they deliberately chose deception; they yielded themselves to Satan, and henceforth they were controlled by his power.—*The Desire of Ages*, pp. 321-323.

Now Is the Time for Repentance

We then, as workers together with him, beseech you also that ye receive not the grace of God in vain. (For he saith, I have heard thee in a time accepted, and in the day of salvation have I succoured thee: behold, now is the accepted time; behold, now is the day of salvation.) 2 Cor. 6:1, 2.

Brother P, you ask if you have committed the sin which has no forgiveness in this life or in the life to come. I answer: I do not see the slightest evidence that this is the case. What constitutes the sin against the Holy Ghost? It is willfully attributing to Satan the work of the Holy Spirit. For example, suppose that one is a witness of the special work of the Spirit of God. He has convincing evidence that the work is in harmony with the Scriptures, and the Spirit witnesses with his spirit that it is of God. Afterward, however, he falls under temptation; pride, self-sufficiency, or some other evil trait controls him; and rejecting all the evidence of its divine character, he declares that that which he had before acknowledged to be the power of the Holy Spirit was the power of Satan.

It is through the medium of His Spirit that God works upon the human heart; and when men willfully reject the Spirit and declare it to be from Satan, they cut off the channel by which God can communicate with them. By denying the evidence which God has been pleased to give them, they shut out the light which had been shining in their hearts, and as the result they are left in darkness. Thus the words of Christ are verified: "If therefore the light that is in thee be darkness, how great is that darkness!" (Matt. 6:23). For a time, persons who have committed this sin may appear to be children of God; but when circumstances arise to develop character and show what manner of spirit they are of, it will be found that they are on the enemy's ground, standing under his black banner.

My brother, the Spirit invites you today. Come with your whole heart to Jesus. Repent of your sins, make confession to God, forsake all iniquity, and you may appropriate to yourself all His promises. "Look unto me, and be ye saved" (Isa. 45:22) is His gracious invitation.—*Testimonies*, vol. 5, p. 634.

THE SPIRIT PATIENTLY WAITS

Behold, I stand at the door, and knock: if any man hear my voice, and open the door, I will come in to him, and will sup with him, and he with me. Rev. 3:20.

All, from the oldest to the youngest, need to be taught of God. We may be taught by man to see the truth clearly, but God alone can teach the heart to receive the truth savingly, which means to receive the words of eternal life into good and honest hearts. The Lord is waiting patiently to instruct every willing soul who will be taught. The fault is not with the willing Instructor, the greatest Teacher the world ever knew, but it is with the learner who holds to his own impressions and ideas, and will not give up his human theories and come in humility to be taught. He will not allow his conscience and his heart to be educated, disciplined, and trained—worked as the husbandman works the earth, and as the architect constructs the building. "Ye are God's husbandry, ye are God's building" (1 Cor. 3:9).

Everyone needs to be worked, molded, and fashioned after the divine similitude. Christ tells you, my dear friends, young and old, the everlasting truth, "Except ye eat the flesh of the Son of man, and drink his blood, ye have no life in you. [If you do not take Christ's word as the man of your counsel, you will not reveal His wisdom or His spiritual life.] Whoso eateth my flesh, and drinketh my blood, hath eternal life. . . . For my flesh is meat indeed, and my blood is drink indeed. He that eateth my flesh, and drinketh my blood, dwelleth in me, and I in him" (John 6:53-56). Said Christ, "It is the spirit that quickeneth; the flesh profiteth nothing: the words that I speak unto you, they are spirit, and they are life" (verse 63).

Those who search the Scriptures, and most earnestly seek to understand them, will reveal the sanctification of the Spirit through the belief of the truth, for they take into their very heart the truth, and have that faith that works by love and purifies the soul. All their spiritual sinew and muscle are nourished by the Bread of Life which they eat.—*Manuscript Releases*, vol. 8, pp. 162, 163.

THE SPIRIT IS EVER WAITING

But the Comforter, which is the Holy Ghost, whom the Father will send in my name, he shall teach you all things, and bring all things to your remembrance, whatsoever I have said unto you. John 14:26.

The Holy Spirit is ever waiting to do His office work upon the human heart. Those who desire to learn can place themselves in close connection with God, and the promise that the Comforter shall teach them all things, and bring all things to their remembrance, whatever Christ had said to His disciples when He was upon the earth will be fulfilled. But if we disconnect from God, we can be no longer students in the school of Christ. Then we shall feel no special burden for the souls for whom Christ has died.

It was most difficult for the disciples of Christ to keep His lessons distinct from the traditions and maxims of the rabbis, the scribes, and pharisees. The teachings which the disciples had been educated to respect as the voice of God held a power over their minds and molded their sentiments. The disciples could not be a living and shining light until they were freed from the influence of the sayings and commandments of men, and the words of Christ were deeply impressed upon their minds and hearts as distinct truths, as precious jewels, to be appreciated, loved, and acted upon.

Jesus came to the world, lived a holy life, and died, to leave to the church His legacy in the valuable treasures He entrusted to them. He made His disciples the depositaries of most precious doctrines, to be placed in the hands of His church unmixed with the errors and traditions of men. He revealed Himself to them as the light of the world, the Sun of righteousness. And He promised them the Comforter, the Holy Spirit, whom the Father was to send in His name.—*Signs of the Times*, Nov. 16, 1891.

"I will not leave you comfortless; I will come to you" (John 14:18). The divine Spirit that the world's Redeemer promised to send is the presence and power of God. He will not leave His people in the world destitute of His grace, to be buffeted by the enemy of God, and harassed by the oppression of the world; but He will come to them.—*Ibid.*, Nov. 23, 1891.

BORN AGAIN

Jesus answered and said unto him, Verily, verily, I say unto thee, Except a man be born again, he cannot see the kingdom of God. John 3:3.

Thy kingdom come. Thy will be done in earth, as it is in heaven" (Matt. 6:10). The whole life of Christ upon earth was lived for the purpose of manifesting the will of God on earth as it is in heaven. Said Christ, "Except a man be born again, he cannot see the kingdom of God. . . . Except a man be born of water and of the Spirit, he cannot enter into the kingdom of God. That which is born of the flesh is flesh; and that which is born of the Spirit is spirit" (John 3:3-6).

Christ does not acknowledge any caste, color, or grade as necessary to become a subject of His kingdom. Admittance to His kingdom does not depend upon wealth or a superior heredity. But those who are born of the Spirit are the subjects of His kingdom. Spiritual character is that which will be recognized by Christ. His kingdom is not of this world. His subjects are those who are partakers of the divine nature, having escaped the corruption that is in the world through lust. And this grace is given them of God.

Christ does not find His subjects fitted for His kingdom, but He qualifies them by His divine power. Those who have been dead in trespasses and sins are quickened to spiritual life. The faculties which God has given them for holy purposes are refined, purified, and exalted, and they are led to form characters after the divine similitude. Though they have misapplied their talents and made them serve sin; though Christ has been to them a stone of stumbling and a rock of offense, because they stumbled at the Word, being disobedient, yet by the drawing of His love they are led at last into the path of duty. Christ said, "I am come that they might have life, and that they might have it more abundantly" (John 10:10).

Christ draws them to Himself by an unseen power. He is the light of life, and He imbues them with His own Spirit. As they are drawn into the spiritual atmosphere, they see that they have been made the sport of Satan's temptations, and that they have been under his dominion; but they break the yoke of fleshly lusts, and refuse to be the servants of sin. Satan strives to hold them. He assails them with various temptations; but the Spirit works to renew them after the image of Him who created them.—*Review and Herald,* Mar. 26, 1895.

CHOSEN TO BE SAVED

According as he hath chosen us in him before the foundation of the world, that we should be holy and without blame before him in love. Eph. 1:4.

We are to believe that we are chosen of God to be saved by the exercise of faith, through the grace of Christ and the work of the Holy Spirit; and we are to praise and glorify God for such a marvelous manifestation of His unmerited favor. It is the love of God that draws the soul to Christ to be graciously received and presented to His Father. Through the work of the Holy Spirit, the divine relationship between God and the sinner is renewed. Our heavenly Father says, "I will be to them a God, and they shall be to Me a people. I will exercise forgiving love toward them, and bestow upon them My joy. They shall be to Me a peculiar treasure; for this people whom I have formed for Myself shall show forth My praise" (see Jer. 30:22; 31:1, 33; Ex. 19:5).

Christ is calling souls to come unto Him, and it is for our present and eternal interest to hear and respond to the call. Jesus says, "Ye have not chosen me, but I have chosen you" (John 15:16). Then let all who would be called children of God respond to the invitation of Christ, and place themselves where the light of heaven will shine upon them, where they will realize what it is to be hearers and doers of the words of Christ, what it is to follow the Light of the world, and be accepted in the Beloved.

Everything that God could do has been done for the salvation of man. In one rich gift He poured out the treasures of heaven. He invites, He pleads, He urges; but He will not compel men to come unto Him. He waits for their cooperation. He waits for the consent of the will, that He may bestow upon the sinner the riches of His grace, reserved for him from the foundation of the world. . . . The Lord does not design that human power should be paralyzed; but that by cooperation with God, man may become a more efficient agent in His hands. . . . The Lord holds out to man the privilege of copartnership with Himself.—*The Messenger*, Apr. 26, 1893.

A TEMPLE FOR THE SPIRIT

What? know ye not that your body is the temple of the Holy Ghost which is in you, which ye have of God, and ye are not your own? For ye are bought with a price: therefore glorify God in your body, and in your spirit, which are God's. 1 Cor. 6:19, 20.

A power above and outside of man is to work upon him, that solid timbers may be brought into his character building. In the inner sanctuary of the soul the presence of God is to abide. "And what agreement hath the temple of God with idols? for ye are the temple of the living God; as God hath said, I will dwell in them, and walk in them; and I will be their God, and they shall be my people" (2 Cor. 6:16). "Know ye not that ye are the temple of God, and that the Spirit of God dwelleth in you? If any man defile the temple of God, him shall God destroy; for the temple of God is holy, which temple ye are" (1 Cor. 3:16, 17). . . .

"For through him we both have access by one Spirit unto the Father. Now therefore ye are no more strangers and foreigners, but fellow-citizens with the saints, and of the household of God; and are built upon the foundation of the apostles and prophets, Jesus Christ himself being the chief corner stone; in whom all the building fitly framed together groweth unto a holy temple in the Lord; . . . in whom ye also are builded together for an habitation of God through the Spirit" (Eph. 2:18-22).

Man does not build himself into a habitation for the Spirit, but unless there is a cooperation of man's will with God's will, the Lord can do nothing for him. The Lord is the great Master Worker, and yet the human agent must cooperate with the Divine Worker, or the heavenly building cannot be completed. All the power is of God, and all the glory is to redound to God, and yet all the responsibility rests with the human agent; for God can do nothing without the cooperation of man.— *Review and Herald*, Oct. 25, 1892.

Partakers of the Divine Nature

Whereby are given unto us exceeding great and precious promises: that by these ye might be partakers of the divine nature, having escaped the corruption that is in the world through lust. 2 Peter 1:4.

A healthy Christian is one who has Christ formed within, the hope of glory. He loves truth, purity, and holiness, and will manifest spiritual vitality, having love for the Word of God, and seeking communion with those who are acquainted with the Word, in order that he may catch every ray of light that God has communicated to them, which reveals Christ and makes Him more precious to the soul. He who has sound faith finds that Christ is the life of the soul, that He is in him as a well of water springing up unto everlasting life, and he delights to conform every power of the soul to the obedience of his Lord. The Holy Spirit with His vivifying influence ever keeps such a soul in the love of God.

To the Christian it is written: "Grace and peace be multiplied unto you through the knowledge of God, and of Jesus our Lord, according as his divine power hath given unto us all things that pertain unto life and godliness, through the knowledge of him that hath called us to glory and virtue: whereby are given unto us exceeding great and precious promises: that by these ye might be partakers of the divine nature, having escaped the corruption that is in the world through lust. And besides this, giving all diligence, add to your faith virtue; and to virtue knowledge; and to knowledge temperance; and to temperance patience; and to patience godliness; and to godliness brotherly kindness; and to brotherly kindness charity. For if these things be in you, and abound, they make you that ye shall neither be barren nor unfruitful in the knowledge of our Lord Jesus Christ. But he that lacketh these things is blind, and cannot see afar off, and hath forgotten that he was purged from his old sins. Wherefore the rather, brethren, give diligence to make your calling and election sure; for if ye do these things, ye shall never fall: for so an entrance shall be ministered unto you abundantly into the everlasting kingdom of our Lord and Saviour Jesus Christ" (2 Peter 1:2-11).— *Review and Herald*, Dec. 11, 1894.

CLAY IN THE HANDS OF THE POTTER

And the vessel that he made of clay was marred in the hand of the potter: so he made it again another vessel, as seemed good to the potter to make it. Then the word of the Lord came to me, saying, O house of Israel, cannot I do with you as this potter? saith the Lord. Behold, as the clay is in the potter's hand, so are ye in mine hand, O house of Israel. Jer. 18:4-6.

I lay down my pen and lift up my soul in prayer, that the Lord would breathe upon His backslidden people, which are as dry bones, that they may live. The end is near, stealing upon us so stealthily, so imperceptibly, so noiselessly, like the muffled tread of the thief in the night to surprise the sleepers off guard and unready. May the Lord grant to bring His Holy Spirit upon hearts that are now at ease, that they may no longer sleep as do others, but watch and be sober.

Who will consent even now, after wasting much of his lifetime, to give his will as clay into the hands of the Potter, and cooperate with God in becoming in His hands molded a vessel unto honor? Oh, how must the clay be in the hands of the Potter, how susceptible to receive divine impressions, standing in the bright beams of righteousness. No earthly, no selfish motives should be suffered to live, for if you give them place, you cannot be hewn into the divine image. The spirit of truth sanctifies the soul.

When the greatness of this work is comprehended, it will bring even the thoughts into captivity to Christ. This is beyond our private comprehension, but thus it will be. Then is it wisdom on our part to put dependence on our own works? We must let God work for us. Is there any excellency that appears in our characters or our conduct? Does it originate with finite human beings? No; it is all from God, the great center or expression of the power of the potter over the clay.

Oh, that those whom the Lord has blessed with the treasures of truth would awake and say from the heart, "Lord, what wilt thou have me to do?" (Acts 9:6). Light is increasing to enlighten every soul who will diffuse the light to others.—*General Conference Bulletin*, Feb. 4, 1893.

DRY BONES VIVIFIED

And [I] shall put my spirit in you, and ye shall live, and I shall place you in your own land: then shall ye know that I the Lord have spoken it, and performed it, saith the Lord. Eze. 37:14.

It is not the human agent that is to inspire with life. The Lord God of Israel will do that part, quickening the lifeless spiritual nature into activity. The breath of the Lord of hosts must enter into the lifeless bodies. In the judgment, when all secrets are laid bare, it will be known that the voice of God spoke through the human agent, and aroused the torpid conscience, and stirred the lifeless faculties, and moved sinners to repentance and contrition, and forsaking of sins. It will then be clearly seen that through the human agent faith in Jesus Christ was imparted to the soul, and spiritual life from heaven was breathed upon one who was dead in trespasses and sins, and he was quickened with spiritual life.

But not only does this simile of the dry bones apply to the world, but also to those who have been blessed with great light; for they also are like the skeletons of the valley. They have the form of men, the framework of the body; but they have not spiritual life. But the parable does not leave the dry bones merely knit together into the forms of men; for it is not enough that there is symmetry of limb and feature. The breath of life must vivify the bodies, that they may stand upright, and spring into activity. These bones represent the house of Israel, the church of God, and the hope of the church is the vivifying influence of the Holy Spirit. The Lord must breathe upon the dry bones, that they may live.

The Spirit of God, with its vivifying power, must be in every human agent, that every spiritual muscle and sinew may be in exercise. Without the Holy Spirit, without the breath of God, there is torpidity of conscience, loss of spiritual life. Many who are without spiritual life have their names on the church records, but they are not written in the Lamb's book of life. They may be joined to the church, but they are not united to the Lord. They may be diligent in the performance of a certain set of duties, and may be regarded as living men; but many are among those who have "a name that thou livest, and art dead" (Rev. 3:1).—*The SDA Bible Commentary*, Ellen G. White Comments, vol. 4, pp. 1165, 1166.

WEAK SOULS STRENGTHENED

Therefore, brethren, we are debtors, not to the flesh, to live after the flesh. For if ye live after the flesh, ye shall die: but if ye through the Spirit do mortify the deeds of the body, ye shall live. Rom. 8:12, 13.

The promise of the Holy Spirit is not limited to any age or to any race. Christ declared that the divine influence of His Spirit was to be with His followers unto the end. From the day of Pentecost to the present time, the Comforter has been sent to all who have yielded themselves fully to the Lord and to His service. To all who have accepted Christ as a personal Saviour, the Holy Spirit has come as a counselor, sanctifier, guide, and witness. The more closely believers have walked with God, the more clearly and powerfully have they testified of their Redeemer's love and of His saving grace. The men and women who through the long centuries of persecution and trial enjoyed a large measure of the presence of the Spirit in their lives have stood as signs and wonders in the world. Before angels and men they have revealed the transforming power of redeeming love.

Those who at Pentecost were endued with power from on high were not thereby freed from further temptation and trial. As they witnessed for truth and righteousness they were repeatedly assailed by the enemy of all truth, who sought to rob them of their Christian experience. They were compelled to strive with all their God-given powers to reach the measure of the stature of men and women in Christ Jesus. Daily they prayed for fresh supplies of grace, that they might reach higher and still higher toward perfection. Under the Holy Spirit's working even the weakest, by exercising faith in God, learned to improve their entrusted powers and to become sanctified, refined, and ennobled. As in humility they submitted to the molding influence of the Holy Spirit, they received of the fullness of the Godhead and were fashioned in the likeness of the divine.—*The Acts of the Apostles*, pp. 49, 50.

DIVINE IMAGE RESTORED

And be renewed in the spirit of your mind; and that ye put on the new man, which after God is created in righteousness and true holiness. Eph. 4:23, 24.

In the plan of restoring in men the divine image, it was provided that the Holy Spirit should move upon human minds, and be as the presence of Christ, a molding agency upon human character. Receiving the truth, men become also recipients of the grace of Christ, and devote their sanctified human ability to the work in which Christ was engaged—men become laborers together with God. It is to make men agents for God, that divine truth is brought home to their understanding. But I would inquire of the church, Have you answered this purpose? Have you fulfilled the design of God in diffusing the light of divine truth, in scattering abroad the precious jewels of truth?

What must be the thoughts of the angels of God as they look upon the church of Christ, and see how slow is the action of those who profess to be the followers of Christ, to impart the light of truth to the world which lies in moral darkness? Heavenly intelligences know that the cross is the great center of attraction. They know that it is through the cross that fallen man is to receive the atonement, and to be brought into unity with God. The councils of heaven are looking upon you who claim to have accepted Christ as your personal Saviour, to see you make known the salvation of God to those who sit in darkness. They are looking to see you making known the significance of the dispensation of the Holy Spirit; how that through the working of this divine agency the minds of men, corrupted and defiled by sin, may become disenchanted with the lies and presentations of Satan, and turn to Christ as their only hope, their personal Saviour.

Christ says: "I have chosen you, and ordained you, that ye should go and bring forth fruit, and that your fruit should remain" (John 15:16). As Christ's ambassador, I would entreat of all who read these lines to take heed while it is called today. "If ye will hear his voice, harden not your hearts" (Heb. 4:7). Without waiting a moment, inquire, What am I to Christ? What is Christ to me? What is my work? What is the character of the fruit I bear?—*Review and Herald,* Feb. 12, 1895.

THE HEART CHANGED

A new heart also will I give you, and a new spirit will I put within you: and I will take away the stony heart out of your flesh, and I will give you an heart of flesh. And I will put my spirit within you, and cause you to walk in my statutes, and ye shall keep my judgments, and do them. Eze. 36:26, 27.

The heart of man may be the abode of the Holy Spirit. The peace of Christ that passeth understanding may rest in your soul, and the transforming power of His grace may work in your life, and fit you for the courts of glory. But if brain and nerve and muscle are all employed in the service of self, you are not making God and heaven the first consideration of your life. It is impossible to be weaving the graces of Christ into your character while you are putting all your energies on the side of the world.

You may be successful in heaping up treasure on the earth, for the glory of self; but "where your treasure is, there will your heart be also" (Matt. 6:21). Eternal considerations will be made of secondary importance. You may take part in the outward forms of worship; but your service will be an abomination to the God of heaven. You cannot serve God and mammon. You will either yield your heart and put your will on the side of God, or you will give your energies to the service of the world. God will accept no half-hearted service.

"The light of the body is the eye: therefore when thine eye is single, thy whole body also is full of light" (Luke 11:34). If the eye is single, if it is directed heavenward, the light of heaven will fill the soul, and earthly things will appear insignificant and uninviting. The purpose of the heart will be changed, and the admonition of Jesus will be heeded. You will lay up your treasure in heaven. Your thoughts will be fixed upon the great rewards of eternity. All your plans will be made in reference to the future, immortal life. You will be drawn toward your treasure. You will not study your worldly interest; but in all your pursuits the silent inquiry will be "Lord, what wilt thou have me to do?" (Acts 9:6).—*Review and Herald*, Jan. 24, 1888.

LIPS ARE SANCTIFIED

And he laid it upon my mouth, and said, Lo, this hath touched thy lips; and thine iniquity is taken away, and thy sin purged. Isa. 6:7.

By His heavenly gifts the Lord has made ample provision for His people. An earthly parent cannot give his child a sanctified character. He cannot transfer his character to his child. God alone can transform us. Christ breathed on His disciples, and said, "Receive ye the Holy Ghost" (John 20:22). This is the great gift of heaven. Christ imparted to them through the Spirit His own sanctification. He imbued them with His power, that they might win souls to the gospel. Henceforth Christ would live through their faculties, and speak through their words. They were privileged to know that hereafter He and they were to be one. They must cherish His principles and be controlled by His Spirit. They were no longer to follow their own way, to speak their own words. The words they spoke were to proceed from a sanctified heart, and fall from sanctified lips. No longer were they to live their own selfish life; Christ was to live in them and speak through them. He would give to them the glory that He had with the Father, that He and they might be one in God.

The Lord Jesus is our great high priest, our advocate in the courts of heaven. The solemn position in which we stand to Him as worshipers is not appreciated. For our present and eternal good we need to understand this relation. If we are His children we are bound together in the bonds of Christian brotherhood, loving one another as He has loved us, united in the sacred relation of those washed in the blood of the Lamb. Bound up with Christ in God, we are to love as brethren.

Thank God that we have a great High Priest, who has passed into the heavens, Jesus the Son of God. Christ has not entered into the holy place made with hands, but into heaven itself, now to appear in the presence of God for us. By virtue of His own blood He entered in once for all into the holy place above, having obtained eternal redemption for us.—*General Conference Bulletin*, fourth quarter 1899.

THE MIND RENEWED

And be not conformed to this world: but be ye transformed by the renewing of your mind, that ye may prove what is that good, and acceptable, and perfect, will of God. Rom. 12:2.

The part man has to act in the salvation of the soul is to believe on Jesus Christ as a perfect Redeemer, not for some other man, but for his own self. He is to trust, to love, to fear the God of heaven. There is a certain work to be accomplished. Man must be delivered from the power of sin. He must be made perfect in every good work. In doing the words of Christ is his only assurance that his house is built upon the solid foundation. To hear, to say, to preach, and not to do the words of Christ is building upon the sand.

Those who do the words of Christ will perfect a Christian character, because Christ's will is their will. Thus is Christ formed within, the hope of glory. They are beholding, as in a glass, the glory of God. By our making Christ the subject of meditation, He will become the subject of conversation; and by beholding, we will actually be changed into the same image, from glory to glory, even by the Spirit of the Lord. Man, fallen man, may be transformed by the renewing of the mind, so that he can "prove what is that good, and acceptable, and perfect, will of God." How does he prove this? By the Holy Spirit taking possession of his mind, spirit, heart, and character. Where does the proving come in? "We are made a spectacle unto the world, and to angels, and to men" (1 Cor. 4:9).

A real work is wrought by the Holy Spirit upon the human character, and its fruits are seen; just as a good tree will bear good fruit, so will the tree that is actually planted in the Lord's garden produce good fruit unto eternal life. Besetting sins are overcome; evil thoughts are not allowed in the mind; evil habits are purged from the soul temple. The tendencies, which have been biased in a wrong direction, are turned in a right direction. Wrong dispositions and feelings are rooted out. Holy tempers and sanctified emotions are now the fruit borne upon the Christian tree. An entire transformation has taken place. This is the work to be wrought.—*Elder E. P. Daniels and the Fresno Church*, pp. 8, 9.

SELF CRUCIFIED

I am crucified with Christ: nevertheless I live; yet not I, but Christ liveth in me: and the life which I now live in the flesh I live by the faith of the Son of God, who loved me, and gave himself for me. Gal. 2:20.

Candidly and seriously we are to consider the question, Have we humbled ourselves before God, that the Holy Spirit may work through us with transforming power? As children of God, it is our privilege to be worked by His Spirit. When self is crucified, the Holy Spirit takes the brokenhearted ones, and makes them vessels unto honor. They are in His hands as clay in the hands of the potter. Jesus Christ will make such men and women superior in mental, physical, and moral power. The graces of the Spirit will give solidity to the character. They will exert an influence for good because Christ is abiding in the soul.

Unless this converting power shall go through our churches, unless the revival of the Spirit of God shall come, all their profession will never make the members of the church Christians. There are sinners in Zion who need to repent of sins that have been cherished as precious treasures. Until these sins are seen, and thrust from the soul, until every faulty, unlovely trait of character is transformed by the Spirit's influence, God cannot manifest Himself in power. There is more hope for the open sinner than for the professedly righteous who are not pure, holy, and undefiled. . . .

Who is willing to take himself in hand? Who is willing to lay his finger upon his cherished idols of sin, and allow Christ to purify the temple by casting out the buyers and sellers? Who is prepared to allow Jesus to enter the soul and cleanse it from everything that tarnishes or corrupts? The standard is "Be ye therefore perfect, even as your Father which is in heaven is perfect" (Matt. 5:48). God calls upon men and women to empty their hearts of self. Then His Spirit can find unobstructed entrance. Stop trying to do the work yourself. Ask God to work in and through you until the words of the apostle become yours, "I live; yet not I, but Christ liveth in me."—*Manuscript Releases*, vol. 1, pp. 366, 367.

THOUGHTS TRANSFORMED

Finally, brethren, whatsoever things are true, whatsoever things are honest, whatsoever things are just, whatsoever things are pure, whatsoever things are lovely, whatsoever things are of good report; if there be any virtue, and if there be any praise, think on these things. Phil. 4:8.

We have each of us an individual work to do, to gird up the loins of our minds, to be sober, to watch unto prayer. The mind must be firmly controlled to dwell upon subjects that will strengthen the moral powers. The youth should begin early to cultivate correct habits of thought. We should discipline the mind to think in a healthful channel, and not permit it to dwell upon things that are evil. The psalmist exclaims, "Let the words of my mouth, and the meditation of my heart, be acceptable in thy sight, O Lord, my strength, and my redeemer" (Ps.19:14).

As God works upon the heart by His Holy Spirit, man must cooperate with Him. The thoughts must be bound about, restricted, withdrawn from branching out and contemplating things that will only weaken and defile the soul. The thoughts must be pure, the meditations of the heart must be clean, if the words of the mouth are to be words acceptable to heaven, and helpful to your associates. Christ said to the Pharisees, "O generation of vipers, how can ye, being evil, speak good things? for out of the abundance of the heart the mouth speaketh. A good man out of the good treasure of the heart bringeth forth good things: and an evil man out of the evil treasure bringeth forth evil things. But I say unto you, That every idle word that men shall speak, they shall give account thereof in the day of judgment. For by thy words thou shalt be justified, and by thy words thou shalt be condemned" (Matt. 12:34-37).

In the Sermon on the Mount, Christ presented before His disciples the far-reaching principles of the law of God. He taught His hearers that the law was transgressed by the thoughts before the evil desire was carried out in actual commission. We are under obligation to control our thoughts, and to bring them into subjection to the law of God.—*Review and Herald,* June 12, 1888.

TASTES ARE CHANGED

That ye put off concerning the former conversation the old man, which is corrupt according to the deceitful lusts. Eph. 4:22.

John says, "The light"—Christ—"shineth in darkness," that is, in the world, "and the darkness comprehended it not. . . . But as many as received him, to them gave he power to become the sons of God, even to them that believe on his name: which were born, not of blood, nor of the will of the flesh, nor of the will of man, but of God" (John 1:5-13). The reason why the unbelieving world are not saved is that they do not choose to be enlightened. The old nature, born of blood and the will of the flesh, cannot inherit the kingdom of God. The old ways, the hereditary tendencies, the former habits, must be given up; for grace is not inherited. The new birth consists in having new motives, new tastes, new tendencies.

Those who are begotten unto a new life by the Holy Spirit have become partakers of the divine nature, and in all their habits and practices, they will give evidence of their relationship to Christ. When men who claim to be Christians retain all their natural defects of character and disposition, in what does their position differ from that of the worldling? They do not appreciate the truth as a sanctifier, a refiner. They have not been born again. . . .

Let none feel that their way needs no changing. Those who decide thus are not fitted to engage in the work of God, for they will not feel the necessity of pressing constantly toward a higher standard, making continual improvement. None can walk safely unless they are distrustful of self, and are constantly looking to the work of God, studying it with willing heart to see their own errors, and to learn the will of Christ, and praying that it may be done in and by and through them. They show that their confidence is not in themselves, but in Christ. They hold the truth as a sacred treasure, able to sanctify and refine, and they are constantly seeking to bring their words and ways into harmony with its principles. They fear and tremble lest something savoring of self shall be idolized, and thus their defects be reproduced in others who confide in them. They are always seeking to subdue self, to put away everything that savors of it, and to supply the place with the meekness and lowliness of Christ. They are looking unto Jesus, growing up into Him, gathering from Him light and grace, that they may diffuse the same to others.—*Review and Herald,* Apr. 12, 1892.

TEMPER IS SUBDUED

Who is a wise man and endued with knowledge among you? Let him shew out of a good conversation his works with meekness of wisdom. James 3:13.

Meekness in the school of Christ is one of the marked fruits of the Spirit. It is a grace wrought by the Holy Spirit as a sanctifier, and enables its possessor at all times to control a rash and impetuous temper. When the grace of meekness is cherished by those who are naturally sour or hasty in disposition, they will put forth the most earnest efforts to subdue their unhappy temper. Every day they will gain self-control, until that which is unlovely and unlike Jesus is conquered. They become assimilated to the Divine Pattern, until they can obey the inspired injunction, "Be swift to hear, slow to speak, slow to wrath" (James 1:19).

When a man professes to be sanctified, and yet in words and works may be represented by the impure fountain sending forth its bitter waters, we may safely say, that man is deceived. He needs to learn the very alphabet of what constitutes the life of a Christian. Some who profess to be servants to Christ have so long cherished the demon of unkindness that they seem to love the unhallowed element, and to take pleasure in speaking words that displease and irritate. These men must be converted, before Christ will acknowledge them as His children.

Meekness is the inward adorning, which God estimates as of great price. The apostle speaks of this as more excellent and valuable than gold, or pearls, or costly array. While the outward adorning beautifies only the mortal body, the ornament of meekness adorns the soul, and connects finite man with the infinite God. This is the ornament of God's own choice. He who garnished the heavens with the orbs of light has by the same Spirit promised that He will "beautify the meek with salvation" (Ps. 149:4). Angels of heaven will register as best adorned, those who put on the Lord Jesus Christ, and walk with Him in meekness and lowliness of mind.—*Review and Herald*, Jan. 18, 1881.

PRIDE IS BROKEN

For I say, through the grace given unto me, to every man that is among you, not to think of himself more highly than he ought to think; but to think soberly, according as God hath dealt to every man the measure of faith. Rom. 12:3.

The acceptance of truth is one of God's means of sanctification. The more clearly we understand the truth that He sends to us, and the more faithfully we obey it, the more humble shall we be in our own estimation, and the more exalted shall we be in the estimation of the heavenly universe. The more unselfish our efforts for God, the more Christlike will be their influence, and the greater will be the good they will accomplish.

There is a wide difference between the spirit of the world and the Spirit of Christ. One leads to self-seeking, to striving for treasures that will be destroyed by the fires of the last day; the other leads to self-denial and self-sacrifice, to striving for the treasures that never perish.

The Holy Spirit, received by faith, breaks stubborn hearts. This is the soul and power of the sanctification of the truth, the source of the faith that works by love and purifies the heart. All true exaltation grows out of the humiliation developed in the life of Christ, shown by the wonderful sacrifice that He made to save perishing souls. He who is exalted by God must first humble himself. God has exalted Christ above every name that is named. But Christ first reached to the very depths of human woe, weaving Himself into the sympathies of the race by His meekness and gentleness. He has set an example that all who engage in His service are to follow.

"Learn of me," said the greatest Teacher that the world has ever known. "Learn of me; for I am meek and lowly in heart: and ye shall find rest unto your souls" (Matt. 11:29). It is not enough for us to read the Word of God. The Scriptures are given for our instruction, and we are to search them carefully and diligently. We are to study the Word of God, comparing one portion with another. Scripture is the key that unlocks scripture. As we read and study and pray, there is beside us a divine Teacher, the Holy Spirit, enlightening our understanding, that we may comprehend the great truths of God's Word.—*Pacific Union Recorder*, Feb. 23, 1905.

THE HOUSE CLEANSED

Create in me a clean heart, O God; and renew a right spirit within me. Ps. 51:10.

"Create in me a clean heart." This is beginning right, at the very foundation of Christian character; for out of the heart are the issues of life. If all, ministers and people, would see to it that their hearts are right with God, we should see much larger results from the labor put forth. The more important and responsible your work, the greater the necessity that you have clean hearts. The needed grace is provided, and the power of the Holy Spirit will work with every effort you make in this direction.

If every child of God would seek Him earnestly and perseveringly, there would be a greater growth in grace. Dissensions would cease; believers would be of one heart and one mind; and purity and love would prevail in the church. By beholding we become changed. The more you contemplate the character of Christ, the more you will become conformed to His image. Come to Jesus just as you are, and He will receive you, and put a new song in your mouth, even praise to God.

"Cast me not away from thy presence; and take not thy holy spirit from me" (Ps. 51:11). Repentance as well as forgiveness is the gift of God through Christ. It is through the influence of the Holy Spirit that we are convinced of sin, and feel our need of pardon. None but the contrite are forgiven; but it is the grace of the Lord that makes the heart penitent. He is acquainted with all our weaknesses and infirmities, and He will help us. He will hear the prayer of faith; but the sincerity of prayer can be proved only by our efforts to bring ourselves into harmony with the great moral standard which will test every man's character.

We need to open our hearts to the influence of the Spirit, and to experience His transforming power. The reason that you do not receive more of the saving help of God is because the channel of communication between Heaven and your own souls is clogged by worldliness, love of display, and desire for supremacy. While some are conforming more and more to the world's customs and maxims, we should be molding our lives after the divine model. And our covenant-keeping God will restore unto us the joys of His salvation, and uphold us by His free Spirit.—*Review and Herald*, June 24, 1884.

A CHRISTLIKE CHARACTER

For ye are dead, and your life is hid with Christ in God. Col. 3:3.

Jesus is the perfect pattern. Instead of trying to please self and have our own way, let us seek to reflect His image. He was kind and courteous, compassionate and tender. Are we like Him in these respects? Do we seek to make our lives fragrant with good works? What we need is the simplicity of Christ. I fear that in many cases a hard, unfeeling spirit, that is entirely unlike that of the divine Pattern, has taken possession of the heart. This cast-iron principle, which has been cherished by so many, and which has even been thought a virtue, must all be removed, that we may love one another as Christ has loved us.

It is not enough that we merely profess the faith; something more than a nominal assent is wanted. There must be a real knowledge, a genuine experience in the principles of the truth as it is in Jesus. The Holy Spirit must work within, bringing these principles into the strong light of distinct consciousness, that we may know their power and make them a living reality. The mind must yield obedience to the royal law of liberty, the law which the Spirit of God impresses upon the heart, and makes plain to the understanding. The expulsion of sin must be the act of the soul itself, in calling into exercise its noblest powers. The only freedom a finite will can enjoy consists in coming into harmony with the will of God, complying with the conditions that make man a partaker of the divine nature, having escaped the corruption that is in the world through lust. . . .

The human character is depraved, deformed by sin, and terribly unlike that of the first man as he came from the hands of the Creator. Jesus proposes to take man's deformity and sin, and to give him, in return, beauty and excellence in his own character. He engages to renovate the soul through the truth. Error cannot do this work of regeneration; therefore we must have spiritual eyesight to discern between truth and falsehood, that we fall not into the snare of the enemy.—*Review and Herald*, Nov. 24, 1885.

HAVING THE MIND OF CHRIST

For who hath known the mind of the Lord, that he may instruct him? But we have the mind of Christ. 1 Cor. 2:16.

As the man is converted by the truth, the work of transformation of character goes on. He has an increased measure of understanding, in becoming a man of obedience to God. The mind and will of God become his will, and by constantly looking to God for counsel, he becomes a man of increased understanding. There is a general development of the mind that is unreservedly placed under the guidance of the Spirit of God.

This is not a one-sided education, which develops a one-sided character; but there is revealed a harmoniously developed character. Weaknesses that have been seen in the powerless, vacillating character are overcome, and continual devotion and piety bring the man in such close relation to Jesus Christ that he has the mind of Christ. He is one with Christ, having soundness and strength of principle, and clearness of perception, which is that wisdom that comes from God, who is the source of all light and understanding.

The grace of God has fallen upon the humble, obedient, conscientious soul like the Sun of righteousness, strengthening the mental faculties, and in the most astonishing manner making those who long to use their capacity in the Master's service, small though it may be, strong continually by obedience and practice, and grow in grace and in the knowledge of Jesus Christ, and be bearers of much fruit to the glory of God, in good works. So that the men of learning and of high accomplishments have learned most precious lessons from the precepts and examples of the unlearned, as the world would call them. But could they have a deeper sight, it would be seen that they had obtained knowledge in the highest graded school, even the school of Jesus Christ. . . . The opening of God's Word is followed by remarkable opening in strengthening a man's faculties; for the entrance of God's Word is the application of divine truth to the heart, purifying and refining the soul through the agency of the Holy Spirit.—*Review and Herald*, July 19, 1887.

ABIDING IN HIM

Abide in me, and I in you. As the branch cannot bear fruit of itself, except it abide in the vine; no more can ye, except ye abide in me. John 15:4.

We need to pray for the impartation of the divine Spirit as the remedy for sin-sick souls. The surface truths of revelation, made plain and easy to be understood, are accepted by many as supplying all that is essential; but the Holy Spirit, working upon the mind, awakens an earnest desire for truth uncorrupted by error. He who is really desirous to know what is truth cannot remain in ignorance; for precious truth rewards the diligent seeker. We need to feel the converting power of God's grace, and I urge all who have closed their heart against God's Spirit to unlock the door, and plead earnestly, Abide with me. Why should we not prostrate ourselves at the throne of divine grace, praying that God's Spirit may be poured out upon us as He was upon the disciples? His presence will soften our hard hearts, and fill us with joy and rejoicing, transforming us into channels of blessing.

The Lord would have every one of His children rich in faith, and this faith is the fruit of the working of the Holy Spirit upon the mind. He dwells with each soul who will receive Him, speaking to the impenitent in words of warning, and pointing them to Jesus, the Lamb of God, that taketh away the sin of the world. He causes light to shine into the minds of those who are seeking to cooperate with God, giving them efficiency and wisdom to do His work.

The Holy Spirit never leaves unassisted a soul who is looking to Jesus. He takes of the things of Christ, and shows them to the seeker. And if the eye is kept fixed upon Jesus, the work of the Spirit ceases not until the soul is conformed to His image. Through the gracious influence of the Spirit the sinner is changed in spirit and purpose, till he becomes one with Christ. His affection for God increases; he hungers and thirsts for righteousness, and by beholding Christ he is changed from glory to glory, from character to character, and becomes more and more like his Master.—*Signs of the Times*, Sept. 27, 1899.

BEHOLDING HIM

Look unto me, and be ye saved, all the ends of the earth: for I am God, and there is none else. Isa. 45:22.

In order to meet the requirement of the law, our faith must grasp the righteousness of Christ, accepting it as our righteousness. Through union with Christ, through acceptance of His righteousness by faith, we may be qualified to work the works of God, to be colaborers with Christ. If you are willing to drift along with the current of evil, and do not cooperate with the heavenly agencies in restraining transgression in your family, and in the church, in order that everlasting righteousness may be brought in, you do not have faith.

Faith works by love and purifies the soul. Through faith the Holy Spirit works in the heart to create holiness therein; but this cannot be done unless the human agent will work with Christ. We can be fitted for heaven only through the work of the Holy Spirit upon the heart; for we must have Christ's righteousness as our credentials if we would find access to the Father. In order that we may have the righteousness of Christ, we need daily to be transformed by the influence of the Spirit, to be a partaker of the divine nature. It is the work of the Holy Spirit to elevate the taste, to sanctify the heart, to ennoble the whole man.

Let the soul look to Jesus. "Behold the Lamb of God, which taketh away the sin of the world" (John 1:29). No one will be forced to look to Christ; but the voice of invitation is sounding in yearning entreaty, "Look and live." In looking to Christ, we shall see that His love is without a parallel, that He has taken the place of the guilty sinner, and has imputed unto him His spotless righteousness.

When the sinner sees his Saviour dying upon the cross under the curse of sin in his stead, beholding His pardoning love, love awakes in his heart. The sinner loves Christ, because Christ has first loved him, and love is the fulfilling of the law. The repenting soul realizes that God "is faithful and just to forgive us our sins, and to cleanse us from all unrighteousness" (1 John 1:9). The Spirit of God works in the believer's soul, enabling him to advance from one line of obedience to another, reaching on from strength to greater strength, from grace to grace in Christ Jesus.—*Review and Herald*, Nov. 1, 1892.

COMPLETE IN HIM

And ye are complete in him, which is the head of all principality and power. Col. 2:10.

You cannot enter heaven with any deformity or imperfection of character, and you must be fitted for heaven now in this probationary life. If you would enter the abode of the righteous when Christ shall come, you must have the deep movings of the Spirit of God, that you may have an individual experience, and be complete in Him who is the fullness of the Godhead bodily. Through the power of the righteousness of Christ, we are to depart from all iniquity. There must be a living connection of the soul with its Redeemer. The channel of communication must be open continually between man and his God, that the soul may grow in grace and in the knowledge of the Lord.

But how many do not pray. They feel under condemnation for sin, and they think they must not come to God until they have done something to merit His favor, or until God has forgotten about their transgressions. They say, "I cannot hold up holy hands before God without wrath or doubting, and therefore I cannot come." So they remain away from Christ, and are committing sin all the time in so doing, for without Him you can do nothing but evil.

Just as soon as you commit sin, you should flee to the throne of grace, and tell Jesus all about it. You should be filled with sorrow for sin, because through sin you have weakened your own spirituality, grieved the heavenly angels, and wounded and bruised the loving heart of your Redeemer. When you have asked Jesus in contrition of soul for His forgiveness, believe that He has forgiven you. Do not doubt His divine mercy, or refuse the comfort of His infinite love.

If your child had disobeyed you, and committed wrong against you, and that child should come with a breaking heart to ask forgiveness, you know what you would do. You know how quickly you would draw your child to your heart, and assure him that your love was unchanged, and his transgressions forgiven. Are you more merciful than your merciful heavenly Father, who so loved the world that He "gave his only begotten Son, that whosoever believeth in him should not perish, but have everlasting life"? (John 3:16). You should go to God as children go to their parents.—*Bible Echo*, Feb. 1, 1892.

RESTING IN HIM

Take my yoke upon you, and learn of me; for I am meek and lowly in heart: and ye shall find rest unto your souls. Matt. 11:29.

While you have been walking in meekness and lowliness of heart, a work has been going on for you, a work which only God could do; for it is God that worketh in you, both to will and to do of His good pleasure. And that good pleasure is to have you abide in Christ, rest in His love. You must not let anything rob your soul of peace, of restfulness, of the assurance that you are accepted just now. Appropriate every promise; all are yours on condition of your complying with the Lord's prescribed terms. Entire surrender of your ways, which seem so very wise, and taking Christ's ways, is the secret of perfect rest in His love.

Giving up one's life to Him means much more than we suppose. We must learn His meekness and lowliness before we realize the fulfillment of the promise "Ye shall find rest unto your souls." It is by learning the habits of Christ, His meekness, His lowliness, that self becomes transformed—by taking Christ's yoke upon you and then submitting to learn. There is no one who has not much to learn. All must come under training by Jesus Christ. When they fall upon Christ, their own hereditary and cultivated traits of character are taken away as hindrances to their being partakers of the divine nature. When self dies, then Christ lives in the human agent. He abides in Christ, and Christ lives in him.

Christ desires all to become His students. He says, Yield yourselves to My training; submit your souls unto Me. I will not extinguish you, but will work out for you such a character that you shall be transferred from the lower school to the higher grade. Submit all things to Me. Let My life, My patience, My longsuffering, My forbearance, My meekness, My lowliness, be worked out in your character, as one that abides in Me. . . . Then you have the promise not only "I will give," but "Ye shall find rest unto your souls."—*Bible Training School*, Aug. 1, 1903.

CONFORMED TO HIS IMAGE

But we all, with open face beholding as in a glass the glory of the Lord, are changed into the same image from glory to glory even as by the Spirit of the Lord. 2 Cor. 3:18.

Sin-burdened, struggling souls, Jesus in His glorified humanity has ascended into the heavens to make intercession for us. "For we have not an high priest which cannot be touched with the feeling of our infirmities; but was in all points tempted like as we are, yet without sin. Let us therefore come boldly unto the throne of grace" (Heb. 4:15, 16). We should be continually looking unto Jesus, the Author and Finisher of our faith; for by beholding Him we shall be changed into His image, our character will be made like His. We should rejoice that all judgment is given to the Son, because in His humanity He has become acquainted with all the difficulties that beset humanity.

To be sanctified is to become a partaker of the divine nature, catching the spirit and mind of Jesus, ever learning in the school of Christ. "But we all, with open face beholding as in a glass the glory of the Lord, are changed into the same image from glory to glory even as by the Spirit of the Lord." It is impossible for any of us by our power or our own efforts to work this change in ourselves. It is the Holy Spirit, the Comforter, which Jesus said He would send into the world, that changes our character into the image of Christ; and when this is accomplished, we reflect, as in a mirror, the glory of the Lord. That is, the character of the one who thus beholds Christ is so like His, that one looking at him sees Christ's own character shining out as from a mirror. Imperceptibly to ourselves, we are changed day by day from our own ways and will into the ways and will of Christ, into the loveliness of His character. Thus we grow up into Christ, and unconsciously reflect His image.

Professed Christians keep altogether too near the lowlands of earth. Their eyes are trained to see only commonplace things, and their minds dwell upon the things their eyes behold. Their religious experience is often shallow and unsatisfying, and their words are light and valueless. How can such reflect the image of Christ? How can they send forth the bright beams of the Sun of righteousness into all the dark places of the earth? To be a Christian is to be Christlike.—*Review and Herald*, Apr. 28, 1891.

IN COOPERATION WITH THE SPIRIT

Wherefore, my beloved, as ye have always obeyed, not as in my presence only, but now much more in my absence, work out your own salvation with fear and trembling. Phil. 2:12.

"I f any man be in Christ, he is a new creature: old things are passed away; behold, all things are become new" (2 Cor. 5:17). Nothing but divine power can regenerate the human heart and imbue souls with the love of Christ, which will ever manifest itself with love for those for whom He died. The fruit of the Spirit is love, joy, peace, long-suffering, goodness, faith, meekness, temperance. When a man is converted to God, a new moral taste is supplied, a new motive power is given, and he loves the things that God loves; for his life is bound up by the golden chain of the immutable promises to the life of Jesus. Love, joy, peace, and inexpressible gratitude will pervade the soul, and the language of him who is blessed will be "Thy gentleness hath made me great" (Ps. 18:35).

But those who are waiting to behold a magical change in their characters without determined effort on their part to overcome sin will be disappointed. We have no reason to fear while looking to Jesus, no reason to doubt but that He is able to save to the uttermost all that come unto Him; but we may constantly fear lest our old nature will again obtain the supremacy, that the enemy shall devise some snare whereby we shall again become his captives.

We are to work out our own salvation with fear and trembling, for it is God that worketh in you to will and to do of His good pleasure. With our limited powers we are to be as holy in our sphere as God is holy in His sphere. To the extent of our ability, we are to make manifest the truth and love and excellence of the divine character. As wax takes the impression of the seal, so the soul is to take the impression of the Spirit of God and retain the image of Christ.

We are to grow daily in spiritual loveliness. We shall fail often in our efforts to copy the divine Pattern. We shall often have to bow down to weep at the feet of Jesus, because of our shortcomings and mistakes; but we are not to be discouraged; we are to pray more fervently, believe more fully, and try again with more steadfastness to grow into the likeness of our Lord.—*Selected Messages*, book 1, pp. 336, 337.

FREE FROM THE CURSE OF SIN

But now being made free from sin, and become servants to God, ye have your fruit unto holiness, and the end everlasting life. Rom. 6:22.

The Lord would have His people sound in the faith—not ignorant of the great salvation so abundantly provided for them. They are not to look forward, thinking that at some future time a great work is to be done for them; for the work is now complete. The believer is not called upon to make his peace with God; he never has nor ever can do this. He is to accept Christ as his peace, for with Christ is God and peace. Christ made an end of sin, bearing its heavy curse in His own body on the tree, and He hath taken away the curse from all those who believe in Him as a personal Saviour. He makes an end of the controlling power of sin in the heart, and the life and character of the believer testify to the genuine character of the grace of Christ.

To those that ask Him, Jesus imparts the Holy Spirit; for it is necessary that every believer should be delivered from pollution, as well as from the curse and condemnation of the law. Through the work of the Holy Spirit, the sanctification of the truth, the believer becomes fitted for the courts of heaven; for Christ works within us, and His righteousness is upon us. Without this no soul will be entitled to heaven. We would not enjoy heaven unless qualified for its holy atmosphere by the influence of the Spirit and the righteousness of Christ.

In order to be candidates for heaven we must meet the requirement of the law: "Thou shalt love the Lord thy God with all thy heart, and with all thy soul, and with all thy strength, and with all thy mind; and thy neighbour as thyself" (Luke 10:27). We can do this only as we grasp by faith the righteousness of Christ. By beholding Jesus we receive a living, expanding principle in the heart, and the Holy Spirit carries on the work, and the believer advances from grace to grace, from strength to strength, from character to character. He conforms to the image of Christ, until in spiritual growth he attains unto the measure of the full stature in Christ Jesus. Thus Christ makes an end of the curse of sin, and sets the believing soul free from its action and effect.—*Selected Messages*, book 1, pp. 394, 395.

SANCTIFIED BUT NOT SINLESS

But of him are ye in Christ Jesus, who of God is made unto us wisdom, and righteousness, and sanctification, and redemption: that, according as it is written, He that glorieth, let him glory in the Lord. 1 Cor. 1:30, 31.

Just here we might distinguish between genuine and false sanctification. Sanctification does not consist in merely professing and teaching the Word of God, but in living in conformity to His will. Those who claim to be sinless, and make their boast of sanctification, are self-confident, and do not realize their peril. They anchor their souls upon the supposition that having once experienced the sanctifying power of God, they are in no danger of falling. While claiming to be rich and increased in goods, and in need of nothing, they know not that they are miserable, and poor, and blind, and naked.

But those who are truly sanctified have a sense of their own weakness. Feeling their need, they will go for light and grace and strength to Jesus, in whom all fullness dwells, and who alone can supply their wants. Conscious of their own imperfections, they seek to become more like Christ, and to live in accordance with the principles of His holy law. This continual sense of inefficiency will lead to such entire dependence upon God that His Spirit will be exemplified in them. The treasures of heaven will be opened to supply the wants of every hungering, thirsting soul. All of this character have the assurance of one day beholding the glory of that kingdom which as yet the imagination can only faintly grasp.

Those who have felt the sanctifying and transforming power of God must not fall into the dangerous error of thinking that they are sinless, that they have reached the highest state of perfection, and are beyond the reach of temptation. The standard the Christian is to keep before him is the purity and loveliness of Christ's character. Day by day he may be putting on new beauties, and reflecting to the world more and still more of the divine image.—*Bible Echo*, Feb. 21, 1898.

ALWAYS GROWING

But the path of the just is as the shining light, that shineth more and more unto the perfect day. Prov. 4:18.

At infinite cost, provision has been made that men shall reach the perfection of Christian character. Those who have been privileged to hear the truth, and have been impressed by the Holy Spirit to receive the Holy Scriptures as the voice of God, have no excuse for becoming dwarfs in the religious life. By exercising the ability which God has given, they are to be daily learning, and daily receiving spiritual fervor and power, which have been provided for every true believer. If we would be growing plants in the Lord's garden, we must have a constant supply of spiritual life and earnestness. Growth will then be seen in the faith and knowledge of our Lord Jesus Christ. There is no halfway house where we may throw off responsibility, and rest by the way. We are to keep advancing heavenward, developing a solid religious character.

The measure of the Holy Spirit we receive will be proportioned to the measure of our desire and the faith exercised for it, and the use we shall make of the light and knowledge that shall be given to us. We shall be entrusted with the Holy Spirit according to our capacity to receive and our ability to impart it to others. Christ says, "Every one that asketh receiveth; and he that seeketh findeth" (Luke 11:10).

He who truly seeks for the precious grace of Christ will be sure not to be disappointed. This promise has been given to us by Him who will not deceive us. It is not stated as a maxim or a theory, but as a fact, as a law of the divine government. We can be assured that we shall receive the Holy Spirit if we individually try the experiment of testing God's Word. God is true; His order is perfect. "He that seeketh findeth; and to him that knocketh it shall be opened" (verse 10). Light and truth will shine forth according to the desire of the soul. Oh, that all would hunger and thirst after righteousness, that they might be filled!—*Review and Herald*, May 5, 1896.

STEP BY STEP TO VICTORY

I therefore so run, not as uncertainly; so fight I, not as one that beateth the air: but I keep under my body, and bring it into subjection: lest that by any means, when I have preached to others, I myself should be a castaway. 1 Cor. 9:26, 27.

God leads His people on step by step. The Christian life is a battle and a march. In this warfare there is no release; the effort must be continuous and persevering. It is by unceasing endeavor that we maintain the victory over the temptations of Satan. Christian integrity must be sought with resistless energy and maintained with a resolute fixedness of purpose. . . .

There is a science of Christianity to be mastered—a science as much deeper, broader, higher than any human science as the heavens are higher than the earth. The mind is to be disciplined, educated, trained; for we are to do service for God in ways that are not in harmony with inborn inclination. There are hereditary and cultivated tendencies to evil that must be overcome. Often the training and education of a lifetime must be discarded, that one may become a learner in the school of Christ. Our hearts must be educated to become steadfast in God. We are to form habits of thought that will enable us to resist temptation. We must learn to look upward. The principles of the Word of God—principles that are as high as heaven, and that compass eternity—we are to understand in their bearing upon our daily life. Every act, every word, every thought, is to be in accord with these principles.

The precious graces of the Holy Spirit are not developed in a moment. Courage, fortitude, meekness, faith, unwavering trust in God's power to save, are acquired by the experience of years. By a life of holy endeavor and firm adherence to the right the children of God are to seal their destiny.

We have no time to lose. We know not how soon our probation may close. Eternity stretches before us. The curtain is about to be lifted. Christ is soon to come. The angels of God are seeking to attract us from ourselves and from earthly things. Let them not labor in vain.—*Testimonies*, vol. 8, pp. 313, 314.

A HOLY FRAGRANCE

Ye have not chosen me, but I have chosen you, and ordained you, that ye should go and bring forth fruit, and that your fruit should remain: that whatsoever ye shall ask of the Father in my name, he may give it you. John 15:16.

In order to bear much fruit, we must make the most of our privileges and opportunities, becoming more and more spiritually minded. We must put away all commonness, all pride, all worldliness, and daily receive divine aid. If you grow spiritually, you must employ all the means which the gospel provides, and be prepared to gain in piety by the influence of the Holy Spirit; for the seed is developed from blade to full corn by unseen and supernatural agencies.

The promise with which Jesus consoled His disciples just before His betrayal and crucifixion was that of the Holy Spirit; and in the doctrine of divine influence and agency, what riches were revealed to them; for this blessing would bring in its train all other blessings. The Holy Spirit breathes upon the soul who humbly rests on Christ as the author and finisher of his faith; and from such a believer fruit will come forth unto life eternal. His influence will be fragrant, and the name of Jesus will be music in his ears, and melody in his heart.

The Christian will be a savor of life unto life to others, although he may not be able to explain the mysteries of his experience. But he will know that when clouds and darkness compassed him about, and he cried unto the Lord, the darkness was dispersed, and peace and joy were in the temple of the soul. He will know what it is to have the pardoning love of God revealed to the heart, to experience the peace that passeth all understanding, to have praise and thanksgiving and adoration welling up in the soul unto Him who has loved us, and washed us from our sins in His own blood. He has peace through Jesus Christ, and joy in the Holy Ghost. One with Christ, his soul is filled with submission to His will, and heaven is enshrined in his heart while he is enfolded in the bosom of infinite love. Christians of this order will bear much fruit to the glory of God. They will rightly interpret the character of God, and manifest His attributes unto the world.—*Signs of the Times*, Apr. 3, 1893.

REPENTANCE, THE FIRST FRUIT

Have mercy upon me, O God, according to thy lovingkindness: according unto the multitude of thy tender mercies blot out my transgressions. Wash me throughly from mine iniquity, and cleanse me from my sin. Ps. 51:1, 2.

Repentance is one of the first fruits of saving grace. Our great Teacher, in His lessons to erring, fallen man, presents the life-giving power of His grace, declaring that through this grace men and women may live the new life of holiness and purity. He who lives this life works out the principles of the kingdom of heaven. Taught of God, he leads others in straight paths. He will not lead the lame into paths of uncertainty. The working of the Holy Spirit in his life shows that he is a partaker of the divine nature. Every soul thus worked by the Spirit of Christ receives so abundant a supply of the rich grace that, beholding his good works, the unbelieving world acknowledges that he is controlled and sustained by divine power, and is led to glorify God.— *God's Amazing Grace*, p. 138.

There are those who, notwithstanding all the gracious invitations of Christ, continue to reveal ungodliness in their lives. To such ones God says: "How long, ye simple ones, will ye love simplicity? . . . Turn you at my reproof: behold, I will pour out my spirit unto you, I will make known my words unto you" (Prov. 1:22, 23).—*Signs of the Times*, June 28, 1905.

Repentance for sin is the first fruits of the working of the Holy Spirit in the life. It is the only process by which infinite purity reflects the image of Christ in His redeemed subjects. In Christ all fullness dwells. Science that is not in harmony with Him is of no value. He teaches us to count all things but loss for the excellency of the knowledge of Christ Jesus our Lord. This knowledge is the highest science that any man can reach.— *The SDA Bible Commentary*, Ellen G. White Comments, vol. 6, p. 1068.

LOVE

Behold, what manner of love the Father hath bestowed upon us, that we should be called the sons of God: therefore the world knoweth us not, because it knew him not. 1 John 3:1.

John says, "Behold, what manner of love the Father hath bestowed upon us, that we should be called the sons of God." No language can express this love; we can describe but a faint degree of love that passeth knowledge. It would require the language of the Infinite to express the love that has made it possible for us to be called the sons of God. In becoming a Christian, a man does not step down. There is no shame in having connection with the living God.

Jesus bore the humiliation and shame and reproach that justly belonged to the sinner. He was the Majesty of heaven, He was the King of glory, He was equal with the Father; and yet He clothed His divinity with humanity, that humanity might touch humanity, that divinity might lay hold of divinity. Had He come as an angel, He could not have been a partaker with us of our sufferings, could not have been tempted in all points like as we are, He could not have sympathized with our sorrows; but He came in the garb of our humanity, that as our substitute and surety, He might overcome the prince of darkness in our behalf, and make us victors through His merits.

[As we stand] under the shadow of the cross of Calvary, the inspiration of His love fills our hearts. When I look upon Him whom my sins have pierced, the inspiration from on high comes upon me; and this inspiration may come upon each one of you through the Holy Spirit. Unless you receive the Holy Spirit, you cannot have the love of God in the soul; but through a living connection with Christ, we are inspired with love and zeal and earnestness.

We are not as a block of marble, which may reflect the light of the sun, but cannot be imbued with life. We are capable of responding to the bright beams of the Sun of righteousness; for as Christ illuminates our souls, He gives light and life. We drink in the love of Christ as the branch draws nourishment from the vine. If we are grafted into Christ, if fiber by fiber we have been united with the living Vine, we shall give evidence of this fact by bearing rich clusters of fruit.—*Review and Herald*, Sept. 27, 1892.

JOY

I will praise thee, O Lord, with my whole heart; I will shew forth all thy marvellous works. I will be glad and rejoice in thee: I will sing praise to thy name, O thou most High. Ps. 9:1, 2.

We must have more faith. Let us begin to believe unto salvation. Let us come to God in faith, fully assured that as we surrender all to Him, He will make us Christlike in character. We must tell this to all over and over again. Then, one with Christ, we can reveal Him to the world. Then all our fitful, haphazard work will cease.

Let us honor God by showing firm faith and unswerving trust. Let us remember that He is not glorified by the manifestation of a fretful, unhappy spirit. The Lord cares for the flowers. He gives them beauty and fragrance. Will He not much more give us the fragrance of a cheerful disposition? Will He not restore in us the divine image? Then let us have faith in Him. Let us now, just now, place ourselves where He can give us His Holy Spirit. Then we can give to the world a revelation of what true religion does for men and women. The joy of a Saviour filling our hearts gives us that peace and confidence which enables us to say, "I know that my Redeemer liveth" (Job 19:25).

In His Word the Lord has made it plain that His people are a joyful people. True faith reaches up the hand and lays hold upon the One who is behind the promise "Great shall be the peace of thy children" (Isa. 54:13). "Thus saith the Lord, Behold, I will extend peace to her like a river" (Isa. 66:12). "Behold, I create Jerusalem a rejoicing, and her people a joy" (Isa. 65:18). In God we may "rejoice with joy unspeakable and full of glory" (1 Peter 1:8). "Men shall be blessed in him: all nations shall call him blessed" (Ps. 72:17). Let us strive to educate the believers to rejoice in the Lord. Spiritual joy is the result of active faith. God's people are to be full of faith and of the Holy Spirit. Then He will be glorified in them.—*Bible Training School*, Apr. 1, 1905.

PEACE

Be careful for nothing; but in every thing by prayer and supplication with thanksgiving let your requests be made known unto God. And the peace of God, which passeth all understanding, shall keep your hearts and minds through Christ Jesus. Phil. 4:6, 7.

The world's Redeemer sought to bring to the hearts of the sorrowing disciples the strongest solace. But from a large field of subjects, He chose the theme of the Holy Spirit, which was to inspire and comfort their hearts. And yet, though Christ made much of this theme concerning the Holy Spirit, how little is it dwelt upon in the churches! The name and presence of the Holy Spirit are almost ignored, yet the divine influence is essential in the work of perfecting the Christian character.

Some are not at peace, not at rest; they are in a state of constant fretfulness, and permit impulse and passion to rule their hearts. They know not what it means to experience peace and rest in Christ. They are as a ship without anchor, driven with the wind and tossed. But those whose minds are controlled by the Holy Spirit walk in humility and meekness; for they work in Christ's lines, and will be kept in perfect peace, while those who are not controlled by the Holy Spirit are like the restless sea.

The Lord has given us a divine directory by which we may know His will. Those who are self-centered, self-sufficient, do not feel their need of searching the Bible, and they are greatly disturbed if others do not have the same defective ideas, and see with the same distorted vision that they do. But he who is guided by the Holy Spirit has cast his anchor within the veil wherein Jesus has entered for us. He searches the Scriptures with eager earnestness, and seeks for light and knowledge to guide him amid the perplexities and perils which at every step compass his path. Those who are restless, complaining, murmuring, read the Bible for the purpose of vindicating their own course of action, and they ignore or pervert the counsels of God. He who has peace has placed his will on the side of God's will, and longs to follow the divine guidance.—*Signs of the Times*, Aug. 14, 1893.

LONG-SUFFERING

Put on therefore, as the elect of God, holy and beloved, bowels of mercies, kindness, humbleness of mind, meekness, longsuffering. Col. 3:12.

The Captain of our salvation made Himself of no reputation, and took upon Him the form of a servant, in order that humanity might be allied to divinity. Man is to represent Christ. He is to be long-suffering toward his fellow men, to be patient, forgiving, and full of Christlike love. He who is truly converted will manifest respect for his brethren; he will do as Christ has commanded. Jesus said, "A new commandment I give unto you, That ye love one another; as I have loved you, that ye also love one another. By this shall all men know that ye are my disciples, if ye have love one to another" (John 13:34, 35). Where the love of Christ abounds in the soul, there will be an expression of that love that will be understood by the world. . . .

Not all who name the name of Christ are one with Christ. Those who do not have the Spirit and the grace of Christ are none of His, no matter what may be their profession. By their fruits ye shall know them. The customs and practices that are after the order of the world do not carry out the principles of God's law, and therefore do not breathe of His Spirit nor express His character. Christlikeness will be revealed only by those who are assimilated to the divine image. Only those who are being molded through the operation of the Holy Spirit are doers of the Word of God, and express the mind and the will of God.

There is counterfeit Christianity in the world as well as genuine Christianity. The true spirit of a man is manifested by the way in which he deals with his fellow man. We may ask the question, Does he represent the character of Christ in spirit and action, or simply manifest the natural, selfish traits of character that belong to the people of this world? Profession weighs nothing with God. Before it is everlastingly too late for wrongs to be righted, let each one ask himself, "What am I?" It depends upon ourselves as to whether we shall form such characters as will constitute us members of God's royal family above.—*Review and Herald*, Apr. 9, 1895.

GENTLENESS

But the fruit of the Spirit is love, joy, peace, longsuffering, gentleness, goodness, faith, meekness, temperance: against such there is no law. Gal. 5:22, 23.

If we have Christ abiding with us, we shall be Christians at home as well as abroad. He who is a Christian will have kind words for his relatives and associates. He will be kind, courteous, loving, sympathetic, and will be educating himself for an abode with the family above. If he is a member of the royal family, he will represent the kingdom to which he is going. He will speak with gentleness to his children, for he will realize that they, too, are heirs of God, members of the heavenly court. Among the children of God no spirit of harshness dwells; for "the fruit of the Spirit is love, joy, peace, longsuffering, gentleness, goodness, faith, meekness, temperance: against such there is no law." The spirit that is cherished in the home is the spirit that will be manifested in the church.

Oh, we must educate the soul to be pitiful, gentle, tender, full of forgiveness and compassion. While we lay aside all vanity, all foolish talking, jesting, and joking, we are not to become cold, unsympathetic, and unsocial. The Spirit of the Lord is to rest upon you until you shall be like a fragrant flower from the garden of God. You are to keep talking of the light, of Jesus, the Sun of righteousness, until you shall change from glory to glory, from character to character, going on from strength to strength, and reflecting more and more of the precious image of Jesus. When you do this, the Lord will write in the books of heaven, "Well done," because you represent Jesus.

Christians should not be hard-hearted, unapproachable; Jesus is to be reflected in our deportment, and we are to have a character beautiful with the graces of heaven. The presence of God is to be an abiding presence with us; and wherever we are, we are to carry light to the world. Those around you are to realize that the atmosphere of heaven surrounds you.—*Review and Herald*, Sept. 20, 1892.

GOODNESS

But I say unto you, That every idle word that men shall speak, they shall give account thereof in the day of judgment. For by thy words thou shalt be justified, and by thy words thou shalt be condemned. Matt. 12:36, 37.

God would have us individually come into that position where He can bestow His love upon us. He has placed a high value upon man, and has redeemed us by the sacrifice of His only begotten Son, and we are to see in our fellow man the purchase of the blood of Christ. If we have this love one for another, we shall be growing in love for God and the truth. We have been pained at heart to see how little love is cherished in our midst. Love is a plant of heavenly origin, and if we would have it flourish in our hearts, we must cultivate it daily. Mildness, gentleness, long-suffering, not being easily provoked, bearing all things, enduring all things—these are the fruits upon the precious tree of love.

When you are associated together, be guarded in your words. Let your conversation be of such a nature that you will have no need of repentance. "Grieve not the holy Spirit of God, whereby ye are sealed unto the day of redemption" (Eph. 4:30). "A good man out of the good treasure of the heart bringeth forth good things: and an evil man out of the evil treasure bringeth forth evil things" (Matt. 12:35). If the love of the truth is in your heart, you will talk of the truth. You will talk of the blessed hope that you have in Jesus. If you have love in your heart, you will seek to establish and build up your brother in the most holy faith. If a word is dropped that is detrimental to the character of your friend or brother, do not encourage this evil-speaking. It is the work of the enemy. Kindly remind the speaker that the Word of God forbids that kind of conversation.

We are to empty the heart of everything that defiles the soul temple, that Christ may dwell within. Our Redeemer has told us how we may reveal Him to the world. If we cherish His Spirit, if we manifest His love to others, if we guard one another's interest, if we are kind, patient, forbearing, the world will have an evidence by the fruits we bear that we are the children of God. It is the unity in the church that enables it to exert a conscious influence upon unbelievers and worldlings.—*Review and Herald*, June 5, 1888.

FAITH

Now faith is the substance of things hoped for, the evidence of things not seen. Heb. 11:1.

In coming to Christ there must be an exercise of faith. We need to bring Him into our everyday life; then we shall have peace and joy, and we shall know by experience the meaning of His word, "If ye keep my commandments, ye shall abide in my love; even as I have kept my Father's commandments, and abide in his love" (John 15:10). Our faith must claim the promise, that we may abide in the love of Jesus. Jesus said, "These things have I spoken unto you, that my joy might remain in you, and that your joy might be full" (verse 11).

Faith works by love and purifies the soul. Through faith the Holy Spirit finds access to the heart, and creates holiness therein. Man cannot become an agent to work the works of Christ unless he is in communion with God through the Holy Spirit. We can be fitted for heaven only through a transformation of character; we must have Christ's righteousness as our credentials, if we would find access to the Father. We must be partakers of the divine nature, having escaped the corruption that is in the world through lust. We must daily be transformed by the influence of the Holy Spirit; for it is the work of the Holy Spirit to elevate the taste, to sanctify the heart, to ennoble the whole man, by presenting to the soul the matchless charms of Jesus.

We are to behold Christ, and by beholding to become changed. We must come to Him, as to an open, inexhaustible fountain, from which we may drink again and again, and ever find a fresh supply. We are to respond to the drawing of His love, to feed on the Bread of Life which came down from heaven, to drink of the Water of Life which flows from the throne of God. We are to keep looking up, that faith may bind us to the throne of God. Do not look down, as though you were bound to the earth. Do not keep up an examination of your faith, pulling it up, as though it were a flower, to see if it has any root. Faith grows imperceptibly.—*Bible Echo*, Feb. 15, 1893.

MEEKNESS

With all lowliness and meekness, with longsuffering, forbearing one another in love. Eph. 4:2.

I invite you to look to the Man of Calvary. Look to Him whose head was crowned with the crown of thorns, who bore the cross of shame, who went step by step down the path of humiliation. Look to Him who was a man of sorrows, and acquainted with grief, who was despised and rejected of men. "Surely he hath borne our griefs, and carried our sorrows" (Isa. 53:4). "He was wounded for our transgressions, he was bruised for our iniquities: the chastisement of our peace was upon him; and with his stripes we are healed" (verse 5). Look to Calvary until your heart melts at the amazing love of the Son of God. He left nothing undone that fallen man might be elevated and purified.

And shall we not confess Him? Will the religion of Christ degrade its receiver? No; it will be no degradation to follow in the footsteps of the Man of Calvary. Day by day let us sit at the feet of Jesus, and learn of Him, that in our conversation, our conduct, our dress, and in all our affairs, we may reveal the fact that Jesus is ruling and reigning over us. God calls upon us to walk in a path that has been cast up for the ransomed of the Lord; we are not to walk in the world. We are to surrender all to God, and confess Christ before men.

"Whosoever shall deny me before men, him will I also deny before my Father which is in heaven" (Matt. 10:33). What right have we to profess to be Christians, and yet deny our Lord in life and deed? "He that taketh not his cross, and followeth after me is not worthy of me. He that findeth his life shall lose it: and he that loseth his life for my sake shall find it" (verses 38, 39). Day by day we are to deny self, to lift the cross and follow in the footsteps of the Master.

Oh, that the baptism of the Holy Spirit might come upon you, that you might be imbued with the Spirit of God! Then day by day you will become more and more conformed to the image of Christ, and in every action of your life, the question would be, "Will it glorify my Master?" By patient continuance in well-doing you would seek for glory and honor, and would receive the gift of immortality.—*Review and Herald*, May 10, 1892.

TEMPERANCE

Whether therefore ye eat, or drink, or whatsoever ye do, do all to the glory of God. 1 Cor. 10:31.

God requires all men to render their bodies to Him a living sacrifice, not a dead or a dying sacrifice, a sacrifice which their own course of action is debilitating, filling with impurities and disease. God calls for a living sacrifice. The body, He tells us, is the temple of the Holy Ghost, the habitation of His Spirit, and He requires all who bear His image to take care of their bodies for the purpose of His service and His glory. "Ye are not your own," says the inspired apostle, "ye are bought with a price"; wherefore "glorify God in your body, and in your spirit, which are God's" (1 Cor. 6:19, 20). In order to do this, add to virtue knowledge, and to knowledge temperance, and to temperance patience.

It is a duty to know how to preserve the body in the very best condition of health, and it is a sacred duty to live up to the light which God has graciously given. If we close our eyes to the light for fear we shall see our wrongs, which we are unwilling to forsake, our sins are not lessened but increased. If light is turned from in one case, it will be disregarded in another.

It is just as much sin to violate the laws of our being as to break one of the Ten Commandments, for we cannot do either without breaking God's law. We cannot love the Lord with all our heart, mind, soul, and strength while we are loving our appetites, our tastes, a great deal better than we love the Lord. We are daily lessening our strength to glorify God, when He requires all our strength, all our mind. By our wrong habits we are lessening our hold on life, and yet professing to be Christ's followers, preparing for the finishing touch of immortality. . . .

Closely examine your own hearts, and in your lives imitate the unerring Pattern, and all will be well with you. Preserve a clear conscience before God. In all you do glorify His name. Divest yourselves of selfishness and selfish love.—*Testimonies*, vol. 2, pp. 70, 71.

SELF-CONTROL

But Daniel purposed in his heart that he would not defile himself with the portion of the king's meat, nor with the wine which he drank: therefore he requested of the prince of the eunuchs that he might not defile himself. Dan. 1:8.

The lesson here presented is one that we would do well to ponder. A strict compliance with the Bible requirements will be a blessing both to body and soul. The fruit of the Spirit is not only love, joy, and peace, but temperance also. We are enjoined not to defile our bodies; for they are the temples of the Holy Spirit.

The Hebrew captives were men of like passions with ourselves. Amid the seductive influences of the luxurious courts of Babylon, they stood firm. The youth of today are surrounded with allurements to self-indulgence. Especially in our large cities, every form of sensual gratification is made easy and inviting. Those who, like Daniel, refuse to defile themselves will reap the reward of temperate habits. With their greater physical stamina and increased power of endurance, they have a bank of deposit upon which to draw in case of emergency.

Right physical habits promote mental superiority. Intellectual power, physical stamina, and length of life depend upon immutable laws. Nature's God will not interfere to preserve men from the consequences of violating nature's requirements. He who strives for the mastery must be temperate in all things. Daniel's clearness of mind and firmness of purpose, his power in acquiring knowledge and in resisting temptation, were due in a great degree to the plainness of his diet, in connection with his life of prayer. . . .

The history of Daniel and his youthful companions has been recorded on the pages of the Inspired Word, for the benefit of the youth of all succeeding ages. Through the record of their fidelity to the principles of temperance, God is speaking today to young men and young women, bidding them gather up the precious rays of light He has given on the subject of Christian temperance, and place themselves in right relation to the laws of health.—*Youth's Instructor*, July 9, 1903.

KINDNESS

She openeth her mouth with wisdom; and in her tongue is the law of kindness. Prov. 31:26.

The Lord will help every one of us where we need help the most in the grand work of overcoming and conquering self. Let the law of kindness be upon your lips and the oil of grace in your heart. This will produce wonderful results. You will be tender, sympathetic, courteous. You need all these graces. The Holy Spirit must be received and brought into your character; then it will be as holy fire, giving forth incense which will rise up to God, not from lips that condemn, but as a healer of the souls of men. Your countenance will express the image of the divine.

No sharp, critical, blunt, or severe words should be spoken. This is common fire, and must be left out of all our councils and intercourse with our brethren. God requires every soul in His service to kindle their censers from the coals of sacred fire. The common, severe, harsh words that come from your lips so readily must be withheld, and the Spirit of God speak through the human agent. By beholding the character of Christ you will become changed into His likeness. The grace of Christ alone can change your heart and then you will reflect the image of the Lord Jesus. God calls upon us to be like Him—pure, holy, and undefiled. We are to bear the divine image.—*The SDA Bible Commentary*, Ellen G. White Comments, vol. 3, p. 1164.

We may talk of the blessings of the Holy Spirit, and pray in regard to receiving them; but unless the human agent is worked by the Spirit of God, He reveals that he has Him not. When the Spirit molds and fashions the character after the divine similitude, He will be unmistakably revealed in every word we speak and in everything we do, showing to the world that there is a marked difference between the children of light and the children of darkness. The Lord wants us to stand stiffly for the faith once delivered to the saints. We are to speak the truth in love. Our great Teacher says, "Take my yoke upon you, and learn of me, for I am meek and lowly in heart: and ye shall find rest unto your souls. For my yoke is easy, and my burden is light" (Matt. 11:29, 30).—Letter 84, 1899.

CHARITY

Is not this the fast that I have chosen? to loose the bands of wickedness, to undo the heavy burdens, and to let the oppressed go free, and that ye break every yoke? Is it not to deal thy bread to the hungry, and that thou bring the poor that are cast out to thy house? when thou seest the naked, that thou cover him; and that thou hide not thyself from thine own flesh? Isa. 58:6, 7.

Truth, precious truth, is sanctifying in its influence. The sanctification of the soul by the operation of the Holy Spirit is the implanting of Christ's nature in humanity. It is the grace of our Lord Jesus Christ revealed in character, and the grace of Christ brought into active exercise in good works. Thus the character is transformed more and more perfectly after the image of Christ in righteousness and true holiness.

There are broad requirements in divine truth stretching out into one line after another of good works. The truths of the gospel are not unconnected; uniting they form one string of heavenly jewels, as in the personal work of Christ, and like threads of gold they run through the whole of Christian work and experience.—*Selected Messages*, book 3, p. 198.

Any neglect on the part of those who claim to be followers of Christ, a failure to relieve the necessities of a brother or a sister who is bearing the yoke of poverty and oppression, is registered in the books of heaven as shown to Christ in the person of His saints. What a reckoning the Lord will have with many, very many, who present the words of Christ to others but fail to manifest tender sympathy and regard for a brother in the faith who is less fortunate and successful than themselves.— *Welfare Ministry*, p. 210.

Many will allow a brother to struggle along unaided under adverse circumstances, and in thus doing they give to one precious soul the impression that they are thus representing Christ. It is no such thing; Jesus, who was rich, for our sake became poor, that we through His poverty might be rich. That He might save the sinner, He withheld not His own life. The heart of Christ is ever touched with human woe.— *Ellen G. White 1888 Materials*, p. 1270.

CONTENTMENT

Not that I speak in respect of want: for I have learned, in whatsoever state I am, therewith to be content. Phil. 4:11.

God has His faithful witnesses who are not attempting to do that which Christ has pronounced impossible—that is, seeking to serve God and mammon at the same time. They are burning and shining lights amid the moral darkness of the world, and amid the gross darkness that covers the people like the pall of death. The members of the church of Christ are individually to be controlled by the Holy Spirit, in order that they may not have a changeable, fluctuating experience. They are to be rooted and grounded in the truth.

When the joy of the saving power of Christ's righteousness is rightly understood by experimental knowledge, there will be vital interest in the church, there will be those who will teach transgressors God's ways, and sinners will be converted to the truth as it is in Jesus. It is the professors of religion that need converting; for Satan has brought his deceptions to bear upon their souls.

The soul that is brought into personal contact with Christ becomes a holy temple unto the Lord; for Jesus is made unto the believer wisdom, righteousness, sanctification, and redemption. He who has fully surrendered to God has a consciousness of Christ's saving presence. He is a possessor of spiritual patience, and has the rest of soul that comes from learning of Him who is meek and lowly of heart. Trusting in Jesus to be his efficiency and righteousness, his soul is filled with a pleasant contentment.

What is the joy of the Christian? It is the result of the consciousness of the presence of Christ. What is the love of the Christian? It is the reflection of the love of Christ. It is the effect of the operation of the Holy Spirit. Looking to the cross of Calvary, we see Jesus dying for the sins of the world, in order that by His death, life and immortality might be brought to light in behalf of the contrite soul. Jesus is all in all, and without Him we can do nothing. Without Christ, spiritual life would be impossible.—*Review and Herald*, Dec. 4, 1894.

THANKFULNESS

In every thing give thanks: for this is the will of God in Christ Jesus concerning you. 1 Thess. 5:18.

There is much needless worrying, much trouble of mind, over things that cannot be helped. The Lord would have His children put their trust fully in Him. Our Lord is a just and righteous God. His children should acknowledge His goodness and His justice in the large and the small things of life. Those who cherish the spirit of worry and complaint are refusing to recognize His guiding hand. Needless anxiety is a foolish thing; and it hinders us from standing in a true position before God.

When the Holy Spirit comes into the soul, there will be no desire to complain and murmur because we do not have everything we want; rather, we will thank God from a full heart for the blessings that we have. There is a great need of more thankfulness among our workers today; and until they have this spirit they will be unprepared for a place in the kingdom of heaven. There is a mighty work to be done for every one of us. We comprehend but little of what God desires to work out through us. We should seek to realize the breadth of His plans, and profit by every lesson that He [has] tried to teach us.

A great deal of mischief is wrought in the imagination of our own hearts and minds when we seek to carry our own way contrary to the law of kindness. Here is where many fail. We do not cultivate a disposition to kindness; we want everything to come in an easy way to ourselves. But the question of greatest importance to each one of us should be not how we can carry our own plans against the plans of others, but how we can have the power to live for Christ every day. Christ came to earth and gave His life that we might have eternal salvation. He wants to encircle each of us with the atmosphere of heaven, that we may give to the world an example that will honor the religion of Christ.—*Loma Linda Messages*, p. 602.

HARMONY

Endeavoring to keep the unity of the Spirit in the bond of peace. There is one body, and one Spirit, even as ye are called in one hope of your calling. Eph. 4:3, 4.

The Holy Spirit will work with the consecrated human instrument; for this is God's purpose. God has opened a door between heaven and earth, which no power can close. He calls upon every human being to be pure, holy, sanctified, in order that the work for this time may be accomplished. When God's people place themselves in proper relation to Him and to one another, there will be a full impartation of the Holy Spirit for the harmonious combination of the whole body.

Nothing so manifestly weakens a church as disunion and strife. Nothing so wars against Christ and the truth as this spirit. "By their fruits ye shall know them" (Matt. 7:20). "Doth a fountain send forth at the same place sweet water and bitter? Can the fig tree, my brethren, bear olive berries? either a vine, figs? so can no fountain both yield salt water and fresh. Who is a wise man and endued with knowledge among you? Let him shew out of a good conversation his works with meekness of wisdom" (James 3:11-13).

"Wherefore lift up the hands which hang down, and the feeble knees; and make straight paths for your feet, lest that which is lame be turned out of the way; but let it rather be healed. Follow peace with all men, and holiness, without which no man shall see the Lord: looking diligently lest any man fail of the grace of God; lest any root of bitterness springing up trouble you, and thereby many be defiled" (Heb. 12:12-15).

As long as we are in this world we must be linked with one another. Humanity is interlaced and interwoven with humanity. As Christians we are members one of another. The Lord has made us thus, and when disappointments come, we are not to think the worse of one another. We are individual members of the general body. In helplessness and disappointment we are fighting the battles of life, and the Lord designs us, as His sons and daughters, whom He calls His friends, to help one another. This is to be a part of our practical Christian work.—*Signs of the Times*, Feb. 7, 1900.

UNITY

Neither pray I for these alone, but for them also which shall believe on me through their word; that they all may be one; as thou, Father, art in me, and I in thee, that they also may be one in us: that the world may believe that thou hast sent me. John 17:20, 21.

Harmony and union existing among men of varied dispositions is the strongest witness that can be borne that God has sent His Son into the world to save sinners. It is our privilege to bear this witness. But, in order to do this, we must place ourselves under Christ's command. Our characters must be molded in harmony with His character, our wills must be surrendered to His will. Then we shall work together without a thought of collision.

Little differences dwelt upon lead to actions that destroy Christian fellowship. Let us not allow the enemy thus to gain the advantage over us. Let us keep drawing nearer to God and to one another. Then we shall be as trees of righteousness, planted by the Lord, and watered by the river of life. And how fruitful we shall be! Did not Christ say: "Herein is my Father glorified, that ye bear much fruit" (John 15:8)?

The heart of the Saviour is set upon His followers' fulfilling God's purpose in all its height and depth. They are to be one in Him, even though they are scattered the world over. But God cannot make them one in Christ unless they are willing to give up their own way for His way.

When Christ's prayer is fully believed, when its instruction is brought into the daily life of God's people, unity of action will be seen in our ranks. Brother will be bound to brother by the golden bonds of the love of Christ. The Spirit of God alone can bring about this oneness. He who sanctified Himself can sanctify His disciples. United with Him, they will be united with one another in the most holy faith. When we strive for this unity as God desires us to strive for it, it will come to us.—*Testimonies*, vol. 8, pp. 242, 243.

ONENESS

And the glory which thou gavest me I have given them; that they may be one, even as we are one: I in them, and thou in me, that they may be made perfect in one; and that the world may know that thou hast sent me, and hast loved them, as thou hast loved me. John 17:22, 23.

What attainments are there presented for the Christian's endeavor, but how far short are our practices. Were our practices in harmony with the command of our Lord, the result would be glorious. He says, "Neither pray I for these alone, but for them also which shall believe on me through their word; that they all may be one; as thou, Father, art in me, and I in thee, that they also may be one in us: that the world may believe that thou hast sent me" (John 17:20, 21). . . .

Jesus did not pray for that which was not attainable by us, and if this unity is possible, why do not those who are professed followers of Christ strive more earnestly for this condition of grace? When we are one with Christ, we shall be one with His followers. The great want of the soul is Jesus, the hope of glory. Through the Holy Spirit this unity may be attained, and love for the brethren will abound, and men will take knowledge of us that we have been with Jesus and learned of Him. Our life will be a reflection of His holy character. As believers in Him we shall represent His meekness of spirit, His gentleness of demeanor. Individually the church of God must answer the prayer of Christ till we all come into the unity of the Spirit.

What is it that causes dissension and discord? It is the result of walking apart from Christ. At a distance from Him, we lose our love for Him, and grow cold toward His followers. The farther the beams of light recede from their center, the wider separated they become. Each believer is as a beam of light from Christ the Sun of righteousness. The more closely we walk with Christ, the center of all love and light, the greater will be our affection for His light-bearers. When the saints are drawn close to Christ, they must of necessity be drawn close to each other, for the sanctifying grace of Christ will bind their hearts together. You cannot love God and yet fail to love your brethren.—*Ellen G. White 1888 Materials*, pp. 1048, 1049.

BROTHERLY LOVE

Be kindly affectioned one to another with brotherly love; in honour prefer-
ring one another. Rom. 12:10.

When the Holy Spirit moves upon human minds, all petty complaints and accusations between man and his fellow man will be put away. The bright beams of the Sun of righteousness will shine into the chambers of the mind and heart. In our worship of God there will be no distinction between rich and poor, white and black. All prejudice will be melted away. When we approach God, it will be as one brotherhood. We are pilgrims and strangers, bound for a better country, even a heavenly. There all pride, all accusation, all self-deception, will forever have an end. Every mask will be laid aside, and we shall "see him as he is" (1 John 3:2). There our songs will catch the inspiring theme, and praise and thanksgiving will go up to God.—*Review and Hearld*, Oct. 24, 1899.

The Lord Jesus came to our world to save men and women of all nationalities. . . . Jesus came to shed light over the whole world. At the beginning of His ministry He declared His mission: "The Spirit of the Lord is upon me, because he hath anointed me to preach the gospel to the poor; he hath sent me to heal the brokenhearted, to preach deliverance to the captives, and recovering of sight to the blind, to set at liberty them that are bruised, to preach the acceptable year of the Lord" (Luke 4:18, 19). . . .

The Lord's eye is upon all His creatures; He loves them all, and makes no difference between white and black, except that He has a special tender pity for those who are called to bear a greater burden than others. Those who love God and believe on Christ as their Redeemer, while they must meet the trials and the difficulties that lie in their path, should yet with a cheerful spirit accept their life as it is, considering that God above regards these things, and for all that the world neglects to bestow, He will Himself make up to them in the best of favors.—*Selected Messages*, book 2, pp. 487, 488.

GENEROSITY

How that in a great trial of affliction the abundance of their joy and their deep poverty abounded unto the riches of their liberality. 2 Cor. 8:2.

It is only when Christian motives are fully acknowledged, and the conscience is awake to duty, when divine light makes impressions upon the heart and character, that selfishness is overcome, and the mind of Christ is exemplified. The Holy Spirit, working upon human hearts and characters, will expel all tendency to covetousness, to deceptive dealing.

When the Lord's messenger bears a message to the church, God is speaking to the people, awakening the conscience to see that they have not been rendering an honest tithe to the Lord, and that when it was not convenient to give, they have failed to present their offerings to Him. They have used the Lord's own money for themselves, in building houses, in purchasing horses, carriages, or lands. They do this in the hope of large returns, and every year they have the same excuse. "Will a man rob God?" (Mal. 3:8). Oh, yes, he has done this many times, because he has not been spiritual, to discern the spiritual things.

On some occasions the Lord has moved decidedly upon worldly, selfish men. Their minds were illuminated by the Holy Spirit, their hearts felt His softening, subduing influence. Under a sense of the abundant mercy and grace of God, they felt it their duty to promote His cause, to build up His kingdom. They remembered the requirement, "Lay not up for yourselves treasures upon earth, where moth and rust doth corrupt, and where thieves break through and steal: but lay up for yourselves treasures in heaven, where neither moth nor rust doth corrupt, and where thieves do not break through nor steal" (Matt. 6:19, 20). They felt a desire to have a share in the kingdom of God, and they pledged to give of their means to some of the various enterprises of the Lord's cause. That pledge was not made to man, but to God in the presence of His angels, who were moving upon the hearts of these selfish, money-loving men.—*Review and Herald*, May 23, 1893.

BENEVOLENCE

Every man according as he purposeth in his heart, so let him give; not grudgingly, or of necessity: for God loveth a cheerful giver. And God is able to make all grace abound toward you; that ye, always having all sufficiency in all things, may abound to every good work. 2 Cor. 9:7, 8.

W hen the hearts of men are softened by the presence of the Spirit of God, they are more susceptible to impressions of the Holy Spirit, and resolves are made to deny self and to sacrifice for the cause of God. It is when divine light shines into the chambers of the mind with unusual clearness and power that the feelings of the natural man are overcome, that selfishness loses its power upon the heart, and that desires are awakened to imitate the Pattern, Jesus Christ, in practicing self-denial and benevolence. The disposition of the naturally selfish man then becomes kind and pitiful toward lost sinners, and he makes a solemn pledge to God, as did Abraham and Jacob.

Heavenly angels are present on such occasions. The love of God and love for souls triumphs over selfishness and love of the world. Especially is this the case when the speaker, in the Spirit and power of God, presents the plan of redemption, laid by the Majesty of heaven in the sacrifice of the cross. . . .

God has given man a part to act in accomplishing the salvation of His fellow men. He can work in connection with Christ by doing acts of mercy and beneficence. But he cannot redeem them, not being able to satisfy the claims of insulted justice. This the Son of God alone can do, by laying aside His honor and glory, clothing His divinity with humanity, and coming to earth to humiliate Himself and shed His blood in behalf of the human race.

In commissioning His disciples to go "into all the world, and preach the gospel to every creature" (Mark 16:15), Christ assigned to men the work of spreading the gospel. But while some go forth to preach, He calls upon others to answer to His claims upon them for tithes and offerings with which to support the ministry and to spread the printed truth all over the land.—*Testimonies*, vol. 4, pp. 470-472.

PURITY

Blessed are the pure in heart: for they shall see God. Matt. 5:8.

When one is fully emptied of self, when every false god is cast out of the soul, the vacuum is supplied by the inflowing of the Spirit of Christ. Such a one has the faith which works by love and purifies the soul from every moral and spiritual defilement. The Holy Spirit, the Comforter, can work upon the heart, influencing and directing, so that he enjoys spiritual things. He is "after the Spirit" (Rom. 8:1), and he minds the things of the Spirit. He has no confidence in self; Christ is all in all. Truth is constantly being unfolded by the Holy Spirit; he receives with meekness the engrafted word, and he gives the Lord all the glory, saying, "God has revealed them unto us by his Spirit" (1 Cor. 2:10). "Now we have received, not the spirit of the world, but the spirit which is of God; that we might know the things that are freely given to us of God" (verse 12).

The Spirit that reveals also works in him the fruits of righteousness. Christ is in him "a well of water springing up into everlasting life" (John 4:14). He is a branch of the True Vine, and bears rich clusters of fruit to the glory of God. What is the character of the fruit borne? "The fruit of the Spirit is love." Mark the words—love, not hatred; it is joy, not discontent and mourning; peace, not irritation, anxiety, and manufactured trials. It is "longsuffering, gentleness, goodness, faith, meekness, temperance: against such there is no law" (Gal. 5:22, 23).

Those who have this Spirit will be earnest laborers together with God; the heavenly intelligences cooperate with them, and they go weighted with the Spirit of the message of truth which they bear. They are a spectacle to the world, to angels, and to men. They are ennobled, refined, through the sanctification of the Spirit and belief of the truth. They have not brought into the treasury of the soul wood, hay, stubble, but gold, silver, and precious stones. They speak words of solid sense, and from the treasures of the heart bring forth pure and sacred things according to the example of Christ.—*Home Missionary*, Nov. 1, 1893.

OUTWARD NEATNESS

She is not afraid of the snow for her household: for all her household are clothed with scarlet. She maketh herself coverings of tapestry; her clothing is silk and purple. Prov. 31:21, 22.

Educate, educate, educate. Parents who receive the truth are to conform their habits and practices to the directions God has given. The Lord desires all to remember that the service of God is a pure and holy service, and that those who receive the truth must be purified in disposition, in temper, in heart, in conversation, in the dress, and in the home, so that the angels of God, unseen by them, shall come in to minister to those who shall be heirs of salvation.

All who join the church should reveal a transformation of character which shows their reverence for holy things. Their whole life should be molded after the refinement of Christ Jesus. Those who join the church are to be humble enough to receive instruction on the points wherein they are remiss, and wherein they can and must change. They must exert a Christian influence. Those who make no change in words or deportment, in their dress or in their homes, are living unto themselves and not unto Christ. They have not been created anew in Christ Jesus, unto the purifying of the heart and the outward surroundings.

Christians will be judged by the fruit they bear in reformatory work. Every true Christian will show what the truth of the gospel has done for him. He who has been made a son of God must practice habits of neatness and cleanliness. Every action, however small, has an influence. The Lord desires to make every human being an agency through whom Christ can manifest His Holy Spirit. Christians are in no case to be careless or indifferent in regard to their outward appearance. They are to be neat and trim, though without adornment. They are to be pure inside and out.—*Testimonies to Southern Africa*, p. 87.

OBEDIENCE

As obedient children, not fashioning yourselves according to the former lusts in your ignorance: but as he which hath called you is holy, so be ye holy in all manner of conversation. 1 Peter 1:14, 15.

What does God require? Perfection, nothing less than perfection. But if we would be perfect, we must put no confidence in self. Daily we must know and understand that self is not to be trusted. We need to grasp God's promises with firm faith. We need to ask for the Holy Spirit with a full realization of our own helplessness. Then when the Holy Spirit works we shall not give self the glory. The Holy Spirit will graciously take the heart into His keeping, bringing to it all the bright beams of the Sun of righteousness. We shall be kept by the power of God through faith.

When we are daily under the control of God's Spirit, we shall be commandment-keeping people. We may show to the world that obedience to God's commands brings its own reward, even in this life, and in the future life eternal blessedness. Notwithstanding our profession of faith, the Lord, by whom our actions are weighed, sees but an imperfect representation of Christ. He has declared that such a condition of things cannot glorify Him.

It means much to commit the keeping of the soul to God. It means that we are to live and walk by faith, not trusting in or glorifying self, but looking to Jesus our advocate as the author and finisher of our faith. The Holy Spirit will do His work upon the heart that is contrite, but never can He work upon a self-important, self-righteous soul. In his own wisdom such a one would mend himself. He interposes between his soul and the Holy Spirit. The Holy Spirit will work if self will not interpose.

Where is our dependence? Where is our help? God's Word tells us: "The Comforter, which is the Holy Ghost, whom the Father will send in my name, he shall teach you all things, and bring all things to your remembrance, whatsoever I have said unto you" (John 14:26). The Holy Spirit is ready to cooperate with all who will receive Him and be taught by Him. All who lay hold on the truth and are sanctified through the truth are so united with Christ that they can represent Him in word and action.—*Manuscript Releases*, vol. 12, pp. 52, 53.

CONFIDENCE

Cast not away therefore your confidence, which hath great recompence of reward. Heb. 10:35.

John says, "This is the confidence that we have in him, that, if we ask anything according to his will, he heareth us: and if we know that he hear us, whatsoever we ask, we know that we have the petitions that we desired of him" (1 John 5:14, 15). Let us dwell much upon these points before the people, that their ideas may be enlarged, their faith increased. They should be encouraged to ask largely, and expect without a doubt the riches of His grace; for through Jesus we can come into the audience chamber of the Most High. Through His merits we have access by one Spirit unto the Father.

Oh, that we may have a deeper experience in prayer! With confidence we may come to God, knowing what it is to have the presence and power of His Holy Spirit. We may confess our sins, and right there, while asking, know that He pardons our transgressions, because He has promised to forgive. We must exercise faith, and manifest true earnestness and humility. We can never do this without the grace of the Holy Spirit. We must lie low at the feet of Jesus, and cherish no selfishness, reveal no self-uplifting, but in simplicity seek the Lord, asking for His Holy Spirit as a little child asks bread of his parents.

We should act our part, take Christ as our personal Saviour, and, standing under the cross of Calvary, "Look and live." God sets His children apart for Himself. And as they connect themselves with Him, they have power with God, and prevail. Of ourselves we can do nothing; but through the grace of His Holy Spirit, life and light are imparted, and the soul is filled with longing, earnest desire for God, for holiness. Then it is that Christ leads us to the throne of grace, and clothes us with His righteousness; for the Lord God of heaven loves us. We would be willfully blind and stubborn to doubt that His heart is toward us. While Jesus, our Intercessor, pleads for us in heaven, the Holy Spirit works in us, to will and to do of His good pleasure. All heaven is interested in the salvation of the soul. Then what reason have we to doubt that the Lord will and does help us?—*Signs of the Times*, Oct. 3, 1892.

GODLINESS

And Enoch walked with God: and he was not; for God took him. Gen. 5:24.

Godliness is the fruit of Christian character. If we abide in the Vine, we shall bear the fruits of the Spirit. The life of the Vine will manifest itself through the branches. We must have a close and intimate connection with heaven, if we bear the grace of godliness. Jesus must be a guest in our homes, a member of our households, if we reflect His image and show that we are sons and daughters of the Most High.

Religion is a beautiful thing in the home. If the Lord abides with us, we shall feel that we are members of Christ's family in heaven. We shall realize that angels are watching us, and our manners will be gentle and forbearing. We shall be fitting up for an entrance into the courts of heaven, by cultivating courtesy and godliness. Our conversation will be holy, and our thoughts will be upon heavenly things.

Enoch walked with God. He honored God in every affair of life. In his home and in his business, he inquired, "Will this be acceptable to the Lord?" And by remembering God, and following His counsel, he was transformed in character, and became a godly man, whose ways pleased the Lord. We are exhorted to add to godliness brotherly kindness. Oh, how much we need to take this step, to add this quality to our characters! In many of our homes there is a hard, combative spirit manifested. Critical words and unkind actions are offensive to God. Dictatorial commands and haughty, overbearing manners are not acceptable to heaven. The reason there are so many differences existing between brethren is that they have failed to add brotherly kindness. We should have that love for others that Christ has had for us.

A man is estimated at his true value by the Lord of heaven. If he is unkind in his earthly home, he is unfit for the heavenly home. If he will have his own way, no matter whom it grieves, he would not be content in heaven, unless he could rule there. The love of Christ must control our hearts, and the peace of God will abide in our homes.—*Review and Herald*, Feb. 21, 1888.

HOLINESS

Follow peace with all men, and holiness, without which no man shall see the Lord. Heb. 12:14.

God has from eternity chosen men to be holy. "This is the will of God [concerning you], even your sanctification" (1 Thess. 4:3). The echo of His voice comes to us, ever saying, "Holier, holier still." And ever our answer is to be "Yes, Lord, holier still."

No man receives holiness as a birthright, or as a gift from any other human being. Holiness is the gift of God through Christ. Those who receive the Saviour become sons of God. They are His spiritual children, born again, renewed in righteousness and true holiness. Their minds are changed. With clearer vision they behold eternal realities. They are adopted into God's family, and they become conformed to His likeness, changed by His Spirit from glory to glory. From cherishing supreme love for self, they come to cherish supreme love for God and for Christ.

"Being justified by faith, we have peace with God through our Lord Jesus Christ" (Rom. 5:1). Justification means pardon. It means that the heart, purged from dead works, is prepared to receive the blessing of sanctification. God has told us what we must do to receive this blessing. "Work out your own salvation with fear and trembling. For it is God which worketh in you both to will and to do of his good pleasure. Do all things without murmuring and disputings; that ye may be blameless and harmless, the sons of God, without rebuke, in the midst of a crooked and perverse nation, among whom ye shine as lights in the world" (Phil. 2:12-15).

The love of God, cherished in the heart and revealed in the words and acts, will do more to elevate and ennoble human beings than all else can. In the life of Christ, this love found full and complete expression. On the cross of Christ the Saviour made an atonement for the fallen race. Holiness is the fruit of this sacrifice. It is because He has died for us that we are promised this great gift. And Christ longs to bestow this gift on us. He longs to make us partakers of His nature. He longs to save those who by sin have separated themselves from God. He calls upon them to choose His service, to give themselves wholly into His control, to learn from Him how to do God's will.—*Signs of the Times*, Dec. 17, 1902.

HUMILITY

And I prayed unto the Lord my God, and made my confession, and said, O Lord, the great and dreadful God, keeping the covenant and mercy to them that love him, and to them that keep his commandments; we have sinned, and have committed iniquity, and have done wickedly, and have rebelled, even by departing from thy precepts and from thy judgments. Dan. 9:4, 5.

Spurious sanctification carries with it a boastful, self-righteous spirit which is foreign to the religion of the Bible. Meekness and humility are the fruits of the Spirit. The prophet Daniel was an example of true sanctification. His long life was filled up with noble service for his Master. He was a man "greatly beloved" (Dan. 10:11) of heaven, and was granted such honors as have rarely been vouchsafed to mortals. Yet his purity of character and unwavering fidelity were equaled only by his humility and contrition.

Instead of claiming to be pure and holy, this honored prophet identified himself with the really sinful of Israel, as he pleaded before God in behalf of his people: "We do not present our supplications before thee for our righteousness, but for thy great mercies" (Dan. 9:18). "We have sinned, we have done wickedly" (verse 15). And "for our sins, and for the iniquities of our fathers, Jerusalem and thy people are become a reproach" (verse 16).

He declares, "I was speaking, and praying, and confessing my sin and the sin of my people" (verse 20). And when at a later time the Son of God appeared in answer to his prayers to give him instruction, he declares, "My comeliness was turned in me into corruption, and I retained no strength" (Dan. 10:8).

Those who are truly seeking to perfect Christian character will never indulge the thought that they are sinless. The more their minds dwell upon the character of Christ, and the nearer they approach to His divine image, the more clearly will they discern Its spotless perfection, and the more deeply will they feel their own weakness and defects. Those who claim to be without sin give evidence that they are far from holy. It is because they have no true knowledge of Christ that they can look upon themselves as reflecting His image. The greater the distance between them and their Saviour, the more righteous they appear in their own eyes.—*The Spirit of Prophecy*, vol. 4, pp. 301, 302.

DEPENDENCE

Not as though I had already attained, either were already perfect: but I follow after, if that I may apprehend that for which also I am apprehended of Christ Jesus. Phil. 3:12.

The experience of the Christian in his earliest love is full of simplicity and freshness; but as his opportunities multiply, his experience should enlarge, and his knowledge increase. He should become strong to bear responsibility, and his maturity should be in proportion to his privileges. . . .

But unless there is an hourly dependence upon Christ, increasing knowledge and privileges will result in self-trust and self-righteousness. The young Christian is in danger of forgetting that it is Christ that has begun the good work in him, and that it is Christ that must finish it. The soul must renounce all merit, and trust wholly in the merit of Him who is too wise to err. Man of himself can do no good thing. Said Jesus, "Without me ye can do nothing" (John 15:5). The soul is to stay itself upon God.

In the gift of Christ all heaven was poured out, and through Christ the Holy Spirit is promised to the believer. Jesus said to His disciples, "The Comforter, which is the Holy Ghost, whom the Father will send in my name, he shall teach you all things, and bring all things to your remembrance, whatsoever I have said unto you" (John 14:26). Christ not only offers pardon to the believing, repenting soul, but He promises him the constant aid of the Holy Spirit.

In the growth of the seed in the soil, man cannot see the working of unseen agencies that develop the plant to perfection, bringing up first the blade, then the ear, then the full corn in the ear. But though young in the faith, you may know that you have passed from death unto life, if the fruits of the Spirit are made manifest in your life. If you are growing in faith and hope and love, you may know that your spiritual vision has been cleared. If you delight to dwell upon the plan of salvation, upon the glorious manifestations of the divine character, if your heart, in contemplation of the love of God, glows with thankfulness and joy, you may be sure that you have been illuminated by the beams of the Holy Spirit, and heavenly agencies are bringing your character up to maturity of Christian life.—*Signs of the Times*, Mar. 27, 1893.

CHRISTLIKENESS

Beloved, now are we the sons of God, and it doth not yet appear what we shall be: but we know that, when he shall appear, we shall be like him; for we shall see him as he is. 1 John 3:2.

Christ is soon coming in the clouds of heaven, and we must be prepared to meet Him, not having spot or wrinkle or any such thing. We are now to accept the invitation of Christ. He says, "Come unto me, all ye that labour and are heavy laden, and I will give you rest. Take my yoke upon you, and learn of me; for I am meek and lowly in heart: and ye shall find rest unto your souls" (Matt. 11:28, 29). The words of Christ to Nicodemus are of practical value to us today: "Except a man be born of water and of the Spirit, he cannot enter into the kingdom of God. That which is born of the flesh is flesh; and that which is born of the Spirit is spirit. Marvel not that I said unto thee, Ye must be born again. The wind bloweth where it listeth, and thou hearest the sound thereof, but canst not tell whence it cometh, and whither it goeth: so is every one that is born of the Spirit" (John 3:5-8).

The converting power of God must be upon our hearts. We must study the life of Christ, and imitate the divine Pattern. We must dwell upon the perfection of His character, and be changed into His image. No one will enter the kingdom of God unless his passions are subdued, unless his will is brought into captivity to the will of Christ.

Heaven is free from all sin, from all defilement and impurity; and if we would live in its atmosphere, if we would behold the glory of Christ, we must be pure in heart, perfect in character through His grace and righteousness. We must not be taken up with pleasure and amusement, but be fitting up for the glorious mansions Christ has gone to prepare for us. If we are faithful, seeking to bless others, patient in well-doing, at His coming Christ will crown us with glory, honor, and immortality.—*Review and Herald*, Apr. 28, 1891.

ENLIGHTENED THROUGH THE SPIRIT

The eyes of your understanding being enlightened; that ye may know what is the hope of his calling, and what the riches of the glory of his inheritance in the saints. Eph. 1:18.

The apostle Paul makes supplication to God: "That the God of our Lord Jesus Christ, the Father of glory, may give unto you the spirit of wisdom and revelation in the knowledge of him: the eyes of your understanding being enlightened; that ye may know what is the hope of his calling, and what the riches of the glory of his inheritance in the saints, and what is the exceeding greatness of his power to us-ward who believe, according to the working of his mighty power" (Eph. 1:17-19). But the mind must first be made adaptable to the nature of the truth to be investigated. The eyes of the understanding must be enlightened, and heart and mind brought into harmony with God, who is truth.

He who beholds Jesus with the eye of faith sees no glory in himself; for the glory of the Redeemer is reflected into the mind and heart. The atonement of His blood is realized, and the taking away of sin stirs his heart with gratitude. Being justified by Christ, the receiver of truth is constrained to make an entire surrender to God, and is admitted into the school of Christ, that he may learn of Him who is meek and lowly of heart. A knowledge of the love of God is shed abroad in his heart. He exclaims, Oh, what love! What condescension! Grasping the rich promises of faith, he becomes a partaker of the divine nature. His heart being emptied of self, the waters of life flow in, and the glory of the Lord shines forth. Perpetually looking unto Jesus, the human is assimilated by the divine. The believer is changed into His likeness.

"We all, with open face beholding as in a glass the glory of the Lord, are changed into the same image from glory to glory [from character to character] even as by the Spirit of the Lord" (2 Cor. 3:18). The human character is changed into the divine. It is the spiritual eye that discerns this glory. It is veiled, shrouded in mystery, until the Holy Spirit imparts this discernment to the soul.—*Review and Herald*, Feb. 18, 1896.

THE SPIRIT ESSENTIAL FOR UNDERSTANDING TRUTH

But God hath revealed them unto us by his Spirit: for the Spirit searcheth all things, yea, the deep things of God. 1 Cor. 2:10.

There is a great work to be done for this time, and we do not half realize what the Lord is willing to do for His people. We talk about the first angel's message, and the second angel's message, and we think we have some understanding of the third angel's message; but we should not be satisfied with our present knowledge. Our petitions, mingled with faith and contrition, should go up to God, for an understanding of the mysteries that God would make known to His saints. We should have a realization that unless taught by the Holy Spirit, we shall not rightly comprehend the Bible; for it is a sealed book even to the learned, who are wise in their own conceit.

Jesus meant just what He said when He directed His disciples to "*search* the Scriptures." Searching means to compare scripture with scripture, and spiritual things with spiritual. We should not be satisfied with a superficial knowledge. We should search for the hidden treasure concealed beneath the surface, as the merchantman seeks for goodly pearls. Light, great light, will reward the diligent searcher for truth.

There are many who have not taxed their mental powers, and who have no experience in putting to the stretch their utmost ability to find out what is truth. It is not possible that the Holy Spirit shall fall upon you unless you feel your need, and are more desirous for its descent than you now are. You should realize that you are living upon the very borders of the eternal world, that Christ is coming very soon, and that all heaven is interested in the work that is in progress in fitting up a people for His coming.

If ever there was a people that needed to heed the counsel of the True Witness to the Laodicean church to be zealous and to repent before God, it is the people who have had opened up before them the stupendous truths for this time, and who have not lived up to their high privileges and responsibilities. We have lost much in not living up to the light of the solemn truths which we profess to believe.—*Review and Herald*, June 4, 1889.

WAYS IN WHICH THE SPIRIT LEADS US

My sheep hear my voice, and I know them, and they follow me. John 10:27.

Jesus expects all who claim to be His soldiers to do service for Him. He expects you to recognize the enemy and to resist him, not to invite him to your confidence and thus betray sacred trust. The Lord has placed you in a position where you may be elevated and ennobled, and be constantly gaining fitness for His work. If you do not obtain these qualifications; you alone are to blame.

There are three ways in which the Lord reveals His will to us, to guide us, and to fit us to guide others. How may we know His voice from that of a stranger? How shall we distinguish it from the voice of a false shepherd? God reveals His will to us in His Word, the Holy Scriptures. His voice is also revealed in His providential workings; and it will be recognized if we do not separate our souls from Him by walking in our own ways, doing according to our own wills, and following the promptings of an unsanctified heart, until the senses have become so confused that eternal things are not discerned, and the voice of Satan is so disguised that it is accepted as the voice of God.

Another way in which God's voice is heard is through the appeals of His Holy Spirit, making impressions upon the heart, which will be wrought out in the character. If you are in doubt upon any subject, you must first consult the Scriptures. If you have truly begun the life of faith, you have given yourself to the Lord to be wholly His, and He has taken you to mold and fashion according to His purpose, that you may be a vessel unto honor. You should have an earnest desire to be pliable in His hands and to follow whithersoever He may lead you. You are then trusting him to work out His designs, while at the same time you are cooperating with Him by working out your own salvation with fear and trembling. You, my brother, will find difficulty here because you have not yet learned by experience to know the voice of the Good Shepherd, and this places you in doubt and peril. You ought to be able to distinguish His voice.—*Testimonies*, vol. 5, pp. 511, 512.

GOING TO THE SOURCE OF LIGHT

The entrance of thy words giveth light; it giveth understanding unto the simple. Ps. 119:130.

It is sometimes the case that men of intellectual ability, improved by education and culture, fail to comprehend certain passages of Scripture, while others who are uneducated, whose understanding seems weak and whose minds are undisciplined, will grasp the meaning, finding strength and comfort in that which the former declare to be mysterious or pass by as unimportant. Why is this? It has been explained to me that the latter class do not rely upon their own understanding. They go to the Source of light, the One who has inspired the Scriptures, and with humility of heart ask God for wisdom, and they receive it. There are mines of truth yet to be discovered by the earnest seeker.

Christ represented the truth as treasure hid in a field. It does not lie right upon the surface; we must dig for it. But our success in finding it does not depend so much on our intellectual ability as on our humility of heart and the faith which will lay hold upon divine aid.

Without the guidance of the Holy Spirit we shall be continually liable to wrest the Scriptures or to misinterpret them. There is much reading of the Bible that is without profit and in many cases is a positive injury. When the Word of God is opened without reverence and without prayer; when the thoughts and affections are not fixed upon God or in harmony with His will, the mind is clouded with doubt; and in the very study of the Bible, skepticism strengthens. The enemy takes control of the thoughts, and he suggests interpretations that are not correct.

Whenever men are not seeking, in word and deed, to be in harmony with God, then, however learned they may be, they are liable to err in their understanding of Scripture, and it is not safe to trust to their explanations. When we are truly seeking to do God's will, the Holy Spirit takes the precepts of His Word and makes them the principles of the life, writing them on the tablets of the soul. And it is only those who are following the light already given that can hope to receive the further illumination of the Spirit.—*Testimonies*, vol. 5, pp. 704, 705.

DEVELOPING SPIRITUAL DISCERNMENT

But the natural man receiveth not the things of the Spirit of God: for they are foolishness unto him: neither can he know them, because they are spiritually discerned. 1 Cor. 2:14.

The jewels of truth lie scattered over the field of revelation; but they have been buried beneath human traditions, beneath the sayings and commandments of men, and the wisdom from heaven has been practically ignored; for Satan has succeeded in making the world believe that the words and achievements of men are of great consequence. The Lord God, the Creator of the worlds, at infinite cost has given the gospel to the world. Through this divine agent, glad, refreshing springs of heavenly comfort and abiding consolation have been opened for those who will come to the fountain of life. There are veins of truth yet to be discovered; but spiritual things are spiritually discerned.

Minds beclouded with evil cannot appreciate the value of the truth as it is in Jesus. When iniquity is cherished, men do not feel the necessity of making diligent effort with prayer and reflection, to understand that they must know or lose heaven. They have so long been under the shadow of the enemy that they view truth as men behold objects through a smoked and imperfect glass; for all things are dark and perverted in their eyes. Their spiritual vision is feeble and untrustworthy; for they look upon the shadow, and turn away from the light.

But those who profess to believe in Jesus should ever press to the light. They should daily pray for the light of the Holy Spirit to shine upon the pages of the sacred book, that they may be enabled to comprehend the things of the Spirit of God. We must have implicit trust in God's Word, or we are lost. The words of men, however great they may be, are not able to make us perfect, to thoroughly furnish unto all good works.

"God hath from the beginning chosen you to salvation through sanctification of the Spirit and belief of the truth" (2 Thess. 2:13). In this text the two agencies in the salvation of man are revealed—the divine influence, the strong, living faith of those who follow Christ. It is through the sanctification of the Spirit and the belief of the truth that we become laborers together with God.—*Review and Herald*, Dec. 1, 1891.

LOOKING FOR TREASURES

Again, the kingdom of heaven is like unto treasure hid in a field; the which when a man hath found, he hideth, and for joy thereof goeth and selleth all that he hath, and buyeth that field. Matt. 13:44.

In our day the church has been to a great degree content with the surface truths of revelation, made so plain and easy to be understood that many have thought these supplied all that was essential, and in accepting them they have been content. But the Holy Spirit, working upon the mind, will not allow it to rest in indolence. He awakens an earnest desire for truth uncorrupted with error and false doctrines. Celestial truths will reward the diligent seeker. The mind that is really desirous to know what is truth cannot be content in indolence.

The kingdom of heaven is likened to treasure hid in a field, "the which when a man hath found, he hideth, and for joy thereof goeth and selleth all that he hath, and buyeth that field." He buys it that he may work it, plow up every part of it, and take possession of its treasures. It is the Holy Spirit's office to direct this search and to reward it. The searcher, while digging the field, finds leads of precious ore of which he seeks to estimate the value, and he sinks the shaft deeper, for still more valuable treasure. Thus many a rich lode is discovered. The gold fields of the earth are not so interlaced with veins of precious ore as is the field of revelation with leads that bring to view the unsearchable riches of Christ.

The Lord would have every one of His believing children rich in faith; and this is the fruit of the working of the Holy Spirit upon the heart. From the heart the Spirit works outward, developing a character that God will approve. What a vast field of the treasures of truth did Christ add to the domain of faith to be appropriated by His disciples! We need greater faith if we would have better knowledge of the Word. The greatest hindrance to our receiving the divine illumination is that we do not depend on the efficiency of the Holy Spirit.—*Ellen G. White 1888 Materials*, pp. 1537, 1538.

SEARCHING FOR TRUTH

Search the scriptures; for in them ye think ye have eternal life: and they are they which testify of me. John 5:39.

Christ came in the form of humanity to live the law of God. He was the Word of life. He came to be the gospel of salvation to the world, and to fulfill every specification of the law. Jesus is the word, the guidebook, which must be received and obeyed in every particular. How necessary that this mine of truth be explored, and the precious treasures of truth be discovered and secured as rich jewels. The incarnation of Christ, His divinity, His atonement, His wonderful life in heaven as our advocate, the office of the Holy Spirit—all these living, vital themes of Christianity are revealed from Genesis to Revelation. The golden links of truth form a chain of evangelical truth, and the first, and staple, is found in the great teachings of Christ Jesus. Why, then, should not the Scriptures be ennobled and exalted in every school in our land? How little children are educated to study the Bible as the Word of God, and feed upon its truths, which are the flesh and blood of the Son of God!

"Except ye eat the flesh of the Son of man, and drink his blood, ye have no life in you. Whoso eateth my flesh, and drinketh my blood [that is, continues to receive the words of Christ and practice them], hath eternal life; and I will raise him up at the last day. For my flesh is meat indeed, and my blood is drink indeed. He that eateth my flesh, and drinketh my blood, dwelleth in me, and I in him" (John 6:53-56), "and he that keepeth his commandments dwelleth in him, and he in him. And hereby we know that he abideth in us, by the Spirit which he hath given us" (1 John 3:24).

There is necessity for every family to make the Bible the book of their study. Christ's sayings are pure gold, without one particle of dross, unless men, with their human understanding, shall try to put it there, and make falsehood appear as a portion of truth. To those who have received the false interpretation of the Word, when they search the Scriptures with the determined effort to obtain the very marrow of truth contained in them, the Holy Spirit opens the eyes of their understanding, and the truths of the Word are to them as a new revelation.— *Fundamentals of Christian Education*, pp. 385, 386.

KNOWING THE UNKNOWN

For what man knoweth the things of a man, save the spirit of man which is in him? even so the things of God knoweth no man, but the Spirit of God. 1 Cor. 2:11.

Revelation is not the creation or invention of something new, but the manifestation of what was, until revealed, unknown to human beings. The great and eternal truths contained in the gospel are revealed through diligent searching and humbling of ourselves before God. The divine Teacher leads the mind of the humble seeker for truth; and by the Holy Spirit's guidance, the truths of the Word are made known to him. And there can be no more certain and efficient way of knowledge than in being thus guided. The promise of the Saviour was "When he, the Spirit of truth, is come, he will guide you into all truth" (John 16:13). It is through the impartation of the Holy Spirit that we are made to understand the Word of God.

The psalmist writes, "Wherewithal shall a young man cleanse his way? by taking heed thereto according to thy word. With my whole heart have I sought thee: O let me not wander from thy commandments. . . . Open thou mine eyes, that I may behold wondrous things out of thy law" (Ps. 119:9-18).

We are admonished to seek for the truth as for hid treasure. The Lord opens the understanding of the true seeker after truth; and the Holy Spirit enables him to grasp the truths of revelation. This is what the psalmist means when he asks that his eyes may be opened to behold wondrous things out of the law. When the soul pants after the excellencies of Jesus Christ, the mind is enabled to grasp the glories of the better world. Only by the aid of the divine Teacher can we understand the truths of the Word of God. In Christ's school we learn to be meek and lowly because there is given to us an understanding of the mysteries of godliness.

He who inspired the Word was the true expositor of the Word. Christ illustrated His teachings by calling the attention of His hearers to the simple laws of nature, and to the familiar objects which they daily saw and handled. Thus He led their minds from the natural to the spiritual.—*Sabbath School Worker*, Dec. 1, 1909.

DIGGING DEEPER INTO THE MINE

These were more noble than those in Thessalonica, in that they received the word with all readiness of mind, and searched the scriptures daily, whether those things were so. Acts 17:11.

It is proper and right to read the Bible; but your duty does not end there; for you are to search its pages for yourselves. The knowledge of God is not to be gained without mental effort, without prayer for wisdom in order that you may separate from the pure grain of truth the chaff with which men and Satan have misrepresented the doctrines of truth. Satan and his confederacy of human agents have endeavored to mix the chaff of error with the wheat of truth. We should diligently seek for the hidden treasure, and seek wisdom from heaven in order to separate human inventions from the divine commands. The Holy Spirit will aid the seeker for great and precious truths which relate to the plan of redemption.

I would impress upon all the fact that a casual reading of the Scriptures is not enough. We must search, and this means the doing of all the Word implies. As the miner eagerly explores the earth to discover its veins of gold, so you are to explore the Word of God for the hidden treasure that Satan has so long sought to hide from man. The Lord says, "If any man willeth to do his will, he shall know of the teaching" (John 7:17, RV).

The Word of God is truth and light, and is to be a lamp unto your feet, to guide you every step of the way to the gates of the city of God. It is for this reason that Satan has made such desperate efforts to obstruct the path that has been cast up for the ransomed of the Lord to walk in. You are not to take your ideas to the Bible, and make your opinions a center around which truth is to revolve. You are to lay aside your ideas at the door of investigation, and with humble, subdued hearts, with self hid in Christ, with earnest prayer, you are to seek wisdom from God. You should feel that you must know the revealed will of God, because it concerns your personal, eternal welfare. The Bible is a directory by which you may know the way to eternal life. You should desire above all things that you may know the will and ways of the Lord.—*Fundamentals of Christian Education*, pp. 307, 308.

WITH HUMBLE HEARTS

For thus saith the high and lofty One that inhabiteth eternity, whose name is Holy; I dwell in the high and holy place, with him also that is of a contrite and humble spirit, to revive the spirit of the humble, and to revive the heart of the contrite ones. Isa. 57:15.

All who will come to the Word of God for guidance, with humble, inquiring minds, determined to know the terms of salvation, will understand what saith the Scriptures. But those who bring to the investigation of the Word a spirit which it does not approve will take away from the search a spirit which it has not imparted. The Lord will not speak to a mind that is unconcerned. He wastes not His instruction on one who is willingly irreverent or polluted. But the tempter educates every mind that yields itself to his suggestions, and is willing to make of none effect God's holy law.

We need to humble our hearts, and with sincerity and reverence search the Word of life; for that mind alone that is humble and contrite can see light. The heart, the mind, the soul, must be prepared to receive light. There must be silence in the soul. The thoughts must be brought into captivity to Jesus Christ. The boastful self-knowledge and self-sufficiency must stand rebuked in the presence of the Word of God.

The Lord speaks to the heart that humbles itself before Him. At the altar of prayer, as the throne of grace is touched by faith, we receive from the hand of God that celestial torch which enlightens our darkness, and convinces us of our spiritual necessity. The Holy Spirit takes of the things of God, and reveals them to the one who is sincerely seeking for the heavenly treasure. If we yield to His guidance, He leads us into all light. As we behold the glory of Christ, we become changed into His image. We have that faith which works by love, and purifies the soul. Our hearts are renewed, and we are made willing to obey God in all things.—*Review and Herald*, Dec. 15, 1896.

WITH A TEACHABLE DISPOSITION

Thus saith the Lord, Stand ye in the ways, and see, and ask for the old paths, where is the good way, and walk therein, and ye shall find rest for your souls. But they said, We will not walk therein. Jer. 6:16.

After asking the Lord for a knowledge of His will, for heavenly wisdom, for the light of the Holy Spirit, the petitioner will search the Scriptures, and find that passages that were dark to his mind have suddenly grown clear, and he understands his duty as never before. Jesus said: "My doctrine is not mine, but his that sent me. If any man will do his will, he shall know of the doctrine, whether it be of God, or whether I speak of myself" (John 7:16, 17).

The knowledge of divine truth is promised to those who will render obedience to the light and truth that have been given to them. An entrance into the strait gate is not dependent upon the possession of learning or riches, but it is dependent upon the possession of a teachable spirit. He who appreciates the first ray of heavenly light, and appropriates it, and walks in it, bringing his actions into harmony with that ray, and becoming sanctified through it, will receive yet more light. He will understand that the gospel is the plan of salvation. . . .

He who has an obedient heart, that is ready to do the will of God, will not only gladly receive truth, but will earnestly seek for truth as for hidden treasure. He will come to the Scriptures with a humble and teachable spirit, seeking to understand how he may walk in the light, and saying, "Lord, what wilt thou have me to do?" (Acts 9:6). He is ready to sacrifice anything and everything, if required, in order that he may be in harmony with the will of God.

It is not always an easy matter to render obedience to the will of God. It demands firmness of purpose to enter in at the strait gate and to travel in the narrow path that leads to eternal life, for on every hand are voices inviting the soul into bye and forbidden paths. Those who love wealth and honor and high position will not enter in at the strait gate unless they part with their idols. There is not room to enter in at the strait gate and carry the things of this world along.

He who would enter in at the strait gate must make an entire consecration of his all to God. Jesus says, "If any man will come after me, let him deny himself, and take up his cross, and follow me" (Matt. 16:24).—*Review and Herald*, Mar. 28, 1912.

WITH EMPTY VESSELS

But we have this treasure in earthen vessels, that the excellency of the power may be of God, and not of us. 2 Cor. 4:7.

The question has been asked, What kind of vessels does the Spirit use? What does Christ say? "Come unto me, all ye that labour and are heavy laden, and I will give you rest. Take my yoke upon you, and learn of me; for I am meek and lowly in heart: and ye shall find rest unto your souls. For my yoke is easy, and my burden is light" (Matt. 11:28-30). What kind of vessels are meet for the Master's use? Empty vessels. When we empty the soul of every defilement, we are ready for use.

Are we emptied of self? Are we cured of selfish planning? Oh, for less self-occupation! May the Lord purify His people, teachers, and churches. He has given a rule for the guidance of all, and from this there can be no careless departure. But there has been, and still is, a swerving from righteous principles. How long shall this condition of things exist? How can the Master use us as vessels for holy service until we empty ourselves, and make room for His Spirit to work?

God calls for His people to reveal Him. Shall the world manifest principles of integrity that the church does not maintain? Shall a selfish ambition to be first be shown by the followers of Christ? Shall not the principles cherished by them be laid upon the true foundation, even Christ Jesus? What material shall we place upon this foundation, that there may no longer be antagonism, but unity, in the church? Shall we bring to it wood, hay, stubble? Shall we not rather bring the most precious material—gold, silver, precious stones? Shall we not distinguish sharply between the chaff and the wheat? Shall we not realize that we must receive the Holy Spirit in our hearts, that it may mold and fashion the life?

We are living in perilous times. In the fear of God I would say that the true exposition of the Scriptures is necessary for the correct moral development of our characters. When mind and heart are worked by the Spirit, when self is dead, the truth is capable of constant expansion and new development. When the truth molds our characters, it will be seen to be truth indeed.—*Review and Herald*, Feb. 28, 1899.

WITH A PRAYERFUL SPIRIT

Open thou mine eyes, that I may behold wondrous things out of thy law.
Ps. 119:18.

Many a portion of Scripture which learned men pronounce a mystery, or pass over as unimportant, is full of comfort and instruction to him who has been taught in the school of Christ. One reason why many theologians have no clearer understanding of God's Word is [that] they close their eyes to truths which they do not wish to practice. An understanding of Bible truth depends not so much on the power of intellect brought to the search as on the singleness of purpose, the earnest longing after righteousness.

The Bible should never be studied without prayer. The Holy Spirit alone can cause us to feel the importance of those things easy to be understood, or prevent us from wresting truths difficult of comprehension. It is the office of heavenly angels to prepare the heart so to comprehend God's Word that we shall be charmed with its beauty, admonished by its warnings, or animated and strengthened by its promises. We should make the psalmist's petition our own: "Open thou mine eyes, that I may behold wondrous things out of thy law".

Temptations often appear irresistible because, through neglect of prayer and the study of the Bible, the tempted one cannot readily remember God's promises and meet Satan with the Scripture weapons. But angels are round about those who are willing to be taught in divine things; and in the time of great necessity they will bring to their remembrance the very truths which are needed. Thus "when the enemy shall come in like a flood, the Spirit of the Lord shall lift up a standard against him" (Isa. 59:19).

Jesus promised His disciples: "The Comforter, which is the Holy Ghost, whom the Father will send in my name, he shall teach you all things, and bring all things to your remembrance, whatsoever I have said unto you" (John 14:26). But the teachings of Christ must previously have been stored in the mind in order for the Spirit of God to bring them to our remembrance in the time of peril. "Thy word have I hid in mine heart," said David, "that I might not sin against thee" (Ps. 119:11).—*The Great Controversy*, pp. 599, 600.

TRUSTING IN HIS ILLUMINATION

Give me understanding, and I shall keep thy law; yea, I shall observe it with my whole heart. Ps. 119:34.

All over the field of revelation are scattered glad springs of heavenly truth, peace, and joy. These fountains of joy are within the reach of every seeker. The words of Inspiration, pondered in the heart, will be as living streams flowing from the river of the water of life. Our Saviour prayed that the mind of His followers might be opened to understand the Scriptures. Whenever we study the Bible with a prayerful heart, the Holy Spirit is near to open to us the meaning of the words we read. The man whose mind is enlightened by the opening of God's Word to his understanding will not only feel that he must more diligently seek to understand that Word, but that he must have a better understanding of the sciences. He will feel that he is called to a high calling in Christ Jesus.

The more closely connected man is with the Source of all knowledge and wisdom, the more he will feel that he must advance in intellectual and spiritual attainments. The opening of God's Word is always followed by a remarkable opening and strengthening of man's faculties; for the entrance of His words giveth light. By contemplation of great truths, the mind is elevated, the affections purified and refined; for the Spirit of God, through the truth of God, quickens the lifeless spiritual faculties, and attracts the soul heavenward.

Then take your Bible and present yourself before your heavenly Father, saying, "Enlighten me; teach me what is truth." The Lord will regard your prayer, and the Holy Spirit will impress the truth upon your soul. In searching the Scriptures for yourself, you will become established in the faith. It is of the greatest importance that you continually search the Scriptures, storing the mind with the truths of God. You may be separated from the companionship of Christians, and placed where you will not have the privilege of meeting with the children of God. You need the treasures of God's Word hidden in your heart, that when opposition comes upon you, you may bring everything to the test of the Scriptures.—*Bible Echo*, Oct. 15, 1892.

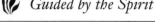

BELIEVING IN HIS GUIDANCE

That your faith should not stand in the wisdom of men, but in the power of God. Howbeit we speak wisdom among them that are perfect: yet not the wisdom of this world, nor of the princes of this world, that come to nought: but we speak the wisdom of God in a mystery, even the hidden wisdom, which God ordained before the world unto our glory. 1 Cor. 2:5-7.

You are accepted in the Beloved. I have had the most earnest desire that you should perfect a Christian character, not in your own strength, but in the strength and in the virtue and righteousness of Christ. The donation of the Holy Spirit was the greatest gift God could bestow upon finite man. This is free to all and in this gift there could be no computation; this endowment specially signalized the enthronement of the only begotten Son of God in His mediatorial kingdom. In this, the gift of the Comforter, the Lord God of heaven demonstrates to man the perfect reconciliation which He had effected between Himself and men. "Which hope," says the apostle, "we have as an anchor of the soul, both sure and stedfast, and which entereth into that within the veil, whither the forerunner is for us entered" (Heb. 6:19, 20).

Has not God said He would give the Holy Spirit to them that ask Him? And is not this Spirit a real, true, actual Guide? Some men seem afraid to take God at His word, as though it would be presumption in them. They pray for the Lord to teach us and yet are afraid to credit the pledged word of God and believe we have been taught of Him. So long as we come to our heavenly Father humbly and with a spirit to be taught, willing and anxious to learn, why should we doubt God's fulfillment of His own promise? You must not for a moment doubt Him and dishonor Him thereby.

When you have sought to know His will, your part in the operation with God is to believe that you will be led and guided and blessed in the doing of His will. We may mistrust ourselves lest we misinterpret His teachings, but make even this a subject of prayer, and trust Him, still trust Him to the uttermost, that His Holy Spirit will lead you to interpret aright His plans and the working of His providence.—*Manuscript Releases*, vol. 6, pp. 223, 224.

MEDITATING ON GOD'S WORD

O how love I thy law! it is my meditation all the day. Ps. 119:97.

Men need not the dim light of tradition and custom to make the Scriptures comprehensible. It is just as sensible to suppose that the sun, shining in the heavens at noonday, needs the glimmerings of the torchlights of earth to increase its glory. In the Bible every duty is made plain, every lesson is comprehensible. The gift of Christ and the illumination of the Holy Spirit reveal to us the Father. The Word is able to make men and women and youth wise unto salvation.

"All Scripture is given by inspiration of God, and is profitable for doctrine, for reproof, for correction, for instruction in righteousness: that the man of God may be perfect, throughly furnished unto all good works" (2 Tim. 3:16, 17). No other book is so potent to elevate the thoughts, to give vigor to the faculties, as the broad, ennobling truths of the Bible. If God's Word were studied as it should be, men would have a breadth of mind, a nobility of character, and a stability of purpose that is rarely seen in these times.

Little benefit is to be derived from a hasty reading of the Scriptures. One may read the whole Bible through, and yet fail to see its beauty or to comprehend its depth of meaning. One passage studied until its significance is clear to the mind, and its relation to the plan of salvation evident, is of more value than the perusal of many chapters with no definite purpose in view and no positive instruction gained. Keep your Bible with you. As you have opportunity, read it; fix the texts in your memory. Even while you are walking in the street, you may read a passage and meditate upon it, thus fixing it on the mind.

Never should the Bible be studied without prayer. Before opening its pages, we should ask for the enlightenment of the Holy Spirit, and it will be given. When Nathanael came to Jesus, the Saviour exclaimed, "Behold an Israelite indeed, in whom is no guile" (John 1:47). Nathanael said, "Whence knowest thou me? Jesus answered and said unto him, Before that Philip called thee, when thou wast under the fig tree, I saw thee" (verse 48). And Jesus will see us also in the secret place of prayer, if we will seek Him for light, that we may know what is truth. Angels from the world of light will be with those who in humility of heart seek for divine guidance.—*Atlantic Union Gleaner*, June 9, 1909.

REJOICING IN THE WORD

Thy words were found, and I did eat them; and thy word was unto me the joy and rejoicing of mine heart: for I am called by thy name, O Lord God of hosts. Jer. 15:16.

There is constant need of patience, gentleness, self-denial, and self-sacrifice in the exercise of Bible religion. But if the Word of God is made an abiding principle in our lives, everything with which we have to do, each word, each trivial act, will reveal that we are subject to Jesus Christ, that even our thoughts have been brought into captivity to Him. If the Word of God is received into the heart, it will empty the soul of self-sufficiency and self-dependence. Our lives will be a power for good, because the Holy Spirit will fill our minds with the things of God. The religion of Christ will be practiced by us; for our wills are in perfect conformity to the will of God.

Some who profess to have true religion sadly neglect the Guidebook given by God to point the way to heaven. They may read the Bible, but merely reading God's Word, as one would read words traced by a human pen, will give only a superficial knowledge. Talking of the truth will not sanctify the receivers. They may profess to be working for God, when, were Christ among them, His voice would be heard, saying, "Ye do err, not knowing the Scriptures, nor the power of God" (Matt. 22:29). Such cannot know what true religion means.

"The words that I speak unto you," said Christ, "they are spirit, and they are life" (John 6:63). Jeremiah testifies to the Word of God, saying, "Thy words were found, and I did eat them; and thy word was unto me the joy and rejoicing of mine heart." There is divine healing in God's Word, which the so-called wise and prudent cannot experience, but which is revealed to babes. "The entrance of thy words giveth light; it giveth understanding unto the simple" (Ps. 119:130). If this Word is enshrined in the heart, it becomes the treasure-house of the mind, from which we bring forth things new and old. We no longer find pleasure in thinking of the common things of earth, but say, "Thy word is a lamp unto my feet, and a light unto my path" (verse 105).—*Review and Herald,* May 4, 1897.

SANCTIFIED THROUGH THE WORD

Sanctify them through thy word: thy word is truth. John 17:17.

The burden of Jesus' request was that those who believed on Him might be kept from the evil of the world, and sanctified through the truth. He does not leave us to vague surmising as to what the truth is, but adds, "Thy word is truth." The Word of God is the means by which our sanctification is to be accomplished. It is of the greatest importance, then, that we acquaint ourselves with the sacred instruction of the Bible. It is as necessary for us to understand the words of life as it was for the early disciples to be informed concerning the plan of salvation.

We shall be inexcusable if, through our own negligence, we are ignorant of the claims of God's Word. God has given us His Word, the revelation of His will, and has promised the Holy Spirit to them that ask Him, to guide them into all truth; and every soul who honestly desires to do the will of God shall know of the doctrine.

The world is full of false teaching; and if we do not resolutely search the Scriptures for ourselves, we shall accept its errors for truth, adopt its customs, and deceive our own hearts. The doctrines and customs of the world are at variance with the truth of God. Those who seek to turn from the service of the world to the service of God will need divine help. They will have to set their faces like a flint toward Zion. They will feel the opposition of the world, the flesh, and the devil, and will have to go contrary to the spirit and influences of the world.

Since the time when the Son of God breasted the haughty prejudices and unbelief of mankind, there has been no change in the attitude of the world toward the religion of Jesus. The servants of Christ must meet the same spirit of opposition and reproach, and must go "without the camp, bearing his reproach" (Heb. 13:13).

The mission of Jesus was demonstrated by convincing miracles. His doctrine astonished the people. It was not the contradictory jargon of the scribes, full of mysticism, burdened with absurd forms and meaningless exactions; but it was a system of truth that met the wants of the heart. His teaching was plain, clear, and comprehensive. The practical truths He uttered had a convincing power, and arrested the attention of the people.—*Review and Herald*, Feb. 7, 1888.

GUIDED THROUGH
THE WRITTEN TESTIMONY

To the law and to the testimony: if they speak not according to this word, it is because there is no light in them. Isa. 8:20.

The Holy Spirit always leads to the written Word, and calls the attention to the great moral standard of righteousness. To be honored of God in thus being privileged to testify of the truth is a wonderful thing. Said Christ to His disciples just before He ascended up and the clouds of angels received Him out of their sight, "Ye shall be witnesses unto me both in Jerusalem, and in all Judea, and in Samaria, and unto the uttermost part of the earth" (Acts 1:8). They were qualified by the heavenly endowment of the Holy Spirit to testify of Christ.

I wish to impress upon you the fact that those who have Jesus abiding in the heart by faith have actually received the Holy Spirit. Every individual who receives Jesus as his personal Saviour just as surely receives the Holy Spirit to be his Counselor, Sanctifier, Guide, and Witness. The more closely the believer walks with God, the clearer his witness, and, as a sure result, the more powerful will be the influence of his testimony upon others of a Saviour's love; the more he will give evidence that he prizes the Word of God. It is his meat, it is his drink, to satisfy the thirsty soul. He prizes the privilege of learning the will of God from His Word.

Some souls who claim to be believers have slighted, and turned from, the Word of God. They have neglected the Bible, the wonderful Guidebook, the true tester of all ideas, and claim that they have the Spirit to teach them, that this renders searching the Scriptures unnecessary. All such are heeding the sophistry of Satan, for the Spirit and the Word agree. Say the Scriptures, "To the law and to the testimony: if they speak not according to this word, it is because there is no light in them." He only is a free man whom the truth makes free.—*Manuscript Releases*, vol. 14, pp. 70, 71.

ILLUMINATION NOT GIVEN
APART FROM THE WORD

For there shall arise false Christs, and false prophets, and shall shew great signs and wonders; insomuch that, if it were possible, they shall deceive the very elect. Matt. 24:24.

In these days of delusion, everyone who is established in the truth will have to contend for the faith once delivered to the saints. Every variety of error will be brought out in the mysterious working of Satan, which would, if it were possible, deceive the very elect, and turn them from the truth. There will be human wisdom to meet—the wisdom of learned men, who, as were the Pharisees, are teachers of the law of God, but do not obey the law themselves. There will be human ignorance and folly to meet in disconnected theories arrayed in new and fantastic dress—theories that it will be all the more difficult to meet because there is no reason in them.

There will be false dreams and false visions, which have some truth, but lead away from the original faith. The Lord has given men a rule by which to detect them: "To the law and to the testimony: if they speak not according to this word, it is because there is no light in them" (Isa. 8:20). If they belittle the law of God, if they pay no heed to His will as revealed in the testimonies of His Spirit, they are deceivers. They are controlled by impulse and impressions, which they believe to be from the Holy Spirit, and consider more reliable than the Inspired Word. They claim that every thought and feeling is an impression of the Spirit; and when they are reasoned with out of the Scriptures, they declare that they have something more reliable. But while they think that they are led by the Spirit of God, they are in reality following an imagination wrought upon by Satan.—*Selected Messages*, book 2, pp. 98, 99.

Satan will work in a most subtle manner to introduce human inventions clothed with angel garments. But the light from the Word is shining amid the moral darkness; and the Bible will never be superseded by miraculous manifestations. The truth must be studied, it must be searched for as hidden treasure. Wonderful illuminations will not be given aside from the Word, or to take the place of it. Cling to the Word, receive the ingrafted Word, which will make men wise unto salvation.—*Ibid.*, p. 100.

NOT RELYING ON OUR OWN IMAGINATION

And my speech and my preaching was not with enticing words of man's wisdom, but in demonstration of the Spirit and of power. 1 Cor. 2:4.

I have seen that danger attends every new phase of experience in the church, because some hear things with such a wrong spirit. While some teachers may be strong and efficient in teaching in the lines of Bible doctrines, they will not all be men who have a knowledge of practical life, and can advise perplexed minds with surety and safety. They do not discern the perplexing situation that must necessarily come to every family who shall make a change. Therefore let all be careful what they say; if they know not the mind of God in some matters, let them never speak from a guess or suppose so. If they know nothing definite, let them say so, and let the individual rely wholly upon God. Let there be much praying done, and even with fasting, that not one shall move in darkness, but move in the light as God is in the light.

We may look for anything now to break forth outside and within our ranks; and there are minds undisciplined by the grace of the Holy Spirit, that have not practiced the words of Christ, and who do not understand the movings of the Spirit of God, who will follow a wrong course of action because they do not follow Jesus fully. They follow impulse and their own imagination.

Let there be nothing done in a disorderly manner, that there shall be a great loss or sacrifice made upon property because of ardent, impulsive speeches which stir up an enthusiasm which is not after the order of God, that a victory that was essential to be gained, shall, for lack of levelheaded moderation and proper contemplation, and sound principles and purposes, be turned into a defeat. Let there be wise generalship in this matter, and all move under the guidance of a wise, unseen Counselor, which is God. Elements that are human will struggle for the mastery, and there may be a work done that does not bear the signature of God.—*Special Testimonies Relating to Various Matters in Battle Creek*, pp. 17, 18.

NOT GUIDED BY EMOTIONS

Thy word is a lamp unto my feet, and a light unto my path. Ps. 119:105.

Sanctification is not a happy flight of feeling, not the work of an instant, but the work of a lifetime. If anyone claims that the Lord has sanctified him, and made him holy, the proof of his claim to the blessing will be seen in the fruits of meekness, patience, long-suffering, truthfulness, and love. If the blessing that those who claim to be sanctified have received leads them to rely upon some particular emotion, and they declare there is no need of searching the Scriptures that they may know God's revealed will, then the supposed blessing is a counterfeit, for it leads its possessors to place value on their own unsanctified emotions and fancies, and to close their ears to the voice of God in His Word.

Why need those who claim they have had special manifestations of the Spirit, and the witness that their sins are all forgiven, conclude that they can lay the Bible aside, and from henceforth walk alone? When we ask those who claim to have been instantaneously sanctified, if they are searching the Scriptures as Jesus told them to do, to see if there is not additional truth for them to accept, they answer, "God makes known His will to us directly in special signs and revelations, and we can afford to lay the Bible aside."

There are thousands who are being deceived by trusting to some special emotion, and discarding the Word of God. They are not building upon the only safe and sure foundation—the Word of God. A religion that is addressed to intelligent creatures will produce reasonable evidences of its genuineness, for there will be marked results in heart and character. The grace of Christ will be made manifest in their daily conduct. We may safely ask those who profess to be sanctified, Do the fruits of the Spirit appear in your life? Do you manifest the meekness and lowliness of Christ, and reveal the fact that you are learning daily in the school of Christ, shaping your life after the pattern of His unselfish life?

The best evidence that any of us can have of our connection with the God of heaven is that we keep His commandments. The best proof of faith in Christ is distrust of self and dependence upon God. The only reliable proof of our abiding in Christ is to reflect His image. Just so far as we do this we give evidence that we are sanctified through the truth, for the truth is exemplified in our daily life.—*Signs of the Times*, Feb. 28, 1895.

NOT TRUSTING IN IMPRESSIONS

I will meditate in thy precepts, and have respect unto thy ways. I will delight myself in thy statutes: I will not forget thy word. Ps. 119:15, 16.

In His Word, God has committed to men the knowledge necessary for salvation. The Holy Scriptures are to be accepted as an authoritative, infallible revelation of His will. They are the standard of character, the revealer of doctrines, and the test of experience. "Every scripture inspired of God is also profitable for teaching, for reproof, for correction, for instruction which is in righteousness: that the man of God may be complete, furnished completely unto every good work" (2 Tim. 3:16, 17, RV).

Yet the fact that God has revealed His will to men through His Word has not rendered needless the continued presence and guiding of the Holy Spirit. On the contrary, the Spirit was promised by our Saviour, to open the Word to His servants, to illuminate and apply Its teachings. And since it was the Spirit of God that inspired the Bible, it is impossible that the teaching of the Spirit should ever be contrary to that of the Word.

The Spirit was not given—nor can it ever be bestowed—to supersede the Bible; for the Scriptures explicitly state that the Word of God is the standard by which all teaching and experience must be tested. Says the apostle John, "Believe not every spirit, but try the spirits whether they are of God: because many false prophets are gone out into the world" (1 John 4:1). And Isaiah declares, "To the law and to the testimony: if they speak not according to this word, it is because there is no light in them" (Isa. 8:20).

Great reproach has been cast upon the work of the Holy Spirit by the errors of a class that, claiming its enlightenment, profess to have no further need of guidance from the Word of God. They are governed by impressions which they regard as the voice of God in the soul. But the spirit that controls them is not the Spirit of God. This following of impressions, to the neglect of the Scriptures, can lead only to confusion, to deception and ruin. It serves only to further the designs of the evil one.

Since the ministry of the Holy Spirit is of vital importance to the church of Christ, it is one of the devices of Satan, through the errors of extremists and fanatics, to cast contempt upon the work of the Spirit and cause the people of God to neglect this source of strength which our Lord Himself has provided.—*The Great Controversy*, pp. vii, viii.

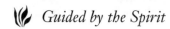

A Clear Voice Amid Other Voices

And thine ears shall hear a word behind thee, saying, This is the way, walk ye in it, when ye turn to the right hand, and when ye turn to the left. Isa. 30:21.

Amid the confusion of delusive doctrines, the Spirit of God will be a guide and a shield to those who have not resisted the evidences of truth. He silences every other voice than that which comes from Him who is the truth and the life. God gives to every soul opportunity to hear the voice of the True Shepherd, to receive the knowledge of God and our Saviour. When the heart receives this truth as a precious treasure, Christ is formed within, the hope of glory, while the whole heavenly universe exclaims, Amen and amen! We have absolute need of the regenerating power of the Holy Spirit. We have no time to confer with flesh and blood.

We have need of divine illumination. Every individual is striving to become a center of influence; and until God works for His people, they will not see that subordination to God is the only safety for any soul. His transforming grace upon human hearts will lead to unity that has not yet been realized; for all who are assimilated to Christ will be in harmony with one another. The Holy Spirit will create unity.

"He shall glorify me" (John 16:14). "This is life eternal, that they might know thee, the only true God, and Jesus Christ, whom thou hast sent" (John 17:3). The Holy Spirit glorifies God by so revealing His character to His people that He becomes the object of their supreme affections, and by making manifest His character in them.

They see clearly that there never was any righteousness in the world but His, no excellence in the world but that derived from Him. When the Spirit was poured out from on high, the church was flooded with light, but Christ was the source of that light; His name was on every tongue, His love filled every heart. So it will be when the angel that comes down from heaven having great power shall lighten the whole earth with His glory. . . .

The gift of His Holy Spirit, rich, full, and abundant, is to His church as an encompassing wall of fire, and the powers of hell shall not prevail against it. In their untainted purity and spotless perfection Christ looks upon His people as the reward of all His suffering, His humiliation, and His love, and the supplement of His glory—Christ the great center from which radiates all glory.—*Home Missionary*, Nov. 1, 1893.

READY TO GIVE REASON OF OUR HOPE

But sanctify the Lord God in your hearts: and be ready always to give an answer to every man that asketh you a reason of the hope that is in you with meekness and fear. 1 Peter 3:15.

This is what we shall see if we are connected with God. God wants us to depend upon Him, and not upon man. He desires us to have a new heart; He would give us revealings of light from the throne of God. We should wrestle with every difficulty, but when some controverted point is presented, are you to go to man to find out his opinion, and then shape your conclusions from his? No, go to God. Tell Him what you want; take your Bible and search as for hidden treasures.

We do not go deep enough in our search for truth. Every soul who believes present truth will be brought where he will be required to give a reason of the hope that is in him. The people of God will be called upon to stand before kings, princes, rulers, and great men of the earth, and they must know that they do know what is truth. They must be converted men and women. God can teach you more in one moment by His Holy Spirit than you could learn from the great men of the earth. The universe is looking upon the controversy that is going on upon the earth. At an infinite cost, God has provided for every man an opportunity to know that which will make him wise unto salvation. How eagerly do angels look to see who will avail himself of this opportunity!

When a message is presented to God's people, they should not rise up in opposition to it; they should go to the Bible, comparing it with the law and the testimony, and if it does not bear this test, it is not true. God wants our minds to expand. He desires to put His grace upon us. We may have a feast of good things every day; for God can open the whole treasure of heaven to us. We are to be one with Christ as He is one with the Father, and the Father will love us as He loves His Son. We may have the same help that Christ had, we may have strength for every emergency; for God will be our front guard and our rearward.—*Selected Messages*, book 1, pp. 415, 416.

CAPABLE TO DISTINGUISH
FALSE THEORIES

Beloved, when I gave all diligence to write unto you of the common salva-tion, it was needful for me to write unto you, and exhort you that ye should earnestly contend for the faith which was once delivered unto the saints. Jude 3.

Jude bears this message to guard believers against the seductive in-fluence of false teachers, men who have a form of godliness but who are not safe leaders. In these last days, false teachers will arise and become actively zealous. All kinds of theories will be presented to divert the minds of men and women from the very truth that defines the position we can occupy with safety in this time when Satan is work-ing with power upon religionists, leading them to make a pretense of being righteous, but to fail of placing themselves under the guidance of the Holy Spirit.

False theories will be mingled with every phase of experience, and advocated with satanic earnestness in order to captivate the mind of every soul who is not rooted and grounded in a full knowledge of the sa-cred principles of the Word. In the very midst of us will arise false teachers, giving heed to seducing spirits whose doctrines are of satanic origin. These teachers will draw away disciples after themselves. Creeping in unawares, they will use flattering words, and make skillful misrepresentations with seductive tact.

The only hope of our churches is to keep wide awake. Those who are well grounded in the truth of the Word, those who test everything by a "Thus saith the Lord" are safe. The Holy Spirit will guide those who prize the wisdom of God above the deceptive sophistries of satanic agencies. Let there be much praying, not in human lines but under the inspiration of love of the truth as it is in Jesus Christ. The families who believe the truth are to speak words of wisdom and intelligence—words that will come to them as the result of searching the Scriptures.

Now is our time of test and trial. Now is the time when the mem-bers of every believing family must close their lips against speaking words of accusation concerning their brethren. Let them speak words that impart courage, and strengthen the faith which works by love and purifies the soul.—*Kress Collection*, p. 5.

ABLE TO DISCERN TRUTH FROM ERROR

For such are false apostles, deceitful workers, transforming themselves into the apostles of Christ. And no marvel; for Satan himself is transformed into an angel of light. 2 Cor. 11:13, 14.

The truth is efficient, and through obedience its power changes the mind into the image of Jesus. It is the truth as it is in Jesus that quickens the conscience and transforms the mind; for it is accompanied to the heart by the Holy Spirit. There are many, who, lacking spiritual discernment, take the bare letter of the Word, and find that unaccompanied by the Spirit of God, it quickens not the soul, it sanctifies not the heart. One may be able to quote from the Old and the New Testament, may be familiar with the commands and promises of the Word of God; but unless the Holy Spirit sends the truth home to the heart, enlightening the mind with divine light, no soul falls upon the Rock and is broken; for it is the divine agency that connects the soul with God.

Without the enlightenment of the Spirit of God, we shall not be able to discern truth from error, and shall fall under the masterful temptations and deceptions that Satan will bring upon the world. We are near the close of the controversy between the Prince of light and the prince of darkness, and soon the delusions of the enemy will try our faith, of what sort it is. Satan will work miracles in the sight of the beast, and deceive "them that dwell on the earth by the means of those miracles which he had power to do in the sight of the beast" (Rev. 13:14).

But though the prince of darkness will work to cover the earth with darkness, and with gross darkness the people, the Lord will manifest His converting power. A work is to be accomplished in the earth similar to that which took place at the outpouring of the Holy Spirit in the days of the early disciples, when they preached Jesus and Him crucified. Many will be converted in a day; for the message will go with power. It can then be said: "Our gospel came not unto you in word only, but also in power, and in the Holy Ghost" (1 Thess. 1:5). It is the Holy Spirit that draws men to Christ; for He takes of the things of God, and shows them unto the sinner. Jesus said: "He shall glorify me: for he shall receive of mine, and shall shew it unto you" (John 16:14).—*Review and Herald*, Nov. 29, 1892.

SEPARATING THE TRUE FROM THE FICTITIOUS

For the time will come when they will not endure sound doctrine; but after their own lusts shall they heap to themselves teachers, having itching ears; and they shall turn away their ears from the truth, and shall be turned unto fables. 2 Tim. 4:3, 4.

Much is being said regarding the impartation of the Holy Spirit, and by some this is being so interpreted that it is an injury to the churches. Eternal life is the receiving of the living elements in the Scriptures and doing the will of God. This is eating the flesh and drinking the blood of the Son of God. To those who do this, life and immortality are brought to light through the gospel, for God's Word is verity and truth, spirit and life. It is the privilege of all who believe in Jesus Christ as their personal Saviour to feed on the Word of God. The Holy Spirit's influence renders that Word, the Bible, an immortal truth, which to the prayerful searcher gives spiritual sinew and muscle.

"Search the scriptures," Christ declared, "for in them ye think ye have eternal life: and they are they which testify of me" (John 5:39). Those who dig beneath the surface discover the hidden gems of truth. The Holy Spirit is present with the earnest searcher. His illumination shines upon the Word, stamping the truth upon the mind with a new, fresh importance. The searcher is filled with a sense of peace and joy never before felt. The preciousness of truth is realized as never before. A new, heavenly light shines upon the Word, illuminating it as though every letter were tinged with gold. God Himself has spoken to the mind and heart, making the Word spirit and life.

Every true searcher of the Word lifts his heart to God, imploring the aid of the Spirit. And he soon discovers that which carries him above all the fictitious statements of the would-be teacher, whose weak, tottering theories are not sustained by the Word of the living God. These theories were invented by men who had not learned the first great lesson, that God's Spirit and life are in His Word. If they had received in the heart the eternal element contained in the Word of God, they would see how tame and expressionless are all efforts to get something new to create a sensation. They need to learn the very first principles of the Word of God.—*Selected Messages*, book 2, pp. 38, 39.

LAYING A FIRM FOUNDATION

That we henceforth be no more children, tossed to and fro, and carried about with every wind of doctrine, by the sleight of men, and cunning craftiness, whereby they lie in wait to deceive. Eph. 4:14.

The voice of God is speaking to us through His Word, and there are many voices that we will hear; but Christ has said we should beware of them who will say, Here is Christ or there is Christ. Then how shall we know that they have not the truth, unless we bring everything to the Scriptures? Christ has warned us to beware of false prophets who will come to us in His name, saying that they are Christ.

Now, if you should take the position that it is not important for you to understand the Scriptures for yourselves, you will be in danger of being led away with these doctrines. Christ has said that there will be a company who in the day of retributive judgment will say, "Lord, Lord, have we not prophesied in thy name? and in thy name have cast out devils? and in thy name done many wonderful works?" But Christ will say, "Depart from me, ye that work iniquity" (Matt. 7:22, 23). . . .

The time is coming when Satan will work miracles right in your sight, claiming that he is Christ; and if your feet are not firmly established upon the truth of God, then you will be led away from your foundation. The only safety for you is to search for the truth as for hid treasures. Dig for the truth as you would for treasures in the earth, and present the Word of God, the Bible, before your heavenly Father, and say, Enlighten me; teach me what is truth.

And when His Holy Spirit shall come into your hearts, to impress the truth into your souls, you will not let it go easily. You have gained such an experience in searching the Scriptures, that every point is established. And it is important that you continually search the Scriptures. You should store the mind with the Word of God; for you may be separated, and placed where you will not have the privilege of meeting with the children of God. Then you will want the treasures of God's Word hidden in your hearts, and when opposition comes around you, you will need to bring everything to the Scriptures.—*Review and Herald*, Apr. 3, 1888.

BUILDING UPON THE ROCK

Therefore whosoever heareth these sayings of mine, and doeth them, I will liken him unto a wise man, which built his house upon a rock. Matt. 7:24.

As you stand here today, and see the defects of your characters in the light of God's great moral standard, will you not say, "I will redeem the past; I will go to work in the Lord's vineyard"? By living faith will you not grasp the promises of God, and appropriate Christ's righteousness, and find the light of heaven shining in your life? You are to bring Christ into your every thought and action. A defective link in a chain makes it worthless, and a defect in your character will unfit you to enter the kingdom of heaven. You must set everything in order. But you cannot do this great work without divine aid. Are you ready to accept the promises of God, and to make them your own by living faith in his immutable word?

You should walk by faith, not by feeling. We do not want a sensational religion; but we want a religion founded on intelligent faith. This faith plants its feet on the eternal rock of God's Word. Those who walk by faith are all the time seeking for perfection of character by constant obedience to Christ. The Captain of our salvation has given us His orders, and we are to yield implicit obedience; but if we close the Book that reveals His will, and do not inquire, or search, or seek to understand, how can we fulfill its obligation? We shall be found wanting at last, if we pursue this course. . . .

We are coming to a crisis, and I am in terror for our souls. Why is it that we find men leaving the faith? Are we in a position where we shall know what we believe, and shall not be shaken out? That souls leave the truth should not discourage us in the least, but only make us seek more earnestly for the blessing of God. It is not the education, or the talents, or the position of men, that is to save them. We are to be kept by the power of God through faith unto salvation.

How do you stand before God today? The question is not How will you stand in the day of trouble, or at some future time? but how is it with your soul today? Will you go to work today? We want a personal, individual experience today. Today, we want Christ abiding with us.— *Review and Herald*, Apr. 9, 1889.

ALWAYS WITH US

I will not leave you comfortless: I will come to you. John 14:18.

Christ desired His disciples to understand that He would not leave them orphans. "I will not leave you comfortless," He declared; "I will come to you. Yet a little while, and the world seeth me no more; but ye see me: because I live, ye shall live also" (John 14:18, 19). Precious, glorious assurance of eternal life! Even though He was to be absent, their relation to Him was to be that of a child to its parent.

"At that day," He said, "ye shall know that I am in my Father, and ye in me, and I in you" (John 14:20). He sought to impress the minds of the disciples with the distinction between those who are of the world and those who are of Christ. He was about to die, but He desired them to realize that He would live again. And although, after His ascension, He would be absent from them, yet by faith they might see and know Him, and He would have the same loving interest in them that He had while with them. . . .

The words spoken to the disciples come to us through their words. The Comforter is ours as well as theirs, at all times and in all places, in all sorrows and in all affliction, when the outlook seems dark and the future perplexing, and we feel helpless and alone. These are times when the Comforter will be sent in answer to the prayer of faith.

There is no comforter like Christ, so tender and so true. He is touched with the feeling of our infirmities. His Spirit speaks to the heart. Circumstances may separate us from our friends; the broad, restless ocean may roll between us and them. Though their sincere friendship may still exist, they may be unable to demonstrate it by doing for us that which would be gratefully received. But no circumstances, no distance, can separate us from the heavenly Comforter. Wherever we are, wherever we may go, He is always there, one given in Christ's place, to act in His stead. He is always at our right hand, to speak soothing, gentle words; to support, sustain, uphold, and cheer.

The influence of the Holy Spirit is the life of Christ in the soul. This Spirit works in and through everyone who receives Christ. Those who know the indwelling of this Spirit reveal its fruit—love, joy, peace, long-suffering, gentleness, goodness, faith.—*Review and Herald*, Oct. 26, 1897.

IN TIMES OF TRIAL

For we have not an high priest which cannot be touched with the feeling of our infirmities; but was in all points tempted like as we are, yet without sin. Heb. 4:15.

Christ dwells in him who receives Him by faith. Though trials may come upon the soul, yet the Lord's presence will be with us. The burning bush in which was the Lord's presence did not consume away. The fire did not extinguish a fiber of the branches. Thus will it be with the feeble human agent who puts his trust in Christ. The furnace fire of temptation may burn, persecution and trial may come, but only the dross will be consumed. The gold will shine brighter because of the process of purification.

Greater is He that is in the heart of the faithful, than he that controls the hearts of unbelievers. Complain not bitterly of the trial which comes upon you, but let your eyes be directed to Christ, who has clothed His divinity with humanity, in order that we may understand how great His interest in us since He has identified Himself with suffering humanity. He tasted the cup of human sorrow, He was afflicted in all our afflictions, He was made perfect through suffering, tempted in all points like as humanity is tempted, in order that He might succor those who are in temptation.

He says, "I will make a man more precious than fine gold; even a man than the golden wedge of Ophir" (Isa. 13:12). He will make a man precious by abiding with him, by giving unto him the Holy Spirit. He says, "If ye then, being evil, know how to give good gifts unto your children: how much more shall your heavenly Father give the Holy Spirit to them that ask him?" (Luke 11:13).

The Lord has instructed us to call God our Father, to regard Him as the fountain of paternal affection, the source of the love that has been flowing from century to century through the channel of the human heart. All the pity, compassion, and love which have been manifested in the earth have emanated from the throne of God, and, compared to the love that dwells in His heart, are as a fountain to an ocean. His love is perpetually flowing forth to make the weak strong, to make the fainthearted firm, and give moral courage to the wavering. God works through Christ, and man may come unto the Father in the name of the Son. Our science and our song is "Hear what the Lord hath done for my soul."—*Signs of the Times*, Mar. 5, 1896.

SURROUNDED BY A DIVINE SHIELD

And call upon me in the day of trouble: I will deliver thee, and thou shalt glorify me. Ps. 50:15.

When trials arise that seem unexplainable, we should not allow our peace to be spoiled. However unjustly we may be treated, let not passion arise. By indulging a spirit of retaliation we injure ourselves. We destroy our own confidence in God, and grieve the Holy Spirit. There is by our side a Witness, a heavenly Messenger, who will lift up for us a standard against the enemy. He will shut us in with the bright beams of the Sun of Righteousness. Beyond this Satan cannot penetrate. He cannot pass this shield of holy light.

While the world is progressing in wickedness, none of us need flatter ourselves that we shall have no difficulties. But it is these very difficulties that bring us into the audience chamber of the Most High. We may seek counsel of One who is infinite in wisdom.

The Lord says, "Call upon me in the day of trouble" (Ps. 50:15). He invites us to present to Him our perplexities and necessities, and our need of divine help. He bids us be instant in prayer. As soon as difficulties arise, we are to offer to Him our sincere, earnest petitions. By our importunate prayers we give evidence of our strong confidence in God. The sense of our need leads us to pray earnestly, and our heavenly Father is moved by our supplications.

Often those who suffer reproach or persecution for their faith are tempted to think themselves forsaken by God. In the eyes of men they are in the minority. To all appearance their enemies triumph over them. But let them not violate their conscience. He who has suffered in their behalf, and has borne their sorrows and afflictions, has not forsaken them.

The children of God are not left alone and defenseless. Prayer moves the arm of Omnipotence. Prayer has "subdued kingdoms, wrought righteousness, obtained promises, stopped the mouths of lions, quenched the violence of fire"—we shall know what it means when we hear the reports of the martyrs who died for their faith—"turned to flight the armies of the aliens" (Heb. 11:33, 34).—*Christ's Object Lessons*, pp. 171, 172.

IN MOMENTS OF DESPAIR

Ask, and it shall be given you; seek, and ye shall find; knock, and it shall be opened unto you: for every one that asketh receiveth; and he that seeketh findeth; and to him that knocketh it shall be opened. Matt. 7:7, 8.

Then come, and seek, and find. The reservoir of power is open, is full and free. Come with humble hearts, not thinking that you must do some good thing to merit the favor of God, or that you must make yourself better before you can come to Christ. You can never do anything to better your condition. In the name of Jesus, come with full assurance of faith, because you are a sinner; for Christ said, "I am not come to call the righteous, but sinners to repentance" (Matt. 9:13). Draw nigh to God, and He will draw nigh to you. You are to ask, to seek, to knock, and to believe that you are accepted through Christ Jesus, trusting Him alone to do those things for you which you can never do for yourself. . . .

Jesus is our atoning sacrifice; we can make no atonement for ourselves, but by faith we can accept the atonement that has been made. "For Christ also hath once suffered for sins, the just for the unjust, that he might bring us to God" (1 Peter 3:18). "Ye were not redeemed with corruptible things, . . . but with the precious blood of Christ, as of a lamb without blemish and without spot" (1 Peter 1:18, 19). "The blood of Jesus Christ his Son cleanseth us from all sin" (1 John 1:7). It is by virtue of this precious blood that the sin-stricken soul can be restored to soundness. While you are putting up your petition to God, the Holy Spirit applies the faithful promises of God to your heart.

In moments of perplexity, when Satan suggests doubt and discouragement, the Spirit of the Lord will lift up as a standard against him the faithful sayings of Christ, and the bright beams of the Sun of righteousness will flash into your mind and soul. When Satan would overwhelm you with despair, the Holy Spirit will point you to the intercession made for you by a living Saviour. Christ is the fragrance, the holy incense, which makes your petitions acceptable to the Father. When the light of Christ's righteousness is fully understood and accepted, love, joy, peace, and inexpressible gratitude will pervade the soul, and the language of him who is blessed will be "Thy gentleness hath made me great" (Ps. 18:35).—*Signs of the Times,* Aug. 22, 1892.

STILL LOVED THOUGH WE ERR

My little children, these things write I unto you, that ye sin not. And if any man sin, we have an advocate with the Father, Jesus Christ the righteous. 1 John 2:1.

Those who are in connection with God are channels for the power of the Holy Spirit. If one who daily communes with God errs from the path, if he turns a moment from looking steadfastly unto Jesus, it is not because he sins willfully; for when he sees his mistake, he turns again, and fastens his eyes upon Jesus, and the fact that he has erred does not make him less dear to the heart of God. He knows that he has communion with the Saviour; and when reproved for his mistake in some matter of judgment, he does not walk sullenly, and complain of God, but turns the mistake into a victory. He learns a lesson from the words of the Master, and takes heed that he be not again deceived.

Those who truly love God have internal evidence that they are beloved of God, that they have communion with Christ, that their hearts are warmed with fervent love toward Him. The truth for this time is believed with sound confidence. They can say with all assurance, "We have not followed cunningly devised fables, when we made known unto you the power and coming of our Lord Jesus Christ, but were eyewitnesses of his majesty. . . . We have also a more sure word of prophecy; whereunto ye do well that ye take heed, as unto a light that shineth in a dark place, until the day dawn, and the day star arise in your hearts" (2 Peter 1:16-19).

The inner life of the soul will reveal itself in the outward conduct. Let the Word of God bear its testimony in behalf of the messenger whom God hath sent with a message in these last days to prepare a people to stand in the day of the Lord. "How beautiful upon the mountains are the feet of him that bringeth good tidings, that publisheth peace; that bringeth good tidings of good, that publisheth salvation; that saith unto Zion, Thy God reigneth!" (Isa. 52:7).

The wisdom of so-called intellectual men cannot be relied upon, unless they have learned and are daily learning lessons in the school of Christ. Men, in their supposed wisdom, may plan and devise theories and systems of philosophy, but the Lord calls them vain and foolish. The Lord says, "The foolishness of God is wiser than men; and the weakness of God is stronger than men" (1 Cor. 1:25).—*Review and Herald*, May 12, 1896.

IN THE DARKEST HOUR

And he said unto me, My grace is sufficient for thee: for my strength is made perfect in weakness. Most gladly therefore will I rather glory in my infirmities, that the power of Christ may rest upon me. 2 Cor. 12:9.

You may be disappointed, and your will and your way may be denied; but be assured that the Lord loves you. The furnace fire may kindle upon you, not for the purpose of destroying you, but to consume the dross, that you may come forth as gold seven times purified. Bear in mind that God will give you songs in the night. Darkness may seem to enclose you, but you are not to look at the clouds. Beyond the darkest cloud there is an ever-shining light. The Lord has light for every soul. Open the door of the heart to hope, peace, and joy. Jesus says, "These things have I spoken unto you, that my joy might remain in you, and that your joy might be full" (John 15:11).

God has a special work for everyone to do, and each one of us may do well the work which God has assigned him. The only thing we have to fear on our part is that we shall not keep our eyes continually fixed upon Jesus, that we shall not have an eye single to the glory of God, so that if we were called to lay down our armor and sleep in death we might not be ready to give an account of our trust. Forget not for a moment that you are Christ's property, bought with an infinite price, and that you are to glorify Him in your spirit, and in your body, which are His. . . .

God has provided a balm for every wound. There is a Balm in Gilead, there is a Physician there. Will you not now as never before study the Scriptures? Seek the Lord for wisdom in every emergency. In every trial plead with Jesus to show you a way out of your troubles, then your eyes will be opened to behold the remedy and to apply to your case the healing promises that have been recorded in His Word. In this way the enemy will find no place to lead you into mourning and unbelief, but instead you will have faith and hope and courage in the Lord. The Holy Spirit will give you clear discernment that you may see and appropriate every blessing that will act as an antidote to grief, as a branch of healing to every draught of bitterness that is placed to your lips.— *Selected Messages*, book 2, pp. 272-274.

WITH CONCERNED PARENTS

Cast me not away from thy presence; and take not thy holy spirit from me. Restore unto me the joy of thy salvation; and uphold me with thy free spirit. Then will I teach transgressors thy ways; and sinners shall be converted unto thee. Ps. 51:11-13.

What a prayer is this! How evident it is that sinners in the household are not to be treated with indifference, but that the Lord looks upon them as the purchase of His blood. In every household where the unconverted are, it should be the work of those who know the Lord to work in wisdom for their conversion. The Lord will surely bless the efforts of parents, as in His fear and love they seek to save the souls of their households. The Lord Jesus is waiting to be gracious.

Oh, that the work might begin at the heart! "For thou desirest not sacrifice; else would I give it: thou delightest not in burnt offering. The sacrifices of God are a broken spirit: a broken and a contrite heart, O God, thou wilt not despise" (Ps. 51:16, 17). Then let it be understood by all the members of the household that the work must begin at the heart. The heart must be subdued and made contrite through the creating, regenerating power of the Holy Spirit. Realizing the aid of this mighty agency, cannot parents work for the conversion of their children with more zeal and love than ever before?

The promise of the Lord is "Then will I sprinkle clean water upon you, and ye shall be clean: from all your filthiness, and from all your idols, will I cleanse you. A new heart also will I give you, and a new spirit will I put within you: and I will take away the stony heart out of your flesh, and I will give you a heart of flesh. And I will put my spirit within you, and cause you to walk in my statutes, and ye shall keep my judgments, and do them" (Eze. 36:25-27).

When the Spirit of the Lord works upon the hearts of the parents, their prayers and tears will come up before God, and they will earnestly entreat, and will receive grace and wisdom from heaven, and will be able to work for their unconverted children. As this Spirit is manifested in the home, it will be brought into the church, and those who are home missionaries will also become agents for God in the church and in the world. The institutions which God has planted will bear an entirely different mold.—*Review and Herald*, Mar. 14, 1893.

BESIDE MOTHERS LEADING THEIR LITTLE ONES

For this child I prayed; and the Lord hath given me my petition which I asked of him: therefore also I have lent him to the Lord; as long as he liveth he shall be lent to the Lord. 1 Sam. 1:27, 28.

Christian mothers should realize that they are coworkers with God when training and disciplining their children in such a manner as will enable them to reflect the character of Christ. In this work they will have the cooperation of heavenly angels; but it is a work that is sadly neglected, and for this reason Christ is robbed of His heritage—the younger members of His family. But through the indwelling of the Holy Spirit, humanity may be a coworker with divinity.

The lessons of Christ upon the occasion of receiving the children should leave a deeper impression upon our minds. The words of Christ encourage parents to bring their little ones to Jesus. They may be wayward, and possess passions like those of humanity, but this should not deter us from bringing them to Christ. He blessed children that were possessed of passions like His own.

We often err in training our children. Parents often indulge their children in that which is selfish and demoralizing, and, instead of having travail of soul for their salvation, they let them drift along, and grow up with perverse tempers and unlovely characters. They do not accept their God-given responsibility to educate and train their children for the glory of God. They become dissatisfied with their children's manners, and disheartened as they realize that their faults are the result of their own neglect, and then they become discouraged.

But if parents would feel that they are never released from their burden of educating and training their children for God, if they would do their work in faith, cooperating with God by earnest prayer and work, they would be successful in bringing their children to the Saviour. Let fathers and mothers devote themselves, soul, body, and spirit, to God before the birth of their children.—*Signs of the Times*, Apr. 9, 1896.

ANSWERING PRAYERS FOR DIVINE HELP

And these words, which I command thee this day, shall be in thine heart: and thou shalt teach them diligently unto thy children, and shalt talk of them when thou sittest in thine house, and when thou walkest by the way, and when thou liest down, and when thou risest up. Deut. 6:6, 7.

Fathers and mothers, how can I find words to describe your great responsibility! By the character you reveal before your children you are educating them to serve God or to serve self. Then offer to heaven your earnest prayers for the aid of the Holy Spirit, that your hearts may be sanctified, and that the course you pursue may honor God and win your children to Christ. It should give to parents a sense of the solemnity and sacredness of their task, when they realize that by careless speech or action they may lead their children astray.

Parents need the guardianship of God and His Word. If they do not heed the counsels of the Word of God, if they do not make the Bible the man of their counsel, the rule of their life, their children will grow careless and will walk in paths of disobedience and unbelief. Christ lived a life of toil and self-denial, and died a death of shame, that He might give an example of the spirit that should inspire and control His followers. As in their home life parents strive to be Christlike, heavenly influences will be shed abroad in the lives of their family.

In every Christian home God should be honored by the morning and evening sacrifices of praise and prayer. Every morning and evening earnest prayers should ascend to God for His blessing and guidance. Will the Lord of heaven pass by such homes, and leave no blessing there? Nay, verily. Angels hear the offering of praise and the prayer of faith, and they bear the petitions to Him who ministers in the sanctuary for His people, and pleads His merits in their behalf. True prayer takes hold upon Omnipotence, and gives men the victory. Upon his knees the Christian obtains strength to resist temptation.—*Review and Herald,* Feb. 1, 1912.

DIRECTING THE SANCTIFICATION OF THE FAMILY

Train up a child in the way he should go: and when he is old, he will not depart from it. Prov. 22:6.

I appeal to parents to prepare themselves and their children to unite with the family above. Get ready, for Christ's sake, get ready to meet your Lord in peace. Begin to work in your family on right lines. Get down to the root of the matter. Bring the truth into your homes, to sanctify and purify them. Do not keep it in the outer court. How blind many professing Christians are to their own interests! How utterly they fail to see what Christ would do for them were He admitted into their homes. Let Christians work as earnestly to win the crown of life as worldlings work to win earthly advantages, and the church of God will certainly move forward with power. . . .

The Holy Spirit produces actions that are in harmony with the law of God. The regenerating work of the Spirit will be seen in families where painstaking efforts are put forth to manifest kindness, patience, and love. Almighty power is at work, preparing minds and hearts to submit to the molding influence of the Holy Spirit, leading parents to sanctify themselves, that their children also may be sanctified.

The home in which the members are polite, courteous Christians exerts a far-reaching influence for good. Other families will mark the results attained by such a home, and will follow the example set, in their turn guarding the home against satanic influences.

The angels of God will often visit the home in which the will of God bears sway. Under the power of divine grace such a home becomes a place of refreshing to worn, weary pilgrims. By watchfully guarding, self is kept from asserting itself. Correct habits are formed. There is a careful recognition of the rights of others. The faith that works by love and purifies the soul stands at the helm, presiding over the whole household. Under the hallowed influence of such a home, the principle of brotherhood laid down in the Word of God is more widely recognized and obeyed.—*Southern Watchman*, Jan. 19, 1904.

VERY CLOSE TO THE CHILDREN

And they brought young children to him, that he should touch them: and his disciples rebuked those that brought them. But when Jesus saw it, he was much displeased, and said unto them, Suffer the little children to come unto me, and forbid them not: for of such is the kingdom of God. Verily I say unto you, Whosoever shall not receive the kingdom of God as a little child, he shall not enter therein. And he took them up in his arms, put his hands upon them, and blessed them. Mark 10:13-16.

God wants every child of tender age to be His child, to be adopted into His family. Young though they may be, the youth may be members of the household of faith, and have a most precious experience. They may have hearts that are tender and ready to receive impressions that will be lasting. They may have their hearts drawn out in confidence and love for Jesus, and live for the Saviour. Christ will make them little missionaries. The whole current of their thoughts may be changed, so that sin will not appear a thing to be enjoyed, but to be hated and shunned.

Small children, as well as those who are older, will be benefited by this instruction; and in thus simplifying the plan of salvation, the teachers will receive as great blessings as those who are taught. The Holy Spirit of God will impress the lessons upon the receptive minds of the children, that they may grasp the ideas of Bible truth in their simplicity. And the Lord will give an experience to these children in missionary lines; He will suggest to them lines of thought that even the teachers did not have. The children who are properly instructed will be witnesses for the truth.—*Counsels to Parents and Teachers*, pp. 169, 170.

Work as if you were working for your life to save children from being drowned in the polluting, corrupting influences of this life.—*Child Guidance*, p. 309.

A teacher should be employed who will educate the children in the truths of the Word of God, which are so essential for these last days, and which it is so important for them to understand. A great test is coming: it will be upon obedience or disobedience to the commandments of God.—*Review and Herald*, July 2, 1908.

THE SPIRIT LOVES TO WORK WITH CHILDREN

And Jesus called a little child unto him, and set him in the midst of them, and said, Verily I say unto you, Except ye be converted, and become as little children, ye shall not enter into the kingdom of heaven. Whosoever therefore shall humble himself as this little child, the same is greatest in the kingdom of heaven. And whoso shall receive one such little child in my name receiveth me. But whoso shall offend one of these little ones which believe in me, it were better for him that a millstone were hanged about his neck, and that he were drowned in the depth of the sea. Matt. 18:2-6.

Oh, for a clear perception of what we might accomplish if we would learn of Jesus! The springs of heavenly peace and joy, unsealed in the soul of the teacher by the magic words of inspiration, will become a mighty river of influence, to bless all who connect with Him. Do not think that the Bible will become a tiresome book to the children. Under a wise instructor the work will become more and more desirable. It will be to them as the bread of life, and will never grow old. There is in it a freshness and beauty that attract and charm the children and youth. It is like the sun shining upon the earth, giving its brightness and warmth, yet never exhausted. By lessons from the Bible history and doctrine, the children and youth can learn that all other books are inferior to this. They can find here a fountain of mercy and of love.

God's holy, educating Spirit is in His Word. A light, a new and precious light, shines forth upon every page. Truth is there revealed, and words and sentences are made bright and appropriate for the occasion, as the voice of God speaking to them.

We need to recognize the Holy Spirit as our enlightener. That Spirit loves to address the children, and discover to them the treasures and beauties of the Word of God. The promises spoken by the Great Teacher will captivate the senses and animate the soul of the child with a spiritual power that is divine. There will grow in the fruitful a familiarity with divine things, which will be as a barricade against the temptations of the enemy.—*General Conference Bulletin*, Apr. 1, 1898.

WITH THE YOUNGER MEMBERS OF GOD'S FAMILY

Remember now thy Creator in the days of thy youth, while the evil days come not, nor the years draw nigh, when thou shalt say, I have no pleasure in them. Eccl. 12:1.

Every blessing the Father has provided for those of more mature experience has been provided for children and youth through Jesus Christ. When the Lord sees the youth studying the life and lessons of Christ, He gives His angels charge over them, to keep them in all their ways, as He gave His angels charge over Jesus, His beloved Son. The angels attended Jesus when He lived upon earth under the guidance of God's Holy Spirit, doing His heavenly Father's will, that He might give a correct sample of character, that might be an example to children and youth. He desired that, in every action of their lives, they should do those things of which God could approve. He knew that every good work, every deed of kindness, every act of obedience to father and mother, would be registered in the books of heaven.

Those who honor their parents would reap a reward in the fulfillment of the promise that they should live long upon the land which the Lord their God giveth them. Children are to continue in well-doing, praying that through the merits of Jesus, the Lord will give them His grace, His mind, and His beauty of character. God has withheld no blessing that is necessary for shaping the character of children and youth after the divine pattern given them in the youth of Jesus. They are to ask for the graces of His character, in simple, trusting faith, and in the name of Jesus, just as a son asks a favor of his earthly parent.

Dear children and youth, you need a new heart. Ask God for this. He says, "A new heart also will I give you" (Eze. 36:26). When you have asked according to His will, doubt not that you will receive; for whatever God has promised, He will fulfill. If you come with true contrition of soul, you need not feel that you are at all presumptuous in asking for what God has promised. Presumption is asking for things to gratify selfish inclination; for human enjoyment in earthly things. But when you ask for the spiritual blessings you so much need in order that you may perfect a character after Christ's likeness, the Lord assures you that you are asking according to a promise that will be verified.—*Youth's Instructor*, Aug. 23, 1894.

YOUTH RECEIVING POWER TO BE OVERCOMERS

Rejoice, O young man, in thy youth; and let thy heart cheer thee in the days of thy youth, and walk in the ways of thine heart, and in the sight of thine eyes: but know thou, that for all these things God will bring thee into judgment. Eccl. 11:9.

In surrendering ourselves to God, we reap great advantages; for if we have weaknesses of character, as we all have, we unite ourselves to One who is mighty to save. Our ignorance will be united to infinite wisdom, our frailty to enduring might, and, like Jacob, we may each become a prince with God. Connected with the Lord God of Israel, we shall have power from above which will enable us to be overcomers; and by the impartation of divine love, we shall find access to the hearts of men. We shall have fastened our trembling grasp upon the throne of the Infinite, and shall say, "I will not let thee go, except thou bless me" (Gen. 32:26).

The assurance is given that He will bless us and make us a blessing; and this is our light, our joy, our triumph. When the youth understand what it is to have the favor and love of God in the heart, they will begin to realize the value of their blood-bought privileges, and will consecrate their ability to God, and strive with all their God-given powers to increase their talents to use in the Master's service.

The only safety for our youth in this age of sin and crime is to have a living connection with God. They must learn how to seek God, that they may be filled with His Holy Spirit, and act as though they realized that the whole host of heaven was looking upon them with interested solicitude, ready to minister unto them in danger and in time of need. The youth should be barricaded by warning and instruction against temptation. They should be taught what are the encouragements held out to them in the Word of God. They should have delineated before them the peril of taking a step into the bypaths of evil. They should be educated to revere the counsels of God in His sacred oracles. They should be so instructed that they will set their resolution against evil, and determine that they will not enter into any path where they could not expect Jesus to accompany them, and His blessing to abide upon them.—*Review and Herald*, Nov. 21, 1893.

HELPING TO BUILD UP A CHARACTER FOR HEAVEN

If it be so, our God whom we serve is able to deliver us from the burning fiery furnace, and he will deliver us out of thine hand, O king. But if not, be it known unto thee, O king, that we will not serve thy gods, nor worship the golden image which thou hast set up. Dan. 3:17, 18.

While these youth were working out their own salvation, God was working in them to will and to do of His good pleasure. Here are revealed the conditions of success. To make God's grace our own, we must act our part. The Lord does not propose to perform for us either the willing or the doing. His grace is given to work in us to will and to do, but never as a substitute for our effort. Our souls are to be aroused to cooperate. The Holy Spirit works in us, that we may work out our own salvation. This is the practical lesson the Holy Spirit is striving to teach us. "It is God which worketh in you both to will and to do of his good pleasure" (Phil. 2:13).

The Lord will cooperate with all who earnestly strive to be faithful in His service, as He cooperated with Daniel and his three companions. Fine mental qualities and a high tone of moral character are not the result of accident. God gives opportunities; success depends upon the use made of them. The openings of Providence must be quickly discerned and eagerly entered. There are many who might become mighty men, if, like Daniel, they would depend upon God for grace to be overcomers, and for strength and efficiency to do their work.

I address you, young men: Be faithful. Put heart into your work. Imitate none who are slothful, and who give divided service. Actions, often repeated, form habits, habits form character. Patiently perform the little duties of life. So long as you undervalue the importance of faithfulness in the little duties, your character-building will be unsatisfactory. In the sight of Omnipotence, every duty is important. The Lord has said, "He that is faithful in that which is least is faithful also in much" (Luke 16:10). In the life of a true Christian there are no nonessentials.—*Messages to Young People*, pp. 147, 148.

MOVING AMONG THE STUDENTS

But if the Spirit of him that raised up Jesus from the dead dwell in you, he that raised up Christ from the dead shall also quicken your mortal bodies by his Spirit that dwelleth in you. Rom. 8:11.

The Lord God of heaven has caused His Holy Spirit from time to time to move upon the students in the school [Battle Creek College], that they might acknowledge Him in all their ways, so that He might direct their paths. At times the manifestation of the Holy Spirit has been so decided that studies were forgotten, and the greatest Teacher the world ever knew made His voice heard, saying, "Come unto me, all ye that labour and are heavy laden, and I will give you rest. Take my yoke upon you, and learn of me; for I am meek and lowly in heart: and ye shall find rest unto your souls. For my yoke is easy, and my burden is light" (Matt. 11:28-30).

The Lord knocked at the door of hearts, and I saw that angels of God were present. There seemed to be no special effort on the part of the teachers to influence the students to give their attention to the things of God, but God had a Watcher in the school, and though His presence was unseen, yet His influence was discernible. Again and again there have been manifest tokens of the presence of the holy Watchman in the school. Again and again the voice of Jesus has spoken to the students, saying, "Behold, I stand at the door, and knock: if any man hear my voice, and open the door, I will come in to him, and will sup with him, and he with me" (Rev. 3:20).

The Lord has been waiting long to impart the greatest, truest joys to the heart. All those who look to Him with undivided hearts, He will greatly bless. Those who have thus looked to Him have caught more distinct views of Jesus as their sin-bearer, their all-sufficient sacrifice, and have been hid in the cleft of the rock, to behold the Lamb of God who taketh away the sins of the world. When we have a sense of His all-sufficient sacrifice, our lips are tuned to the highest, loftiest themes of praise.—*Special Testimonies on Education*, pp. 77, 78.

EAGER TO HELP TEACHERS

And when the sons of the prophets which were to view at Jericho saw him, they said, The spirit of Elijah doth rest on Elisha. And they came to meet him, and bowed themselves to the ground before him. 2 Kings 2:15.

The Holy Spirit came into the schools of the prophets, bringing even the thoughts of the students into harmony with the will of God. There was a living connection between heaven and these schools, and the joy and thanksgiving of loving hearts found expression in songs of praise in which the angels joined. If teachers would open their hearts to receive the Spirit, they would be prepared to cooperate with Him in working for their students; and when He is given free course, He will effect wonderful transformations. He will work in each heart, correcting selfishness, molding and refining the character, and bringing even the thoughts into captivity to Christ. . . .

Instead of being repressed and driven back, the Holy Spirit should be welcomed, and His presence encouraged. When teachers sanctify themselves through obedience to the Word, the Holy Spirit will give them glimpses of heavenly things. When they seek God with humility and earnestness, the words which they have spoken in freezing accents will burn in their hearts; the truth will not then languish upon their tongues.

The agency of the Spirit of God does not remove from us the necessity of exercising our faculties and talents, but teaches us how to use every power to the glory of God. The human faculties when under the special direction of the grace of God are capable of being used to the best purpose on earth. Ignorance does not increase the humility or spirituality of any professed follower of Christ. The truths of the divine Word can be best appreciated by an intellectual Christian. Christ can be best glorified by those who serve Him intelligently. The great object of education is to enable us to use the powers which God has given us in such a manner as to represent the religion of the Bible and promote the glory of God.—*North Pacific Union Gleaner*, May 26, 1909.

GOING HOUSE TO HOUSE WITH THE GOSPEL WORKER

Then he called his twelve disciples together, and gave them power and authority over all devils, and to cure diseases. And he sent them to preach the kingdom of God, and to heal the sick. And he said unto them, Take nothing for your journey, neither staves, nor script, neither bread, neither money; neither have two coats apiece. And whatsoever house ye enter into, there abide, and thence depart. Luke 9:1-4.

The Lord is calling upon His people to take up different lines of missionary service. Those in the highways and byways of life are to hear the gospel message. Church members are to do evangelistic work in the homes of their neighbors who have not yet received full evidence of the truth for this time.

Let those who take up this work make the life of Christ their constant study. Let them be intensely in earnest, using every capability in the Lord's service. Precious results will follow sincere, unselfish efforts. From the Great Teacher the workers will receive the highest of all education. But those who do not impart the light they have received will one day realize that they have sustained a fearful loss.

Many of God's people are to go forth with our publications into places where the third angel's message has never been proclaimed. The work of the canvasser-evangelist whose heart is imbued with the Holy Spirit is fraught with wonderful possibilities for good. The presentation of the truth, in love and simplicity, from house to house, is in harmony with the instruction that Christ gave His disciples when He sent them out on their first missionary tour. By songs of praise, humble, heartfelt prayers, and a simple presentation of truth in the family circle, many will be reached. The divine Worker will be present to send conviction to hearts. "I am with you alway" (Matt. 28:20) is His promise. With the assurance of the abiding presence of such a Helper, we may labor with faith and hope and courage.

The monotony of our service for God needs to be broken up. Every church member should be engaged in some special service for the Master. Let those who are well established in the truth go into neighboring places, and hold meetings. Let God's Word be read, and let the ideas expressed be such that they will be readily comprehended by all.—*Review and Herald*, May 5, 1904.

MAKING LASTING IMPRESSIONS THROUGH THE CANVASSER

How beautiful upon the mountains are the feet of him that bringeth good tidings, that publisheth peace; that bringeth good tidings of good, that publisheth salvation; that saith unto Zion, Thy God reigneth! Isa. 52:7.

Humble, fervent prayer would do more in behalf of the circulation of our books than all the expensive pictures in the world. If the workers will turn their attention to that which is true and living and real; if they will pray for, believe for, and trust in the Holy Spirit, it will be poured upon them in strong, heavenly currents, and right and lasting impressions will be made upon the human heart. Then pray and work, and work and pray, and the Lord will work with you.

Every canvasser has positive and constant need of the angelic ministration; for he has an important work to do, a work that he cannot do in his own strength. Those who are born again, who are willing to be guided by the Holy Spirit, doing in Christ's way that which they can do, those who will work as if they could see the heavenly universe watching them, will be accompanied and instructed by holy angels, who will go before them to the dwellings of the people, preparing the way for them. . . .

When men realize the times in which we are living, they will work as in the sight of heaven. The canvasser will handle these books that bring light and strength to the soul. He will drink in the spirit of these books, and put his whole soul into the work of presenting them to the people. His strength, his courage, his success will depend upon how fully the truth presented in the books is woven into his own experience and developed in his character. When his own life is thus molded he can go forward representing to others the sacred truth he is handling in the books for which he is finding a place in homes. Imbued with the Spirit of God, he will gain a deep, rich experience, and heavenly angels will give him success in the work.—*Australasian Union Conference Record*, May 1, 1901.

DIRECTING THE PUBLISHING MINISTRY

And the Gentiles shall come to thy light, and kings to the brightness of thy rising. Isa. 60:3.

Our publishing houses were erected to do a work for the Lord, to send heavenly light to all parts of the world, to bring precious souls into the fold. Let the [publishing house] office be a missionary plant to do a work for the Master in the conversion of souls. Work, and watch, and pray for souls as they that must give an account. This year try the Lord's prescribed remedy for evil. Let every man do that which the Lord requires him to do, looking unto Jesus, who is the owner of every soul.

Let the workers who have to act a part in this firm remember that God calls them to be a convention of Christian workers, a spectacle to the world, to angels, and to men. Let small companies assemble together in the evening or early morning to study the Bible for themselves. Let them have a season of prayer that they may be strengthened and enlightened and sanctified by the Holy Spirit. This is the work Christ wants to have done in the heart of everyone who is engaged in any department of the publishing work. If you will do this, a great blessing will come to you from the One who gave His whole life to service, the One who redeemed you by His own life.

You must have the power of the Holy Spirit, else you cannot be an overcomer. What testimonies you should bear of the loving acquaintance you have made with your fellow workers in these precious seasons when seeking the blessing of God. Let each tell his experience in simple words. This will bring more comfort and joy to the soul than all the pleasant instruments of song that can be produced in the Tabernacle. Let Christ come into your hearts.

The work of every believer is aggressive. It is a daily warfare. Christ is saying to the managers and workers in the office, "Ye are my witnesses" (Isa. 43:10). Think it; speak it; act it. Heaven is just next door. Open the door heavenward and close the door earthward. God is calling the workers in every department of the office. Will you hear His voice and open the door of the heart to Jesus? Will you love Him who gave His life for you?—*Manuscript Releases*, vol. 12, pp. 46, 47.

IMPRESSING MINDS
THROUGH THE BOOKS

Also I heard the voice of the Lord, saying, Whom shall I send, and who will go for us? Then said I, Here am I; send me. Isa. 6:8.

Pray and work. More will be accomplished by the Christlike humble prayer than by many words without prayer. Work in simplicity, and the Lord will work with the canvasser. The Holy Spirit will impress minds just as He impresses the minds of those who listen to the words of God's delegated ministers, who preach His Word. The same ministry of holy angels attends the one who gives himself to canvassing for books for the educating of the people as to what is truth.

Men and women can work in lines effectually if they feel in their hearts that they are doing the work of the Lord in ministering to the souls who know not the truth for this time. They are sounding the note of warning in the byways and highways to prepare a people for the great day of God which is about to break upon the world. We have no time to lose. We must encourage this work. Who will go forth now with our publications? Let them read the sixth chapter of Isaiah, and take its lesson home to their hearts.

"Then said I, Woe is me! for I am undone; because I am a man of unclean lips, and I dwell in the midst of a people of unclean lips: for mine eyes have seen the King, the Lord of hosts. Then flew one of the seraphims unto me, having a live coal in his hand, which he had taken with the tongs from off the altar: and he laid it upon my mouth, and said, Lo, this hath touched thy lips; and thine iniquity is taken away, and thy sin purged. Also I heard the voice of the Lord, saying, Whom shall I send, and who will go for us? Then said I, Here am I; send me" (Isa. 6:5-8).

This representation will be acted over and over again if the canvassers are pressing close to the side of Christ, wearing His yoke, and daily learning of Him how to carry messages of peace and comfort to the sorrowing, disappointed ones, the sad and brokenhearted. By imbuing them with His own Spirit, Christ the great teacher is fitting them to do a good and important work.—*Bible Echo*, Sept. 18, 1899.

TRAVELING WITH THE MISSIONARIES

As they ministered to the Lord, and fasted, the Holy Ghost said, Separate me Barnabas and Saul for the work whereunto I have called them. And when they had fasted and prayed, and laid their hands on them, they sent them away. So they, being sent forth by the Holy Ghost, departed unto Seleucia; and from thence they sailed to Cyprus. Acts 13:2-4.

Oh, how we need the divine Presence! For the baptism of the Holy Spirit, every worker should be breathing out his prayers to God. Companies should be gathered together to call upon God for special help, for heavenly wisdom, that the people of God may know how to plan and devise and execute the work. Especially should men pray that the Lord will choose His agents, and baptize His missionaries with the Holy Spirit.

For ten days the disciples prayed before the Pentecostal blessing came. It needed all that time to bring them to an understanding of what is meant to offer effectual prayer, drawing nearer and nearer to God, confessing their sins, humbling their hearts before God, and by faith beholding Jesus, and becoming changed into His image. When the blessing did come, it filled all the place where they were assembled; and endowed with power, they went forth to do effectual work for the Master.

We should pray as earnestly for the descent of the Holy Spirit as the disciples prayed on the day of Pentecost. If they needed [the Spirit] at that time, we need Him more today. Moral darkness, like a funeral pall, covers the earth. All manner of false doctrines, heresies, and satanic deceptions are misleading the minds of men. Without the Spirit and power of God, it will be in vain that we labor to present the truth. We must have the Holy Spirit to sustain us in the conflict; "for we wrestle not against flesh and blood, but against principalities, against powers, against the rulers of the darkness of this world, against spiritual wickedness in high places" (Eph. 6:12).

We cannot fall as long as we hope and trust in God. Let every soul of us, ministers and people, say, as did Paul, "I therefore so run, not as uncertainly; so fight I, not as one that beateth the air" (1 Cor. 9:26), but with a holy faith and hope, in expectation of winning the prize.—*Home Missionary*, Nov. 1, 1893.

DISPELLING DARKNESS

Arise, shine; for thy light is come, and the glory of the Lord is risen upon thee. For, behold, the darkness shall cover the earth, and gross darkness the people: but the Lord shall arise upon thee, and his glory shall be seen upon thee. Isa. 60:1, 2.

The church has been appointed as the medium through which divine light is to shine into the moral darkness of this world, and the peace-giving beams of the Sun of righteousness fall upon the hearts of men. Personal labor with individuals and with families constitutes a part of the work to be done in God's moral vineyard. The meekness, the patience, the forbearance, the love of Christ must be revealed in the homes of the land. The church must arise and shine. Radiant with the Spirit and power of the truth, the people of God must go forth to a world lying in darkness, to make manifest the light of the glory of God. God has given to men noble powers of mind to be employed to His honor; and in the missionary work these powers of mind are called into active exercise. Wise improvement and development of the gifts of God will be seen in His servants. Day by day there will be growth in the knowledge of Christ.

He who once spake as never man spake, who wore the garb of humanity, is still the Great Teacher. As you follow in His footsteps, seeking the lost, angels will draw near, and through the illumination of the Spirit of God, greater knowledge will be obtained as to the best ways and means for accomplishing the work committed to your hands. . . .

Those who should have been the light of the world have shed forth but feeble and sickly beams. What is light? It is piety, goodness, truth, mercy, love; it is the revealing of the truth in the character and life. The gospel is dependent on the personal piety of its believers for its aggressive power, and God has made provision through the death of His beloved Son, that every soul may be thoroughly furnished unto every good work. Every soul is to be a bright and shining light, showing forth the praises of Him who has called us out of darkness into His marvelous light.—*Review and Herald*, Mar. 24, 1891.

ENCOURAGING THE HERALDS
OF THE GOSPEL

Not that we are sufficient of ourselves to think any thing as of ourselves; but our sufficiency is of God; who also hath made us able ministers of the new testament; not of the letter, but of the spirit: for the letter killeth, but the spirit giveth life. 2 Cor. 3:5, 6.

Those only who are constantly receiving fresh supplies of grace will have power proportionate to their daily need and their ability to use that power. Instead of looking forward to some future time when, through a special endowment of spiritual power, they will receive a miraculous fitting up for soul winning, they are yielding themselves daily to God, that He may make them vessels meet for His use. Daily they are improving the opportunities for service that lie within their reach. Daily they are witnessing for the Master wherever they may be, whether in some humble sphere of labor in the home, or in a public field of usefulness.

To the consecrated worker there is wonderful consolation in the knowledge that even Christ during His life on earth sought His Father daily for fresh supplies of needed grace; and from this communion with God He went forth to strengthen and bless others. Behold the Son of God bowed in prayer to His Father! Though He is the Son of God, He strengthens His faith by prayer, and by communion with heaven gathers to Himself power to resist evil and to minister to the needs of men.

As the elder brother of our race He knows the necessities of those who, compassed with infirmity and living in a world of sin and temptation, still desire to serve Him. He knows that the messengers whom He sees fit to send are weak, erring men; but to all who give themselves wholly to His service He promises divine aid. His own example is an assurance that earnest, persevering supplication to God in faith—faith that leads to entire dependence upon God, and unreserved consecration to His work—will avail to bring to men the Holy Spirit's aid in the battle against sin.—*The Acts of the Apostles*, pp. 55, 56.

WORKING THROUGH HUMBLE INSTRUMENTS

Because the foolishness of God is wiser than men; and the weakness of God is stronger than men. 1 Cor. 1:25.

God will move upon men of humble position in society, men who have not become insensible to the bright rays of light through so long contemplating the light of truth, and refusing to make any improvement or advancement therein. Many such will be seen hurrying hither and thither, constrained by the Spirit of God to bring the light to others. The truth, the word of God, is as a fire in their bones, filling them with a burning desire to enlighten those who sit in darkness.

Many, even among the uneducated, now proclaim the words of the Lord. Children are impelled by the Spirit to go forth and declare the message from heaven. The Spirit is poured out upon all who will yield to its promptings, and, casting off all man's machinery, his binding rules and cautious methods, they will declare the truth with the might of the Spirit's power. Multitudes will receive the faith and join the armies of the Lord.

Many of those who are professedly followers of the Lord at the present time do not submit themselves to the guidance of His Spirit, but try to harness up the Holy Spirit, and drive Him in their way. All such must abandon their self-sufficiency, and yield themselves unreservedly to the Lord, that He may work out His good pleasure in and through them.

The seven last plagues are about to descend upon the disobedient. Many have let the gospel invitation go unheeded; they have been tested and tried; but mountainous obstacles have seemed to loom up before their faces, blocking their onward march. Through faith, perseverance, and courage, many will surmount these obstructions and walk out into the glorious light. Almost unconsciously barriers have been erected in the strait and narrow way; stones of stumbling have been placed in the path; these will all be rolled away. The safeguards which false shepherds have thrown around their flocks will become as naught; thousands will step out into the light, and work to spread the light.—*Review and Herald*, July 23, 1895.

WITH CONSECRATED MEN AND WOMEN

For ye see your calling, brethren, how that not many wise men after the flesh, not many mighty, not many noble, are called. 1 Cor. 1:26.

Not all can fill the same place; but everyone who yields himself to the consecrating influence of the Holy Spirit will be under the control of Christ, and for consecrated men and women God has made full provision. He will carry on His work by a variety of ways and instruments. It is not alone the most talented, not alone those who hold high positions of trust, or are the most highly educated, that the Lord will use in His work of soul-saving. He will use many who have had few advantages. By the use of simple means He will bring those who own property and land to a belief of the truth; and these will become God's helping hand in the advancement of His work. It is not always the brightest talent that accomplishes the most for God. The Lord can speak through anyone who is consecrated to His service.

When we catch the Spirit of the message that is to lead souls to choose between life and death, we shall see a work done that we do not now dream of. Once let the missionary spirit take hold of men and women, young and old, and we shall see many going into the highways and hedges, and compelling the honest in heart to come in.

Let those who labor for souls remember that they are pledged to co-operate with Christ, to obey His directions, to follow His guidance. Every day they are to ask for and receive power from on high. They are to cherish a constant sense of the Saviour's love, His efficiency, His watchfulness, His tenderness. They are to look to Him as the shepherd and bishop of their souls. Then they will have the sympathy and support of the heavenly angels. Christ will be their joy and crown of rejoicing. Their hearts will then be controlled by the Holy Spirit. They will go forth clothed with holy zeal, and their efforts will be accompanied by a power proportionate to the importance of the message they proclaim.—*Review and Herald*, Oct. 27, 1910.

DIVINE HELP IN DOING SAMARITAN WORK

But a certain Samaritan, as he journeyed, came where he was: and when he saw him, he had compassion on him, and went to him, and bound up his wounds, pouring in oil and wine, and set him on his own beast, and brought him to an inn, and took care of him. Luke 10:33, 34.

I have been shown that the medical missionary work will discover, in the very depths of degradation, men who once possessed fine minds, richest qualifications, who will be rescued, by proper labor, from their fallen condition. It is the truth as it is in Jesus that is to be brought before human minds after they have been sympathetically cared for and their physical necessities met. The Holy Spirit is working and cooperating with the human agencies that are laboring for such souls, and some will appreciate the foundation upon a rock for their religious faith.

There is to be no startling communication of strange doctrine to these subjects whom God loves and pities; but as they are helped physically by the medical missionary workers, the Holy Spirit cooperates with the minister of human agencies to arouse the moral powers. The mental powers are awakened into activity, and these poor souls will, many of them, be saved in the kingdom of God.

Nothing can, or ever will, give character to the work in the presentation of truth to help the people just where they are so well as Samaritan work. A work properly conducted to save poor sinners that have been passed by the churches will be the entering wedge whereby the truth will find standing room. A different order of things needs to be established among us as a people, and as this class of work is done, there will be created an entirely different atmosphere surrounding the souls of the workers; for the Holy Spirit communicates to all those who are doing God's service, and those who are worked by the Holy Spirit will be a power for God in lifting up, strengthening, and saving the souls that are ready to perish.—*Welfare Ministry*, pp. 131, 132.

PITY AND COMPASSION:
GOD'S SPIRIT AT WORK

Which now of these three, thinkest thou, was neighbour unto him that fell among the thieves? And he said, He that shewed mercy on him. Then said Jesus unto him, Go, and do thou likewise. Luke 10:36, 37.

It is not possible for the heart in which Christ abides to be destitute of love. If we love God because He first loved us, we shall love all for whom Christ died. We cannot come in touch with divinity without coming in touch with humanity; for in Him who sits upon the throne of the universe, divinity and humanity are combined. Connected with Christ, we are connected with our fellow men by the golden links of the chain of love. Then the pity and compassion of Christ will be manifest in our life. We shall not wait to have the needy and unfortunate brought to us. We shall not need to be entreated to feel for the woes of others. It will be as natural for us to minister to the needy and suffering as it was for Christ to go about doing good.

Wherever there is an impulse of love and sympathy, wherever the heart reaches out to bless and uplift others, there is revealed the working of God's Holy Spirit. In the depths of heathenism, men who have had no knowledge of the written law of God, who have never even heard the name of Christ, have been kind to His servants, protecting them at the risk of their own lives. Their acts show the working of a divine power. . . .

The glory of heaven is in lifting up the fallen, comforting the distressed. And wherever Christ abides in human hearts, He will be revealed in the same way. Wherever it acts, the religion of Christ will bless. Wherever it works, there is brightness.

No distinction on account of nationality, race, or caste is recognized by God. He is the Maker of all mankind. All men are of one family by creation, and all are one through redemption.—*Christ's Object Lessons*, pp. 384-386.

EARNEST TO GIVE THE FINAL WARNING

And after these things I saw another angel come down from heaven, having great power; and the earth was lightened with his glory. Rev. 18:1.

Day after day is passing into eternity, bringing us nearer to the close of probation. Now we must pray as never before for the Holy Spirit to be more abundantly bestowed upon us, and we must look for its sanctifying influence to come upon the workers, that the people for whom they labor may know that they have been with Jesus and learned of Him. We need spiritual eyesight now as never before, that we may see afar off, and that we may discern the snares and designs of the enemy, and as faithful watchmen proclaim the danger. We need spiritual power that we may take in, as far as the human mind can, the great subjects of Christianity, and how far-reaching are its principles.

When God's people humble the soul before Him, individually seeking His Holy Spirit with all the heart, there will be heard from human lips such a testimony as is represented in this scripture: "After these things I saw another angel come down from heaven, having great power; and the earth was lightened with his glory." There will be faces aglow with the love of God, there will be lips touched with holy fire, saying, "The blood of Jesus Christ his Son cleanseth us from all sin" (1 John 1:7).

Those who are under the influence of the Spirit of God will not be fanatical, but calm, steadfast, free from extravagance. But let all who have had the light of truth shining clear and distinct upon their pathway be careful how they cry peace and safety. Be careful what influence you exert at this time. . . .

Jesus longs to bestow the heavenly endowment in large measure upon His people. Prayers are ascending to God daily for the fulfillment of the promise; and not one of the prayers put up in faith is lost. Christ ascended on high, leading captivity captive, and gave gifts unto men. When, after Christ's ascension, the Spirit came down as promised, like a rushing, mighty wind, filling the whole place where the disciples were assembled, what was the effect?

Thousands were converted in a day. We have taught, we have expected that an angel is to come down from heaven, that the earth will be lightened with his glory, when we shall behold an ingathering of souls similar to that witnessed on the day of Pentecost.—*Home Missionary*, Nov. 1, 1893.

THE TIME IS NEAR FOR
THE SPIRIT'S DEPARTING

*And the Spirit and the bride say, Come. And let him that heareth say,
Come. And let him that is athirst come. And whosoever will, let him take
the water of life freely. Rev. 22:17.*

Probationary time will not continue much longer. Now God is withdrawing His restraining hand from the earth. Long has He been speaking to men and women through the agency of His Holy Spirit; but they have not heeded the call. Now He is speaking to His people, and to the world, by His judgments. The time of these judgments is a time of mercy for those who have not yet had opportunity to learn what is truth. Tenderly will the Lord look upon them. His heart of mercy is touched; His hand is still stretched out to save. Large numbers will be admitted to the fold of safety who in these last days will hear the truth for the first time.

The Lord calls upon those who believe in Him to be workers together with Him. While life shall last, they are not to feel that their work is done. Shall we allow the signs of the end to be fulfilled without telling people of what is coming upon the earth? Shall we allow them to go down in darkness without having urged upon them the need of a preparation to meet their Lord? Unless we ourselves do our duty to those around us, the day of God will come upon us as a thief. Confusion fills the world, and a great terror is soon to come upon human beings. The end is very near. We who know the truth should be preparing for what is soon to break upon the world as an overwhelming surprise.

As a people, we must prepare the way of the Lord, under the overruling guidance of the Holy Spirit. The gospel is to be proclaimed in its purity. The stream of living water is to deepen and widen in its course. In fields nigh and afar off, men will be called from the plow, and from the more common commercial business vocations, and will be educated in connection with men of experience. As they learn to labor effectively, they will proclaim the truth with power. Through most wonderful workings of divine providence, mountains of difficulty will be removed.

The message that means so much to the dwellers upon earth will be heard and understood. Men will know what is truth. Onward, and still onward, the work will advance, until the whole earth shall have been warned. And then shall the end come.—*Review and Herald*, Nov. 22, 1906.

THE SPIRIT FINALLY WITHDRAWN

He that is unjust, let him be unjust still: and he which is filthy, let him be filthy still: and he that is righteous, let him be righteous still: and he that is holy, let him be holy still. Rev. 22:11.

When the third angel's message closes, mercy no longer pleads for the guilty inhabitants of the earth. The people of God have accomplished their work. They have received "the latter rain," the "refreshing from the presence of the Lord" (Acts 3:19), and they are prepared for the trying hour before them. Angels are hastening to and fro in heaven. An angel returning from the earth announces that his work is done; the final test has been brought upon the world, and all who have proved themselves loyal to the divine precepts have received "the seal of the living God" (Rev. 7:2).

Then Jesus ceases His intercession in the sanctuary above. He lifts His hands and with a loud voice says, "It is done," and all the angelic host lay off their crowns as He makes the solemn announcement: "He that is unjust, let him be unjust still: and he which is filthy, let him be filthy still: and he that is righteous, let him be righteous still: and he that is holy, let him be holy still." Every case has been decided for life or death. Christ has made the atonement for His people and blotted out their sins. The number of His subjects is made up; "the kingdom and dominion, and the greatness of the kingdom under the whole heaven" (Dan. 7:27), is about to be given to the heirs of salvation, and Jesus is to reign as King of kings and Lord of lords.

When He leaves the sanctuary, darkness covers the inhabitants of the earth. In that fearful time the righteous must live in the sight of a holy God without an intercessor. The restraint which has been upon the wicked is removed, and Satan has entire control of the finally impenitent. God's long-suffering has ended. The world has rejected His mercy, despised His love, and trampled upon His law. The wicked have passed the boundary of their probation; the Spirit of God, persistently resisted, has been at last withdrawn.—*The Great Controversy*, pp. 613, 614.

THE GREATEST WORK ON EARTH

For the Son of man is come to seek and to save that which was lost.
Luke 19:10.

Everyone who believes in Christ as a personal Saviour is under bonds to God to be pure and holy, to be a spiritual worker, seeking to save the lost, whether they are great or small, rich or poor, bond or free. The greatest work on earth is to seek and to save those who are lost, for whom Christ has paid the infinite price of His own blood. Everyone is to do active service, and if those who have been blessed with light do not diffuse light to others, they will lose the rich grace which has been bestowed upon them, because they neglect a sacred duty plainly marked out in the Word of God. As the light of the unfaithful one diminishes, his own soul is brought into peril; and the ones to whom he should have been a shining light miss the labor that God intended that they should have through the human instrument. Thus the sheep unsought is not brought back to the fold.

God depends upon you, the human agent, to fulfill your duty to the best of your ability, and He Himself will give the increase. If human agents would but cooperate with the divine intelligences, thousands of souls would be rescued. The Holy Spirit would give devoted workers glimpses of Jesus that would brace them for every conflict, that would elevate and strengthen them, and make them more than conquerors. When two or three are met together to unite their counsel, and to send up their petitions, the promise is for them: "Ask, and it shall be given you; seek, and ye shall find; knock, and it shall be opened unto you" (Luke 11:9). "If ye then, being evil, know how to give good gifts unto your children: how much more shall your heavenly Father give the Holy Spirit to them that ask him?" (verse 13). The Lord has promised that where two or three are met together in His name, there will He be in the midst. Those who meet together for prayer will receive an unction from the Holy One.—*Review and Herald,* June 30, 1896.

THE LIGHT OF THE WORLD

Ye are the light of the world. A city that is set on an hill cannot be hid. Matt. 5:14.

Our fidelity to Christian principles calls us to active service for God. Those who do not use their talents in the cause and work of God will have no part with Jesus in His glory. Light is to shine forth from every soul that is a recipient of the grace of God. There are many souls in darkness, but what rest, and ease, and quietude many feel in this matter! Thousands enjoy great light and precious opportunities, but do nothing with their influence or their money, to enlighten others. They do not even take the responsibility of keeping their own souls in the love of God, that they may not become a burden to the church. Such ones would be a burden and a clog in heaven. For Christ's sake, for the truth's sake, for their own sakes, such should arouse and make diligent work for eternity. Heavenly mansions are preparing for all who will comply with the conditions laid down in the Word of God.

In behalf of the souls for whom Christ has died, who are in the darkness of error, it is enjoined upon all true followers of Christ to be a light to the world. God has done His part in the great work, and is waiting for the cooperation of His followers. The plan of salvation is fully developed. The blood of Jesus Christ is offered for the sins of the world, the Word of God is speaking to man in counsels, in reproofs, in warnings, in promises, and in encouragement, and the efficacy of the Holy Spirit is extended to help him in all his efforts. But with all this light the world is still perishing in darkness, buried in error and sin.

Who will be laborers together with God, to win these souls to the truth? Who will bear to them the good tidings of salvation? The people whom God has blessed with light and truth are to be the messengers of mercy. Their means are to flow into the divine channel. Their earnest efforts are to be put forth. They are to become laborers together with God, self-denying, self-sacrificing, like Jesus, who for our sakes became poor, that we through His poverty might be made rich.—*Review and Herald*, Mar. 1, 1887.

THE SALT OF THE EARTH

Ye are the salt of the earth: but if the salt have lost his savour, wherewith shall it be salted? it is thenceforth good for nothing, but to be cast out, and to be trodden under foot of men. Matt. 5:13.

God will work with the church, but not without their cooperation. May every one of you who have tasted the good Word of God "let your light so shine before men, that they may see your good works, and glorify your Father which is in heaven" (Matt. 5:16). Jesus says, "Ye are the salt of the earth: but if the salt have lost his savour, wherewith shall it be salted? it is thenceforth good for nothing, but to be cast out, and to be trodden under foot of men." The saving salt, the savor of the Christian, is the love of Jesus in the heart, the righteousness of Christ pervading the soul. If the professor of religion would keep the saving efficacy of his faith, he must ever keep the righteousness of Christ before him, and have the glory of God for his rearward. Then the power of Christ will be revealed in life and character.

Oh, when we come to the pearly gates, and have an entrance into the city of God, will anyone who enters there regret that he devoted his life unreservedly to Jesus? Let us now love Him with undivided affections, and cooperate with the heavenly intelligences, that we may be laborers together with God, and by partaking of the divine nature, be able to reveal Christ to others. Oh, for the baptism of the Holy Spirit! Oh, that the bright beams of the Sun of righteousness might shine into the chambers of mind and heart, that every idol might be dethroned and expelled from the soul temple! Oh, that our tongues might be loosened to speak of His goodness, to tell of His power!

If you respond to the drawing of Jesus, you will not fail to have an influence on somebody through the beauty and power of the grace of Christ. Let us behold Him and become changed into the image of Him in whom dwelleth all the fullness of the Godhead bodily, and realize that we are accepted in the Beloved, "complete in him, which is the head of all principality and power" (Col. 2:10).—*Bible Echo*, Feb. 15, 1892.

AMBASSADORS FOR CHRIST

Now then we are ambassadors for Christ, as though God did beseech you by us: we pray you in Christ's stead, be ye reconciled to God. 2 Cor. 5:20.

We are ambassadors for Christ, and we are to live, not to save our reputation, but to save perishing souls from perdition. Our daily endeavor should be to show them that they may gain truth and righteousness. Instead of trying to elicit sympathy for ourselves, by giving others the impression that we are not appreciated, we are to forget self entirely; and if we fail to do this, through want of spiritual discernment and vital piety, God will require at our hands the souls of those for whom we should have labored. He has made provision that every worker in His service may have grace and wisdom, that he may become a living epistle, known and read of all men.

By watchfulness and prayer we may accomplish just what the Lord designs that we shall. By faithful, painstaking discharge of our duty, by watching for souls as they that must give account, we may remove every stumbling block out of the way of others. By earnest warnings and entreaties, with our own souls drawn out in tender solicitude for those that are ready to perish, we may win souls to Christ.

I would that all my brethren and sisters would remember that it is a serious thing to grieve the Holy Spirit, and He is grieved when the human agent seeks to work himself, and refuses to enter the service of the Lord because the cross is too heavy or the self-denial too great. The Holy Spirit seeks to abide in each soul. If He is welcomed as an honored guest, those who receive Him will be made complete in Christ. The good work begun will be finished; the holy thoughts, heavenly affections, and Christlike actions will take the place of impure thoughts, perverse sentiments, and rebellious acts.

The Holy Spirit is a divine teacher. If we heed His lessons, we shall become wise unto salvation. But we need to guard well our hearts; for too often we forget the heavenly instruction we have received, and seek to act out the natural inclinations of our unconsecrated minds. Each one must fight his own battle against self. Heed the teachings of the Holy Spirit. If this is done, they will be repeated again and again until the impressions are as it were "laid in the rock forever."—*Counsels on Health*, pp. 560, 561.

WITNESSES FOR THE CROSS

And ye are witnesses of these things. And, behold, I send the promise of my Father upon you: but tarry ye in the city of Jerusalem, until ye be endued with power from on high. Luke 24:48, 49.

After the outpouring of the Holy Spirit, the disciples, clothed with the divine panoply, went forth as witnesses to tell the wonderful story of the manger and the cross. They were humble men, but they went forth with the truth. After the death of their Lord, they were a helpless, disappointed, discouraged company—as sheep without a shepherd: but now they go forth as witnesses for the truth, with no weapons but the Word and Spirit of God, to triumph over all opposition. Their Saviour had been rejected and condemned and nailed to the ignominious cross. The Jewish priests and rulers had declared in scorn, "He saved others; himself he cannot save. If he be the king of Israel, let him now come down from the cross, and we will believe him" (Matt. 27:42).

But that cross, that instrument of shame and torture, brought hope and salvation to the world. The believers rallied; their hopelessness and conscious helplessness had left them. They were transformed in character, and united in the bonds of Christian love. Although without wealth, though counted by the world as mere ignorant fishermen, they were made by the Holy Spirit witnesses for Christ. Without earthly honor or recognition, they were heroes of faith. From their lips came words of divine eloquence and power that shook the world.

The third, fourth, and fifth chapters of Acts give an account of their witnessing. Those who had rejected and crucified the Saviour expected to find His disciples discouraged, crestfallen, and ready to disown their Lord. With amazement they heard the clear, bold testimony given under the power of the Holy Spirit. The words and works of the disciples represented the words and works of their Teacher; and all who heard them said, They have learned of Jesus, they talk as He talked. "And with great power gave the apostles witness of the resurrection of the Lord Jesus: and great grace was upon them all" (Acts 4:33).—*Ellen G. White 1888 Materials*, p. 1543.

COOPERATING WITH THE DIVINE POWER

But ye shall receive power, after that the Holy Ghost is come upon you: and ye shall be witnesses unto me both in Jerusalem, and in all Judea, and in Samaria, and unto the uttermost part of the earth. Acts 1:8.

God has determined to leave nothing undone to recover man from the toils of the enemy. *After* Christ's ascension, the Holy Spirit was given to man to assist all who would cooperate with Him in the reshaping and remodeling of the human character. The Holy Spirit's part of the work has been defined by our Saviour. He says, "He will reprove the world of sin, and of righteousness, and of judgment" (John 16:8). The Holy Spirit is the convicter, and sanctifier as well.

As none can repent of their sins until they are convicted, the necessity of uniting the Spirit with us in our labor to reach the fallen is apparent. All of our human abilities will be exercised in vain unless we are united to the heavenly intelligences. It is through the lack of knowledge of the vitalizing truth, and the corrupting influence of error, that men are fallen so low, sunk in the depths of sinful degradation. Angels and men are to work in harmony to teach the truth of God to those who are unlearned therein, that they may be set free from the bonds of sin. It is the truth alone that makes men free. This liberty, this freedom through the knowledge of the truth, is to be proclaimed to every creature.

Jesus Christ, God Himself, and the angels of heaven are interested in this grand and holy work. Man has been given the exalted privilege of revealing the divine character by unselfishly engaging in the effort to rescue man from the pit of ruin into which he has been plunged. Every human being who will submit to be enlightened by the Holy Spirit is to be used for the accomplishment of this divinely conceived purpose. Christ is the head of His church, and it will glorify Him the more to have every portion of that church engaged in the work for the salvation of souls.

But the human workers need to leave more room for the Holy Spirit to work, that the laborers may be bound together, and move forward in the strength of a united body of soldiers. Let all remember that we are "a spectacle unto the world, and to angels, and to men" (1 Cor. 4:9).— *Australasian Union Conference Record*, Apr. 1, 1898.

LABORERS TOGETHER WITH GOD

For we are labourers together with God: ye are God's husbandry, ye are God's building. 1 Cor. 3:9.

The Holy Spirit must be the living agency to convince of sin. The divine agent presents to the speaker the benefits of the sacrifice made upon the cross; and as the truth is brought in contact with the souls present, Christ wins them to Himself, and works to transform their nature. He is ready to help our infirmities, to teach, to lead, to inspire us with ideas that are of heavenly birth.

How little can men do in the work of saving souls, and yet how much through Christ, if they are imbued with His Spirit! The human teacher cannot read the hearts of his hearers; but Jesus dispenses the grace that every soul needs. He understands the capabilities of man, his weakness and his strength. The Lord is working on the human heart; and a minister can be to the souls who are listening to his words a savor of death unto death, turning them away from Christ; or, if he is consecrated, devotional, distrustful of self, but looking unto Jesus, he may be a savor of life unto life to souls who are already under the convicting power of the Holy Spirit, and in whose hearts the Lord is preparing the way for the messages which He has given to the human agent. Thus the heart of the unbeliever is touched, and it responds to the message of truth.

"We are labourers together with God." The convictions implanted in the heart, and the enlightenment of the understanding by the entrance of the Word, work in perfect harmony. The truth brought before the mind has power to arouse the dormant energies of the soul. The Spirit of God working in the heart cooperates with the working of God through His human instrumentalities.

Again and again I have been shown that the people of God in these last days could not be safe in trusting in men, and making flesh their arm. The mighty cleaver of truth has taken them out of the world as rough stones that are to be hewed and squared and polished for the heavenly building. They must be hewed by the prophets with reproof, warning, admonition, and advice, that they may be fashioned after the divine Pattern; this is the specified work of the Comforter—to transform heart and character, that men may keep the way of the Lord.—*Home Missionary*, Nov. 1, 1893.

HUMAN COOPERATION ESSENTIAL

For whosoever shall call upon the name of the Lord shall be saved. How then shall they call on him in whom they have not believed? and how shall they believe in him of whom they have not heard? and how shall they hear without a preacher? Rom. 10:13, 14.

God has expended amazing sacrifices upon men, and mighty energies for the reclaiming of man from transgression and sin to loyalty and obedience; but I have been shown that He does nothing without the cooperation of human agencies. Every endowment of grace and power and efficiency has been liberally provided, and the strongest motives presented to arouse and keep living in the human heart the missionary spirit, that divine and human agency may be combined. . . .

What use have you made of the gift of God? He has supplied the motive forces of which He has made a lodgment in your hearts, that with patience and hope and untiring vigilance you might set forth Jesus Christ and Him crucified, that you might send the note of warning that Christ is coming the second time with power and great glory, calling men to repent of their sins. . . .

How did the Holy Spirit work upon your hearts? By the energies of the Holy Spirit it was stimulating you to the exercise of the talents God has given you, that every man and woman and youth should employ them to set forth the truth for this time, making personal efforts, going into the cities where truth has never been and lifting the standard. In the blessing God has bestowed upon you, have not your energies been quickened, and the truth been more deeply impressed upon your soul, and its important relation to perishing souls out of Christ? Are ye witnesses for Christ in a more distinct and decided manner, after the manifest revealing of God's blessing upon you?

The Holy Spirit's office is to bring decidedly to your minds the important, vital truths. Is this extra endowment to be bound up in a napkin and hidden in the earth? No, no, it is to be put out to the exchangers; and as man uses his talents, however small, the Holy Spirit takes the things of God, and presents them anew to the mind. He makes the neglected Word to be a vivifying agency. Through the Spirit, it is quick and powerful upon human minds, not because of the smartness, the educational power of the human agency, but because the divine power works with the human, and to the divine belongs all the credit.—*Home Missionary*, Nov. 1, 1893.

INSTRUMENTALITIES FOR THE SAVING OF SOULS

I have planted, Apollos watered; but God gave the increase. So then nei-ther is he that planteth any thing, neither he that watereth; but God that giveth the increase. 1 Cor. 3:6, 7.

Here are the mighty agencies for moving the world. The cross of Calvary brings under tribute every power of those who believe on Christ, that they may be instrumentalities for the saving of souls. Human effort is to be united with the divine; it must derive its ef-ficacy from heaven. We are to be laborers together with God. The Lord is represented as opening the hearts of men and women to receive the Word, and the Holy Spirit makes the Word effective.

Those who receive the truth have that faith which leads to decided action, which works by love, and purifies the soul. Thus the truth is a sanctifier. Its transforming power is seen on the character. When it has been admitted into the inner sanctuary of the soul, it does not operate superficially, leaving the heart unchanged; it does not awaken the emo-tions merely, to the neglect of the judgment and will; but it goes down to the very depths of the nature, and brings the whole being into har-monious action.

Now the work of him who is truly converted begins in earnest. He must work as Christ worked. He must not live any longer to himself, but wholly for the Lord. The world has lost him; for his life is hid with Christ in God. That means that self no longer has the supremacy. The light shining from the cross of Calvary holds him in its bright rays, and the Spirit has taken of the things of Christ, and revealed them to him in such an attractive light as to have a transforming effect on his habits and practices, showing that he is a new creature in Christ Jesus. Every dol-lar he recognizes as of value, not to gratify his taste or lust, not for him to hide in the earth, but to do good with, to help win souls to the truth, to build up the kingdom of Christ. His enjoyment is the same as that of Christ—in seeing souls saved. Why are we doing so little for the salva-tion of men, when there is so much to do? Why are we doing so little to draw men and women and children to Christ?—*Review and Herald,* Oct. 6, 1891.

UNWORTHY BUT USEFUL

But God hath chosen the foolish things of the world to confound the wise; and God hath chosen the weak things of the world to confound the things which are mighty; and base things of the world, and things which are despised, hath God chosen, yea, and things which are not, to bring to nought things that are: that no flesh should glory in his presence. 1 Cor. 1:27-29.

If we had a just appreciation of the importance and greatness of our work, and could see ourselves as we are at this time, we should be filled with wonder that God could use us, unworthy as we are, in the work of bringing souls into the truth. There are many things that we ought to be able to understand, that we do not comprehend because we are so far behind our privileges.

Christ said to His disciples, "I have yet many things to say unto you, but ye cannot bear them now" (John 16:12). This is our condition. Would they not have been able to understand what He had to say to them, if they had been doers of His word—if they had improved point after point of the truth which He had presented to them? But although they could not then understand, He told them that He would send the Comforter, who would lead them into all truth. We should be in a position where we can comprehend the teaching, leading, and working of the Spirit of Christ. We must not measure God or His truth by our finite understanding, or by our preconceived opinions.

There are many who do not realize where they are standing; for they are spiritually blinded. "Examine yourselves, whether ye be in the faith; prove your own selves. Know ye not your own selves, how that Jesus Christ is in you, except ye be reprobates?" (2 Cor. 13:5). I trust that none of us will be found to be reprobates. Is Christ abiding in your hearts by faith? Is His Spirit in you? If it is, there will be such a yearning in your soul for the salvation of those for whom Christ has died, that self will sink into insignificance, and Christ alone will be exalted. . . .

Those who profess to be united to Christ should be laborers together with God. The people of God are to warn the world, and to prepare a people to stand in the day of wrath when the Son of man shall come in the clouds of heaven. The members of the church of Christ should gather up the divine rays of light from Jesus, and reflect them to others, leaving a bright track heavenward in the world.—*Review and Herald*, Oct. 8, 1889.

ALL MEMBERS
CALLED TO BE MISSIONARIES

But ye are a chosen generation, a royal priesthood, an holy nation, a peculiar people; that ye should shew forth the praises of him who hath called you out of darkness into his marvellous light. 1 Peter 2:9.

The Holy Spirit, Christ's representative, arms the weakest with might to press forward unto victory. God has organized His instrumentalities to draw all men unto Him. He sends forth to His work many who have not been dedicated by the laying on of hands. He answers objections that would arise against this method of labor, even before they arise. God sees the end from the beginning. He knows and anticipates every want, and provides for every emergency. If finite men to whom He commits His work do not bar the way, God will send forth laborers into His vineyard.

To every converted soul He says: "Go ye into all the world, and preach the gospel to every creature" (Mark 16:15). It is not necessary that the Lord should first sit in earthly legislative councils, and inquire of those who think they must plan for His work, "Will you permit men whom I have chosen, to unite with you in working in some part of My moral vineyard?" Christ was standing only a few steps from His heavenly throne when He gave His commission to His disciples, and included as missionaries all who would believe on His name.

Jesus wants every minister to whom He has committed a sacred trust to remember His injunctions, to consider the vastness of His work, and to place the obligation of preaching the gospel to the world upon the large number to whom it belongs. "Thus it is written, and thus it behoved Christ to suffer, and to rise from the dead the third day; and that repentance and remission of sins should be preached in his name among all nations, beginning at Jerusalem" (Luke 24:46, 47). The power of God was to go with those that proclaimed the gospel. If those who claim to have a living experience in the things of God had done their appointed duty as God ordained, the whole world would have been warned, and the Lord Jesus would have come to our world with power and great glory.—*Home Missionary*, Aug. 1, 1896.

GOD MAY CHOOSE AND FIT ANYBODY

Thus saith the Lord, Let not the wise man glory in his wisdom, neither let the mighty man glory in his might, let not the rich man glory in his riches: but let him that glorieth glory in this, that he understandeth and knoweth me, that I am the Lord which exercise lovingkindness, judgment, and righteousness, in the earth: for in these things I delight, saith the Lord. Jer. 9:23, 24.

The Lord works in His own way, in order that men shall not lift themselves up in pride of intellect, and take the credit and the glory to themselves. The Lord would have every human being understand that his capabilities and endowments are from the Lord. God works by whom He will. He takes those whom He pleases to do His work, and He does not consult those to whom He will send His messenger as to what are their preferences concerning whom or what manner of person they would like to bring the message of God to them.

God will use men who are willing to be used. The Lord would use men of intelligence if they would permit Him to mold and fashion them, and to shape their testimony after His own order. Men high or low, learned or ignorant, would better let the Lord manage and take care of the safety of His own ark. The work of men is to obey the voice of God.

Whoever has a connection with the work and cause of God is to be continually under the discipline of God. "Thus saith the Lord, Let not the wise man glory in his wisdom, neither let the mighty man glory in his might, let not the rich man glory in his riches: but let him that glorieth glory in this, that he understandeth and knoweth me, that I am the Lord which exercise lovingkindness, judgment, and righteousness, in the earth: for in these things I delight, saith the Lord." . . .

There are souls famishing for the bread of life, thirsting for the waters of salvation; and woe unto that man who by pen or voice shall turn them aside into false paths! The Spirit of God is appealing to men, presenting to them their moral obligation to love and serve Him with heart, might, mind, and strength, and to love their neighbors as themselves. The Holy Spirit moves upon the inner self until it becomes conscious of the divine power of God, and every spiritual faculty is quickened to decided action.—*Review and Herald*, May 12, 1896.

EVEN CHILDREN MAY
SHARE THEIR FAITH

And when the chief priests and scribes saw the wonderful things that he did, and the children crying in the temple, and saying, Hosanna to the son of David; they were sore displeased, and said unto him, Hearest thou what these say? And Jesus saith unto them, Yea; have ye never read, Out of the mouth of babes and sucklings thou hast perfected praise? Matt. 21:15, 16.

The standard of truth may be raised by humble men and women; and the youth, and even children, may be a blessing to others, by revealing what the truth has done for them. God will use the most feeble instruments if they are wholly submitted to Him. He can work through them to reach souls to whom the minister could not obtain access. There are the highways and byways to be searched. With your Bible in your hand, with your heart warm and glowing with the love of God, you may go out and tell others your experience; you may make known to them the truth that has impressed your heart, praying with faith that God will make your efforts successful in their salvation. Communicate light, and you will have more light to communicate. Thus you may become laborers together with God.

God desires that His children shall make use of all their powers, that in working to bless others, they may grow strong in the strength of Jesus. You may not be learned; you may not be thought capable of doing a great work for God; but there are things which you can do. You can let your light shine forth to others. . . .

Everyone may have an understanding of the truth, and exert an influence for good. Then go to work, my brethren and sisters. Gain an experience by working for others. You may make mistakes; but this is not more than the most intelligent, and those in positions of trust, have done again and again. You will not always meet with success; but you can never know the result of humble, disinterested effort to help those who are in darkness. Through the agency of the Holy Spirit, you may win souls from error to truth, and in so doing your own souls will be filled with the love of God.—*Review and Herald*, Jan. 12, 1897.

GLOBAL MISSION:
THE SPIRIT OPENS DOORS

And this gospel of the kingdom shall be preached in all the world for a witness unto all nations; and then shall the end come. Matt. 24:14.

The whole world is a vast missionary field, and yet we who have long been established in the truth should be encouraged with the thought that fields which were once difficult of access are now easily entered. Every church in our land should seek for the revival of the missionary spirit. They should seek for steady growth in zeal and activity. All should pray that the indifference which has caused both men and means to be withheld from the work may be banished, and that Christ may abide in the soul. For our sake He became poor, that we through His poverty might be made rich.

The office work of the Holy Spirit is to convince of sin, and I know that it is a sin for any one of us to be indifferent now. As we look around at the different fields that have been entered, we are led to inquire, "What hath God wrought?" What more could He have done for His vineyard than He has done? God has made provision to supply His rich grace, to give divine power for the performance of His work. Nothing is wanting on the part of God; the lack is on the part of the human agency, who refuses to cooperate with divine intelligences. Through the plan He has devised, nothing can be done for the salvation of man save through the cooperation of man. Sinners who have been blessed with light and evidence, who know that through grace that can be supplied to them, they may meet the conditions upon which salvation is promised, and yet who decline to make the attempt, have but themselves to blame for their own destruction. We feel that of such it may be said that Christ has died for them in vain.

But who is to blame for the loss of souls who know not God, and who have had no opportunity for hearing the reasons of our faith? What obligation rests upon the church in reference to a world that is perishing without the gospel? Unless there is more decided self-denial on the part of those who claim to believe the truth, unless there is more decided faithfulness in bringing all the tithes and offerings into the treasury, unless broader plans are laid than have yet been carried into execution, we shall not fulfill the gospel commission to go into all the world, and preach Christ to every creature.—*Home Missionary*, Apr. 1, 1895.

THE CITIES: FIELDS WHITE FOR HARVEST

Say not ye, There are yet four months, and then cometh harvest? behold, I say unto you, Lift up your eyes, and look on the fields; for they are white already to harvest. John 4:35.

To us, as surely as to the disciples of that time, Christ speaks these words. Time is passing, and the Lord calls upon the workers in all lines of His work to lift up their eyes and behold the fields all ripe for the harvest.

Our workers are not branching out as they should in their efforts. Our leading men are not awake to the work that must yet be accomplished. When I think of the cities in which so little work has been done, in which there are so many thousands to be warned of the soon coming of the Saviour, I feel an intensity of desire to see men and women going forth to the work in the power of the Spirit, filled with Christ's love for perishing souls.

The heathen in the cities at our doors have been strangely neglected. Organized effort should be made to save them. We are now to work to convert the heathen who are in the midst of us—those who are living within the shadow of our doors. A new song is to be put in their mouths, and they are to go forth to impart to others now in darkness the light of the third angel's message.

We all need to be wide awake that, as the way opens, we may advance the work in the large cities. We are far behind in following the light given us to enter the cities and erect memorials for God. Step by step we are to lead souls into the full light of truth. Many are longing for spiritual food. We are to continue working until a church is organized and a humble house of worship built. I am greatly encouraged to believe that many persons not of our faith will help considerably by their means. The light given me is that in many places, especially in the great cities of America, help will be given by such persons.—*Pacific Union Recorder*, Oct. 23, 1902.

THE NEIGHBORHOOD:
A LARGE FIELD OF WORK

Return to thine own house, and shew how great things God hath done unto thee. And he went his way, and published throughout the whole city how great things Jesus had done unto him. Luke 8:39.

The fields are opening everywhere, calling for the living preacher. At home and abroad are openings that there seems no way to fill. Yet there is a large number who have the light of truth, and if these would do all in their power to give light to others, how much might be accomplished! All cannot be preachers of the Word, but in their own homes all might do something for Christ. They could do a good work among their neighbors. If they would put their minds and hearts to the work, they might devise plans by which they could be useful in a small way, whatever their position.

The ever-increasing opportunities for usefulness, the providential openings for the Word of God to be presented, demand our offerings of time and intellect and money, gifts large and small, as God has prospered us, to make a way for the truth in the dark places of the earth, to set up the standard of righteousness, and to advance the interests of the kingdom of Christ. The heavenly angels are waiting to unite with the human agent, that many souls may hear and be impressed by the Holy Spirit, and be converted.

We have long been looking and waiting for the coming of the Lord; but are we doing all in our power to hasten His coming? "The Lord is not slack concerning his promise, as some men count slackness; but is longsuffering to us-ward, not willing that any should perish, but that all should come to repentance" (2 Peter 3:9). While the Lord is ever working, while all heaven is engaged in the work on earth to draw men to Christ and repentance, what are the human agents doing to be channels of light, that they may co-operate with the divine agencies? Are they daily inquiring, "Lord, what wilt thou have me to do?" (Acts 9:6). Are they practicing self-denial, as did Jesus? Are they deeply stirred, their hearts drawn out in prayer to God that they may be receiving of His grace, the Holy Spirit of God, that they may have wisdom to work with their ability and their means to save souls that are perishing out of Christ?—*Review and Herald*, May 16, 1893.

FILLED WITH THE SPIRIT

And the disciples were filled with joy, and with the Holy Ghost. Acts 13:52.

The work of the Holy Spirit is immeasurably great. It is from this Source that power and efficiency come to the worker for God; and the Holy Spirit is the Comforter, as the personal presence of Christ to the soul. He who looks to Christ in simple, childlike faith is made a partaker of the divine nature through the agency of the Holy Spirit. When led by the Spirit of God, the Christian may know that he is made complete in Him who is the head of all things. As Christ was glorified on the day of Pentecost, so will He again be glorified in the closing work of the gospel, when He shall prepare a people to stand the final test, in the closing conflict of the great controversy.

When the earth is lightened with the glory of God, we shall see a work similar to that which was wrought when the disciples, filled with the Holy Spirit, proclaimed the power of a risen Saviour. The light of heaven penetrated the darkened minds of those who had been deceived by the enemies of Christ, and the false representation of Him was rejected; for through the efficacy of the Holy Spirit, they now saw Him exalted to be a Prince and Saviour, to give repentance unto Israel, and remission of sins. Christ was glorified through the power of the Holy Spirit resting upon men.

The revelation of Christ by the Holy Spirit brought to them a realizing sense of His power and majesty, and they stretched forth their hands unto Him by faith, saying, "I believe." Thus it was in the time of the early rain; but the latter rain will be more abundant. The Saviour of men will be glorified, and the earth will be lightened with the bright shining of the beams of His righteousness. He is the fountain of light, and light from the gates ajar has been shining upon the people of God, that they may lift Him up in His glorious character before those who sit in darkness.—*Home Missionary*, Nov. 1, 1893.

TOUCHED WITH SACRED FIRE

John answered, saying unto them all, I indeed baptize you with water; but one mightier than I cometh, the latchet of whose shoes I am not worthy to unloose: he shall baptize you with the Holy Ghost and with fire. Luke 3:16.

It was a sin in the ancient economy to offer a sacrifice upon the wrong altar, or to allow incense to be kindled from a strange fire. We are in danger of commingling the sacred and the common. The holy fire from God is to be used with our offerings. The true altar is Christ, and the true fire is the Holy Spirit. The Holy Spirit is to inspire, to teach, to lead, and to guide men, and make them safe counselors. If we turn aside from God's chosen ones, we are in danger of inquiring from strange gods, and of offering upon a strange altar. . . .

The most powerful preaching of the Word will avail nothing unless the Spirit teaches and enlightens those who hear. Unless the Spirit works with and through the human agent, souls will not be saved or characters transformed by the reading of the Scriptures. The planning and devising that is done in connection with the work should not be of a character to draw attention to self. The Word is a power, a sword in the hand of the human agent. But the Holy Spirit is its efficiency, its vital power in impressing the mind.

"They shall be all taught of God" (John 6:45). It is God that causeth the light to shine into the hearts of men. Will my ministering brethren remember that it is essential that God be recognized as the source of our strength, and the Spirit as the Comforter? The great reason why God can do so little for us is that we forget that living virtue comes through our cooperation with the Holy Spirit.—*Manuscript Releases*, vol. 2, pp. 45, 46.

The Spirit is constantly showing to the soul glimpses of the things of God. A divine presence seems to hover near, and then if the mind responds, if the door of the heart is opened, Jesus abides with the human agent. The Spirit's energy is working in the heart and leading the inclination of the will to Jesus by living faith and complete dependence on divine power to will and to do of His good pleasure. The Spirit taketh the things of God, just as fast as the soul resolves and acts in accordance with the light revealed.—*Ibid.*, p. 46.

THE SPIRIT GIVES THE RIGHT WORDS

For it is not ye that speak, but the Spirit of your Father which speaketh in you. Matt. 10:20.

Of all the gifts which God has given to man, none is more precious than the gift of speech, if it is sanctified by the Holy Spirit. It is with the tongue that we convince and persuade: with it we offer prayer and praise to God, and with it we convey rich thoughts of the Redeemer's love. Those who are fitted to enlighten minds will often have opportunity to read from the Bible or from books which teach the truth, and thus bring the evidence to enlighten souls. . . .

When the Lord's voice calls, "Whom shall I send? and who will go for us?" the divine Spirit puts it into hearts to respond, "Here am I; send me" (Isa. 6:8). But bear in mind that the live coal from the altar must first touch your lips. Then the words you speak will be wise and holy words. Then you will have wisdom to know what to say and what to leave unsaid. You will not try to reveal your smartness as theologians. You will be careful not to arouse a combative spirit or excite prejudice, by introducing indiscriminately all the points of our faith. You will find enough to talk about that will not excite opposition, but that will open the heart to desire a deeper knowledge of God's Word.

The Lord desires you to be soul winners; therefore, while you should not force doctrinal points upon the people, you should "be ready always to give an answer to every man that asketh you a reason of the hope that is in you with meekness and fear" (1 Peter 3:15). Why fear? Fear lest your words should savor of self-importance, lest unadvised words be spoken, lest the words and manner should not be after Christ's likeness. Connect firmly with Christ, and present the truth as it is in Him. Hearts cannot fail to be touched by the story of the atonement.

As you learn the meekness and lowliness of Christ, you will know what you should say to the people; for the Holy Spirit will tell you what words you ought to speak. Those who realize the necessity of keeping the heart under the control of the Holy Spirit will be enabled to sow seed that will spring up into eternal life. This is the work of the gospel evangelist.—*Australasian Union Conference Record*, July 1, 1902.

HUMAN VOICE A CHANNEL FOR DIVINE VOICE

And thou shalt speak unto him, and put words in his mouth: and I will be with thy mouth, and with his mouth, and will teach you what ye shall do. Ex. 4:15.

W hen he who is a colaborer with Christ presses home the truth to the sinner's heart in humility and love, the voice of love speaks through the human instrumentality. Heavenly intelligences work with a consecrated human agent, and the Spirit operates upon the soul of the unbeliever. Efficiency to believe comes from God to the heart, and the sinner accepts the evidence of God's Word.

Through the gracious influence of the Holy Spirit he is changed and becomes one with Christ in spirit and purpose. His affection for God increases, he hungers after righteousness and longs to be more like his Master. By beholding Christ, he is changed from glory to glory, from character to character, and becomes more and more like Jesus. He is imbued with love for Christ and filled with a deep, unresting love for perishing souls, and Christ is formed within, the hope of glory. "As many as received him, to them gave he power to become the sons of God, even to them that believe on his name" (John 1:12).—*Testimonies to Ministers*, pp. 220, 221.

We need more of the working of the Infinite and far less trust in human agencies. We are to prepare a people to stand in the day of God's preparation; we are to call men's attention to the cross of Calvary, to make clear the reason why Christ made His great sacrifice. We are to show men that it is possible for them to come back to their allegiance to God and to their obedience to His commandments. When the sinner looks upon Christ as the propitiation for his sins, let men step aside. Let them declare to the sinner that Christ "is the propitiation for our sins: and not for ours only, but also for the sins of the whole world" (1 John 2:2).

Encourage him to seek wisdom from God; for through earnest prayer he will learn the way of the Lord more perfectly than if instructed by some human counselor. He will see that it was the transgression of the law that caused the death of the Son of the infinite God, and he will hate the sins that wounded Jesus. As he looks upon Christ as a compassionate, tender High Priest, his heart will be preserved in contrition.—*Ibid*., p. 220.

LOVE: THE BEST
ADVERTISEMENT FOR TRUTH

By this shall all men know that ye are my disciples, if ye have love one to another. John 13:35.

Man may become a fellow laborer with God in carrying out the great work of redemption. God allows each man his own sphere of action while He has given His Word as the guide of life. He has also given the Holy Spirit as a sufficient power to overcome all hereditary and cultivated tendencies to evil, and to impress His own character on the human agent, and, through him, upon all who shall come within the sphere of his influence.

The human agent is urged to cooperate with God, to work out His mercy, His goodness, and His love, thus impressing other minds. Every man is to become an instrumentality through which the Holy Spirit can work. He can become this only by yielding all his capabilities to the control of the Spirit. God gave His Spirit upon the day of Pentecost, and through [the Spirit's] working upon receptive hearts [God] could impress all with whom the believers came in contact.

Through our relation of friendship and familiarity with human beings like ourselves, we may exert an uplifting influence. Those who are united in a common hope and faith in Christ Jesus can be a blessing to one another. Jesus says, "Love one another; as I have loved you" (John 13:34). Love is not simply an impulse, a transitory emotion, dependent upon circumstances; it is a living principle, a permanent power. The soul is fed by the streams of pure love that flow from the heart of Christ, as a wellspring that never fails.

Oh, how is the heart quickened, how are its motives ennobled, its affections deepened, by this communion! Under the education and discipline of the Holy Spirit, the children of God love one another, truly, sincerely, unaffectedly, "without partiality, and without hypocrisy" (James 3:17). And this because the heart is in love with Jesus. Our affection for one another springs from our common relation to God. We are one family, we love one another as He loved us. When compared with this true, sanctified, disciplined affection, the shallow courtesy of the world, the meaningless expressions of effusive friendship, are as chaff to the wheat.—*Ellen G. White 1888 Materials*, pp. 1508, 1509.

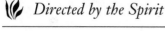

EARNEST WORK:
A RECIPE FOR LESSENING BURDENS

Therefore I take pleasure in infirmities, in reproaches, in necessities, in persecutions, in distresses for Christ's sake: for when I am weak, then am I strong. 2 Cor. 12:10.

There have been altogether too many looking in upon their own trials and difficulties. But when they forget self, and look upon the suffering necessity of others, there will be no time to magnify their own griefs. Earnest work for the Lord is a recipe for mind ailments; and the helpful hand to lift the burdens Christ has borne for all His heritage will lessen our burdens, and they will not seem worth mentioning. True, honest work will give healthy action to the mind by giving healthy action to the muscles. It is the constant manufacturing of ills and burdens that kills. We are to be content to bear the strain of daily duties; and the great pressure of tomorrow's liabilities—leave these cares for the time when we must take them.

We are called now to be educated, that we may do the work that God has assigned to us, and it will not crush out our life. The humblest can have a share in the work, and a share in the reward when the coronation shall take place, and Christ, our Advocate and Redeemer, becomes the king of His redeemed subjects. We must now do all in our power to seek personal consecration to God. It is not more mighty men, not more talented men, not more learned men, that we need in the presentation of the truth for this time; but men who have a knowledge of God and Jesus Christ, whom He has sent.

Personal piety will qualify any worker, for the Holy Spirit takes possession of him, and the truth for this time becomes a power, because his everyday thoughts and all his activities are running in Christ's lines. He has an abiding Christ; and the humblest soul, linked with Christ Jesus, is a power, and his work will abide. May the Lord help us to understand His divine will, and do it heartily, unflinchingly, and there will be joy in the Lord.—*Home Missionary*, Nov. 1, 1897.

HUMAN WORK
MADE EFFECTIVE BY THE SPIRIT

If ye then, being evil, know how to give good gifts unto your children: how much more shall your heavenly Father give the Holy Spirit to them that ask him? Luke 11:13.

The promise of the gift of the Holy Spirit is not comprehended as it should be; the privileges to be enjoyed through its acceptance are not appreciated as they might be. God desires that His church should lay hold by faith upon His promises, and ask for the power of the Holy Spirit to help them in every place. He assures us that He is more willing to give the Holy Spirit to those that ask Him, than parents are to give good gifts unto their children. Since it is possible for everyone to have the heavenly unction, "ye need not that any man teach you" (1 John 2:27), and there is no excuse for shunning responsibilities; no duty should be unwelcome, no obligation evaded. Christ Himself is the renewing power, working in and through every soldier by the agency of the Holy Spirit. The efficiency of the Spirit of God will make effective the labors of all who are willing to submit to His guidance.

God is moving upon every mind that is open to receive the impressions of His Holy Spirit. He is sending out messengers that they may give the warnings in every locality. God is testing the devotion of His churches, and their willingness to render obedience to the Spirit's guidance. Knowledge is to be increased. The messengers of heaven are to be seen running to and fro, seeking in every way possible to warn the people of the coming judgments, and presenting the glad tidings of salvation through our Lord Jesus Christ. The standard of righteousness is to be exalted.

The Spirit of God is moving upon men's hearts, and those who respond to His influence will become lights in the world. Everywhere they are seen going forth to communicate to others the light they have received, as they did after the descent of the Holy Spirit on the day of Pentecost. And as they let their light shine they receive more and more of the Spirit's power. The earth is lighted with the glory of God.— *Australasian Union Conference Record*, Apr. 1, 1898.

KEEPING TOTAL DEPENDENCY ON GOD

And I, brethren, when I came to you, came not with excellency of speech or of wisdom, declaring unto you the testimony of God. For I determined not to know any thing among you, save Jesus Christ, and him crucified. And I was with you in weakness, and in fear, and in much trembling. 1 Cor. 2:1-3.

There will come times when the church will be stirred by divine power, and earnest activity will be the result; for the life-giving power of the Holy Spirit will inspire its members to go forth and bring souls to Christ. But when this activity is manifested, the most earnest workers will be safe only as they depend upon God through constant, earnest prayer. They will need to make earnest supplication that through the grace of Christ they may be saved from taking pride in their work, or of making a savior of their activity. They must constantly look to Jesus, that they may realize that it is His power which does the work, and thus be able to ascribe all the glory to God.

We shall be called upon to make most decided efforts to extend the work of God, and prayer to our heavenly Father will be most essential. It will be necessary to engage in prayer in the closet, in the family, and in the church. Our households must be set in order, and earnest efforts must be made to interest every member of the family in missionary enterprises. We must seek to engage the sympathies of our children in earnest work for the unsaved, that they may do their best at all times and in all places to represent Christ.

But let us not forget that as activity increases, and we become successful in doing the work that must be accomplished, there is danger of our trusting in human plans and methods. There will be a tendency to pray less, and to have less faith. We shall be in danger of losing our sense of dependence upon God, who alone can make our work succeed; but although this is the tendency, let no one think that the human instrument is to do less. No, he is not to do less, but to do more by accepting the heavenly gift, the Holy Spirit. The world in its own wisdom knew not God, and every human power is naturally, to a greater or less degree, opposed to God. We are to look to Jesus, and cooperate with heavenly agencies, offering our petitions to the Father in Jesus' name.—*Review and Herald*, July 4, 1893.

FOLLOWING THE CAPTAIN'S ORDERS

Thou therefore endure hardness, as a good soldier of Jesus Christ. No man that warreth entangleth himself with the affairs of this life; that he may please him who hath chosen him to be a soldier. 2 Tim. 2:3, 4.

We have only a little while to urge the warfare; then Christ will come, and this scene of rebellion will close. Then our last efforts will have been made to work with Christ and advance His kingdom. Some who have stood in the forefront of the battle, zealously resisting incoming evil, fall at the post of duty; others gaze sorrowfully at the fallen heroes, but have no time to cease work. They must close up the ranks, seize the banner from the hand palsied by death, and with renewed energy vindicate the truth and the honor of Christ. As never before, resistance must be made against sin—against the powers of darkness. The time demands energetic and determined activity on the part of those who believe present truth. They should teach the truth by both precept and example.

If the time seems long to wait for our Deliverer to come, if, bowed by affliction and worn with toil, we feel impatient for our commission to close, and to receive an honorable release from the warfare, let us remember—and let the remembrance check every murmur—that God leaves us on earth to encounter storms and conflicts, to perfect Christian character, to become better acquainted with God our Father and Christ our Elder Brother, and to do work for the Master in winning many souls to Christ, that with glad heart we may hear the words: "Well done, thou good and faithful servant: . . . enter thou into the joy of thy Lord" (Matt. 25:21).

Be patient, Christian soldier. Yet a little while, and He that shall come will come. The night of weary waiting, and watching, and mourning is nearly over. The reward will soon be given; the eternal day will dawn. There is no time to sleep now—no time to indulge in useless regrets. He who ventures to slumber now will miss precious opportunities of doing good. We are granted the blessed privilege of gathering sheaves in the great harvest; and every soul saved will be an additional star in the crown of Jesus, our adorable Redeemer. Who is eager to lay off the armor, when by pushing the battle a little longer he will achieve new victories and gather new trophies for eternity?—*Review and Herald*, Oct. 25, 1881.

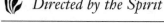

KEEPING THE WATCHERS AWAKE

And that, knowing the time, that now it is high time to awake out of sleep: for now is our salvation nearer than when we believed. Rom. 13:11.

My brethren, you must have Jesus enthroned within, and self must die. We must be baptized with the Holy Spirit, and then we shall not sit down, saying unconcernedly, "What is to be will be; prophecy must be fulfilled." Oh, awake, I pray you, awake! for you bear the most sacred responsibilities. As faithful watchmen, you should see the sword coming, and give the warning, that men and women may not pursue a course through ignorance that they would avoid if they knew the truth.

The Lord has enlightened us in regard to what is coming upon the earth, that we may enlighten others, and we shall not be held guiltless if we are content to sit at ease, with folded hands, and quibble over matters of minor importance. The minds of many have been engrossed with contentions, and they have rejected the light given through the Testimonies, because it did not agree with their own opinions.

God does not force any man into His service. Every soul must decide for himself whether or not he will fall on the Rock and be broken. Heaven has been amazed to see the spiritual stupidity that has prevailed. You need individually to open your proud hearts to the Spirit of God. You need to have your intellectual ability sanctified to the service of God. The transforming power of God must be upon you, that your minds may be renewed by the Holy Spirit, that you may have the mind that was in Christ.

If the watchmen sleep under an opiate of Satan's and do not recognize the voice of the true Shepherd, and do not take up the warning, I tell you in the fear of God, they will be charged with the blood of souls. The watchmen must be wide awake, men who will not slumber at their post of duty, day nor night. They must give the trumpet a certain sound, that the people may shun the evil, and choose the good. Stupidity and careless indifference cannot be excused. On every side of us there are breakers and hidden rocks which will dash our bark in pieces, and leave us helpless wrecks, unless we make God our refuge and help.—*Review and Herald*, Dec. 24, 1889.

ALL HEAVEN INTERESTED IN SAVING SOULS

To wit, that God was in Christ, reconciling the world unto himself, not imputing their trespasses unto them; and hath committed unto us the word of reconciliation. 2 Cor. 5:19.

In the work of saving men, men and angels are to work in harmony, teaching the truth of God to those who are unlearned therein, in order that they may be set free from the bonds of sin. Truth alone can make men free. The liberty that comes through a knowledge of truth is to be proclaimed to every creature. Our heavenly Father, Jesus Christ, and the angels of heaven are all interested in this grand and holy work.

To man has been given the exalted privilege of revealing the divine character by unselfishly seeking to rescue man from the pit of ruin into which he has been plunged. Every human being who will submit to be enlightened by the Holy Spirit is to be used for the accomplishment of this divinely conceived purpose. Christ is the head of His church, and it will glorify Him the more to have every portion of that church engaged in the work for the salvation of souls. . . .

There is more joy in heaven over one sinner that repents, than over the ninety and nine who suppose they need no repentance. When we hear of the success of the truth in any locality, let the whole church join in songs of rejoicing, let praises ascend to God. Let the name of the Lord be glorified by us, and we shall be inspired with greater zeal to become workers together with God. The Lord urges us to fulfill the injunction "Go ye into all the world, and preach the gospel to every creature" (Mark 16:15). But we need to leave more room for the working of the Holy Spirit, in order that laborers may be bound together and may move forward in the strength of a united body of soldiers.

Let all remember that we are "a spectacle unto the world, and to angels, and to men" (1 Cor. 4:9). Therefore each one should inquire with meekness and fear, What is my path of duty? Entire consecration to the service of God will reveal the molding influence of the Holy Spirit at every step along the way.—*Review and Herald*, July 16, 1895.

HEAVENLY AGENCIES WAITING FOR US

That if thou shalt confess with thy mouth the Lord Jesus, and shalt believe in thine heart that God hath raised him from the dead, thou shalt be saved. For with the heart man believeth unto righteousness; and with the mouth confession is made unto salvation. Rom. 10:9, 10.

The Lord calls for every talent and ability to be put to use. When the reproach of indolence and slothfulness shall have been wiped away from the church, the Spirit of the Lord will be graciously manifested; divine power will combine with human effort, the church will see the providential interpositions of the Lord God of hosts, the light of truth will be diffused, the knowledge of God and of Jesus Christ whom He has sent. As in the apostles' time, many souls will turn unto the Lord. The earth will be lighted with the glory of the angel from heaven.

If the world is to be convinced of sin as transgressors of God's law, the agency must be the Holy Spirit working through human instrumentalities. The church needs now to shake off her death-like slumber; for the Lord is waiting to bless His people who will recognize the blessing when it comes, and diffuse it in clear, strong rays of light. "Then will I sprinkle clean water upon you, and ye shall be clean. . . . And I will put my spirit within you, and cause you to walk in my statutes" (Eze. 36:25-27).

If the wilderness of the church is to become as a fruitful field, and the fruitful field to be as a forest, it is through the Holy Spirit of God poured out upon His people. The heavenly agencies have long been waiting for the human agents, the members of the church, to cooperate with them in the great work to be done. They are waiting for you. So vast is the field, so comprehensive the design, that every sanctified heart will be pressed into service as an agent of divine power. . . .

Let all who believe the truth for this time put away their differences; put away envy and evil speaking and evil thinking. Press together, press together. "Seeing ye have purified your souls in obeying the truth through the Spirit unto unfeigned love of the brethren, see that ye love one another with a pure heart fervently" (1 Peter 1:22).—*General Conference Bulletin*, Feb. 28, 1893.

NO TIME TO LOSE

The harvest is past, the summer is ended, and we are not saved. Jer. 8:20.

The Lord is coming. The earth's history is soon to close. Are you prepared to meet the Judge of the earth? Bear in mind that "he shall have judgment without mercy, that hath shewed no mercy" (James 2:13). How terrible it will be in the last great day to find that those with whom we have been familiarly associated are separated from us forever; to see the members of our family, perhaps our own children, unsaved; to find those who have visited our homes, and eaten at our tables, among the lost. Then we shall ask ourselves the question Was it because of my impatience, my un-Christlike disposition; was it because self was not under control, that the religion of Christ became distasteful to them?

The world must be warned of the soon coming of the Lord. We have but a little time in which to work. Years have passed into eternity that might have been improved in seeking first the kingdom of God and His righteousness, and in diffusing the light to others. God calls upon His people who have great light, much labor bestowed upon them, and are established in the truth to now work for themselves and others as they have never done before. Make use of every ability; bring into exercise every power, every entrusted talent; use all the light that God has given you to do others good. Do not try to be preachers; but become ministers for God.

As the truth is better understood by the workers, it will ever appear in a more striking light; as you seek to enlighten others, with your minds under the holy influence of the Spirit of God, your attention will be directed toward those things that are of eternal interest. In such efforts, mingled with prayers for divine light, your own hearts will throb with the quickening influence of the grace of God; your own affections will glow with more divine fervor, and your whole Christian life will be more of a reality, more earnest, more prayerful. Thus by Christ abiding in the heart, you may become laborers together with God.—*Home Missionary*, Feb. 1, 1898.

A Prayer for the Outpouring of the Spirit

As thou hast sent me into the world, even so have I also sent them into the world. And for their sakes I sanctify myself, that they also might be sanctified through the truth. Neither pray I for these alone, but for them also which shall believe on me through their word. John 17:18-20.

My heavenly Father, I come to Thee at this time, just as I am, poor and needy, and dependent upon Thee. I ask Thee to give me and give this people the grace that perfects Christian character. Wilt Thou have compassion upon this people? Let Thy light shine into the chambers of the mind, and into the soul temple. My Saviour, Thou hast given Thy life to purchase Thine inheritance, that, as overcomers, they may enter the kingdom of God, where they shall go no more out forever. Bless those who have signified their desire to serve Thee. Put Thy Spirit upon them.

I ask Thee, heavenly Father, to let Thy Holy Spirit come to this people. May Thy salvation be revealed. Touch their hearts, and make them very tender. Soften them by Thy Holy Spirit, and help them to see the work to be done for their neighbors, and for souls that are perishing all around them. Oh, awaken them to their responsibilities! May they wash their robes of character, and make them white in the blood of the Lamb. Wilt Thou encircle them in the arms of Thy mercy? Plead with them through the impressions of Thy Holy Spirit, that they may try to let their light shine to those that have not known the truth. Put Thy church in order, O Lord, that they may labor for souls.

My Saviour, reveal Thyself to this people. Let Thy love be expressed. Oh, let it be revealed! Hold Thy people, that Satan may not have his will and way with them. Help them to press through all opposition, that at last they may lay their crowns at the feet of Jesus in the city of God; and Thy name shall have all the glory. Amen.—*Review and Herald*, July 16, 1908.

BEAUTY IN DIVERSITY

Now concerning spiritual gifts, brethren, I would not have you ignorant. . . . Now there are diversities of gifts, but the same Spirit. And there are differences of administrations, but the same Lord. And there are diversities of operations, but it is the same God which worketh all in all. 1 Cor. 12:1-6.

The talents that Christ entrusts to His church represent especially the gifts and blessings imparted by the Holy Spirit. "To one is given by the Spirit the word of wisdom; to another the word of knowledge by the same Spirit; to another faith by the same Spirit; to another the gifts of healing by the same Spirit; to another the working of miracles; to another prophecy; to another discerning of spirits; to another divers kinds of tongues; to another the interpretation of tongues: but all these worketh that one and the selfsame Spirit, dividing to every man severally as he will" (1 Cor. 12:8-11). . . .

In all the Lord's arrangements, there is nothing more beautiful than His plan of giving to men and women a diversity of gifts. The church is His garden, adorned with a variety of trees, plants, and flowers. He does not expect the hyssop to assume the proportions of the cedar, nor the olive to reach the height of the stately palm. Many have received but a limited religious and intellectual training, but God has a work for this class to do, if they will labor in humility, trusting in Him. . . .

Different gifts are imparted to different ones, that the workers may feel their need of one another. God bestows these gifts, and they are employed in His service, not to glorify the possessor, not to uplift man, but to uplift the world's Redeemer. They are to be used for the good of all mankind, by representing the truth, not testifying to a falsehood. . . . In every word and act, kindness and love will be revealed; and as each worker fills his appointed place faithfully, the prayer of Christ for the unity of His followers will be answered, and the world will know that these are His disciples.—*Signs of the Times*, Mar. 15, 1910.

TO BE GOD'S INSTRUMENTALITIES

Who then is Paul, and who is Apollos, but ministers by whom ye believed, even as the Lord gave to every man? 1 Cor. 3:5.

God's servants do not all possess the same gifts, but they are all His workmen. Each is to learn of the Great Teacher, and then to communicate what he has learned. All do not do the same work, but under the sanctifying influence of the Holy Spirit they are all God's instrumentalities. God employs a diversity of gifts in His work of winning souls from Satan's army.

"Now he that planteth and he that watereth are one: and every man shall receive his own reward according to his own labor" (1 Cor. 3:8). God, and not man, is the judge of man's work, and He will apportion to each his just reward. It is not given to any human being to judge between the different servants of God. The Lord alone is the judge and rewarder of every good work.

"He that planteth and he that watereth are one," engaged in the same work—the salvation of souls. "We are labourers together with God: ye are God's husbandry, ye are God's building" (verse 9). In these words the church is compared to a cultivated field, in which the husbandmen are to labor, caring for the vines of the Lord's planting; and to a building, which is to become a holy temple for the Lord. Christ is the Master Workman. All are to work under His supervision, letting Him work for and through His workmen. He gives them tact and skill, and if they heed His instructions, crowns their labor with success.

None are to complain against God, who has appointed to each man his work. He who murmurs and frets, who wants his own way, who desires to mold his fellow laborers to suit his own ideas, needs the divine touch before he is qualified to labor in any line. Unless he is changed, he will surely mar the work.

Remember that we are laborers together with God. God is the all-powerful, effectual mover. His servants are His instruments.—*Review and Herald*, Dec. 11, 1900.

TO BECOME AGENTS OF SALVATION

For God, who commanded the light to shine out of darkness, hath shined in our hearts, to give the light of the knowledge of the glory of God in the face of Jesus Christ. 2 Cor. 4:6.

Christians are to be indeed the representatives of Jesus Christ; they are not to be pretenders. Shall the world form its conceptions of God by the course of those who only take the name of Christ, and do not His works? Shall they point to those who claim to be believers, but who are not believers at heart, who betray sacred trusts, and work the works of the enemy, and say, "Oh, these are Christians, and they will cheat and lie, and they cannot be trusted"? These are not the ones who truly represent God.

But God will not leave the world to be deceived. The Lord has a peculiar people on the earth, and He is not ashamed to call them brethren; for they do the works of Christ. They make it manifest that they love God, because they keep His commandments. They bear the divine image. They are a spectacle unto the world, to angels, and to men. They cooperate with heavenly intelligences, and the Lord is most honored and glorified by those who do the most good works.

True piety of heart is made manifest by good words and good works, and men see the works of those who love God, and they are led thereby to glorify God. The true Christian abounds in good works; he brings forth much fruit. He feeds the hungry, clothes the naked, visits the sick, and ministers to the afflicted. Christians take a heartfelt interest in the children that are about them, who, through the subtle temptations of the enemy, are ready to perish. . . . There are youth all around us to whom the members of the church owe a duty; for Christ has died for them upon the cross of Calvary to purchase for them the gift of salvation. They are precious in the sight of God, and He desires their eternal happiness.

The saving work of Christ is complete only when the members of the church do their part, arising and shining because their light is come, and the glory of the Lord is risen upon them. Christ calls for voluntary cooperation on the part of His agents in doing earnest, consistent work for the salvation of souls.—*Review and Herald,* Jan. 29, 1895.

USED AS A POWER FOR GOD

But the manifestation of the Spirit is given to every man to profit withal. For to one is given by the Spirit the word of wisdom; to another the word of knowledge by the same Spirit. 1 Cor. 12:7, 8.

One worker may be a ready speaker; another a ready writer; another may have the gift of sincere, earnest, fervent prayer; another the gift of singing; another may have special power to explain the Word of God with clearness. And each gift is to become a power for God because He works with the laborer. To one God gives the word of wisdom, to another knowledge, to another faith; but all are to work under the same Head. The diversity of gifts leads to a diversity of operations, but "it is the same God which worketh all in all" (1 Cor. 12:6).

The Lord desires His chosen servants to learn how to unite together in harmonious effort. It may seem to some that the contrast between their gifts and the gifts of a fellow laborer is too great to allow them to unite in harmonious effort; but when they remember that there are varied minds to be reached, and that some will reject the truth as it is presented by one laborer, only to open their hearts to God's truth as it is presented in a different manner by another laborer, they will hopefully endeavor to labor together in unity. Their talents, however diverse, may all be under the control of the same Spirit. In every word and act, kindness and love will be revealed; and as each worker fills his appointed place faithfully, the prayer of Christ for the unity of His followers will be answered, and the world will know that these are His disciples.

In loving sympathy and confidence God's workers are to unite with one another. He who says or does anything that tends to separate the members of Christ's church is counterworking the Lord's purpose. Wrangling and dissension in the church, the encouragement of suspicion and unbelief, are dishonoring to Christ. God desires His servants to cultivate Christian affection for one another.—*Testimonies*, vol. 9, pp. 144, 145.

A God-given Faith

To another faith by the same Spirit; to another the gifts of healing by the same Spirit. 1 Cor. 12:9.

Faith, too, is the gift of God. Faith is the assent of man's understanding to God's words, that binds the heart to God's service. And whose is man's understanding, if it be not God's? Whose the heart, if it be not God's? To have faith is to render to God the intellect, the energy, that we have received from Him; therefore those who exercise faith do not themselves deserve any credit. Those who believe so firmly in a heavenly Father that they can trust Him with unlimited confidence; those who by faith can reach beyond the grave to the eternal realities beyond, must pour forth to their Maker the confession "All things come of thee, and of thine own have we given thee" (1 Chron. 29:14).

No man has a right to call himself his own. And no man possesses any good thing that he can call his own. Every man, every thing, is the property of the Lord. All that man receives from the bounty of heaven is still the Lord's. Whatever knowledge he has that in any way helps him to be an intelligent workman in God's cause is from the Lord, and should be imparted by him to his fellow men, in order that they, too, may become valuable workmen. He to whom God has entrusted unusual gifts should return to the Lord's storehouse that which he has received, by freely giving to others the benefit of his blessings. Thus God will be honored and glorified. . . .

Heavenly bestowed capabilities should not be made to serve selfish ends. Every energy, every endowment, is a talent that should contribute to God's glory by being used in His service. His gifts are to be put out to the exchangers, that He may receive His own, with usury. The talents that fit a man for service are entrusted to him not only that he may be an acceptable worker himself, but that he may also be enabled to teach others who in some respects are deficient.—*Review and Herald*, Dec. 1, 1904.

FAITH THAT WORKS

*And what shall I more say? for the time would fail me to tell of Gedeon,
and of Barak, and of Samson, and of Jephthae; of David also, and Samuel,
and of the prophets: who through faith subdued kingdoms, wrought righteousness, obtained promises, stopped the mouths of lions, quenched the violence of fire, escaped the edge of the sword, out of weakness were made
strong, waxed valiant in fight, turned to flight the armies of the aliens.
Heb. 11:32-34.*

Faith is trusting God—believing that He loves us and knows best
what is for our good. Thus, instead of our own, it leads us to
choose His way. In place of our ignorance, it accepts His wisdom;
in place of our weakness, His strength; in place of our sinfulness, His
righteousness. Our lives, ourselves, are already His; faith acknowledges
His ownership and accepts its blessing. Truth, uprightness, purity, have
been pointed out as secrets of life's success. It is faith that puts us in possession of these principles.

Every good impulse or aspiration is the gift of God; faith receives
from God the life that alone can produce true growth and efficiency.

How to exercise faith should be made very plain. To every promise
of God there are conditions. If we are willing to do His will, all His
strength is ours. Whatever gift He promises is in the promise itself.
"The seed is the word of God" (Luke 8:11). As surely as the oak is in the
acorn, so surely is the gift of God in His promise. If we receive the
promise, we have the gift.

Faith that enables us to receive God's gifts is itself a gift, of which
some measure is imparted to every human being. It grows as exercised
in appropriating the Word of God. In order to strengthen faith, we
must often bring it in contact with the Word.

In the study of the Bible the student should be led to see the power
of God's word. In the creation, "He spake, and it was done; he commanded, and it stood fast." He "calleth those things which be not as
though they were" (Ps. 33:9; Rom. 4:17); for when He calls them, they
are.—*Education*, pp. 253, 254.

THE GIFT OF SPEECH

Preach the word; be instant in season, out of season; reprove, rebuke, exhort with all longsuffering and doctrine. 2 Tim. 4:2.

The power of speech is a talent that should be diligently cultivated. Of all the gifts we have received from God, none is capable of being a greater blessing than this. With the voice we convince and persuade; with it we offer praise and prayer to God; and with it we tell others of the Redeemer's love. Not one word is to be spoken unadvisedly. No evil speaking, no frivolous talk, no fretful repining or impure suggestions, will escape the lips of him who is following Christ.

The apostle Paul, writing by the Holy Spirit, says, "Let no corrupt communication proceed out of your mouth" (Eph. 4:29). A corrupt communication does not mean only words that are vile. It means any expression contrary to holy principles and pure and undefiled religion. It includes impure hints and covert suggestions of evil. Unless instantly resisted, these lead to great sin.

Upon every family, upon every individual Christian, is laid the duty of barring the way against corrupt speech. When [we are] in the company of those who indulge in foolish talk, it is our duty to change the subject of conversation if possible. By the help of the grace of God, we should try to drop words or introduce a subject that will turn the conversation into a profitable channel.

Our words should be words of praise and thanksgiving. If the mind and heart are full of the love of God, this will be revealed in the conversation. It will not be a difficult matter to impart that which enters into our spiritual life. Great thoughts, noble aspirations, clear perceptions of truth, unselfish purposes, yearnings for piety and holiness, will bear fruit in words that reveal the character of the heart treasure. When Christ is thus revealed in our speech, it will have a power in winning souls to Him.

We should speak of Christ to those who know Him not. We should do as Christ did. Wherever He was, in the synagogue, by the wayside, in the boat thrust out a little from the land, at the Pharisee's feast or the table of the publican, He spoke to men of the things pertaining to the higher life.—*Signs of the Times*, July 2, 1902.

THE GIFT OF SINGING

What is it then? I will pray with the spirit, and I will pray with the understanding also: I will sing with the spirit, and I will sing with the understanding also. 1 Cor. 14:15.

The Lord is calling upon His people to take up different lines of missionary work, to sow beside all waters. We do but a small part of the work that He desires us to do among our neighbors and friends. By kindness to the poor, the sick, or the bereaved we may obtain an influence over them, so that divine truth will find access to their hearts. No such opportunity for service should be allowed to pass unimproved. It is the highest missionary work that we can do. The presentation of the truth in love and sympathy from house to house is in harmony with the instruction of Christ to His disciples when He sent them out on their first missionary tour.

Those who have the gift of song are needed. Song is one of the most effective means of impressing spiritual truth upon the heart. Often by the words of sacred song, the springs of penitence and faith have been unsealed. Church members, young and old, should be educated to go forth to proclaim this last message to the world. If they go in humility, angels of God will go with them, teaching them how to lift up the voice in prayer, how to raise the voice in song, and how to proclaim the gospel message for this time.

Young men and women, take up the work to which God calls you. Christ will teach you to use your abilities to good purpose. As you receive the quickening influence of the Holy Spirit, and seek to teach others, your minds will be refreshed, and you will be able to present words that are new and strangely beautiful to your hearers. Pray and sing, and speak the Word. . . .

God wants His people to receive to impart. As impartial, unselfish witnesses, they are to give to others what the Lord has given them. And as you enter into this work, and by whatever means in your power seek to reach hearts, be sure to work in a way that will remove prejudice instead of creating it. Make the life of Christ your constant study, and labor as He did, following His example.—*Review and Herald*, June 6, 1912.

THE GIFT OF HEALING

Is any sick among you? let him call for the elders of the church; and let them pray over him, anointing him with oil in the name of the Lord: and the prayer of faith shall save the sick, and the Lord shall raise him up; and if he have committed sins, they shall be forgiven him. James 5:14, 15.

The power of Christ to stay disease has been revealed in the past in a remarkable manner. Before we were blessed with institutions where the sick could get help from suffering, by diligent treatment and earnest prayer in faith to God, we carried the most seemingly hopeless cases through successfully. Today the Lord invites the suffering ones to have faith in Him. Man's necessity is God's opportunity.

"And he went out from thence, and came into his own country; and his disciples follow him. And when the sabbath day was come, he began to teach in the synagogue: and many hearing him were astonished, saying, From whence hath this man these things? and what wisdom is this which is given unto him, that even such mighty works are wrought by his hands? Is not this the carpenter, the son of Mary, the brother of James, and Joses, and of Judah, and Simon? and are not his sisters here with us? And they were offended at him. But Jesus said unto them, A prophet is not without honour, but in his own country, and among his own kin, and in his own house. And he could there do no mighty work, save that he laid his hands upon a few sick folk, and healed them" (Mark 6:1-6).

With all our treatments given to the sick, simple fervent prayer should be offered for the blessing of healing. We are to point the sick to the compassionate Saviour, and His power to forgive and to heal. Through His gracious providence they may be restored. Point the sufferers to their Advocate in the heavenly courts. Tell them that Christ will heal the sick, if they will repent and cease to transgress the laws of God. There is a Saviour who will reveal Himself in our sanitariums to save those who will submit themselves to Him. The suffering ones can unite with you in prayer, confessing their sin, and receiving pardon.—*Manuscript Releases*, vol. 8, pp. 267, 268.

HEALING POWER
THROUGH THE GREAT PHYSICIAN

And at even, when the sun did set, they brought unto him all that were diseased, and them that were possessed with devils. And all the city was gathered together at the door. And he healed many that were sick of divers diseases, and cast out many devils; and suffered not the devils to speak, because they knew him. Mark 1:32-34.

In giving us His Son, the Father gave the most costly gift that heaven could bestow. This gift it is our privilege to use in our ministration to the sick. Let Christ be your dependence. Commit every case to the Great Healer; let Him guide in every operation. The prayer offered in sincerity and in faith will be heard. This will give confidence to the physicians and courage to the sufferer.

I have been instructed that we should lead the sick in our institutions to expect large things because of the faith of the physician in the Great Healer, who, in the years of His earthly ministry, went through the towns and villages of the land and healed all who came to Him. None were turned away; He healed them all. Let the sick realize that, although unseen, Christ is present to bring relief and healing.

After His resurrection, Christ met with His disciples, and for forty days instructed them concerning their future work. On the day of His ascension, He met with the disciples in a mountain in Galilee, where He had appointed them. And He said to them, "All power is given unto me in heaven and in earth; go ye therefore, and teach all nations; baptizing them in the name of the Father, and of the Son, and of the Holy Ghost: teaching them to observe all things whatsoever I have commanded you: and, lo, I am with you alway, even unto the end of the world" (Matt. 28:18-20). It is the privilege of every physician and every sufferer to believe this promise; it is life to all who believe.—*Loma Linda Messages*, p. 355.

HEALING GIFT DOES NOT REPLACE INSTITUTIONS

And he put forth his hand, and touched him, saying, I will: be thou clean. And immediately the leprosy departed from him. And he charged him to tell no man: but go, and shew thyself to the priest, and offer for thy cleansing, according as Moses commanded, for a testimony unto them. Luke 5:13, 14.

The remark is often made, by one and another, "Why depend so much on sanitariums? Why do we not pray for the miraculous healing of the sick, as the people of God used to do?" In the early history of our work many were healed by prayer. And some, after they were healed, pursued the same course in the indulgence of appetite that they had followed in the past. They did not live and work in such a way as to avoid sickness. They did not show that they appreciated the Lord's goodness to them. Again and again they were brought to suffering through their own careless, thoughtless course of action. How could the Lord be glorified in bestowing on them the gift of health?

When the light came that we should have a sanitarium, the reason was plainly given. There were many who needed to be educated in regard to healthful living. A place must be provided to which the sick could be taken, where they could be taught how to live so as to preserve health. . . .

Lectures should be diligently kept up as a means of teaching the patients how to prevent disease by a wise course of action. By means of these lectures the patients may be shown the responsibility resting on them to keep the body in the most healthful condition because it is the Lord's purchased possession. Mind, soul, and body are bought with a price. . . . "Therefore glorify God in your body, and in your spirit, which are God's" (1 Cor. 6:20). . . .

In the providence of God, instruction has been given that sanitariums be established, in order that the sick may be drawn to them, and learn how to live healthfully. The establishment of sanitariums is a providential arrangement, whereby people from all churches are to be reached, and made acquainted with the saving truth for this time.—*Manuscript Releases*, vol. 7, pp. 378, 379.

NOT ALL HEALING COMES FROM THE SPIRIT

Many will say to me in that day, Lord, Lord, have we not prophesied in thy name? and in thy name have cast out devils? and in thy name done many wonderful works? And then will I profess unto them, I never knew you: depart from me, ye that work iniquity. Matt. 7:22, 23.

We need to be anchored in Christ, rooted and grounded in the faith. Satan works through agents. He selects those who have not been drinking of the living waters, whose souls are athirst for something new and strange, and who are ever ready to drink at any fountain that may present itself. Voices will be heard, saying, "Lo, here is Christ," or "Lo, . . . there"; but we must believe them not (Matt. 24:23). We have unmistakable evidence of the voice of the True Shepherd, and He is calling upon us to follow Him. He says, "I have kept my Father's commandments" (John 15:10). He leads His sheep in the path of humble obedience to the law of God, but He never encourages them in the transgression of that law.

"The voice of a stranger" is the voice of one who neither respects nor obeys God's holy, just, and good law. Many make great pretensions to holiness, and boast of the wonders they perform in healing the sick, when they do not regard this great standard of righteousness. But through whose power are these cures wrought?. . .

If those through whom cures are performed are disposed, on account of these manifestations, to excuse their neglect of the law of God, and continue in disobedience, though they have power to any and every extent, it does not follow that they have the great power of God. On the contrary, it is the miracle-working power of the great deceiver. He is a transgressor of the moral law, and employs every device that he can master to blind men to its true character. We are warned that in the last days he will work with signs and lying wonders. And he will continue these wonders until the close of probation, that he may point to them as evidence that he is an angel of light and not of darkness.—*Review and Herald*, Nov. 17, 1885.

TRUE MIRACLES WILL HAPPEN AGAIN

Here is the patience of the saints: here are they that keep the command-ments of God, and the faith of Jesus. Rev. 14:12.

The great work of the gospel is not to close with less manifesta-tion of the power of God than marked its opening. The prophecies which were fulfilled in the outpouring of the former rain at the opening of the gospel are again to be fulfilled in the latter rain at its close. Here are "the times of refreshing" to which the apostle Peter looked forward when he said: "Repent ye therefore, and be con-verted, that your sins may be blotted out, when the times of refreshing shall come from the presence of the Lord; and he shall send Jesus Christ, which before was preached unto you" (Acts 3:19, 20).

Servants of God, with their faces lighted up and shining with holy consecration, will hasten from place to place to proclaim the message from heaven. By thousands of voices, all over the earth, the warning will be given. Miracles will be wrought, the sick will be healed, and signs and wonders will follow the believers. Satan also works, with lying wonders, even bringing down fire from heaven in the sight of men (Rev. 13:13). Thus the inhabitants of the earth will be brought to take their stand.

The message will be carried not so much by argument as by the deep conviction of the Spirit of God. The arguments have been presented. The seed has been sown, and now it will spring up and bear fruit. The publications distributed by missionary workers have exerted their influ-ence, yet many whose minds were impressed have been prevented from fully comprehending the truth or from yielding obedience. Now the rays of light penetrate everywhere, the truth is seen in its clearness, and the honest children of God sever the bands which have held them. Family connections, church relations, are powerless to stay them now. Truth is more precious than all besides. Notwithstanding the agencies combined against the truth, a large number take their stand upon the Lord's side.—*The Great Controversy*, pp. 611, 612.

THE GIFT OF TONGUES:
FLUENCY IN FOREIGN LANGUAGES

And there were dwelling at Jerusalem Jews, devout men, out of every nation under heaven. Now when this was noised abroad, the multitude came together, and were confounded, because that every man heard them speak in his own language. And they were all amazed and marvelled, saying one to another, Behold, are not all these which speak Galileans? And how hear we every man in our own tongue, wherein we were born? Acts 2:5-8.

A nd there appeared unto them cloven tongues like as of fire, and it sat upon each of them. And they were all filled with the Holy Ghost, and began to speak with other tongues, as the Spirit gave them utterance" (Acts 2:3, 4). The Holy Spirit, assuming the form of tongues of fire, rested upon those assembled. This was an emblem of the gift then bestowed on the disciples, which enabled them to speak with fluency languages with which they had heretofore been unacquainted. The appearance of fire signified the fervent zeal with which the apostles would labor and the power that would attend their work.

"There were dwelling at Jerusalem Jews, devout men, out of every nation under heaven" (verse 5). During the dispersion the Jews had been scattered to almost every part of the inhabited world, and in their exile they had learned to speak various languages. Many of these Jews were on this occasion in Jerusalem, attending the religious festivals then in progress. Every known tongue was represented by those assembled. This diversity of languages would have been a great hindrance to the proclamation of the gospel; God therefore in a miraculous manner supplied the deficiency of the apostles. The Holy Spirit did for them that which they could not have accomplished for themselves in a lifetime. They could now proclaim the truths of the gospel abroad, speaking with accuracy the languages of those for whom they were laboring.

This miraculous gift was a strong evidence to the world that their commission bore the signet of Heaven. From this time forth the language of the disciples was pure, simple, and accurate, whether they spoke in their native tongue or in a foreign language.—*The Acts of the Apostles*, pp. 39, 40.

TONGUES: TO PREACH THE GOSPEL

So likewise ye, except ye utter by the tongue words easy to be understood, how shall it be known what is spoken? for ye shall speak into the air. There are, it may be, so many kinds of voices in the world, and none of them is without signification. Therefore if I know not the meaning of the voice, I shall be unto him that speaketh a barbarian, and he that speaketh shall be a barbarian unto me. 1 Cor. 14:9-11.

Ministers who labor in word and doctrine should be thorough workmen, and should present the truth in its purity, yet with simplicity. They should feed the flock with clean provender, thoroughly winnowed. There are wandering stars professing to be ministers sent of God who are preaching the Sabbath from place to place, but who have truth mixed up with error and are throwing out their mass of discordant views to the people. Satan has pushed them in to disgust intelligent and sensible unbelievers.

Some of these have much to say upon the gifts and are often especially exercised. They give themselves up to wild, excitable feelings and make unintelligible sounds which they call the gift of tongues, and a certain class seem to be charmed with these strange manifestations. A strange spirit rules with this class, which would bear down and run over anyone who would reprove them. God's Spirit is not in the work and does not attend such workmen. They have another spirit. Still, such preachers have success among a certain class. But this will greatly increase the labor of those servants whom God shall send, who are qualified to present before the people the Sabbath and the gifts in their proper light, and whose influence and example are worthy of imitation.

The truth should be presented in a manner which will make it attractive to the intelligent mind. We are not understood as a people, but are looked upon as poor, weak-minded, low, and degraded. Then how important for all who teach, and all who believe the truth, to be so affected by its sanctifying influence that their consistent, elevated lives shall show unbelievers that they have been deceived in this people. How important that the cause of truth be stripped of everything like a false and fanatical excitement, that the truth may stand upon its own merits, revealing its native purity and exalted character.—*Testimonies*, vol. 1, pp. 414, 415.

PREACHING CHRIST: MORE IMPORTANT THAN TONGUES AND MIRACLES

How is it then, brethren? when ye come together, every one of you hath a psalm, hath a doctrine, hath a tongue, hath a revelation, hath an interpretation. Let all things be done unto edifying. 1 Cor. 14:26.

There is a great work to be done in our world. Men and women are to be converted, not by the gift of tongues nor by the working of miracles, but by the preaching of Christ crucified. Why delay the effort to make the world better? Why wait for some wonderful thing to be done, some costly apparatus to be provided? However humble your sphere, however lowly your work, if you labor in harmony with the teachings of the Saviour, He will reveal Himself through you, and your influence will draw souls to Him. He will honor the meek and lowly ones, who seek earnestly to do service for Him. Into all that we do, whether our work be in the shop, on the farm, or in the office, we are to bring the endeavor to save souls.

We are to sow beside all waters, keeping our souls in the love of God, working while it is day, using the means entrusted to us in the Master's service. Whatever our hands find to do, we are to do it with cheerfulness; whatever sacrifice we are called upon to make, we are to make it cheerfully. As we sow beside all waters, we shall realize the truth of the words "He which soweth bountifully shall reap also bountifully" (2 Cor. 9:6).

We owe everything to grace, sovereign grace. Grace ordained our redemption, our regeneration, and our adoption to heirship with Jesus Christ. Let this grace be revealed to others.

The Saviour takes those whom He finds will be molded, and uses them for His own name's glory. He uses material that others would pass by, and works in all who will give themselves to Him. He delights to take apparently hopeless material, those whom Satan has debased, and through whom he has worked, and make them the subjects of His grace. He rejoices to deliver them from suffering, and from the wrath that is to fall upon the disobedient. He makes His children His agents in the accomplishment of this work, and in its success, even in this life, they find a precious reward.—*Review and Herald*, Jan. 5, 1905.

LOOKING FOR A MORE EXCELLENT WAY

But covet earnestly the best gifts: and yet shew I unto you a more excellent way. 1 Cor. 12:31.

Some are in danger of giving way to envy lest another shall have the supremacy. They are liable not to recognize the gifts of their fellow workers as being as necessary to the success of the work as are their own gifts. But true love for God carries with it true, reverential trust. And he who loves God will love his brother also.

There is to be no ordering, no domineering, no masterly authority. The love of God, in a healing, life-giving current, is to flow through the life. The spirit and words and deeds of every worker are to show that he realizes that he is acting in Christ's place. The power that he receives from the Great Teacher is the power to educate others, not the power to order or dictate. He is to come to Christ as one who desires to know how to teach and help others.

Patient, cheerful contentment is one of the "best gifts." So also is courage to follow in the path of duty, even when this path separates us from friends. But courage of conviction must never lead to stubbornness, which leads a man to adhere to his own ideas. Let all watch and pray.

The talent of speech is a wonderful gift—a gift that can be a great power for good or for evil.

Intellectual ability, good taste, skill, refinement, true elevation—these God uses in His work. But they must first be placed under His jurisdiction. The Lord's presence is to be a controlling power. He whose heart blends with the heart of Christ is, in desires and practices, conformed to the will of Christ.

We are to covet earnestly the best gifts, but this does not mean that we are to seek to be first. We are to strive earnestly for power to follow Christ's example, that we may be heralds of His gospel. This is true religion. Temptations come; suspicions and evil surmising make it hard for us to preserve the spirit of the higher life; nevertheless the Lord desires us to walk straight forward in His blessed, holy light.—*Pacific Union Recorder*, July 26, 1906.

GOD CAN USE COMMON SKILLS

And Moses said unto the children of Israel, See, the Lord hath called by name Bezaleel the son of Uri, the son of Hur, of the tribe of Judah; and he hath filled him with the spirit of God, in wisdom, in understanding, and in knowledge, and in all manner of workmanship. Ex. 35:30, 31.

Skill in the common arts is a gift from God. He provides both the gift and wisdom to use the gift aright. When He desired a work done on the tabernacle, He said, "See, I have called by name Bezaleel the son of Uri, the son of Hur, of the tribe of Judah: and I have filled him with the spirit of God, in wisdom, and in understanding, and in knowledge, and in all manner of workmanship" (Ex. 31:2, 3). Through the prophet Isaiah the Lord said, "Give ye ear, and hear my voice; hearken, and hear my speech. Doth the plowman plow all day to sow? doth he open and break the clods of his ground?

"When he hath made plain the face thereof, doth he not cast abroad the fitches, and scatter the cumin, and cast in the principal wheat and the appointed barley and the rie in their place? For his God doth instruct him to discretion, and doth teach him. For the fitches are not threshed with a threshing instrument, neither is a cart wheel turned about upon the cumin; but the fitches are beaten out with a staff, and the cumin with a rod. Bread corn is bruised; because he will not ever be threshing it, nor break it with the wheel of his cart, nor bruise it with his horsemen. This also cometh forth from the Lord of hosts, which is wonderful in counsel, and excellent in working" (Isa. 28:23-29).

God dispenses His gifts as it pleases Him. He bestows one gift upon one, and another gift upon another, but all for the good of the whole body. It is in God's order that some shall be of service in one line of work, and others in other lines—all working under the selfsame Spirit. The recognition of this plan will be a safeguard against emulation, pride, envy, or contempt of one another. It will strengthen unity and mutual love.—*Counsels to Parents and Teachers*, pp. 314, 315.

COMMON INDIVIDUALS GIFTED TO SERVE

But the Lord said unto Samuel, Look not on his countenance, or on the height of his stature; because I have refused him: for the Lord seeth not as man seeth; for man looketh on the outward appearance, but the Lord looketh on the heart. 1 Sam. 16:7.

God does not accept men because of their capabilities, but because they seek His face, desiring His help. God sees not as man sees. He judges not from appearances. He searches the heart, and judges righteously. "To this man will I look," He declares, "even to him that is poor and of a contrite spirit, and trembleth at my word" (Isa. 66:2).

He accepts and communes with His lowly, unpretentious followers; for in them He sees the most precious material, which will stand the test of storm and tempest, heat and pressure.

Our object in working for the Master should be that His name may be glorified in the conversion of sinners. Those who labor to gain applause are not approved of God.

The Lord uses many gifts in the work of saving sinners. In the future, common men will be impressed by the Spirit of God to leave their ordinary employment to go forth and proclaim the last message of mercy. They are to be strengthened and encouraged, and as fast as possible prepared for labor, that success may crown their efforts. They cooperate with unseen, heavenly agencies, for they are willing to spend and be spent in the service of the Master. They are laborers together with God, and their brethren should bid them Godspeed, praying for them as they go forth to fulfill the great commission. No one is authorized to hinder such workers. They are to be treated with the greatest respect. No taunting word is to be spoken of them as in the rough places of the earth they sow the gospel seed.—*Review and Herald*, July 4, 1907.

NO GIFT SUPERIOR OR INFERIOR

For the Son of man is as a man taking a far journey, who left his house, and gave authority to his servants, and to every man his work, and commanded the porter to watch. Mark 13:34.

Jesus is ministering in the heavenly sanctuary, but He is with His workers also; for He declares, "Lo, I am with you alway, even unto the end of the world" (Matt. 28:20). He is spiritual director of His church on earth, and He longs to see the members filled with a determination to labor harmoniously for the advancement of His kingdom. He has raised up a succession of workers who derive their authority from Him, the Great Teacher. He has chosen for His work men of varied talents and varied capabilities. Some of these might not be the men you would choose, but you will pass through an experience that will lead you to see that God exalts men whom you would regard as inferior to yourselves.

When the judgment shall sit, and the books are opened, many will be surprised by God's estimate of character. They will realize that God sees not as man sees, that He judges not as human beings judge. He reads the heart. He knows the motives that prompt the action, and He recognizes and commends every faithful effort put forth for Him. The Lord uses various gifts in His work. Let no worker think that his gifts are superior to those of another worker. Let God be the judge. He tests and approves His workers, and He places a just estimate on their qualifications. He has placed in the church a variety of gifts, to meet the varied wants of the many minds with which His workers are brought in contact.

The Lord has given to every man his work, and every man is to do the work that the Lord has given him. All have not the same gifts or the same disposition. All need to feel daily the converting power of the Holy Spirit, that they may bear much fruit for the Lord. It is not the one who preaches the gospel that provides the efficiency that makes his efforts successful. It is the unseen Worker standing behind the minister who brings conviction and conversion to souls.—*Bible Training School*, Nov. 1, 1909.

MORE GIFTS: MORE RESPONSIBILITY

For the kingdom of heaven is as a man travelling into a far country, who called his own servants, and delivered unto them his goods. And unto one he gave five talents, to another two, and to another one; to every man according to his several ability; and straightway took his journey. Matt. 25:14, 15.

To every man is given his work. One man may not be able to do the work for which another man has been trained and educated. But the work of every man must begin at the heart, not resting in a theory of the truth. The work of him who surrenders the soul to God and cooperates with divine agencies will reveal an able, wise workman, who discerns how to adapt himself to the situation. The root must be holy, or there will be no holy fruit. All are to be workers together with God. Self must not become prominent. The Lord has entrusted talents and capabilities to every individual, and those who are most highly favored with opportunities and privileges to hear the Spirit's voice are under the heaviest responsibility to God.

Those who are represented as having but one talent have also their work to do. By trading, not with pounds, but with pence, they are diligently to employ their ability, determined not to fail nor be discouraged. They are to ask in faith, and depend upon the Holy Spirit to work upon unbelieving hearts. If they depend upon their own capabilities, they will fail. Those who faithfully trade upon the one talent will hear the gracious commendations spoken to them with as much heartiness as to those who have been gifted with many talents, and who have wisely improved them, "Well done, thou good and faithful servant: thou hast been faithful over a few things, I will make thee ruler over many things" (Matt. 25:21).

It is the spirit of humility in which the work is done which God regards. He who had but one talent had an influence to exert, and his work was needed. In perfecting his own character, in learning in the school of Christ, he was exerting an influence that helped to perfect the character of those who had larger responsibilities, who were in danger of building themselves up, and of neglecting some important little things, which that faithful man with his one talent was regarding with diligent care.— *Notebook Leaflets*, vol. 1, pp. 129, 130.

YOUTH GIFTED TO
BE A LIVING CHANNEL

Let no man despise thy youth; but be thou an example of the believers, in word, in conversation, in charity, in spirit, in faith, in purity. Till I come, give attendance to reading, to exhortation, to doctrine. Neglect not the gift that is in thee, which was given thee by prophecy, with the laying on of the hands of the presbytery. 1 Tim. 4:12-14.

Every youth should consider himself of value with God, because he has been entrusted with the richest gift that can be given. It is his privilege to be a living channel, through which God can communicate the treasures of His grace, the unsearchable riches of Christ.

Our sins may be as mountains before us, but if we humble our hearts in confession of them, trusting in the merits of a crucified and risen Saviour, we shall be forgiven, and shall be cleansed from all unrighteousness. The depth of a Saviour's love is revealed in our salvation. If we will accept this salvation, our testimony will be "We have redemption through his blood" (Eph. 1:7). The law of the Spirit of life in Christ Jesus has made us free from the law of sin and death. We are more than conquerors through Him that loved us, and gave Himself for us.

It is here, right here in the world, that our talents are to be used. We are to lead souls to "the Lamb of God, which taketh away the sin of the world" (John 1:29). It is our work, and should be our pleasure, to present in our lives the unsearchable riches of Christ. We may make daily progress in the path of holiness, and still find greater heights to be reached; but every stretch of the spiritual muscles, every tax on heart and brain, will bring to light the abundance of the supply of grace essential for us as we advance. The more we contemplate eternal things, the more we shall reveal the merits of a Saviour's sacrifice, the protection of His righteousness, the fullness of His wisdom, and His power to present us before the Father without spot, or wrinkle, or any such thing.—*Youth's Instructor*, Nov. 30, 1899.

WOMEN GIFTED TO BENEFIT HUMANITY

And many of the Samaritans of that city believed on him for the saying of the woman, which testified, He told me all that ever I did. So when the Samaritans were come unto him, they besought him that he would tarry with them: and he abode there two days. And many more believed because of his own word; and said unto the woman, Now we believe, not because of thy saying: for we have heard him ourselves, and know that this is indeed the Christ, the Saviour of the world. John 4:39-42.

Women may accomplish a good work for God, if they will first learn the precious, all-important lesson of meekness in the school of Christ. They will be able to benefit humanity by presenting to them the all-sufficiency of Jesus. When each member of the church realizes his own individual responsibility, when he humbly takes up the work which presents itself before him, the work will go on to success. God has given to every man his work according to his several ability.

It will not be an easy task to work for the Master in this age. But how much perplexity might be saved, if workers continually relied upon God, and duly considered the directions that God has given. He says, "Having then gifts differing according to the grace that is given to us, whether prophecy, let us prophesy according to the proportion of faith; or ministry, let us wait on our ministering: or he that teacheth, on teaching; or he that exhorteth, on exhortation: he that giveth, let him do it with simplicity; he that ruleth, with diligence; he that sheweth mercy, with cheerfulness" (Rom. 12:6-8).

This is a subject that demands close, critical study. Many mistakes are made because men do not heed this instruction. Many who are entrusted with some humble line of work to do for the Master soon become dissatisfied, and think that they should be teachers and leaders. They want to leave their humble ministering, which is just as important in its place as the larger responsibilities. Those who are set to do visiting soon come to think that anyone can do that work, that anyone can speak words of sympathy and encouragement, and lead men in a humble, quiet way to a correct understanding of the Scriptures. But it is a work that demands much grace, much patience, and an ever-increasing stock of wisdom.—*Manuscript Releases*, vol. 11, pp. 278, 279.

MOTHERS GIFTED TO
NURTURE THEIR CHILDREN

When I call to remembrance the unfeigned faith that is in thee, which dwelt first in thy grandmother Lois, and thy mother Eunice; and I am persuaded that in thee also. 2 Tim. 1:5.

The mother's work is given her of God, to bring up her children in the nurture and admonition of the Lord. The love and fear of God should ever be kept before their tender minds. When corrected, they should be taught to feel that they are admonished of God, that He is displeased with deception, untruthfulness, and wrongdoing. Thus the minds of little ones may be so connected with God that all they do and say will be in reference to His glory; and in afteryears they will not be like the reed in the wind, continually wavering between inclination and duty.

If in their tender years, the minds of children are filled with pleasant images of truth, of purity and goodness, a taste will be formed for that which is pure and elevated, and their imagination will not become easily corrupted or defiled. While if the opposite course is pursued, if the minds of the parents are continually dwelling upon low scenes; if their conversation lingers over objectional features of character; if they form a habit of speaking complainingly of the course others have pursued, the little ones will take lessons from the words and expressions of contempt, and will follow the pernicious example. The evil impress, like the taint of the leprosy, will cleave to them in afterlife.

The seeds sown in infancy by the careful, God-fearing mother will become trees of righteousness, which will blossom and bear fruit; and the lessons given by a God-fearing father by precept and example will, as in the case of Joseph, yield an abundant harvest by and by.

Will parents review their work in the educating and training of their children, and consider whether they have done their whole duty in hope and faith that these children may be a crown of rejoicing in the day of the Lord Jesus? Have they so labored for the welfare of their children that Jesus can look down from heaven and by the gift of His Spirit sanctify their efforts? Parents, it may be yours to prepare your children for the highest usefulness in this life, and to share at last the glory of that which is to come.—*Good Health*, Jan. 1, 1880.

STUDENTS GIFTED TO BE WITNESSES

Study to shew thyself approved unto God, a workman that needeth not to be ashamed, rightly dividing the word of truth. 2 Tim. 2:15.

Let teachers and students watch for opportunities to confess Christ in their conversation. Such witness will be more effective than many sermons. . . .

Students, make your school life as perfect as possible. You will pass over the way but once, and precious are the opportunities granted you. You are not only to learn but to practice the lessons of Christ. While obtaining your education, you have the opportunity to tell of the wonderful truths of God's Word. Improve every such opportunity. God will bless every minute spent in this way. Maintain your simplicity and your love for souls, and the Lord will lead you in safe paths. The rich experience you gain will be of more value to you than gold or silver or precious stones.

You know not to what position you may be called in the future. God may use you as He used Daniel, to take the knowledge of the truth to the mighty of the earth. It rests with you to say whether you will have skill and knowledge to do this work. God can give you skill in all your learning. He can help you to adapt yourself to the line of study you take up. Make it your first interest to gather up right, noble, uplifting principles. God desires you to witness for Him. He does not want you to stand still; He wants you to run in the way of His commandments.

Christ desires to use every student as His agent. You are to cooperate with the One who gave His life for you. What rich blessings would come to our schools if teachers and students would consecrate themselves, heart, mind, soul, and strength, to God's service as His helping hand! His helping hand—this is what you may be if you will yield yourselves to His keeping. He will lead you safely, and enable you to make straight paths for yourselves and for others. He will give you knowledge and wisdom, and a fitness for fuller service.—*Counsels to Parents and Teachers*, pp. 554, 555.

THE CANVASSER GIFTED TO TESTIFY

Serving the Lord with all humility of mind, and with many tears, and temptations, which befell me by the lying in wait of the Jews: and how I kept back nothing that was profitable unto you, but have shewed you, and have taught you publickly, and from house to house. Acts 20:19, 20.

From the light which God has given me, there is much responsibility resting upon the canvassers. They should go to their work prepared to explain the Scriptures, and nothing should be said or done to bind their hands. If they put their trust in the Lord as they travel from place to place, the angels of God will be round about them, giving them words to speak which will bring light and hope and courage to many souls. Were it not for the work of the canvassers, many would never hear the truth.

Of all the gifts which God has given to man, none is more noble or a greater blessing than the gift of speech, if it is sanctified by the Holy Spirit. It is with the tongue we convince and persuade; with it we offer prayer and praise to God, and with it we convey rich thoughts of the Redeemer's love. By this work the canvasser can scatter the seeds of truth, causing the light from the Word of God to shine into many minds.

I sincerely hope that no mind will receive the impression that it belittles a minister of the gospel to canvass. Hear the apostle Paul's testimony: "Ye know, from the first day that I came into Asia, after what manner I have been with you at all seasons, serving the Lord with all humility of mind, and with many tears, and temptations, which befell me by the lying in wait of the Jews: and how I kept back nothing that was profitable unto you, but have shewed you, and have taught you publickly, and from house to house, testifying both to the Jews, and also to the Greeks, repentance toward God, and faith toward our Lord Jesus Christ" (Acts 20:18-21). The eloquent Paul, to whom God manifested Himself in a remarkable manner, went from house to house, with all humility of mind, and with many tears and temptations.—*Home Missionary*, Nov. 1, 1896.

PASTORS AND TEACHERS TO PURSUE UNITY

And he gave some, apostles; and some, prophets; and some, evangelists; and some, pastors and teachers; for the perfecting of the saints, for the work of the ministry, for the edifying of the body of Christ: till we all come in the unity of the faith, and of the knowledge of the Son of God, unto a perfect man, unto the measure of the stature of the fullness of Christ. Eph. 4:11-13.

The Lord has given to those who should be His human agents talents of means, capacity, and influence, according to their ability to employ these gifts in a wise manner for His service. He has given to every man his work. "And he gave some, apostles; and some, prophets; and some, evangelists; and some, pastors and teachers."

Why were these various workers appointed? "For the perfecting of the saints, for the work of the ministry, for the edifying of the body of Christ: till we all come in the unity of the faith, and of the knowledge of the Son of God, unto a perfect man, unto the measure of the stature of the fullness of Christ: that we henceforth be no more children, tossed to and fro, and carried about with every wind of doctrine, by the sleight of men, and cunning craftiness, whereby they lie in wait to deceive; but speaking the truth in love, may grow up into him in all things, which is the head, even Christ" (Eph. 4:12-15).

We can see from this scripture that the Lord has His appointed workers, and that the work committed unto them has in view a definite object. Prophets, apostles, evangelists, pastors, teachers, are all to work for the perfecting of the saints, for the work of the ministry, for the edifying of the body of Christ. Is not this object worthy of careful attention? Can we not discern that there has been neglect in some special work for the church, in that the saints have not attained the perfection that God would have them attain? Had the work of the ministry been done, the church would have been edified, and educated for the great work that devolves upon them. The truth would have been presented in such a way that the Spirit of the Lord would have moved upon hearts, and sinners would have been convicted and converted, and would have taken their position as followers of Christ.—*Review and Herald*, Mar. 7, 1893.

EVERY MAN, WOMAN, AND CHILD IS RESPONSIBLE

And so he that had received five talents came and brought other five talents, saying, Lord, thou deliveredst unto me five talents: behold, I have gained beside them five talents more. His lord said unto him, Well done, thou good and faithful servant: thou hast been faithful over a few things, I will make thee ruler over many things: enter thou into the joy of thy lord. Matt. 25:20, 21.

The parable of the talents should be a matter of the most careful and prayerful study; for it has a personal and individual application to every man, woman, and child possessed of the powers of reason. Your obligation and responsibility are in proportion to the talents God has bestowed upon you. There is not a follower of Christ but has some peculiar gift for the use of which he is accountable to God.

Many have excused themselves from rendering their gift to the service of Christ, because others were possessed of superior endowments and advantages. The opinion has prevailed that only those who are especially talented are required to sanctify their abilities to the service of God. It has come to be understood that talents are given only to a certain favored class, to the exclusion of others who, of course, are not called upon to share in the toils or rewards. But it is not so represented in the parable. When the master of the house called his servants, he gave to every man his work.

The whole family of God are included in the responsibility of using their Lord's goods. Every individual, from the lowliest and most obscure to the greatest and most exalted, is a moral agent endowed with abilities for which he is accountable to God. To a greater or less degree, all are placed in charge of the talents of their Lord. The spiritual, mental, and physical ability, the influence, station, possessions, affections, sympathies, all are precious talents to be used in the cause of the Master for the salvation of souls for whom Christ died. How few appreciate these blessings! How few seek to improve their talent, and increase their usefulness in the world! The Master has given to every man his work. He has given to every man according to his ability, and his trust is in proportion to his capacity. God requires everyone to be a worker in His vineyard. You are to take up the work that has been placed in your charge, and to do it faithfully.— *Review and Herald*, May 1, 1888.

ASKING FOR THE GIFTS

If any of you lack wisdom, let him ask of God, that giveth to all men liberally, and upbraideth not; and it shall be given him. James 1:5.

Those who ask because they wish to impart to others will not be disappointed. God will reward those who come to Him in earnest faith. He assures us that the thought of His majesty and sovereignty should not keep us in fear. He will do much more graciously than we suppose if we will come to the footstool of His mercy. He urges His sovereignty as a reason for His great and merciful bountifulness in supplying the demands upon Him. He pledges Himself to hear our prayers, declaring that He *will* hear them. He condescends to appeal from the instinct of parental tenderness to the infinite benevolence of Him whose we are by creation and by redemption. He says, "If ye then, being evil, know how to give good gifts unto your children; how much more shall your heavenly Father give the Holy Spirit to them that ask him" (Luke 11:13). The needy and soul-hungry never plead with God in vain. . . .

In view of this, tell me who should wear countenances more bright and cheerful, more full of sunshine, than those who live by faith in the Son of God. In Him the needy and hungry find all their wants supplied. But let us not forget that those whom God has blessed with the good things of this life are to be His helping hand, to supply the necessities of His needy ones. They are to be laborers together with Him. They are His stewards in trust, and are to use their goods for the advancement of His work, that His name may be glorified.

The Lord desires to employ the church as a channel through which to communicate His bounties. If His people would keep the channel open, receiving the spiritual and temporal gifts of His grace, and imparting them to the needy, there would be no sick ones neglected, no orphans crying for food. The hearts of the widow and the fatherless would sing for joy.

God has given man the richest of His gifts. This He has done that man may dispense His bounties.—*Bible Echo*, Aug. 12, 1901.

GUIDANCE PROMISED TO FIND YOUR GIFT

But all these worketh that one and the selfsame Spirit, dividing to every man severally as he will. 1 Cor. 12:11.

We are to be guided and controlled by the same Spirit, but in order for this to be, it is not necessary that we all have the same gifts. "There are diversities of gifts, but the same Spirit. And there are differences of administrations, but the same Lord. And there are diversities of operations, but it is the same God which worketh all in all" (1 Cor. 12:4-6), to bring these different operations into perfect harmony. "God hath set the members every one of them in the body as it hath pleased Him" (verse 18). He has placed every man at his post of duty, assigning to him a given work. If you have any question as to your post of duty, pray to God for guidance, and your work will be assigned. God has told us expressly that He has placed every man at his post.

"To one is given by the Spirit the word of wisdom; to another the word of knowledge by the same Spirit; to another faith by the same Spirit; to another the gifts of healing by the same Spirit; to another the working of miracles; to another prophecy; to another discerning of spirits; to another divers kinds of tongues; to another the interpretation of tongues: but all these worketh that one and the selfsame Spirit" (1 Cor. 12:8-11).

"But unto every one of us is given grace according to the measure of the gift of Christ. . . . When he ascended up on high, he led captivity captive, and gave gifts unto men. . . . He gave some, apostles; and some, prophets; and some, evangelists; and some, pastors and teachers; for the perfecting of the saints, for the work of the ministry, for the edifying of the body of Christ: till we all come in the unity of the faith, and of the knowledge of the Son of God, unto a perfect man, unto the measure of the stature of the fulness of Christ" (Eph. 4:7-13). Here the members of the church of God are shown acting their different parts, all under the supervision of the great Master Worker, who knows just what each one in His service should do to meet the necessities that arise.—*Bible Training School*, Apr. 1, 1903.

FEELING THE NEED FOR THE SPIRITUAL GIFTS

And I thank Christ Jesus our Lord, who hath enabled me, for that he counted me faithful, putting me into the ministry; who was before a blasphemer, and a persecutor, and injurious: but I obtained mercy, because I did it ignorantly in unbelief. And the grace of our Lord was exceeding abundant with faith and love which is in Christ Jesus. 1 Tim. 1:12-14.

Those who would be successful in winning souls to Christ must carry with them the divine influence of the Holy Spirit. But how little is known concerning the operation of the Spirit of God. How little has been said of the importance of being endowed by the Holy Spirit, and yet it is through the agency of the Holy Spirit that men are to be drawn to Christ, and through His power alone can the soul be made pure. The Saviour said: "And when he is come, he will reprove the world of sin, and of righteousness, and of judgment" (John 16:8).

Christ has promised the gift of the Holy Spirit to His church, but how little is this promise appreciated. How seldom is [the Spirit's] power felt in the church; how little is His power spoken of before the people. The Saviour has said: "Ye shall receive power, after that the Holy Ghost is come upon you: and ye shall be witnesses unto me" (Acts 1:8). With the reception of this gift, all other gifts would be ours; for we are to have this gift according to the plentitude of the riches of the grace of Christ, and He is ready to supply every soul according to the capacity to receive. Then let us not be satisfied with only a little of this blessing, only that amount which will keep us from the slumber of death, but let us diligently seek for the abundance of the grace of God.

God grant that His converting power may be felt throughout this large assembly. Oh, that the power of God may rest upon the people. What we need is daily piety. We need to search the Scriptures daily, to pray earnestly that by the power of the Holy Spirit God may fit every one of us up to work in our place in His vineyard. No one is prepared to educate and strengthen the church unless he has received the gift of the Holy Spirit.—*Review and Herald*, Mar. 29, 1892.

GIVEN BY INSPIRATION OF GOD

All scripture is given by inspiration of God, and is profitable for doctrine, for reproof, for correction, for instruction in righteousness. 2 Tim. 3:16.

The Bible points to God as its author; yet it was written by human hands; and in the varied style of its different books it presents the characteristics of the several writers. The truths revealed are all "given by inspiration of God"; yet they are expressed in the words of men. The Infinite One by His Holy Spirit has shed light into the minds and hearts of His servants. He has given dreams and visions, symbols and figures; and those to whom the truth was thus revealed have themselves embodied the thought in human language.

The Ten Commandments were spoken by God Himself, and were written by His own hand. They are of divine and not of human composition. But the Bible, with its God-given truths expressed in the language of men, presents a union of the divine and the human. Such a union existed in the nature of Christ, who was the Son of God and the Son of man. Thus it is true of the Bible, as it was of Christ, that "the Word was made flesh, and dwelt among us" (John 1:14).

Written in different ages, by men who differed widely in rank and occupation, and in mental and spiritual endowments, the books of the Bible present a wide contrast in style, as well as a diversity in the nature of the subjects unfolded. Different forms of expression are employed by different writers; often the same truth is more strikingly presented by one than by another. And as several writers present a subject under varied aspects and relations, there may appear, to the superficial, careless, or prejudiced reader, to be discrepancy or contradiction, where the thoughtful, reverent student, with clearer insight, discerns the underlying harmony.—*The Great Controversy*, pp. v, vi.

VARIETY IN STYLES

We have also a more sure word of prophecy; whereunto ye do well that ye take heed, as unto a light that shineth in a dark place, until the day dawn, and the day star arise in your hearts. 2 Peter 1:19.

The writers of the Bible had to express their ideas in human language. It was written by human men. These men were inspired of the Holy Spirit. Because of the imperfections of human understanding of language, or the perversity of the human mind, ingenious in evading truth, many read and understand the Bible to please themselves. It is not that the difficulty is in the Bible. Opposing politicians argue points of law in the statute book, and take opposite views in their application and in these laws.

The Scriptures were given to men, not in a continuous chain of unbroken utterances, but piece by piece through successive generations, as God in His providence saw a fitting opportunity to impress man at sundry times and divers places. Men wrote as they were moved upon by the Holy Ghost. There is "first the bud, then the blossom, and next the fruit," "first the blade, then the ear, after that the full corn in the ear" (Mark 4:28). This is exactly what the Bible utterances are to us.

There is not always perfect order or apparent unity in the Scriptures. The miracles of Christ are not given in exact order, but are given just as the circumstances occurred, which called for this divine revealing of the power of Christ. The truths of the Bible are as pearls hidden. They must be searched, dug out by painstaking effort. Those who take only a surface view of the Scriptures will, with their superficial knowledge, which they think is very deep, talk of the contradictions of the Bible, and question the authority of the Scriptures. But those whose hearts are in harmony with truth and duty will search the Scriptures with a heart prepared to receive divine impressions.—*Selected Messages*, book 1, pp. 19, 20.

WRITERS IMPRESSED
BY DIFFERENT ASPECTS

For the prophecy came not in old time by the will of man: but holy men of God spake as they were moved by the Holy Ghost. 2 Peter 1:21.

As presented through different individuals [in the Bible], the truth is brought out in its varied aspects. One writer is more strongly impressed with one phase of the subject; he grasps those points that harmonize with his experience or with his power of perception and appreciation; another seizes upon a different phase; and each, under the guidance of the Holy Spirit, presents what is most forcibly impressed upon his own mind—a different aspect of the truth in each, but a perfect harmony through all. And the truths thus revealed unite to form a perfect whole, adapted to meet the wants of men in all the circumstances and experiences of life.

God has been pleased to communicate His truth to the world by human agencies, and He Himself, by His Holy Spirit, qualified men and enabled them to do this work. He guided the mind in the selection of what to speak and what to write. The treasure was entrusted to earthen vessels, yet it is, nonetheless, from heaven. The testimony is conveyed through the imperfect expression of human language, yet it is the testimony of God; and the obedient, believing child of God beholds in it the glory of a divine power, full of grace and truth.

In His Word, God has committed to men the knowledge necessary for salvation. The Holy Scriptures are to be accepted as an authoritative, infallible revelation of His will. They are the standard of character, the revealer of doctrines, and the test of experience. "Every scripture inspired of God is also profitable for teaching, for reproof, for correction, for instruction which is in righteousness: that the man of God may be complete, furnished completely unto every good work" (2 Tim. 3:16, 17, RV).—*The Great Controversy*, pp. vi, vii.

DIVINE MESSAGE IN HUMAN LANGUAGE

God, who at sundry times and in divers manners spake in time past unto the fathers by the prophets, hath in these last days spoken unto us by his Son, whom he hath appointed heir of all things, by whom also he made the worlds. Heb. 1:1, 2.

The Bible is not given to us in grand superhuman language. Jesus, in order to reach man where he is, took humanity. The Bible must be given in the language of men. Everything that is human is imperfect. Different meanings are expressed by the same word; there is not one word for each distinct idea. The Bible was given for practical purposes.

The stamps of minds are different. All do not understand expressions and statements alike. Some understand the statements of the Scriptures to suit their own particular minds and cases. Prepossessions, prejudices, and passions have a strong influence to darken the understanding and confuse the mind even in reading the words of Holy Writ. . . .

The Bible is written by inspired men, but it is not God's mode of thought and expression. It is that of humanity. God, as a writer, is not represented. Men will often say such an expression is not like God. But God has not put Himself in words, in logic, in rhetoric, on trial in the Bible. The writers of the Bible were God's penmen, not His pen. Look at the different writers.

It is not the words of the Bible that are inspired, but the men that were inspired. Inspiration acts not on the man's words or his expressions but on the man himself, who, under the influence of the Holy Ghost, is imbued with thoughts. But the words receive the impress of the individual mind. The divine mind is diffused. The divine mind and will is combined with the human mind and will; thus the utterances of the man are the Word of God.—*Selected Messages*, book 1, pp. 20, 21.

THEOPHANIES:
DIVINE PRESENCE WITH HUMANS

And the angel of the Lord appeared unto him in a flame of fire out of the midst of a bush: and he looked, and, behold, the bush burned with fire, and the bush was not consumed. Ex. 3:2.

Friday, March 20 [1896], I arose early, about half past three o'clock in the morning. While [I was] writing upon the fifteenth chapter of John suddenly a wonderful peace came upon me. The whole room seemed to be filled with the atmosphere of heaven. A holy, sacred Presence seemed to be in my room. I laid down my pen and was in a waiting attitude to see what the Spirit would say unto me. I saw no person. I heard no audible voice, but a heavenly Watcher seemed close beside me; I felt that I was in the presence of Jesus.

The sweet peace and light which seemed to be in my room it is impossible for me to explain or describe. A sacred, holy atmosphere surrounded me, and there were presented to my mind and understanding matters of intense interest and importance. A line of action was laid out before me as if the unseen Presence was speaking with me. The matter I had been writing upon seemed to be lost to my mind and another matter distinctly opened before me. A great awe seemed to be upon me as matters were imprinted upon my mind.—*Selected Messages*, book 3, pp. 35, 36.

I arose early Thursday morning, about two o'clock, and was writing busily upon [the subject of] the True Vine, when I felt a Presence in my room, as I have many times before, and I lost all recollection of what I was about. I seemed to be in the presence of Jesus. He was communicating to me that in which I was to be instructed. Everything was so plain that I could not misunderstand.—*Ibid.*, p. 36.

DIVERSE WAYS OF
INSPIRATION: THE VISIONARY

It is not expedient for me doubtless to glory. I will come to visions and revelations of the Lord. I knew a man in Christ above fourteen years ago, (whether in the body, I cannot tell; or whether out of the body, I cannot tell: God knoweth;) such an one caught up to the third heaven. 2 Cor. 12:1, 2.

As inquiries are frequently made as to my state in vision, and after I come out, I would say that when the Lord sees fit to give a vision, I am taken into the presence of Jesus and angels, and am entirely lost to earthly things. I can see no farther than the angel directs me. My attention is often directed to scenes transpiring upon earth.

At times I am carried far ahead into the future and shown what is to take place. Then again I am shown things as they have occurred in the past. After I come out of vision I do not at once remember all that I have seen, and the matter is not so clear before me until I write, then the scene rises before me as was presented in vision, and I can write with freedom.

Sometimes the things which I have seen are hid from me after I come out of vision, and I cannot call them to mind until I am brought before a company where that vision applies, then the things which I have seen come to my mind with force. I am just as dependent upon the Spirit of the Lord in relating or writing a vision, as in having the vision. It is impossible for me to call up things which have been shown me unless the Lord brings them before me at the time that He is pleased to have me relate or write them.—*Selected Messages*, book 1, pp. 36, 37.

Although I am as dependent upon the Spirit of the Lord in writing my views as I am in receiving them, yet the words I employ in describing what I have seen are my own, unless they be those spoken to me by an angel, which I always enclose in marks of quotation.—*Ibid.*, p. 37.

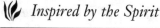

THE HISTORIAN:
USING SECULAR SOURCES

Forasmuch as many have taken in hand to set forth in order a declaration of those things which are most surely believed among us, even as they delivered them unto us, which from the beginning were eyewitnesses, and ministers of the word; it seemed good to me also, having had perfect understanding of all things from the very first, to write unto thee in order, most excellent Theophilus. Luke 1:1-3.

As the Spirit of God has opened to my mind the great truths of His Word, and the scenes of the past and the future, I have been bidden to make known to others that which has thus been revealed—to trace the history of the controversy in past ages, and especially so to present it as to shed a light on the fast-approaching struggle of the future. In pursuance of this purpose, I have endeavored to select and group together events in the history of the church in such a manner as to trace the unfolding of the great testing truths that at different periods have been given to the world, that have excited the wrath of Satan, and the enmity of a world-loving church, and that have been maintained by the witness of those who "loved not their lives unto the death" (Rev. 12:11). . . .

The great events which have marked the progress of reform in past ages are matters of history, well known and universally acknowledged by the Protestant world; they are facts which none can gainsay. This history I have presented briefly, in accordance with the scope of the book, and the brevity which must necessarily be observed, the facts having been condensed into as little space as seemed consistent with a proper understanding of their application.

In some cases where a historian has so grouped together events as to afford, in brief, a comprehensive view of the subject, or has summarized details in a convenient manner, his words have been quoted; but in some instances no specific credit has been given, since the quotations are not given for the purpose of citing that writer as authority, but because his statement affords a ready and forcible presentation of the subject.

In narrating the experience and views of those carrying forward the work of reform in our own time, similar use has been made of their published works.—*The Great Controversy*, pp. xi, xii.

THE EYEWITNESS:
INSPIRED TO GIVE TESTIMONY

That which we have seen and heard declare we unto you, that ye also may have fellowship with us: and truly our fellowship is with the Father, and with his Son Jesus Christ. 1 John 1:3.

The work begun in feebleness and obscurity has continued to increase and strengthen. Publishing houses and missions in many lands attest its growth. In place of the edition of our first paper carried to the post office in a carpetbag, many hundreds of thousands of copies of our various periodicals are now sent out monthly from the offices of publication. The hand of God has been with His work to prosper and build it up.

The later history of my life would involve the history of many of the enterprises which have arisen among us, and with which my lifework has been closely intermingled. For the upbuilding of these institutions, my husband and [I] labored with pen and voice. To notice, even briefly, the experiences of these active and busy years would far exceed the limits of this sketch. Satan's efforts to hinder the work and to destroy the workmen have not ceased; but God has had a care for His servants and for His work.

In reviewing our past history, having traveled over every step of advance to our present standing, I can say, Praise God! As I see what the Lord has wrought, I am filled with astonishment, and with confidence in Christ as leader. We have nothing to fear for the future, except as we shall forget the way the Lord has led us, and His teaching in our past history.

We are debtors to God to use every advantage He has entrusted to us to beautify the truth by holiness of character, and to send the messages of warning, and of comfort, of hope and love, to those who are in the darkness of error and sin.—*Life Sketches*, pp. 195, 196.

THE COUNSELOR:
GIVING INSPIRED ADVICE

For out of much affliction and anguish of heart I wrote unto you with many tears; not that ye should be grieved, but that ye might know the love which I have more abundantly unto you. 2 Cor. 2:4.

When I went to Colorado I was so burdened for you that, in my weakness, I wrote many pages to be read at your camp meeting. Weak and trembling, I arose at three o'clock in the morning to write to you. God was speaking through clay. You might say that this communication was only a letter. Yes, it was a letter, but prompted by the Spirit of God, to bring before your minds things that had been shown me. In these letters which I write, in the testimonies I bear, I am presenting to you that which the Lord has presented to me. I do not write one article in the paper, expressing merely my own ideas. They are what God has opened before me in vision—the precious rays of light shining from the throne. . . .

What voice will you acknowledge as the voice of God? What power has the Lord in reserve to correct your errors and show you your course as it is? What power to work in the church? If you refuse to believe until every shadow of uncertainty and every possibility of doubt is removed, you will never believe. The doubt that demands perfect knowledge will never yield to faith. Faith rests upon evidence, not demonstration. The Lord requires us to obey the voice of duty, when there are other voices all around us urging us to pursue an opposite course. It requires earnest attention from us to distinguish the voice which speaks from God. We must resist and conquer inclination, and obey the voice of conscience without parleying or compromise, lest its promptings cease, and will and impulse control.

The word of the Lord comes to us all who have not resisted His Spirit by determining not to hear and obey. This voice is heard in warnings, in counsels, in reproof. It is the Lord's message of light to His people. If we wait for louder calls or better opportunities, the light may be withdrawn, and we left in darkness.—*Selected Messages*, book 1, pp. 27, 28.

THE LEADER:
CALLING FOR COMMITMENT

And if it seem evil unto you to serve the Lord, choose you this day whom ye will serve; whether the gods which your fathers served that were on the other side of the flood, or the gods of the Amorites, in whose land ye dwell: but as for me and my house, we will serve the Lord. Joshua 24:15.

I feel a special interest in the movements and decisions that shall be made at this conference [the 1901 General Conference session] regarding the things that should have been done years ago, and especially ten years ago, when we were assembled in conference, and the Spirit and power of God came into our meeting, testifying that God was ready to work for this people if they would come into working order. . . .

The light then given me was that this people should stand higher than any other people on the face of the whole earth, that they should be a loyal people, a people who would rightly represent truth. The sanctifying power of the truth, revealed in their lives, was to distinguish them from the world. They were to stand in moral dignity, having such a close connection with heaven that the Lord God of Israel could give them a place in the earth.

Year after year the same acknowledgment was made, but the principles which exalt a people were not woven into the work. God gave them clear light as to what they should do, and what they should not do, but they departed from that light, and it is a marvel to me that we stand in as much prosperity as we do today. It is because of the great mercy of our God, not because of our righteousness, but that His name should not be dishonored in the world. . . .

The Word of God is to be our guide. Have you given heed to the Word? The Testimonies are not by any means to take the place of the Word. They are to bring you to that neglected Word, that you may eat the words of Christ, that you may feed upon them, that by living faith you may be built up from that upon which you feed. If you live in obedience to Christ and His Word, you are eating the leaves of the tree of life, which are for the healing of the nations.—*General Conference Bulletin,* Apr. 3, 1901.

THE WRITER:
PUBLISHING BY GOD'S ORDERS

And he that sat upon the throne said, Behold, I make all things new. And he said unto me, Write: for these words are true and faithful. Rev. 21:5.

Sister White is not the originator of these books. They contain the instruction that during her lifework God has been giving her. They contain the precious, comforting light that God has graciously given His servant to be given to the world. From their pages this light is to shine into the hearts of men and women, leading them to the Saviour. The Lord has declared that these books are to be scattered throughout the world. There is in them truth which to the receiver is a savor of life unto life. They are silent witnesses for God.

In the past they have been the means in His hands of convicting and converting many souls. Many have read them with eager expectation, and, by reading them, have been led to see the efficacy of Christ's atonement, and to trust in its power. They have been led to commit the keeping of their souls to their Creator, waiting and hoping for the coming of the Saviour to take His loved ones to their eternal home. In the future, these books are to make the gospel plain to many others, revealing to them the way of salvation.

The Lord has sent His people much instruction, line upon line, precept upon precept, here a little, and there a little. Little heed is given to the Bible, and the Lord has given a lesser light to lead men and women to the greater light. Oh, how much good would be accomplished if the books containing this light were read with a determination to carry out the principles they contain! There would be a thousandfold greater vigilance, a thousandfold more self-denial and resolute effort. And many more would now be rejoicing in the light of present truth.

My brethren and sisters, work earnestly to circulate these books. Put your hearts into this work, and the blessing of God will be with you. Go forth in faith, praying that God will prepare hearts to receive the light. Be pleasant and courteous. Show by a consistent course that you are true Christians. Walk and work in the light of heaven, and your path will be as the path of the just, shining more and more unto the perfect day.—*Review and Herald*, Jan. 20, 1903.

REASONS FOR THE GIFT: TO DEFINE TRUTH

At the beginning of thy supplications the commandment came forth, and I am come to shew thee; for thou art greatly beloved: therefore understand the matter, and consider the vision. Dan. 9:23.

After the passing of the time in 1844 we searched for the truth as for hidden treasure. I met with the brethren, and we studied and prayed earnestly. Often we remained together until late at night, and sometimes through the entire night, praying for light and studying the Word. Again and again these brethren came together to study the Bible, in order that they might know its meaning, and be prepared to teach it with power. When they came to the point in their study where they said, "We can do nothing more," the Spirit of the Lord would come upon me. I would be taken off in vision, and a clear explanation of the passages we had been studying would be given me, with instruction as to how we were to labor and teach effectively. Thus light was given that helped us to understand the scriptures in regard to Christ, His mission, and His priesthood. A line of truth extending from that time to the time when we shall enter the city of God was made plain to me, and I gave to others the instruction that the Lord had given me.

During this whole time I could not understand the reasoning of the brethren. My mind was locked, as it were, and I could not comprehend the meaning of the scriptures we were studying. This was one of the greatest sorrows of my life. I was in this condition of mind until all the principal points of our faith were made clear to our minds, in harmony with the Word of God. The brethren knew that, when not in vision, I could not understand these matters, and they accepted, as light directly from heaven, the revelations given.

Many errors arose, and though I was then little more than a child, I was sent by the Lord from place to place to rebuke those who were holding these false doctrines. There were those who were in danger of going into fanaticism, and I was bidden in the name of the Lord to give them a warning from heaven.—*Review and Herald*, May 25, 1905.

TO ESTABLISH BIBLE TRUTH

That the God of our Lord Jesus Christ, the Father of glory, may give unto you the spirit of wisdom and revelation in the knowledge of him. Eph. 1:17.

The truths that have been unfolding in their order, as we have advanced along the line of prophecy revealed in the Word of God, are truth, sacred, eternal truth today. Those who passed over the ground step by step in the past history of our experience, seeing the chain of truth in the prophecies, were prepared to accept and obey every ray of light. They were praying, fasting, searching, digging for the truth as for hidden treasures, and the Holy Spirit, we know, was teaching and guiding us.

Many theories were advanced, bearing a semblance of truth, but so mingled with misinterpreted and misapplied scriptures that they led to dangerous errors. Very well do we know how every point of truth was established, and the seal set upon it by the Holy Spirit of God. And all the time voices were heard, "Here is the truth," "I have the truth; follow me." But the warnings came, "Go not ye after them. I have not sent them, but they ran" (see Jer. 23:21).

The leadings of the Lord were marked, and most wonderful were His revelations of what is truth. Point after point was established by the Lord God of heaven. That which was truth then is truth today. But the voices do not cease to be heard—"This is truth. I have new light." But these new lights in prophetic lines are manifest in misapplying the Word and setting the people of God adrift without an anchor to hold them. If the student of the Word would take the truths which God has revealed in the leadings of His people, and appropriate these truths, digest them, and bring them into their practical life, they would then be living channels of light. But those who have set themselves to study out new theories have a mixture of truth and error combined, and, after trying to make these things prominent, have demonstrated that they have not kindled their taper from the divine altar, and it has gone out in darkness.—*Manuscript Releases*, vol. 17, pp. 4, 5.

To Build Upon the Foundation

And are built upon the foundation of the apostles and prophets, Jesus Christ himself being the chief corner stone. Eph. 2:20.

Let not any man enter upon the work of tearing down the foundations of the truth that have made us what we are. God has led His people forward step by step though there were pitfalls of error on every side. Under the wonderful guidance of a plain "Thus saith the Lord," a truth has been established that has stood the test of trial. When men arise and attempt to draw away disciples after them, meet them with the truths that have been tried as by fire.

"And unto the angel of the church in Sardis write: These things saith he that hath the seven Spirits of God, and the seven stars; I know thy works, that thou hast a name that thou livest, and art dead. Be watchful, and strengthen the things which remain, that are ready to die: for I have not found thy works perfect before God. Remember therefore how thou hast received and heard, and hold fast, and repent. If therefore thou shalt not watch, I will come on thee as a thief, and thou shalt not know what hour I will come upon thee" (Rev. 3:1-3).

Those who seek to remove the old landmarks are not holding fast; they are not remembering how they have received and heard. Those who try to bring in theories that would remove the pillars of our faith concerning the sanctuary or concerning the personality of God or of Christ are working as blind men. They are seeking to bring in uncertainties and to set the people of God adrift without an anchor.

Those who claim to be identified with the message that God has given us should have keen, clear spiritual perceptions, that they may distinguish truth from error. The word spoken by the messenger of God is "Wake up the watchmen." If men will discern the spirit of the messages given and strive to find out from what source they come, the Lord God of Israel will guard them from being led astray.—Manuscript Release 760, pp. 9, 10.

TO MEET FANATICISM

For we have not followed cunningly devised fables, when we made known unto you the power and coming of our Lord Jesus Christ, but were eyewitnesses of his majesty. 2 Peter 1:16.

Again and again in past years I have been bidden to speak in protest against the fanciful and forbidden schemes that have been presented by one and another. My message has ever been, Preach the Word in simplicity and all humility; present clear, unadulterated truth to the people. Open no door to fanatical movements, for the influence of these is to bring confusion of mind and discouragement and lack of faith to God's people. . . .

Whenever I have been called to meet fanaticism in its varied forms, I have received clear, positive, and definite instruction to lift my voice against its influence. With some the evil has revealed itself in the form of man-made tests for ascertaining a knowledge of the will of God; and I was shown that this was a delusion which became an infatuation, and that it is contrary to the will of the Lord. If we follow such methods, we shall be found aiding the enemy's plans. In times past certain among the believers had great faith in the setting of signs by which to decide their duty. Some had such confidence in these signs that men went so far as to exchange wives, thus bringing adultery into the church.

I have been shown that deceptions like those we were called to meet in the early experiences of the message would be repeated, and that we shall have to meet them again in the closing days of the work. At this time we are required to bring all our powers under the control of God, exercising our faculties in accordance with the light He has given. Read the fourth and fifth chapters of Matthew. Study Matthew 4:8-10; also chapter 5:13. Meditate upon the sacred work that was carried forward by Christ. It is thus that the principles of the Word of God are to be brought into our labors.—*Selected Messages*, book 2, pp. 28, 29.

To Prevent Fanaticism

Take heed therefore unto yourselves, and to all the flock, over the which the Holy Ghost hath made you overseers, to feed the church of God, which he hath purchased with his own blood. For I know this, that after my departing shall grievous wolves enter in among you, not sparing the flock. Also of your own selves shall men arise, speaking perverse things, to draw away disciples after them. Acts 20:28-30.

Fanaticism will appear in the very midst of us. Deceptions will come, and of such a character that if it were possible they would mislead the very elect. If marked inconsistencies and untruthful utterances were apparent in these manifestations, the words from the lips of the Great Teacher would not be needed. It is because of the many and varied dangers that would arise, that this warning is given.

The reason why I hang out the danger signal is that through the enlightenment of the Spirit of God I can see that which my brethren do not discern. It may not be a positive necessity for me to point out all these peculiar phases of deception that they will need to guard against. It is enough for me to tell you, Be on your guard; and as faithful sentinels keep the flock of God from accepting indiscriminately all that professes to be communicated to them from the Lord. If we work to create an excitement of feeling, we shall have all we want, and more than we can possibly know how to manage. Calmly and clearly "Preach the Word." We must not regard it as our work to create an excitement.

The Holy Spirit of God alone can create a healthy enthusiasm. Let God work, and let the human agent walk softly before Him, watching, waiting, praying, looking unto Jesus every moment, led and controlled by the precious Spirit, which is light and life.—*Selected Messages*, book 2, pp. 16, 17.

TO AVOID DOCTRINAL ERRORS

And account that the longsuffering of our Lord is salvation; even as our beloved brother Paul also according to the wisdom given unto him hath written unto you; as also in all his epistles, speaking in them of these things; in which are some things hard to be understood, which they that are unlearned and unstable wrest, as they do also the other scriptures, unto their own destruction. 2 Peter 3:15, 16.

The Lord will certainly do great things for us if we will hunger and thirst after righteousness. We are the purchased property of Jesus Christ. We must not lose our devotion, our consecration. We are in conflict with the errors and delusions that have to be swept away from the minds of those who have not acted upon the light they already have. Bible truth is our only safety.

I know and understand that we are to be established in the faith, in the light of the truth given us in our early experience. At that time one error after another pressed in upon us, and ministers and doctors brought in new doctrines. We would search the Scriptures with much prayer and the Holy Spirit would bring the truth to our minds. Sometimes whole nights would be devoted to searching the Scriptures and earnestly asking God for guidance. Companies of earnest, devoted men and women assembled for this purpose. The power of God would come upon me and I was enabled clearly to define what is truth and what is error.

As the points of our faith were thus established, our feet were placed upon a solid foundation. We accepted the truth point by point under the demonstration of the Holy Spirit. I would be taken off in vision and explanations would be given me. I was given illustrations of heavenly things and of the sanctuary, so that we were placed where light was shining on us in clear, distinct rays.

All these truths are immortalized in my writings. The Lord never denies His Word. Men may get up scheme after scheme, and the enemy will seek to seduce souls from the truth, but all who believe that the Lord has spoken through Sister White, and has given her a message, will be safe from the many delusions that will come in in these last days.—Manuscript Release 760, pp. 22, 23.

TO WARN ABOUT FUTURE DECEPTIONS

But there were false prophets also among the people, even as there shall be false teachers among you, who privily shall bring in damnable heresies, even denying the Lord that bought them, and bring upon themselves swift destruction. 2 Peter 2:1.

In the future, deception of every kind is to arise, and we want solid ground for our feet. We want solid pillars for the building. Not one pin is to be removed from that which the Lord has established. The enemy will bring in false theories, such as the doctrine that there is no sanctuary. This is one of the points on which there will be a departing from the faith. Where shall we find safety unless it be in the truths that the Lord has been giving for the last fifty years?

I want to tell you that Christ lives. He makes intercession for us, and He will save everyone who will come to Him in faith and obey His directions. But remember that He does not want you to give your energies to criticism of your brethren. Attend to the salvation of your own soul. Do the work God has given you. You will find so much to do that you will have no inclination to criticize someone else. Use the talent of speech to help and bless. If you do the work God has given you, you will have a message to bear, and you will understand what is meant by the sanctification of the Spirit.

Do not think that Satan is not doing anything. Do not think that his army is passive. He and his agencies are on the ground today. We are to put on the whole armor of God. Having done all, we are to stand, meeting principalities and powers and spiritual wickedness in high places. And if we have on the heavenly armor, we shall find that the assaults of the enemy will not have power over us. Angels of God will be round about us to protect us. I have the assurance of God that thus it will be.

In the name of the Lord God of Israel I ask you to come up to the help of the Lord, to the help of the Lord against the mighty. If you do this, you will have on your side a strong Helper, a personal Saviour. You will be covered with the shield of providence. God will make a way for you, so that you will never be overtaken by the enemy.—*Review and Herald*, May 25, 1905.

GOD'S PLANS FOR THE WORK OF THE CHURCH: EDUCATIONAL WORK

The fear of the Lord is the beginning of wisdom: and the knowledge of the holy is understanding. Prov. 9:10.

The true object of education is to fit men and women for service by developing and bringing into active exercise all their faculties. The work at our colleges and training schools should be strengthened year by year, for in them our youth are to be prepared to go forth to serve the Lord as efficient laborers. The Lord calls upon the youth to enter our schools, and quickly fit themselves for active work. Time is short. Workers for Christ are needed everywhere. Urgent inducements should be held out to those who ought now to be engaged in earnest effort for the Master.

Our schools have been established by the Lord; and if they are conducted in harmony with His purpose, the youth sent to them will be quickly prepared to engage in various branches of missionary work. Some will be trained to enter the field as missionary nurses, some as canvassers, some as evangelists, and some as gospel ministers. Some are to be prepared to take charge of church schools, in which the children shall be taught the first principles of education. This is a very important work, demanding high ability and careful study.

Satan is trying to lead men and women away from right principles. The enemy of all good, he desires to see human beings so trained that they will exert their influence on the side of error, instead of using their talents to bless their fellow men. And multitudes who profess to belong to God's true church are falling under his deceptions. They are being led to turn away from their allegiance to the King of heaven. . . .

It is to fortify the youth against the temptations of the enemy that we have established schools where they may be qualified for usefulness in this life and for the service of God throughout eternity. Those who have an eye single to God's glory will earnestly desire to fit themselves for special service; for the love of Christ will have a controlling influence upon them. This love imparts more than finite energy, and qualifies human beings for divine achievement.—*Counsels to Parents and Teachers*, pp. 493-495.

THE MEDICAL MINISTRY

How God anointed Jesus of Nazareth with the Holy Ghost and with power: who went about doing good, and healing all that were oppressed of the devil; for God was with him. Acts 10:38.

Our work is clearly defined. As the Father sent His only-begotten Son into our world, even so Christ sends us, His disciples, as His medical missionary workers. In fulfilling this high and holy mission, we are to do the will of God. No one man's mind or judgment is to be our criterion of what constitutes genuine medical missionary work. . . .

True medical missionary work is of heavenly origin. It was not originated by any person who lives. But in connection with this work we see so much which dishonors God that I am instructed to say, The medical missionary work is of divine origin, and has a most glorious mission to fulfill. In all its bearings it is to be in conformity with Christ's work. Those who are workers together with God will just as surely represent the character of Christ as Christ represented the character of His Father while in this world.

I am instructed to say that God will have the medical missionary work cleansed from the tarnish of earthliness, and elevated to stand in its true position before the world. When schemes that imperil souls are brought into connection with this work, its influence is destroyed. This is why there have arisen in the carrying forward of medical missionary work many perplexities that demand our careful consideration. . . .

Nothing will help us more at this stage of our work than to understand and to fulfill the mission of the greatest Medical Missionary that ever trod the earth; nothing will help us more than to realize how sacred is this kind of work and how perfectly it corresponds with the lifework of the Great Missionary. The object of our mission is the same as the object of Christ's mission. Why did God send His Son to the fallen world? To make known and to demonstrate to mankind His love for them. Christ came as a Redeemer. Throughout His ministry He was to keep prominent His mission to save sinners.—*Medical Ministry*, p. 24.

THE PUBLISHING WORK

And he said unto me, Thou must prophesy again before many peoples, and nations, and tongues, and kings. Rev. 10:11.

Our publishing work was established by the direction of God and under His special supervision. It was designed to accomplish a specific purpose. Seventh-day Adventists have been chosen by God as a peculiar people, separate from the world. By the great cleaver of truth He has cut them out from the quarry of the world and brought them into connection with Himself. He has made them His representatives and has called them to be ambassadors for Him in the last work of salvation. The greatest wealth of truth ever entrusted to mortals, the most solemn and fearful warnings ever sent by God to man, have been committed to them to be given to the world; and in the accomplishment of this work our publishing houses are among the most effective agencies.

These institutions are to stand as witnesses for God, teachers of righteousness to the people. From them truth is to go forth as a lamp that burneth. Like a great light in a lighthouse on a dangerous coast, they are constantly to send forth beams of light into the darkness of the world, to warn men of the dangers that threaten them with destruction.

The publications sent forth from our printing houses are to prepare a people to meet God. Throughout the world they are to do the same work that was done by John the Baptist for the Jewish nation. By startling messages of warning, God's prophet awakened men from worldly dreaming. Through him God called backsliding Israel to repentance. By his presentation of truth he exposed popular delusions. In contrast with the false theories of his time, truth in his teaching stood forth as an eternal certainty. "Repent ye: for the kingdom of heaven is at hand" was John's message (Matt. 3:2). This same message, through the publications from our printing houses, is to be given to the world today.—*Testimonies*, vol. 7, pp. 138, 139.

WELFARE MINISTRY

And Jesus went about all the cities and villages, teaching in their syna-gogues, and preaching the gospel of the kingdom, and healing every sick-ness and every disease among the people. But when he saw the multitudes, he was moved with compassion on them, because they fainted, and were scattered abroad, as sheep having no shepherd. Matt. 9:35, 36.

The Lord continually performed deeds of loving ministry, and this every minister of the gospel should do. He has appointed us to be His ambassadors, to carry forward His work in the world. To every true, self-sacrificing worker is given the commission "Go ye into all the world, and preach the gospel to every creature" (Mark 16:15).

Read carefully the instruction given in the New Testament. The work that the Great Teacher did in connection with His disciples is the example we are to follow in our medical missionary work. But have we followed this example? The glad tidings of salvation are to be pro-claimed in every village, town, and city. But where are the missionaries? In the name of God I ask, Where are the laborers together with God?

It is only by an unselfish interest in those in need of help that we can give a practical demonstration of the truths of the gospel. "If a brother or sister be naked, and destitute of daily food, and one of you say unto them, Depart in peace, be ye warmed and filled; notwithstanding ye give them not those things which are needful to the body; what doth it profit? Even so faith, if it hath not works, is dead, being alone" (James 2:15-17). "And now abideth faith, hope, charity, these three; but the greatest of these is charity" (1 Cor. 13:13).

Much more than mere sermonizing is included in preaching the gospel. The ignorant are to be enlightened; the discouraged are to be uplifted; the sick are to be healed. The human voice is to act its part in God's work. Words of tenderness, sympathy, and love are to witness to the truth. Earnest, heartfelt prayers are to bring the angels near.

The evangelization of the world is the work that God has given to those who go forth in His name. They are to be colaborers with Christ, revealing to those ready to perish His tender, pitying love.—*Review and Herald*, Mar. 4, 1902.

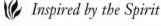

THE HEALTH FOOD MINISTRY

And when it was evening, his disciples came to him, saying, This is a desert place, and the time is now past; send the multitude away, that they may go into the villages, and buy themselves victuals. But Jesus said unto them, They need not depart; give ye them to eat. Matt. 14:15, 16.

I have earnest words to speak to those who shall engage in the health food business. There is to be an entirely different feature brought into the work of our food stores, restaurants, and into every line in which our food productions are handled. This work must be carried forward as a means of gospel enlightenment to those who have not given themselves to the Lord. Those who handle these foods need daily the counsel of the One who created food for the five thousand hungry men. The work of our food stores and restaurants must be carried on in such a way that there will be no loss financially. We must not forget that this line of work needs to live. But all corrupting influences must be weeded out from it.

Keep on the gaining side we must. But what is the use of carrying on this work if we have to sacrifice principles of justice, mercy, and the love of God? What is the use of carrying it on if through its influence, no souls are enlightened and prepared to lay hold upon the Word that is their spiritual food? Upon those connected with this work there should be urged the necessity of calling the attention of the people with whom they are brought into contact [to] the truths of heavenly origin.

There should be appointed to the health food work men who are well qualified to speak words in season, and out of season, and who can enlighten the minds of men and women in regard to the truth. Special wisdom is needed in order to understand when to speak, and when to keep silent. Let each worker pray much for spiritual understanding.—*The Health Food Ministry*, p. 89.

THE SUPPORT OF MISSIONS

That they do good, that they be rich in good works, ready to distribute, willing to communicate; laying up in store for themselves a good foundation against the time to come, that they may lay hold on eternal life. 1 Tim. 6:18, 19.

The mission of the church of Christ is to save perishing sinners. It is to make known the love of God to men, and to win them to Christ by the efficacy of that love. The truth for this time must be carried into the dark corners of the earth, and this work may begin at home.

The followers of Christ should not live selfish lives; but, imbued with the Spirit of Christ, they should work in harmony with Him.

He has given His people a plan for raising sums sufficient to make the enterprise self-sustaining. God's plan in the tithing system is beautiful in its simplicity and equality. All may take hold of it in faith and courage, for it is of divine origin. In it are combined simplicity and utility, and it does not require depth of learning to understand and execute it.

All may feel that they can act a part in carrying forward the precious work of salvation. Every man, woman, and youth may become a treasurer for God; and there would be no want of means with which to carry forward the great work of sounding the last message of warning to the [world].

The treasury will be full if all adopt this system, and the contributors will be left none the poorer. Through every investment made they will become more wedded to the cause of present truth. They will be "laying up in store for themselves a good foundation against the time to come, that they may lay hold on eternal life" (1 Tim. 6:19).

If the plan of systematic benevolence was adopted by every individual and fully carried out, there would be a constant supply in the treasury. The income would flow in like a steady stream constantly supplied by overflowing springs of benevolence.—*East Michigan Banner*, Jan. 18, 1905.

ADVICE FOR THE LEADERS

Feed the flock of God which is among you, taking the oversight thereof, not by constraint, but willingly; not for filthy lucre, but of a ready mind; neither as being lords over God's heritage, but being ensamples to the flock. 1 Peter 5:2, 3.

I am instructed to say to our ministering brethren, Let the messages that come from your lips be charged with the power of the Spirit of God. If ever there was a time when we needed the special guidance of the Holy Spirit, it is now. We need a thorough consecration. It is fully time that we gave to the world a demonstration of the power of God in our own lives and in our ministry.

The Lord desires to see the work of proclaiming the third angel's message carried forward with increasing efficiency. As He has worked in all ages to give victories to His people, so in this age He longs to carry to a triumphant fulfillment His purposes for His church. He bids His believing saints to advance unitedly, going from strength to greater strength, from faith to increased assurance and confidence in the truth and righteousness of His cause.

We are to stand firm as a rock to the principles of the Word of God, remembering that God is with us to give us strength to meet each new experience. Let us ever maintain in our lives the principles of righteousness, that we may go forward from strength to strength in the name of the Lord. We are to hold as very sacred the faith that has been substantiated by the instruction and approval of the Spirit of God from our earliest experience until the present time. We are to cherish as very precious the work that the Lord has been carrying forward through His command-keeping people, and which, through the power of His grace, will grow stronger and more efficient as time advances.

The enemy is seeking to becloud the discernment of God's people, and to weaken their efficiency, but if they will labor as the Spirit of God shall direct, He will open doors of opportunity before them for the work of building up the old waste places. Their experience will be one of constant growth, until the Lord shall descend from heaven with power and great glory to set His seal of final triumph upon His faithful ones.—*Review and Herald*, June 12, 1913.

DIVINE COUNSEL FOR PARENTS

I have written unto you, fathers, because ye have known him that is from the beginning. I have written unto you, young men, because ye are strong, and the word of God abideth in you, and ye have overcome the wicked one. 1 John 2:14.

Parents may understand that as they follow God's directions in the training of their children, they will receive help from on high. They receive much benefit; for as they teach, they learn. Their children will achieve victories through the knowledge that they have acquired in keeping the way of the Lord. They are enabled to overcome natural and hereditary tendencies to evil. By setting an example of kindness and patience, by molding the characters of their children after the divine Pattern, fathers and mothers become qualified to help the youth outside of their homes.

Parents, it is your work to develop in your children patience, constancy, and genuine love. In dealing aright with the children God has given you, you are helping them lay the foundation for pure, well-balanced characters. You are instilling into their minds principles which they will one day follow in their own families. The effect of your well-directed efforts will be seen as they conduct their households in the way of the Lord.

Blessed is the family where father and mother have surrendered themselves to God to do His will! One well-ordered, well-disciplined family tells more in behalf of Christianity than all the sermons that can be preached. Such a family gives evidence that the parents have been successful in following God's directions, and that their children will serve Him in the church. Their influence grows; for as they impart, they receive to impart again. The father and mother find helpers in their children, who give to others the instruction received in the home. The neighborhood in which they live is helped, for in it they have become enriched for time and for eternity. The whole family is engaged in the service of the Master; and by their godly example, others are inspired to be faithful and true to God in dealing with His flock, His beautiful flock.—*Review and Herald*, June 6, 1899.

ENCOURAGEMENT FOR THE ERRING

This then is the message which we have heard of him, and declare unto you, that God is light, and in him is no darkness at all. If we say that we have fellowship with him, and walk in darkness, we lie, and do not the truth: but if we walk in the light, as he is in the light, we have fellowship one with another, and the blood of Jesus Christ his Son cleanseth us from all sin. 1 John 1:5-7.

For half a century I have been the Lord's messenger, and as long as my life shall last I shall continue to bear the messages that God gives me for His people. I take no glory to myself; in my youth the Lord made me His messenger, to communicate to His people testimonies of encouragement, warning, and reproof. For sixty years I have been in communication with heavenly messengers, and I have been constantly learning in reference to divine things, and in reference to the way in which God is constantly working to bring souls from the error of their ways to the light in God's light.

Many souls have been helped because they have believed that the messages given me were sent in mercy to the erring. When I have seen those who needed a different phase of Christian experience, I have told them so, for their present and eternal good. And so long as the Lord spares my life, I will do my work faithfully, whether or not men and women shall hear and receive and obey. My work is clearly given me to do, and I shall receive grace in being obedient.

I love God. I love Jesus Christ, the Son of God, and I feel an intense interest in every soul who claims to be a child of God. I am determined to be a faithful steward so long as the Lord shall spare my life. I will not fail nor be discouraged. . . .

I love the Lord; I love my Saviour, and my life is wholly in the hands of God. As long as He sustains me, I shall bear a decided testimony.—*Manuscript Releases*, vol. 5, pp. 152, 153.

DIRECTIONS FOR THE YOUTH

In all thy ways acknowledge him, and he shall direct thy paths. Prov. 3:6.

There are great things expected from the sons and daughters of God. I look upon the youth of today, and my heart yearns over them. What possibilities are open before them! If they sincerely seek to learn of Christ, He will give them wisdom, as He gave wisdom to Daniel. They may obtain directions from Him who is mighty in counsel. "The fear of the Lord is the beginning of wisdom" (Ps. 111:10). Says the psalmist, "The entrance of thy words giveth light; it giveth understanding unto the simple" (Ps. 119:130). And the wise man writes, "In all thy ways acknowledge him, and he shall direct thy paths."

Let the youth try to appreciate the privilege that may be theirs, to be directed by the unerring wisdom of God. Let them take the Word of truth as the man of their counsel, and become skillful in the use of "the sword of the Spirit." Satan is a wise general; but the humble, devoted soldier of Jesus Christ may overcome him. It is written of the victors, that "they overcame him by the blood of the Lamb, and by the word of their testimony" (Rev. 12:11).

We must not trust in self. Our finite strength is only weakness. Says Jesus, "Without me ye can do nothing"; but He promises, "If ye abide in me, and my words abide in you, ye shall ask what ye will, and it shall be done unto you" (John 15:5, 7).

It is thought a great honor to be invited into the presence of a king of this earth. But let us consider the amazing privilege that is proffered to us. If we obey the requirements of God, we may become the sons and daughters of the King of the universe. Through a crucified and risen Saviour, we may be filled with the fruits of righteousness, and be fitted to shine in the courts of the King of kings through unending ages. . . . Our work is to seek the closest union with the Son of God, to learn in His school, to become meek and lowly of heart, to work the works of Christ, advancing His kingdom and hastening His coming.—*Review and Herald*, Feb. 28, 1888.

CLOSING MESSAGE
ADDRESSED TO YOUTH

For I am now ready to be offered, and the time of my departure is at hand. I have fought a good fight, I have finished my course, I have kept the faith: henceforth there is laid up for me a crown of righteousness, which the Lord, the righteous judge, shall give me at that day: and not to me only, but unto all them also that love his appearing. 2 Tim. 4:6-8.

I do not expect to live long. My work is nearly done. Tell our young people that I want my words to encourage them in that manner of life that will be most attractive to the heavenly intelligences, and that their influence upon others may be most ennobling.

In the night season I was selecting and laying aside books that are of no advantage to the young. We should select for them books that will encourage them to sincerity of life, and lead them to the opening of the Word. This has been presented to me in the past, and I thought I would get it before you and make it secure. We cannot afford to give to young people valueless reading. Books that are a blessing to mind and soul are needed. These things are too lightly regarded; therefore our people should become acquainted with what I am saying.

I do not think I shall have more testimonies for our people. Our men of solid minds know what is good for the uplifting and upbuilding of the work. But with the love of God in their hearts, they need to go deeper and deeper into the study of the things of God. I am very anxious that our young people shall have the proper class of reading; then the old people will get it also. We must keep our eyes on the religious attraction of the truth. We are to keep mind and brain open to the truths of God's Word. Satan comes when men are unaware. We are not to be satisfied because the message of warning has been once presented. We must present it again and again.—*Review and Herald*, Apr. 15, 1915.

LIGHT LASTING UNTIL THE END

And I heard a voice from heaven saying unto me, Write, Blessed are the dead which die in the Lord from henceforth: Yea, saith the Spirit, that they may rest from their labours; and their works do follow them. Rev. 14:13.

A bundant light has been given to our people in these last days. Whether or not my life is spared, my writings will constantly speak, and their work will go forward as long as time shall last. My writings are kept on file in the office, and even though I should not live, these words that have been given to me by the Lord will still have life and will speak to the people. But my strength is yet spared, and I hope to continue to do much useful work. I may live until the coming of the Lord; but if I should not, I trust it may be said of me, "Blessed are the dead which die in the Lord from henceforth: Yea, saith the Spirit, that they may rest from their labours; and their works do follow them." . . .

I thank God for the assurance of His love, and that I have daily His leading and guidance. I am very busy with my writing. Early and late, I am writing out the matters that the Lord opens before me. The burden of my work is to prepare a people to stand in the day of the Lord. The promise of Christ is sure. The time is not long. We must work and watch and wait for the Lord Jesus. We are called upon to be steadfast, unmovable, always abounding in the work of the Lord. All our hopes have their foundation in Christ.

Are our people reviewing the past and the present and the future, as it is unfolding before the world? Are they heeding the messages of warning given them? Is it our greatest concern today that our lives shall be refined and purified, and that we shall reflect the similitude of the divine? This must be the experience of all who join that company who are washed and made white in the blood of the Lamb. They must be arrayed in the righteousness of Christ. His name must be written in their foreheads.—*Selected Messages*, book 1, pp. 55, 56.

THE PROPER ATTITUDE

Look to yourselves, that we lose not those things which we have wrought, but that we receive a full reward. Whosoever transgresseth, and abideth not in the doctrine of Christ, hath not God. He that abideth in the doctrine of Christ, he hath both the Father and the Son. 2 John 8, 9.

Soon every possible effort will be made to discount and pervert the truth of the testimonies of God's Spirit. We must have in readiness the clear, straight messages that since 1846 have been coming to God's people.

There will be those once united with us in the faith who will search for new, strange doctrines, for something odd and sensational to present to the people. They will bring in all conceivable fallacies, and will present them as coming from Mrs. White, that they may beguile souls. . . .

Those who have treated the light that the Lord has given as a common thing will not be benefited by the instruction presented.

There are those who will misinterpret the messages that God has given, in accordance with their spiritual blindness.

Some will yield their faith, and will deny the truth of the messages, pointing to them as falsehoods.

Some will hold them up to ridicule, working against the light that God has been giving for years, and some who are weak in the faith will thus be led astray.

But others will be greatly helped by the messages. Though not personally addressed, they will be corrected, and will be led to shun the evils specified. . . . The Spirit of the Lord will be in the instruction, and doubts existing in many minds will be swept away. The testimonies themselves will be the key that will explain the messages given, as scripture is explained by scripture. Many will read with eagerness the messages reproving wrong, that they may learn what they may do to be saved. . . . These messages are to find their place in hearts, and transformations will take place.—*Selected Messages*, book 1, pp. 41, 42.

ENOCH

By faith Enoch was translated that he should not see death; and was not found, because God had translated him: for before his translation he had this testimony, that he pleased God. Heb. 11:5.

E noch was a public teacher of the truth in the age in which he lived. He taught the truth; he lived the truth; and the character of the teacher who walked with God was in every way harmonious with the greatness and sacredness of his mission. Enoch was a prophet who spake as he was moved by the Holy Ghost. He was a light amid the moral darkness, a pattern man, a man who walked with God, being obedient to God's law—that law which Satan had refused to obey, which Adam had transgressed, which Abel obeyed, and because of his obedience was murdered.

And now God would demonstrate to the universe the falsity of Satan's charge that man cannot keep God's law. He would demonstrate that though man had sinned, he could so relate himself to God that he would have the mind and Spirit of God and would be a representative symbol of Christ. This holy man was selected of God to denounce the wickedness of the world, and to evidence to the world that it is possible for men to keep all the law of God. . . .

Enoch not only meditated and prayed, and put on the armor of watchfulness, but he came forth from his pleadings with God to plead with his fellow men. He did not mask the truth to find favor with unbelievers, thus neglecting their souls. This close connection with God gave him courage to work the works of God. Enoch walked with God and "had this testimony that his ways pleased God" (Heb. 11:5).

This is the privilege of every believer today. It is man dwelling with God, and God taking up His abode with man. "I in them, and thou in me" (John 17:23), says Jesus. To walk with God and have the witness that their ways please Him is an experience not to be confined to Enoch, to Elijah, to patriarchs, to prophets, to apostles, and to martyrs. It is not only the privilege but the duty of every follower of Christ to have Jesus enshrined in the heart, to carry Him with them in their lives; and they will indeed be fruit-bearing trees.—*The Upward Look*, p. 228.

NOAH

*And the Lord said unto Noah, Come thou and all thy house into the ark;
for thee have I seen righteous before me in this generation. Gen. 7:1.*

I n the days of Noah, the wickedness of the world became so great
that God could no longer bear with it; and He said, "I will destroy
man whom I have created from the face of the earth" (Gen. 6:7). But
He pitied the race, and in His love provided a refuge for all who would
accept it. He gave the message to Noah to be given to the people: "My
spirit shall not always strive with man" (verse 3).

Noah was directed to build an ark, and at the same time to preach
that God would bring a flood of waters upon the earth to destroy the
wicked. Those who would believe the message, and would prepare for
that event by repentance and reformation, should find pardon and be
saved; but a continued resistance of the entreaties and warnings from
God through His servant Noah would separate them from God, and as
a result infinite mercy and love would cease its pleadings.

The Spirit of God continued to strive with rebellious man until the
time specified had nearly expired, when Noah and his family entered the
ark, and the hand of God closed its door. Mercy had stepped from the
golden throne, no longer to intercede for the guilty sinner.

All the men of that generation were not in the fullest sense of the
term heathen idolaters. Many had a knowledge of God and His law; but
they not only rejected the message of the faithful preacher of righteousness themselves, but used all their influence to prevent others from
being obedient to God. To everyone comes a day of trial and of trust.
That generation had their day of opportunity and privilege while Noah
was sounding the note of warning of the coming destruction; but they
yielded their minds to the control of Satan rather than of God, and he
deceived them, as he did our first parents. He set before them darkness
and falsehood in the place of light and truth; and they accepted his
sophistry and lies, because they were acceptable to them, and in harmony with their corrupt lives, while truth that would have saved them
was rejected as a delusion.—*Signs of the Times*, Apr. 1, 1886.

ABRAHAM

After these things the word of the Lord came unto Abram in a vision, saying, Fear not, Abram: I am thy shield, and thy exceeding great reward. . . . And he brought him forth abroad, and said, Look now toward heaven, and tell the stars, if thou be able to number them: and he said unto him, So shall thy seed be. And he believed in the Lord; and he counted it to him for righteousness. Gen. 15:1-6.

God designed that Abraham should be a channel of light and blessing, that he should have a gathering influence, and that God should have a people on the earth. Abraham was to be in the world, reflecting in his life the character of Jesus. When he received the divine call, Abraham was not a man of renown, neither a lawgiver, nor a conqueror. He was a simple herdsman, dwelling in tents, but employing a large number of workmen to carry on his humble employment. And the honor which he received was because of his faithfulness to God, his strict integrity and just dealing.

The Lord said of him: "Shall I hide from Abraham that thing which I do; seeing that Abraham shall surely become a great and mighty nation, and all the nations of the earth shall be blessed in him? For I know him, that he will command his children and his household after him, and they shall keep the way of the Lord, to do justice and judgment; that the Lord may bring upon Abraham that which he hath spoken of him" (Gen. 18:17-19).

Abraham's unselfish life made him indeed a "spectacle unto the world, and to angels, and to men" (1 Cor. 4:9). And the Lord declared He would bless those who blessed Abraham, and that He would punish those who misused or injured him. Through Abraham's experience in his religious life a correct knowledge of Jehovah has been communicated to thousands; and his light will shed its beams all along the path of those who practice the piety, the faith, the devotion, and the obedience of Abraham.

Abraham had a knowledge of Christ; for the Lord had enlightened him in regard to the world's Redeemer. And he made known to his household and his children that the sacrificial offerings prefigured Christ, the Lamb of God, who was to be slain for the sins of the world. Thus he gathered converts to believe in the only true and living God.— *Youth's Instructor*, Mar. 4, 1897.

JOSEPH

And God sent me before you to preserve you a posterity in the earth, and to save your lives by a great deliverance. So now it was not you that sent me hither, but God: and he hath made me a father to Pharaoh, and lord of all his house, and a ruler throughout all the land of Egypt. Gen. 45:7, 8.

It was God's design that through Joseph, Bible religion should be introduced among the Egyptians. This faithful witness was to represent Christ in the court of kings. Through dreams, God communicated with Joseph in his youth, giving him an intimation of the high position he would be called to fill. The brothers of Joseph, to prevent the fulfillment of his dreams, sold him as a slave, but their cruel act resulted in bringing about the very thing the dreams had foretold.

Those who seek to turn aside the purpose of God, and oppose His will, may appear for a time to prosper; but God is at work to fulfill His own purposes, and He will make manifest who is the ruler of the heavens and the earth.

Joseph regarded his being sold into Egypt as the greatest calamity that could have befallen him; but he saw the necessity of trusting in God as he had never done when protected by his father's love. Joseph brought God with him into Egypt, and the fact was made apparent by his cheerful demeanor amid his sorrow. As the ark of God brought rest and prosperity to Israel, so did this God-loving, God-fearing youth bring a blessing to Egypt. This was manifested in so marked a manner that Potiphar, in whose house he served, attributed all his blessings to his purchased slave, and made him a son rather than a servant. It is God's purpose that those who love and honor His name shall be honored also themselves, and that the glory given to God through them shall be reflected upon themselves.

Joseph's character did not change when he was exalted to a position of trust. He was brought where his virtue would shine in distinct light in good works. The blessing of God rested upon him in the house and in the field. All the responsibilities of Potiphar's house were placed upon him. And in all this he manifested steadfast integrity; for he loved and feared God.—*Youth's Instructor*, Mar. 11, 1897.

MOSES

And Moses said unto God, Who am I, that I should go unto Pharaoh, and that I should bring forth the children of Israel out of Egypt? And he said, Certainly I will be with thee; and this shall be a token unto thee, that I have sent thee: When thou hast brought forth the people out of Egypt, ye shall serve God upon this mountain. Ex. 3:11, 12.

Devotion and humility have ever characterized the men with whom God has entrusted important responsibilities in His work. The divine call to Moses in the desert found him distrustful of self. He realized his unfitness for the position to which God had called him; but having accepted the trust, he became a polished instrument in the hand of God to accomplish the greatest work ever committed to mortals.

Had Moses trusted to his own strength and wisdom, and eagerly accepted the great charge, he would have evinced his entire unfitness for such a work. The fact that a man feels his own weakness is at least some evidence that he realizes the magnitude of the work appointed him, and this gives room for hope that he will make God his counselor and his strength. Such a person will move no farther nor faster than he knows God is leading him.

A man will gain power and efficiency as he accepts the responsibilities which God places upon him, and with his whole soul seeks to qualify himself to bear them aright. However humble his position or limited his ability, that individual will attain true greatness who cheerfully responds to the call of duty, and, trusting to the divine strength, seeks to perform his work with fidelity. He will feel that he has a sacred commission to battle against wrong, to strengthen the right, to elevate, comfort, and bless his fellow men. Indolence, selfishness, and love of worldly approbation must yield to this high and holy calling.

Engaged in such a work, the weak man will become strong; the timid, brave; the irresolute, firm and decided. Each sees the importance of his position and his course, inasmuch as heaven has chosen him to do a special work for the King of kings. Such men will leave the world better for their having lived in it. Their influence is exerted to elevate, to purify, and to ennoble all with whom they come in contact, and thus they help to prepare their fellow men for the heavenly courts.—*Signs of the Times*, Aug. 11, 1881.

JOSHUA

There shall not any man be able to stand before thee all the days of thy life: as I was with Moses, so I will be with thee: I will not fail thee, nor forsake thee. Joshua 1:5.

After the death of Moses, Joshua was appointed the leader of Israel to conduct them to the Promised Land. He was well qualified for this important office. He had been prime minister to Moses during the greater part of the time the Israelites had wandered in the wilderness. He had seen the wonderful works of God wrought by Moses and well understood the disposition of the people. He was one of the twelve spies who were sent out to search the Promised Land, and one of the two who gave a faithful account of its richness, and who encouraged the people to go up and possess it in the strength of God.

The Lord promised Joshua that He would be with him as He had been with Moses, and He would make Canaan an easy conquest to him, provided he would be faithful to observe all His commandments. Joshua had been anxious concerning the execution of his commission to lead the people into the land of Canaan; but this assurance removed his fears. He commanded the children of Israel to make ready for a three days' journey and all the men of war to prepare for battle.

"And they answered Joshua, saying, All that thou commandest us we will do, and whithersoever thou sendest us, we will go. According as we hearkened unto Moses in all things, so will we hearken unto thee: only the Lord thy God be with thee, as he was with Moses. Whosoever he be that doth rebel against thy commandment, and will not hearken unto thy words in all that thou commandest him, he shall be put to death: only be strong and of a good courage" (Joshua 1:16-18).

God willed that the passage of the Israelites over Jordan should be miraculous. Joshua commanded the people to sanctify themselves, for upon the morrow the Lord would do wonders among them. At the appointed time, he directed the priests to take up the ark containing the law of God and bear it before the people. "And the Lord said unto Joshua, This day will I begin to magnify thee in the sight of all Israel, that they may know that, as I was with Moses, so I will be with thee" (Joshua 3:7).—*Testimonies*, vol. 4, pp. 156, 157.

DEBORAH AND BARAK

Then sang Deborah and Barak the son of Abinoam on that day, saying,
Praise ye the Lord for the avenging of Israel, when the people willingly of-
fered themselves. Judges 5:1, 2.

The Israelites, having again separated themselves from God by idolatry, were grievously oppressed by these enemies. The property and even the lives of the people were in constant danger. Hence the villages and lonely dwellings were deserted, and the people congregated in the walled cities. The high roads were unoccupied, and the people went from place to place by unfrequented byways. At the places for drawing water, many were robbed and even murdered, and to add to their distress, the Israelites were unarmed. Among forty thousand men, not a sword or a spear could be found.

For twenty years, the Israelites groaned under the yoke of the oppressor; then they turned from their idolatry, and with humiliation and repentance cried unto the Lord for deliverance. They did not cry in vain. There was dwelling in Israel a woman illustrious for her piety, and through her the Lord chose to deliver His people. Her name was Deborah. She was known as a prophetess, and in the absence of the usual magistrates, the people had sought to her for counsel and justice.

The Lord communicated to Deborah His purpose to destroy the enemies of Israel, and bade her send for a man named Barak, of the tribe of Naphtali, and make known to him the instructions which she had received. She accordingly sent for Barak, and directed him to assemble ten thousand men of the tribes of Naphtali and Zebulun, and make war upon the armies of King Jabin. . . .

Deborah celebrated the triumph of Israel in a most sublime and impassioned song. She ascribed to God all the glory of their deliverance, and bade the people praise Him for His wonderful works.—*Signs of the Times*, June 16, 1881.

GIDEON

And the Lord looked upon him, and said, Go in this thy might, and thou shalt save Israel from the hand of the Midianites: have not I sent thee? And he said unto him, Oh my Lord, wherewith shall I save Israel? behold, my family is poor in Manasseh, and I am the least in my father's house. And the Lord said unto him, Surely I will be with thee, and thou shalt smite the Midianites as one man. Judges 6:14-16.

All the wonders which God has wrought for His people have been performed by the most simple means. When the people of God are wholly consecrated to Him, then He will employ them to carry forward His work on the earth. But we should remember that whatever success may attend us, the glory and honor belongs to God; for every faculty and every power is a gift from Him.

God will test, to the utmost, the faith and courage of those to whom He has entrusted responsibilities in His work. Appearances will often be forbidding. Although God has given repeated assurance of His help, yet faith will almost stagger. "Thus saith the Lord" must be our firm reliance, independent of human reasonings, or apparent impossibilities.

The experience of Gideon and his army was designed to teach a lesson of simplicity and faith. The leader whom God had chosen occupied no prominent position in Israel. He was not a ruler, a Levite, or a priest. He thought himself the least in his father's house. Human wisdom would not have selected him; but God saw in Gideon a man of integrity and moral courage. He was distrustful of self, and willing to listen to the teachings of God, and carry out His purposes.

The Lord is not dependent upon men of high position, of great intellect, or extensive knowledge. Such men are frequently proud and self-sufficient. They feel themselves competent to devise and execute plans without counsel from God. They separate themselves from the True Vine, and hence become dry and fruitless, as withered branches.

The Lord would put to shame the vaunting of men. He will give success to the feeblest efforts, the most unpromising methods, when divinely appointed, and entered upon with humility and trust.—*Signs of the Times*, June 30, 1881.

SAMUEL

And Samuel grew, and the Lord was with him, and did let none of his words fall to the ground. And all Israel from Dan even to Beer-sheba knew that Samuel was established to be a prophet of the Lord. 1 Sam. 3:19, 20.

During the years since the Lord first manifested Himself to the son of Hannah, Samuel's call to the prophetic office had come to be acknowledged by the whole nation. By faithfully delivering the divine warning to the house of Eli, painful and trying as the duty had been, Samuel had given proof of his fidelity as Jehovah's messenger; "and the Lord was with him, and did let none of his words fall to the ground. And all Israel from Dan even to Beer-sheba knew that Samuel was established to be a prophet of the Lord."

The Israelites as a nation still continued in a state of irreligion and idolatry, and as a punishment they remained in subjection to the Philistines. During this time Samuel visited the cities and villages throughout the land, seeking to turn the hearts of the people to the God of their fathers; and his efforts were not without good results. After suffering the oppression of their enemies for twenty years, the Israelites "mourned after the Lord." Samuel counseled them, "If ye do return unto the Lord with all your hearts, then put away the strange gods and Ashtaroth from among you, and prepare your hearts unto the Lord, and serve him only" (1 Sam. 7:3).

Here we see that practical piety, heart religion, was taught in the days of Samuel as taught by Christ when He was upon the earth. Without the grace of Christ the outward forms of religion were valueless to ancient Israel. They are the same to modern Israel.

There is need today of such a revival of true heart religion as was experienced by ancient Israel. Repentance is the first step that must be taken by all who would return to God. No one can do this work for another. We must individually humble our souls before God and put away our idols. When we have done all that we can do, the Lord will manifest to us His salvation.—*Patriarchs and Prophets*, pp. 589, 590.

DAVID

Now these be the last words of David. David the son of Jesse said, and the man who was raised up on high, the anointed of the God of Jacob, and the sweet psalmist of Israel, said, The spirit of the Lord spake by me, and his word was in my tongue. 2 Sam. 23:1, 2.

Who can measure the results of those years of toil and wandering among the lonely hills? The communion with nature and with God, the care of his flocks, the perils and deliverances, the griefs and joys, of his lowly lot, were not only to mold the character of David and to influence his future life, but through the psalms of Israel's sweet singer they were in all coming ages to kindle love and faith in the hearts of God's people, bringing them nearer to the ever-loving heart of Him in whom all His creatures live.

David, in the beauty and vigor of his young manhood, was preparing to take a high position with the noblest of the earth. His talents, as precious gifts from God, were employed to extol the glory of the divine Giver. His opportunities of contemplation and meditation served to enrich him with that wisdom and piety that made him beloved of God and angels. As he contemplated the perfections of his Creator, clearer conceptions of God opened before his soul. Obscure themes were illuminated, difficulties were made plain, perplexities were harmonized, and each ray of new light called forth fresh bursts of rapture, and sweeter anthems of devotion, to the glory of God and the Redeemer.

The love that moved him, the sorrows that beset him, the triumphs that attended him, were all themes for his active thought; and as he beheld the love of God in all the providences of his life, his heart throbbed with more fervent adoration and gratitude, his voice rang out in a richer melody, his harp was swept with more exultant joy; and the shepherd boy proceeded from strength to strength, from knowledge to knowledge; for the Spirit of the Lord was upon him.—*Patriarchs and Prophets*, p. 642.

SOLOMON

And now, O Lord my God, thou hast made thy servant king instead of David my father: and I am but a little child: I know not how to go out or come in. And thy servant is in the midst of thy people which thou hast chosen, a great people, that cannot be numbered nor counted for multitude. Give therefore thy servant an understanding heart to judge thy people, that I may discern between good and bad: for who is able to judge this thy so great a people? 1 Kings 3:7-9.

The name of Jehovah was greatly honored during the first part of Solomon's reign. The wisdom and righteousness revealed by the king bore witness to all nations of the excellency of the attributes of the God whom he served. For a time Israel was as the light of the world, showing forth the greatness of Jehovah. Not in the surpassing wisdom, the fabulous riches, the far-reaching power and fame that were his, lay the real glory of Solomon's early reign; but in the honor that he brought to the name of the God of Israel through a wise use of the gifts of heaven.

As the years went by and Solomon's fame increased, he sought to honor God by adding to his mental and spiritual strength, and by continuing to impart to others the blessings he received. None understood better than he that it was through the favor of Jehovah that he had come into possession of power and wisdom and understanding, and that these gifts were bestowed that he might give to the world a knowledge of the King of kings.

Solomon took an especial interest in natural history, but his researches were not confined to any one branch of learning. Through a diligent study of all created things, both animate and inanimate, he gained a clear conception of the Creator. In the forces of nature, in the mineral and the animal world, and in every tree and shrub and flower, he saw a revelation of God's wisdom; and as he sought to learn more and more, his knowledge of God and his love for Him constantly increased.—*Prophets and Kings*, pp. 32, 33.

ELIJAH

And Elijah came unto all the people, and said, How long halt ye between two opinions? if the Lord be God, follow him: but if Baal, then follow him. And the people answered him not a word. 1 Kings 18:21.

Among the mountains of Gilead, east of the Jordan, there dwelt in the days of Ahab a man of faith and prayer whose fearless ministry was destined to check the rapid spread of apostasy in Israel. Far removed from any city of renown, and occupying no high station in life, Elijah the Tishbite nevertheless entered upon his mission confident in God's purpose to prepare the way before him and to give him abundant success. The word of faith and power was upon his lips, and his whole life was devoted to the work of reform. His was the voice of one crying in the wilderness to rebuke sin and press back the tide of evil. And while he came to the people as a reprover of sin, his message offered the balm of Gilead to the sin-sick souls of all who desired to be healed.

As Elijah saw Israel going deeper and deeper into idolatry, his soul was distressed and his indignation aroused. God had done great things for His people. He had delivered them from bondage and given them "the lands of the heathen: . . . that they might observe his statutes, and keep his laws" (Ps. 105:44, 45). But the beneficent designs of Jehovah were now well-nigh forgotten. Unbelief was fast separating the chosen nation from the Source of their strength.

Viewing this apostasy from his mountain retreat, Elijah was overwhelmed with sorrow. In anguish of soul he besought God to arrest the once-favored people in their wicked course, to visit them with judgments, if need be, that they might be led to see in its true light their departure from Heaven. He longed to see them brought to repentance before they should go to such lengths in evil-doing as to provoke the Lord to destroy them utterly.—*Prophets and Kings*, pp. 119, 120.

ELISHA

And it came to pass, when they were gone over, that Elijah said unto Elisha, Ask what I shall do for thee, before I be taken away from thee. And Elisha said, I pray thee, let a double portion of thy spirit be upon me. 2 Kings 2:9.

We may learn valuable lessons from the experience of the prophet Elisha. Elisha was chosen by the Lord as Elijah's helper, and through test and trial he proved himself true to his trust. He was willing to be and do anything the Lord directed. He did not seek to shun the humblest service, but was as faithful in the performance of smaller duties as of larger responsibilities. He was always willing to serve in any position to which the Lord pointed him, however disagreeable it might be to his natural inclinations. And at every step he learned lessons of humility and service. . . .

"And it came to pass, when they were gone over, that Elijah said unto Elisha, Ask what I shall do for thee, before I be taken away from thee. And Elisha said, I pray thee, let a double portion of thy spirit be upon me." He did not ask for worldly honor, for a high place among the great men of the earth. That for which he craved was a double portion of the Spirit given to the one God was about to honor with translation. He knew that nothing but a double portion of the Spirit that had rested on Elijah could fit him to fill the place Elijah had filled, because Elijah had the experience and wisdom of age, which cannot by any method be imparted to the young. . . .

When the Lord in His providence sees fit to remove from His work those to whom He has given wisdom, He helps and strengthens their successors, if they will look to Him for aid and will walk in His ways. They may be even wiser than their predecessors; for they may profit by their experience and learn wisdom from their mistakes.

The Lord has a special care for His church. Those who will seek wisdom from Him will be lights in the world, shining brighter and brighter unto the perfect day.—Manuscript 114, 1901.

ISAIAH

And he said, Go, and tell this people, Hear ye indeed, but understand not; and see ye indeed, but perceive not. Make the heart of this people fat, and make their ears heavy, and shut their eyes; lest they see with their eyes, and hear with their ears, and understand with their heart, and convert, and be healed. Isa. 6:9, 10.

The prophet's duty was plain; he was to lift his voice in protest against the prevailing evils. But he dreaded to undertake the work without some assurance of hope. "Lord, how long?" (Isa. 6:11) he inquired. Are none of Thy chosen people ever to understand, and repent, and be healed?

His burden of soul in behalf of erring Judah was not to be borne in vain. His mission was not to be wholly fruitless. Yet the evils that had been multiplying for many generations could not be removed in his day. Throughout his lifetime he must be a patient, courageous teacher—a prophet of hope as well as of doom. The divine purpose finally accomplished, the full fruitage of his efforts, and of the labors of all God's faithful messengers, would appear. A remnant should be saved. That this might be brought about, the messages of warning and entreaty were to be delivered to the rebellious, the Lord declared, "until the cities be wasted without inhabitant, and the houses without man, and the land be utterly desolate, and the Lord have removed men far away, and there be a great forsaking in the midst of the land" (verses 11, 12).

The heavy judgments that were to befall the impenitent—war, exile, oppression, the loss of power and prestige among the nations—all these were to come in order that those who would recognize in them the hand of an offended God might be led to repent. The ten tribes of the northern kingdom were soon to be scattered among the nations, and their cities left desolate; the destroying armies of hostile nations were to sweep over their land again and again; even Jerusalem was finally to fall, and Judah was to be carried away captive; yet the Promised Land was not to remain wholly forsaken forever.—*Review and Herald,* Mar. 11, 1915.

JEREMIAH

Then the word of the Lord came unto me, saying, Before I formed thee in the belly I knew thee; and before thou camest forth out of the womb I sanctified thee, and I ordained thee a prophet unto the nations. Jer. 1:4, 5.

The Lord gave Jeremiah a message of reproof to bear to His people, charging them with the continual rejection of God's counsel; saying, "I have spoken unto you, rising early and speaking; but ye hearkened not unto me. I have sent also unto you all my servants the prophets, rising up early and sending them, saying, Return ye now every man from his evil way, and amend your doings, and go not after other gods to serve them, and ye shall dwell in the land which I have given to you and to your fathers" (Jer. 35:14, 15).

God pleaded with them not to provoke Him to anger with the work of their hands and hearts; but they "hearkened not." Jeremiah then predicted the captivity of the Jews, as their punishment for not heeding the word of the Lord. The Chaldeans were to be used as the instrument by which God would chastise His disobedient people. Their punishment was to be in proportion to their intelligence, and the warnings they had despised. God had long delayed His judgments, because of His unwillingness to humiliate His chosen people; but now He would visit His displeasure upon them, as a last effort to check them in their evil course.

In these days He has instituted no new plan to preserve the purity of His people. He entreats the erring ones who profess His name to repent and turn from their evil ways, in the same manner that He did of old. He predicts the dangers before them by the mouth of His chosen servants now as then. He sounds His note of warning, and reproves sin just as faithfully as in the days of Jeremiah. But the Israel of our time have the same temptations to scorn reproof and hate counsel as did ancient Israel. They too often turn a deaf ear to the words that God has given His servants for the benefit of those who profess the truth.—*Signs of the Times*, Feb. 12, 1880.

JOSIAH AND HULDAH

Go ye, inquire of the Lord for me, and for the people, and for all Judah, concerning the words of this book that is found: for great is the wrath of the Lord that is kindled against us, because our fathers have not hearkened unto the words of this book, to do according unto all that which is written concerning us. 2 Kings 22:13.

Josiah, from his earliest manhood, had endeavored to take advantage of his position as king to exalt the principles of God's holy law. And now, while Shaphan the scribe was reading to him out of the book of the Law, the king discerned in this volume a treasure of knowledge, a powerful ally, in the work of reform he so much desired to see wrought in the land. He resolved to walk in the light of its counsels, and also to do all in his power to acquaint his people with its teachings, and to lead them, if possible, to cultivate reverence and love for the law of heaven.

But was it possible to bring about the needed reform? From all that he could learn from the reading of the volume before him, Israel had almost reached the limit of divine forbearance; soon God would arise to punish those who had brought dishonor upon His name. Already the anger of the Lord was kindled against the people. Overwhelmed with sorrow and dismay, Josiah rent his garments, and bowed before God in agony of spirit, seeking pardon for the sins of an impenitent nation.

At that time the prophetess Huldah was living in Jerusalem, near the Temple. The mind of the king, filled with anxious foreboding, reverted to her; and he determined to inquire of the Lord through this chosen messenger, to learn, if possible, whether by any means within his power he might save erring Judah, now on the verge of ruin.

The gravity of the situation, and the respect in which he held the prophetess, led him to choose as his messengers to her the first men of the kingdom. "Go ye," he bade them, "inquire of the Lord for me, and for the people, and for all Judah, concerning the words of this book that is found: for great is the wrath of the Lord that is kindled against us, because our fathers have not hearkened unto the words of this book, to do according unto all that which is written concerning us."—*Review and Herald*, July 22, 1915.

DANIEL

Then the king made Daniel a great man, and gave him many great gifts, and made him ruler over the whole province of Babylon, and chief of the governors over all the wise men of Babylon. Dan. 2:48.

A confession of Christ means something more than bearing testimony in social meeting. Daniel is an example to believers as to what it means to confess Christ. He held the responsible position of prime minister in the kingdom of Babylon, and there were those who were envious of Daniel among the great men of the court, and they wanted to find something against him that they might bring an accusation against him to the king. But he was a faithful statesman, and they could find no flaw in his character or life.

"Then said these men, we shall not find any occasion against this Daniel, except we find it against him concerning the law of his God" (Dan. 6:5). So they agreed together to ask the king to make a decree that no one should ask any petition of any God or man for thirty days save of the king, and if any disobeyed this decree, he was to be cast into the den of lions.

But did Daniel cease to pray because this decree was to go into force? No, that was just the time when he needed to pray. "When Daniel knew that the writing was signed, he went into his house; and his windows being open in his chamber toward Jerusalem, he kneeled upon his knees three times a day, and prayed, and gave thanks before his God, as he did aforetime" (verse 10). Daniel did not seek to hide his loyalty to God. He did not pray in his heart, but with his voice, aloud, with his window open toward Jerusalem, he offered up his petition to heaven. . . .

We may know that if our life is hid with Christ in God, when we are brought into trial because of our faith, Jesus will be with us. When we are brought before rulers and dignitaries to answer for our faith, the Spirit of the Lord will illuminate our understanding, and we shall be able to bear a testimony to the glory of God. And if we are called to suffer for Christ's sake, we shall be able to go to prison trusting in Him as a little child trusts in its parents. Now is the time to cultivate faith in God.—*Review and Herald*, May 3, 1892.

ESTHER

Then Mordecai commanded to answer Esther, Think not with thyself that thou shalt escape in the king's house, more than all the Jews. For if thou altogether holdest thy peace at this time, then shall there enlargement and deliverance arise to the Jews from another place; but thou and thy father's house shall be destroyed: and who knoweth whether thou art come to the kingdom for such a time as this? Esther 4:13, 14.

In ancient times the Lord worked in a wonderful way through consecrated women who united in His work with men whom He had chosen to stand as His representatives. He used women to gain great and decisive victories. More than once, in times of emergency, He brought them to the front and worked through them for the salvation of many lives. Through Esther the queen, the Lord accomplished a mighty deliverance for His people. At a time when it seemed that no power could save them, Esther and the women associated with her, by fasting and prayer and prompt action, met the issue, and brought salvation to their people.

A study of women's work in connection with the cause of God in Old Testament times will teach us lessons that will enable us to meet emergencies in the work today. We may not be brought into such a critical and prominent place as were the people of God in the time of Esther; but often converted women can act an important part in more humble positions. This many have been doing, and are still ready to do. It is a woman's duty to unite with her husband in the disciplining and training of her sons and daughters, that they may be converted, and their powers consecrated to the service of God. There are many who have ability to stand with their husbands in sanitarium work, to give treatments to the sick and to speak words of counsel and encouragement to others. There are those who should seek an education that will fit them to act the part of physicians.—*Special Testomonies*, Series B, No. 15, pp. 1, 2.

EZRA AND NEHEMIAH

So they read in the book in the law of God distinctly, and gave the sense, and caused them to understand the reading. And Nehemiah, which is the Tirshatha, and Ezra the priest the scribe, and the Levites that taught the people, said unto all the people, This day is holy unto the Lord your God; mourn not, nor weep. For all the people wept, when they heard the words of the law. Neh. 8:8, 9.

Nehemiah and Ezra are men of opportunity. The Lord had a special work for them to do. They were to call upon the people to consider their ways, and to see where they had made their mistake; for the Lord had not suffered His people to become powerless and confused and to be taken into captivity without a cause. The Lord especially blessed these men for standing up for the right. Nehemiah was not set apart as a priest or a prophet, but the Lord used him to do a special work. He was chosen as a leader of the people. But his fidelity to God did not depend upon his position.

The Lord will not allow His work to be hindered, even though the workmen may prove unworthy. God has men in reserve, prepared to meet the demand, that His work may be preserved from all contaminating influences. God will be honored and glorified. When the divine Spirit impresses the mind of the man appointed by God as fit for the work, he responds, saying, "Here am I; send me."

God demonstrated to the people for whom He had done so much that He would not serve with their sins. He wrought, not through those who refused to serve Him with singleness of purpose, who had corrupted their ways before Him, but through Nehemiah; for he was registered in the books of heaven as a *man*. God has said, "Them that honour me I will honour" (1 Sam. 2:30). Nehemiah showed himself to be a man whom God could use to put down false principles and to restore heaven-born principles; and God honored him. The Lord will use in His work men who are as true as steel to principle, who will not be swayed by the sophistries of those who have lost their spiritual eyesight.—*Review and Herald*, May 2, 1899.

ZERUBBABEL AND ZECHARIAH

Then the prophets, Haggai the prophet, and Zechariah the son of Iddo, prophesied unto the Jews that were in Judah and Jerusalem in the name of the God of Israel, even unto them. Then rose up Zerubbabel the son of Shealtiel, and Jeshua the son of Jozadak, and began to build the house of God which is at Jerusalem: and with them were the prophets of God helping them. Ezra 5:1, 2.

In rebuilding the house of the Lord, Zerubbabel had been encompassed with manifold difficulties. In former years, adversaries had "weakened the hands of the people of Judah, and troubled them in building," "and made them to cease by force and power" (Ezra 4:4, 23). But the Lord interposed in behalf of the faithful builders, and now He speaks through His prophet, Zechariah, to Zerubbabel, saying, "Not by might, nor by power, but by my Spirit, saith the Lord of hosts. Who art thou, O great mountain? before Zerubbabel thou shalt become a plain: and he shall bring forth the headstone thereof with shoutings, crying, Grace, grace unto it" (Zech. 4:6, 7).

Throughout the history of God's people, great mountains of difficulty, apparently insurmountable, have loomed up before those who were advancing in the opening providences of God. Such obstacles to progress are permitted by the Lord as a test of faith. When [we are] hedged about on every side, this is the time above all others to trust in God and in the power of His Holy Spirit. We are not to walk in our own strength, but in the strength of the Lord God of Israel. It is folly to trust in man or to make flesh our arm. We must trust in Jehovah; for in Him is everlasting strength. The One who, in response to words and deeds of faith, made the way plain before His servant Zerubbabel, is able to clear away every obstacle devised by Satan to hinder the progress of His cause. Through the exercise of persevering faith, every mountain of difficulty may be removed.

Sometimes God trains His workers by bringing to them disappointment and apparent failure. It is His purpose that they shall learn to master difficulty. He seeks to inspire them with a determination to make every apparent failure prove a success.—*Review and Herald,* Jan. 16, 1908.

JOHN THE BAPTIST

Then said they unto him, Who art thou? that we may give an answer to them that sent us. What sayest thou of thyself? He said, I am the voice of one crying in the wilderness, Make straight the way of the Lord, as said the prophet Esaias. John 1:22, 23.

Verily I say unto you, Among them that are born of women there hath not risen a greater than John the Baptist" (Matt. 11:11). In the announcement to Zacharias before the birth of John, the angel had declared, "He shall be great in the sight of the Lord" (Luke 1:15). In the estimation of Heaven, what is it that constitutes greatness? Not that which the world accounts greatness; not wealth, or rank, or noble descent, or intellectual gifts, in themselves considered. If intellectual greatness, apart from any higher consideration, is worthy of honor, then our homage is due to Satan, whose intellectual power no man has ever equaled. But when perverted to self-serving, the greater the gift, the greater curse it becomes.

It is moral worth that God values. Love and purity are the attributes He prizes most. John was great in the sight of the Lord, when, before the messengers from the Sanhedrin, before the people, and before his own disciples, he refrained from seeking honor for himself, but pointed all to Jesus as the Promised One. His unselfish joy in the ministry of Christ presents the highest type of nobility ever revealed in man.

The witness borne of him after his death, by those who had heard his testimony to Jesus, was "John did no miracle: but all things that John spake of this man were true" (John 10:41). It was not given to John to call down fire from heaven, or to raise the dead, as Elijah did, nor to wield Moses' rod of power in the name of God. He was sent to herald the Saviour's advent, and to call upon the people to prepare for His coming. So faithfully did he fulfill his mission, that as the people recalled what he had taught them of Jesus, they could say, "All things that John spake of this man were true." Such witness to Christ every disciple of the Master is called upon to bear.—*The Desire of Ages*, pp. 219, 220.

JESUS OUR LORD

The Spirit of the Lord is upon me, because he hath anointed me to preach the gospel to the poor; he hath sent me to heal the brokenhearted, to preach deliverance to the captives, and recovering of sight to the blind, to set at liberty them that are bruised, to preach the acceptable year of the Lord. Luke 4:18, 19.

Christ spoke no words revealing His importance, or showing His superiority; He did not ignore His fellow beings. He made no assumption of authority because of His relation to God, but His words and actions showed Him to be possessed of a knowledge of His mission and character. He spoke of heavenly things as one to whom everything heavenly was familiar. He spoke of His intimacy and oneness with the Father as a child would speak of its connection with its parents. He spoke as one who had come to enlighten the world with His glory. He never patronized the schools of the rabbis; for He was the teacher sent by God to instruct mankind. As one in whom all restorative power is found, Christ spoke of drawing all men unto Him, and of giving the life everlasting. In Him there is power to heal every physical and every spiritual disease.

Christ came to our world with a consciousness of more than human greatness, to accomplish a work that was to be infinite in its results. Where do you find Him when doing this work? In the house of Peter the fisherman. Resting by Jacob's well, telling the Samaritan woman of the living water. He generally taught in the open air, but sometimes in the Temple, for He attended the gatherings of the Jewish people. But oftenest He taught when sitting on a mountainside, or in a fisherman's boat. He entered into the lives of these humble fishermen. His sympathy was enlisted in behalf of the needy, the suffering, the despised; and many were attracted to Him.

When the plan of redemption was laid, it was decided that Christ should not appear in accordance with His divine character; for He could not then associate with the distressed and the suffering. He must come as a poor man. He could have appeared in accordance with His exalted station in the heavenly courts; but no, He must reach to the very lowest depths of human suffering and poverty, that His voice might be heard by the burdened and disappointed.—*Signs of the Times*, June 24, 1897.

THE DISCIPLES

And with great power gave the apostles witness of the resurrection of the Lord Jesus: and great grace was upon them all. Acts 4:33.

After the crucifixion of Christ, the disciples were a helpless, discouraged company—as sheep without a shepherd. Their Master had been rejected, condemned, and nailed to the ignominious cross. Scornfully the Jewish priests and rulers had declared: "He saved others; himself he cannot save. If he be the King of Israel, let him now come down from the cross, and we will believe him" (Matt. 27:42).

But the cross, that instrument of shame and torture, brought hope and salvation to the world. The disciples rallied; their hopelessness and helplessness left them. They were transformed in character, and united in bonds of Christian love. They were but humble men, without wealth, and with no weapon but the Word and Spirit of God, counted by the Jews as mere fishermen. Yet in Christ's strength they went forth to witness for the truth, and to triumph over all opposition. Clothed with the divine panoply, they went forth to tell the wonderful story of the manger and the cross. Without earthly honor or recognition, they were heroes of faith. From their lips came words of divine eloquence that shook the world.

Those who had rejected and crucified the Saviour expected to find the disciples discouraged and crestfallen, ready to disown their Lord. They heard with amazement the clear, bold testimony of the apostles, given under the power of the Holy Spirit. The disciples worked and spoke as their Master had worked and spoken, and all who heard them said, "They have been with Jesus, and learned of Him."

As the apostles went forth, preaching Jesus everywhere, they did many things that the Jewish rulers did not approve. The people brought their sick, and those vexed with unclean spirits, into the streets; crowds collected round them, and those who had been healed shouted the praises of God, and glorified the name of Him whom the Jews had condemned, crowned with thorns, and caused to be scourged and crucified.—*Signs of the Times*, Sept. 20, 1899.

STEPHEN

And Stephen, full of faith and power, did great wonders and miracles among the people. Acts 6:8.

Stephen was very active in the cause of God, and declared his faith boldly. "Then there arose certain of the synagogue, which is called the synagogue of the Libertines, and Cyrenians, and Alexandrians, and of them of Cilicia and of Asia, disputing with Stephen. And they were not able to resist the wisdom and the spirit by which he spake" (Acts 6:9, 10). These students of the great rabbis had felt confident that in a public discussion they could obtain a complete victory over Stephen, because of his supposed ignorance. But he not only spoke with the power of the Holy Ghost, but it was plain to all the vast assembly that he was also a student of the prophecies, and learned in all matters of the law. He ably defended the truths he advocated, and utterly defeated his opponents.

The priests and rulers who witnessed the wonderful manifestation of the power that attended the ministration of Stephen were filled with bitter hatred. Instead of yielding to the weight of evidence he presented, they determined to silence his voice by putting him to death. They had on several occasions bribed the Roman authorities to pass over without comment instances where the Jews had taken the law into their own hands, and tried, condemned, and executed prisoners according to their national custom. The enemies of Stephen did not doubt that they could pursue such a course without danger to themselves. They determined to risk the consequences at all events, and they therefore seized Stephen and brought him before the Sanhedrin council for trial. . . .

As Stephen stood face to face with his judges, to answer to the crime of blasphemy, a holy radiance shone upon his countenance. "And all that sat in the council, looking stedfastly on him, saw his face as it had been the face of an angel" (verse 15). Those who exalted Moses might have seen in the face of the prisoner the same holy light which radiated the face of that ancient prophet. The Shekinah was a spectacle which they would never again witness in the Temple whose glory had departed forever. Many who beheld the lighted countenance of Stephen trembled and veiled their faces; but stubborn unbelief and prejudice never faltered.—*The Spirit of Prophecy*, vol. 3, pp. 294-296.

PHILIP THE DEACON

Then the Spirit said unto Philip, Go near, and join thyself to this chariot. And Philip ran thither to him, and heard him read the prophet Esaias, and said, Understandest thou what thou readest? Acts 8:29, 30.

God is looking down from His throne, and is sending His angels to this earth to cooperate with those who are teaching the truth. Read the record of the experience of Philip and the eunuch. "The angel of the Lord spake unto Philip, saying, Arise, and go toward the south unto the way that goeth down from Jerusalem unto Gaza, which is desert. And he arose and went: and, behold, a man of Ethiopia, an eunuch of great authority under Candace queen of the Ethiopians, who had the charge of all her treasure, and had come to Jerusalem for to worship, was returning, and sitting in his chariot read Esaias the prophet" (Acts 8:26-28). . . .

This incident shows the care that the Lord has over every mind that is susceptible to the truth. We see how closely the ministration of heavenly angels is connected with the work of the Lord's servants on this earth.

A burden was placed upon Philip to enter new places, to break up fresh ground. Direction was given him by an angel who was watching for every opportunity to bring men into connection with their fellow men. Philip was sent "toward the south unto the way that goeth down from Jerusalem unto Gaza, which is desert" (verse 26). This brought him into touch with a man of wide influence, who, when converted, would communicate to others the light of truth. By the Lord's working through Philip, the man was convinced of the truth, and was converted and baptized. He was a highway hearer, a man of good standing, who would exert a strong influence in favor of the truth.

Today, as then, angels of heaven are waiting to lead men to their fellow men. An angel showed Philip where to find this man, who was so ready to receive the truth, and today angels of God will guide and direct the footsteps of those workers who will allow the Holy Spirit to sanctify their tongues and refine and ennoble their hearts.—*Review and Herald*, Apr. 20, 1905.

DORCAS

Now there was at Joppa a certain disciple named Tabitha, which by interpretation is called Dorcas: this woman was full of good works and almsdeeds which she did. Acts 9:36.

At Joppa, which was near Lydda, there lived a woman named Dorcas, whose good deeds had made her greatly beloved. . . . Her life was filled with acts of kindness. Her skillful fingers were more active than her tongue. She knew who needed comfortable clothing and who needed sympathy, and she freely ministered to the poor and the sorrowful.

"And it came to pass in those days, that she was sick, and died" (Acts 9:37). The church in Joppa realized their loss. And in view of the life of service that Dorcas had lived, it is little wonder that they mourned, or that warm teardrops fell upon the inanimate clay.

Hearing that Peter was at Lydda, the believers in Joppa sent messengers to him, "desiring him that he would not delay to come to them" (verse 38).

"Then Peter arose and went with them. When he was come, they brought him into the upper chamber: and all the widows stood by him weeping, and shewing the coats and garments which Dorcas made while she was with them" (verse 39).

Peter directed that the weeping friends be sent from the room, and then kneeling down, he prayed fervently to God to restore Dorcas to life and health. Turning to the body, he said: "Tabitha, arise. And she opened her eyes: and when she saw Peter, she sat up" (verse 40).

Dorcas was of great service to the church, and God saw fit to bring her back from the land of the enemy, that her skill and energy might still be a blessing to others, and that by this manifestation of His power, the cause of Christ might be strengthened.—*Review and Herald*, Apr. 6, 1911.

PAUL

But rise, and stand upon thy feet: for I have appeared unto thee for this purpose, to make thee a minister and a witness both of these things which thou hast seen, and of those things in the which I will appear unto thee. Acts 26:16.

The solemn charge that had been given Paul on the occasion of his interview with Ananias rested with increasing weight upon his heart. When, in response to the invitation "Brother Saul, receive thy sight," Paul had for the first time looked upon the face of this devout man, Ananias under the inspiration of the Holy Spirit said to him: "The God of our fathers hath chosen thee, that thou shouldest know his will, and see that Just One, and shouldest hear the voice of his mouth. For thou shalt be his witness unto all men of what thou hast seen and heard. And now why tarriest thou? arise, and be baptized, and wash away thy sins, calling on the name of the Lord" (Acts 22:13-16).

These words were in harmony with the words of Jesus Himself, who, when He arrested Saul on the journey to Damascus, declared: "I have appeared unto thee for this purpose, to make thee a minister and a witness both of these things which thou hast seen, and of those things in the which I will appear unto thee; delivering thee from the people, and from the Gentiles, unto whom now I send thee, to open their eyes, and to turn them from darkness to light, and from the power of Satan unto God, that they may receive forgiveness of sins, and inheritance among them which are sanctified by faith that is in me" (Acts 26:16-18).

As he pondered these things in his heart, Paul understood more and more the meaning of his call to be "an apostle of Jesus Christ by the will of God" (Eph. 1:1). His call had come "not of men, neither by man, but by Jesus Christ, and God the Father" (Gal. 1:1). The greatness of the work before him led him to give much study to the Holy Scriptures, in order that he might preach the gospel "not with wisdom of words, lest the cross of Christ should be made of none effect" (1 Cor. 1:17), "but in demonstration of the Spirit and of power," that the faith of all who heard "should not stand in the wisdom of men, but in the power of God" (1 Cor. 2:4, 5).—*Review and Herald*, Mar. 30, 1911.

TIMOTHY

I charge thee therefore before God, and the Lord Jesus Christ, who shall judge the quick and the dead at his appearing and his kingdom; preach the word; be instant in season, out of season; reprove, rebuke, exhort with all longsuffering and doctrine. 2 Tim. 4:1, 2.

This solemn charge to one so zealous and faithful as was Timothy is a strong testimony to the importance and responsibility of the work of the gospel minister. Summoning Timothy before the bar of God, Paul bids him preach the Word, not the sayings and customs of men; to be ready to witness for God whenever opportunity should present itself—before large congregations and private circles, by the way and at the fireside, to friends and to enemies, whether in safety or exposed to hardship and peril, reproach and loss.

Fearing that Timothy's mild, yielding disposition might lead him to shun an essential part of his work, Paul exhorted him to be faithful in reproving sin and even to rebuke with sharpness those who are guilty of gross evils. Yet he was to do this "with all longsuffering and doctrine." He was to reveal the patience and love of Christ, explaining and enforcing his reproofs by the truths of the Word.

To hate and reprove sin, and at the same time to show pity and tenderness for the sinner, is a difficult attainment. The more earnest our own efforts to attain to holiness of heart and life, the more acute will be our perception of sin and the more decided our disapproval of any deviation from the right. We must guard against undue severity toward the wrongdoer, but we must also be careful not to lose sight of the exceeding sinfulness of sin. There is need of showing Christlike patience and love for the erring one, but there is also danger of showing so great toleration for his error that he will look upon himself as undeserving of reproof, and will reject it as uncalled for and unjust.—*The Acts of the Apostles*, pp. 503, 504.

AQUILA AND PRISCILLA:
SELF-SUPPORTING MISSIONARIES

Greet Priscilla and Aquila my helpers in Christ Jesus: who have for my life laid down their own necks: unto whom not only I give thanks, but also all the churches of the Gentiles. Rom. 16:3, 4.

Paul set an example against the sentiment, then gaining influence in the church, that the gospel could be proclaimed successfully only by those who were wholly freed from the necessity of physical toil. He illustrated in a practical way what might be done by consecrated laymen in many places where the people were unacquainted with the truths of the gospel. His course inspired many humble toilers with a desire to do what they could do to advance the cause of God, while at the same time they supported themselves in daily labor.

Aquila and Priscilla were not called to give their whole time to the ministry of the gospel, yet these humble laborers were used by God to show Apollos the way of truth more perfectly. The Lord employs various instrumentalities for the accomplishment of His purpose, and while some with special talents are chosen to devote all their energies to the work of teaching and preaching the gospel, many others, upon whom human hands have never been laid in ordination, are called to act an important part in soulsaving.

There is a large field open before the self-supporting gospel worker. Many may gain valuable experiences in ministry while toiling a portion of the time at some form of manual labor, and by this method strong workers may be developed for important service in needy fields.

The self-sacrificing servant of God who labors untiringly in word and doctrine carries on his heart a heavy burden. He does not measure his work by hours. His wages do not influence him in his labor, nor is he turned from his duty because of unfavorable conditions. From heaven he received his commission, and to heaven he looks for his recompense when the work entrusted to him is done.—*The Acts of the Apostles*, pp. 355, 356.

JOHN THE REVELATOR

I John, who also am your brother, and companion in tribulation, and in the kingdom and patience of Jesus Christ, was in the isle that is called Patmos, for the word of God, and for the testimony of Jesus Christ. Rev. 1:9.

To outward appearances the enemies of truth were triumphing; but God's hand was moving unseen in the darkness. The Lord permitted His servant to be placed where Christ could give him a more wonderful revelation of Himself than he had ever yet received; where he could receive most precious enlightenment of the churches. He permitted him to be placed in solitude, that his ear and heart might be more fully prepared to hear and receive the revelations that he was to be given. The man who exiled John was not released from responsibility in the matter. But he became an instrument in the hands of God to carry out His eternal purpose; and the very effort to extinguish light placed the truth in bold relief.

John was deprived of the companionship of his brethren, but no man could deprive him of the companionship of Christ. A great light was to shine from Christ to His servant. The Lord watched over His banished disciple, and gave him a wonderful revelation of Himself. Richly favored was this beloved disciple. With the other disciples he had walked and talked with Jesus, learning of Him and feasting on His words. His head had often rested on his Saviour's bosom. But he must see Him also in Patmos.

God and Christ and the heavenly host were John's companions on the lonely island, and from them he received instruction of infinite importance. There he wrote out the visions and revelations he received of God, telling of the things that would take place in the closing scenes of this earth's history. When his voice could no longer witness to the truth, the messages given him in Patmos were to go forth as a lamp that burneth. From them men and women were to learn the purposes of God, not concerning the Jewish nation merely, but concerning every nation upon the earth.—*Signs of the Times*, Mar. 22, 1905.

THE GREATEST NEED

Purge me with hyssop, and I shall be clean: wash me, and I shall be whiter than snow. Ps. 51:7.

A revival of true godliness among us is the greatest and most urgent of all our needs. To seek this should be our first work. There must be earnest effort to obtain the blessing of the Lord, not because God is not willing to bestow His blessing upon us, but because we are unprepared to receive it. Our heavenly Father is more willing to give His Holy Spirit to them that ask Him than are earthly parents to give good gifts to their children. But it is our work, by confession, humiliation, repentance, and earnest prayer, to fulfill the conditions upon which God has promised to grant us His blessing.

A revival need be expected only in answer to prayer. While the people are so destitute of God's Holy Spirit, they cannot appreciate the preaching of the Word; but when the Spirit's power touches their hearts, then the discourses given will not be without effect. Guided by the teachings of God's Word, with the manifestation of His Spirit, in the exercise of sound discretion, those who attend our meetings will gain a precious experience, and returning home will be prepared to exert a healthful influence.

The old standard-bearers knew what it was to wrestle with God in prayer, and to enjoy the outpouring of His Spirit. But these are passing off from the stage of action; and who are coming up to fill their places? How is it with the rising generation? Are they converted to God? Are we awake to the work that is going on in the heavenly sanctuary, or are we waiting for some compelling power to come upon the church before we shall arouse? Are we hoping to see the whole church revived? That time will never come.

There are persons in the church who are not converted, and who will not unite in earnest, prevailing prayer. We must enter upon the work individually. We must pray more, and talk less.—*Review and Herald*, Mar. 22, 1887.

THE GREATEST GIFT

Now he which stablisheth us with you in Christ, and hath anointed us, is God; who hath also sealed us, and given the earnest of the Spirit in our hearts. 2 Cor. 1:21, 22.

In giving the Holy Spirit, it was impossible for God to give more. To this gift nothing could be added. By it all needs are supplied. The Holy Spirit is the vital presence of God, and if appreciated will call forth praise and thanksgiving, and will ever be springing up unto everlasting life. The restoration of the Spirit is the covenant of grace. Yet how few appreciate this great gift, so costly, yet so free to all who will accept it? When faith takes hold of the blessing, there comes rich spiritual good. But too often the blessing is not appreciated. We need an enlarged conception in order to comprehend its value. . . .

Oh, what amazing love and condescension! The Lord Jesus encourages His believing ones to ask for the Holy Spirit. By presenting the parental tenderness of God, He seeks to encourage faith in the reception of the gift. The heavenly Parent is more willing to give the Holy Spirit to them that ask Him than earthly parents are to give good gifts to their children.

What greater thing could be promised? What more is necessary to awaken a response in every soul, to inspire us with a longing for the great gift? Shall not our halfhearted supplications be turned into petitions of intense desire for this great blessing?

We do not ask for enough of the good things God has promised. If we would reach up higher and expect more, our petitions would reveal the quickening influence that comes to every soul who asks with the full expectation of being heard and answered. The Lord is not glorified by the tame supplications which show that nothing is expected. He desires everyone who believes to approach the throne of grace with earnestness and assurance.—*Signs of the Times*, Aug. 7, 1901.

A THOROUGH REFORMATION

Fulfil ye my joy, that ye be likeminded, having the same love, being of one accord, of one mind. Phil. 2:2.

The time has come for a thorough reformation to take place. When this reformation begins, the spirit of prayer will actuate every believer and will banish from the church the spirit of discord and strife. Those who have not been living in Christian fellowship will draw close to one another. One member working in right lines will lead other members to unite with him in making intercession for the revelation of the Holy Spirit. There will be no confusion, because all will be in harmony with the mind of the Spirit. The barriers separating believer from believer will be broken down, and God's servants will speak the same things. The Lord will cooperate with His servants. All will pray understandingly the prayer that Christ taught His servants: "Thy kingdom come. Thy will be done in earth, as it is in heaven" (Matt. 6:10).

As I hear of the terrible calamities that from week to week are taking place, I ask myself: What do these things mean? The most awful disasters are following one another in quick succession. How frequently we hear of earthquakes and tornadoes, of destruction by fire and flood, with great loss of life and property! Apparently these calamities are capricious outbreaks of seemingly disorganized, unregulated forces, but in them God's purpose may be read. They are one of the means by which He seeks to arouse men and women to a sense of their danger.

The coming of Christ is nearer than when we first believed. The great controversy is nearing its end. The judgments of God are in the land. They speak in solemn warning, saying: "Be ye also ready: for in such an hour as ye think not the Son of man cometh" (Matt. 24:44).— *Testimonies*, vol. 8, pp. 251, 252.

HEART SEARCHING AND SELF-EXAMINATION

Search me, O God, and know my heart: try me, and know my thoughts: and see if there be any wicked way in me, and lead me in the way everlasting. Ps. 139:23, 24.

After Christ's ascension, the disciples were gathered together in one place to make humble supplication to God. And after ten days of heart searching and self-examination, the way was prepared for the Holy Spirit to enter the cleansed, consecrated soul temples. Every heart was filled with the Spirit, as though God desired to show His people that it was His prerogative to bless them with the choicest of heaven's blessings.

What was the result? Thousands were converted in a day. The sword of the Spirit flashed right and left. Newly edged with power, it pierced even to the dividing asunder of soul and spirit, and of the joints and marrow. The idolatry that had been mingled with the worship of the people was overthrown. New territory was added to the kingdom of God. Places that had been barren and desolate sounded forth His praises. Believers, reconverted, born again, were a living power for God. A new song was put in their mouths, even praise to the Most High.

Controlled by the Spirit, they saw Christ in their brethren. One interest prevailed. One subject of emulation swallowed up all others—to be like Christ, to do the works of Christ. The earnest zeal felt was expressed by loving helpfulness, by kindly words and unselfish deeds. All strove to see who could do the most for the enlargement of Christ's kingdom. "The multitude of them that believed were of one heart and of one soul" (Acts 4:32).

In the twelve disciples the leaven of truth was hidden by the Great Teacher. These disciples were to be the instruments in God's hands for revealing truth to the world. Divine power was given them; for a risen Saviour breathed on them, saying, "Receive ye the Holy Ghost." Imbued with this Spirit, they went forth to witness for the truth. And so God desires His servants to go forth today with the message He has given them. But till they receive the Holy Spirit, they cannot bear this message with power. Till they receive the Spirit, they cannot realize what God can do through them.—*Review and Herald*, June 10, 1902.

WITH ONE ACCORD

And when the day of Pentecost was fully come, they were all with one accord in one place. Acts 2:1.

To us today, as verily as to the first disciples, the promise of the Spirit belongs. God will today endow men and women with power from above, as He endowed those who on the day of Pentecost heard the word of salvation. At this very hour His Spirit and His grace are for all who need them and will take Him at His word.

Notice that it was after the disciples had come into perfect unity, when they were no longer striving for the highest place, that the Spirit was poured out. They were of one accord. All differences had been put away. And the testimony borne of them after the Spirit had been given is the same. Mark the word: "The multitude of them that believed were of one heart and of one soul" (Acts 4:32). The Spirit of Him who died that sinners might live animated the entire congregation of believers.

The disciples did not ask for a blessing for themselves. They were weighted with the burden of souls. The gospel was to be carried to the ends of the earth, and they claimed the endowment of power that Christ had promised. Then it was that the Holy Spirit was poured out, and thousands were converted in a day.

So it may be now. Let Christians put away all dissension and give themselves to God for the saving of the lost. Let them ask in faith for the promised blessing, and it will come. The outpouring of the Spirit in the days of the apostles was "the former rain," and glorious was the result. But the latter rain will be more abundant. What is the promise to those living in these last days? "Turn you to the strong hold, ye prisoners of hope: even today do I declare that I will render double unto thee" (Zech. 9:12) "Ask ye of the Lord rain in the time of the latter rain; so the Lord shall make bright clouds, and give them showers of rain, to every one grass in the field" (Zech. 10:1).—*Testimonies*, vol. 8, pp. 20, 21.

SEEKING HARMONY

Let nothing be done through strife or vainglory; but in lowliness of mind let each esteem other better than themselves. Phil. 2:3.

God's servants are to labor in perfect harmony. Contention brings alienation and strife and discord. I am instructed that our churches have no need to spend their time in strife. When a spirit of contention struggles for the supremacy, call a halt, and make things right, else Christ will come quickly, and will remove your candlestick out of its place. Let an earnest work of repentance be done. Let the Spirit of God search through mind and heart, and cleanse away all that hinders the needed reformation. Until this is done, God cannot bestow on us His power and grace. And while we are without His power and grace, men will stumble and fall, and will not know at what they stumble.

The love of Christ is the bond that is to unite believers heart to heart and mind to mind.

The blood of Christ has been shed for the whole human family. None need be lost. Those who are lost will perish because they chose to forfeit an eternity of bliss for the satisfaction of having their own way. This was Satan's choice, and today his work and his kingdom testify to the character of his choice. The crime and misery that fill our world, the horrible murders that are of daily occurrence, are the fruit of man's submission to Satan's principles.

My brethren, read the book of Revelation from beginning to end, and ask yourselves whether you might not better spend less time in strife and contention, and begin to think of how fast we are approaching the last great crisis. Those who seek to make it appear that there is no special meaning attached to the judgments that the Lord is now sending upon the earth will soon be forced to understand that which now they do not choose to understand.—*Review and Herald*, Aug. 20, 1903.

FEELING OUR SPIRITUAL NEED

And the publican, standing afar off, would not lift up so much as his eyes unto heaven, but smote upon his breast, saying, God be merciful to me a sinner. Luke 18:13.

We should be often in prayer. The outpouring of the Spirit of God came in answer to earnest prayer. But mark this fact concerning the disciples. The record says, "They were all with one accord in one place. And suddenly there came a sound from heaven as of a rushing mighty wind, and it filled all the house where they were sitting. And there appeared unto them cloven tongues like as of fire, and it sat upon each of them. And they were all filled with the Holy Ghost" (Acts 2:1-4).

They were not assembled to relate tidbits of scandal. They were not seeking to expose every stain they could find on a brother's character. They felt their spiritual need, and cried to the Lord for the holy unction to help them in overcoming their own infirmities, and to fit them for the work of saving others. They prayed with intense earnestness that the love of Christ might be shed abroad in their hearts.

This is our great need today in every church in our land. For "if any man be in Christ, he is a new creature: old things are passed away; behold, all things are become new" (2 Cor. 5:17). That which was objectionable in the character is purified from the soul by the love of Jesus. All selfishness is expelled, all envy, all evil-speaking, is rooted out, and a radical transformation is wrought in the heart. "The fruit of the Spirit is love, joy, peace, longsuffering, gentleness, goodness, faith, meekness, temperance: against such there is no law" (Gal. 5:22, 23). "The fruit of righteousness is sown in peace of them that make peace" (James 3:18).

Paul says that "as touching the law"—as far as outward acts were concerned—he was "blameless," but when the spiritual character of the law was discerned, when he looked into the holy mirror, he saw himself a sinner. Judged by a human standard, he had abstained from sin, but when he looked into the depths of God's law, and saw himself as God saw him, he bowed in humiliation, and confessed his guilt.—*Review and Herald*, July 22, 1890.

PLACING SELF ASIDE

But what things were gain to me, those I counted loss for Christ. Phil. 3:7.

I t is through the church that the self-sacrificing love of Jesus is to be made manifest to the world; but by the present example of the church the character of Christ is misrepresented, and a false conception of Him is given to the world. Self-love excludes the love of Jesus from the soul, and this is why there is not in the church greater zeal and more fervent love for Him who first loved us. Self is supreme in so many hearts. Their thoughts, their time, their money, are given to self-gratification, while souls for whom Christ died are perishing.

This is why the Lord cannot impart to His church the fullness of His blessing. To honor them in a distinguished manner before the world would be to put His seal upon their works, confirming their false representation of His character. When the church shall come out from the world, and be separate from its maxims, habits, and practices, the Lord Jesus will work with His people; He will pour a large measure of His Spirit upon them, and the world will know that the Father loves them. Will the people of God continue to be so stupefied with selfishness? His blessing hangs over them, but it cannot be bestowed in its fullness because they are so corrupted with the spirit and practices of the world. There is spiritual pride among them; and should the Lord work as His heart longs to do, it would but confirm them in their self-esteem and self-exaltation.

Shall Christ continue to be misrepresented by our people? Shall the grace of God, the divine enlightenment, be shut away from His church, because of their lukewarmness? It will be, unless there is most thorough seeking of God, renunciation of the world, and humbling of the soul before God. The converting power of God must pass through our churches.—*Home Missionary*, Nov. 1, 1890.

OPENING THE HEART

I am the vine, ye are the branches: He that abideth in me, and I in him, the same bringeth forth much fruit: for without me ye can do nothing. John 15:5.

The Lord desires to make man the repository of divine influence, and the only thing that hinders the accomplishment of God's designs is that men close their hearts to the Light of life. Apostasy caused the withdrawal of the Holy Spirit from man, but through the plan of redemption this blessing of heaven is to be restored to those who sincerely desire it. The Lord has promised to give all good things to those who ask Him, and all good things are defined as given with the gift of the Holy Spirit.

The more we discover our real need, our real poverty, the more will we desire the gift of the Holy Spirit; our souls will be turned, not into the channel of ambition and presumption, but into the channel of earnest supplication for the enlightenment of heaven. It is because we do not see our need, do not realize our poverty, that we do not pour forth earnest entreaties, looking unto Jesus, the author and finisher of our faith, for the bestowal of the blessing. . . .

Jesus has said, "Ask, and it shall be given you; seek, and ye shall find; knock, and it shall be opened unto you" (Matt. 7:7). It is in proportion to our appreciation of the necessity and value of spiritual things that we seek for their attainment. "Without me ye can do nothing," says Jesus, and yet many think that man can do very much in his own finite strength and wisdom. Satan is ready to offer his counsel that he may win souls in the game of life.

When men do not feel the need of counseling with their brethren, something is wrong; they trust to their wisdom. It is essential that brethren should counsel together. This I have been compelled to urge for the last forty-five years. Again and again the instruction has been repeated that those who are engaged in important work in the cause of God should not walk in their own ideas, but counsel together. —*Manuscript Releases*, vol. 2, p. 333.

EMPTYING THE VESSEL

That ye may be blameless and harmless, the sons of God, without rebuke, in the midst of a crooked and perverse nation, among whom ye shine as lights in the world. Phil. 2:15.

Transformation of character is to be the testimony to the world of the indwelling love of Christ. The Lord expects His people to show that the redeeming power of grace can work upon the faulty character and cause it to develop in symmetry and abundant fruitfulness.

But in order for us to fulfill God's purpose, there is a preparatory work to be done. The Lord bids us empty our hearts of the selfishness which is the root of alienation. He longs to pour upon us His Holy Spirit in rich measure, and He bids us clear the way by self-renunciation. When self is surrendered to God, our eyes will be opened to see the stumbling stones which our un-Christlikeness has placed in the way of others. All these God bids us remove. He says: "Confess your faults one to another, and pray one for another, that ye may be healed" (James 5:16). Then we may have the assurance that David had when, after confession of his sin, he prayed: "Restore unto me the joy of thy salvation; and uphold me with thy free spirit. Then will I teach transgressors thy ways; and sinners shall be converted unto thee" (Ps. 51:12, 13).

When the grace of God reigns within, the soul will be surrounded with an atmosphere of faith and courage and Christlike love, an atmosphere invigorating to the spiritual life of all who inhale it. . . . Everyone who is a partaker of Christ's pardoning love, everyone who has been enlightened by the Spirit of God and converted to the truth, will feel that for these precious blessings he owes a debt to every soul with whom he comes in contact. Those who are humble in heart the Lord will use to reach souls whom the ordained ministers cannot approach. They will be moved to speak words which reveal the saving grace of Christ.—*Testimonies*, vol. 6, p. 43.

WINDOWS WIDE OPEN

That ye might walk worthy of the Lord unto all pleasing, being fruitful in every good work, and increasing in the knowledge of God. Col. 1:10.

There are some who talk in a regretful way concerning the restraints that the religion of the Bible imposes upon those who would follow its teachings. They seem to think that restraint is a great disadvantage, but we have reason to thank God with all our heart that He has raised a heavenly barrier between us and the ground of the enemy. There are certain tendencies of the natural heart that many think must be followed in order that the best development of the individual may result, but that which man thinks essential God sees would not be the blessing to humanity which men imagine, for the development of these very traits of character would unfit them for the mansions above.

The Lord places men under test and trial that the dross may be separated from the gold, but He forces none. He does not bind with fetters and cords and barriers, for they increase disaffection rather than decrease it. The remedy for evil is found in Christ as an indwelling Saviour. But in order that Christ may be in the soul, it must first be emptied of self, then there is a vacuum created that may be supplied by the Holy Spirit.

The Lord purifies the heart very much as we air a room. We do not close the doors and windows and throw in some purifying substance; but we open the doors and throw wide the windows, and let heaven's purifying atmosphere flow in. The Lord says, "He that doeth truth cometh to the light" (John 3:21). The windows of impulse, of feeling, must be opened up toward heaven, and the dust of selfishness and earthliness must be expelled. The grace of God must sweep through the chambers of the mind, the imagination must have heavenly themes for contemplation, and every element of the nature must be purified and vitalized by the Spirit of God.—*Manuscript Releases*, vol. 2, p. 338.

THE SUN OF RIGHTEOUSNESS PURIFIES THE SOUL

Giving thanks unto the Father, which hath made us meet to be partakers of the inheritance of the saints in light: who hath delivered us from the power of darkness, and hath translated us into the kingdom of his dear Son. Col. 1:12, 13.

It is the privilege of every earnest seeker for truth and righteousness to rely upon the sure promises of God. The Lord Jesus makes manifest the fact that the treasures of divine grace are placed entirely at our disposal, in order that we may become channels of light. We cannot receive the riches of the grace of Christ without desiring to impart them to others. When we have the love of Christ in our hearts, we shall feel that it is our duty and privilege to communicate it. The sun shining in the heavens pours its bright beams into all the highways and byways of life. It has sufficient light for thousands of worlds like ours. And so it is with the Sun of righteousness; His bright beams of healing and gladness are amply sufficient to save our little world, and are efficacious in establishing security in every world that has been created. . . .

Those who realize their need of repentance toward God, and faith toward our Lord Jesus Christ, will have contrition of soul, will repent for their resistance of the Spirit of the Lord. They will confess their sin in refusing the light that heaven has so graciously sent them, and they will forsake the sin that grieved and insulted the Spirit of the Lord. They will humble self, and accept the power and grace of Christ, acknowledging the messages of warning, reproof, and encouragement. Then their faith in the work of God will be made manifest, and they will rely upon the atoning sacrifice. They will make a personal appropriation of Christ's abundant grace and righteousness, and He will become to them a present Saviour; for they will realize their need of Him, and with complete trust will rest in Him. They will drink of the water of life from the divine, inexhaustible Fountain. In a new and blessed experience, they will cast themselves upon Christ, and become partakers of the divine nature.—*Review and Herald*, Aug. 26, 1890.

EYES LOOKING HEAVENWARD

For our conversation is in heaven; from whence also we look for the Saviour, the Lord Jesus Christ. Phil. 3:20.

Shall we not break off our sins by righteousness, and have our conversation in heaven, whence we look for our Saviour? Shall we not talk of our Saviour until it becomes natural for us to do so? If we do not order our conversation aright, we shall not see the salvation of God. Satan will take possession of the heart, and we shall become low and sensual. Let us elevate the thoughts, and take hold upon things that are of real value, gaining an education here that will be of value in the world to come. Shall we not seek the Lord with earnestness, repent of our backslidings, mourn that we have neglected His Word, that we do not know the truth better, and turn to Him with all the heart, that He may heal us, and love us freely? Today let us take a step toward heaven. . . .

The latter rain is to fall upon the people of God. A mighty angel is to come down from heaven, and the whole earth is to be lighted with His glory. Are we ready to take part in the glorious work of the third angel? Are our vessels ready to receive the heavenly dew? Have we defilement and sin in the heart? If so, let us cleanse the soul temple, and prepare for the showers of the latter rain. The refreshing from the presence of the Lord will never come to hearts filled with impurity. May God help us to die to self, that Christ, the hope of glory, may be formed within!

I must have the Spirit of God in my heart. I can never go forward to do the great work of God, unless the Holy Spirit rests upon my soul. "As the hart panteth after the water brooks, so panteth my soul after thee, O God" (Ps. 42:1). The day of judgment is upon us. Oh, that we may wash our robes of character, and make them white in the blood of the Lamb!—*Review and Herald*, Apr. 21, 1891.

FROM SCARLET TO WHITE

Come now, and let us reason together, saith the Lord: though your sins be as scarlet, they shall be as white as snow; though they be red like crimson, they shall be as wool. Isa. 1:18.

When you remember that Christ has paid the price of His own blood for your redemption and for the redemption of others, you will be moved to catch the bright rays of His righteousness, that you may shed them upon the pathway of those around you. You are not to look to the future, thinking that at some distant day you are to be made holy; it is now that you are to be sanctified through the truth. The prophet exhorts: "Seek ye the Lord while he may be found, call ye upon him while he is near: let the wicked forsake his way, and the unrighteous man his thoughts: and let him return unto the Lord, and he will have mercy upon him; and to our God, for he will abundantly pardon" (Isa. 55:6, 7). And Jesus said, "But ye shall receive power, after that the Holy Ghost is come upon you: and ye shall be witnesses unto me . . . unto the uttermost part of the earth" (Acts 1:8).

We are to receive the Holy Ghost. We have had an idea that this gift of God was not for such as we are, that the gift of the Holy Spirit was too sacred, too holy for us; but the Holy Spirit is the Comforter that Christ promised to His disciples to bring all things to their remembrance, whatsoever He had said unto them. Then let us cease to look to ourselves, but look to Him from whom all virtue comes. No one can make himself better, but we are to come to Jesus as we are, earnestly desiring to be cleansed from every spot and stain of sin, and receive the gift of the Holy Spirit. We are not to doubt His mercy, and say, "I do not know whether I shall be saved or not." By living faith we must lay hold of His promise, for He has said, "Though your sins be as scarlet, they shall be as white as snow; though they be red like crimson, they shall be as wool."

We are to be witnesses for Christ, reflecting upon others the light which the Lord permits to shine upon us. We are to be as faithful soldiers marching under the bloodstained banner of Prince Emmanuel. —*Signs of the Times*, Apr. 4, 1892.

GARMENT CHANGED

And when the king came in to see the guests, he saw there a man which had not on a wedding garment: and he saith unto him, Friend, how camest thou in hither not having a wedding garment? And he was speechless. Matt. 22:11, 12.

Discard your citizen's dress, and put on the wedding garment which Christ has prepared. Then you can sit in heavenly places with Christ Jesus. God welcomes all who come to Him just as they are, not building themselves up in self-righteousness, not seeking to justify self, not claiming merits for what they call good actions, not priding themselves on their supposed knowledge. While you have been walking and working in meekness and lowliness of heart, a work has been done for you—a work that only God could do. It is God who works in you, both to will and to do of His good pleasure. That good pleasure is to see you abiding in Christ, resting in His love.

Let not anything rob your soul of peace, of restfulness, of the assurance that you are accepted just now. Claim every promise; all are yours if you will comply with the prescribed terms. Entire self-surrender, an acceptance of Christ's ways, is the secret of perfect rest in His love.

The abiding rest—who has it? That rest is found when all self-justification, all reasoning from a selfish standpoint, is put away. Entire self-surrender, an acceptance of His ways, is the secret of perfect rest in His love. We must learn His meekness and lowliness before we experience the fulfillment of the promise "Ye shall find rest unto your souls" (Matt. 11:29). It is by learning the habits of Christ that self becomes transformed—by taking His yoke, and then submitting to learn.

Giving up the life to Christ means much more than many suppose. God calls for an entire surrender. We cannot receive the Holy Spirit until we break every yoke that binds us to our objectionable traits of character. These are the great hindrances to wearing Christ's yoke and learning of Him. There is no one who has not much to learn. All must be trained by Christ.—*Review and Herald*, Apr. 25, 1899.

THE WILL SURRENDERED

For it is God which worketh in you both to will and to do of his good pleasure. Phil. 2:13.

Christ has promised the gift of the Holy Spirit to His church, and the promise belongs to us as much as to the first disciples. But like every other promise, it is given on conditions. There are many who believe and profess to claim the Lord's promise; they talk about Christ and the Holy Spirit, yet receive no benefit. They do not surrender the soul to be guided and controlled by divine agencies. We cannot use the Holy Spirit. The Spirit is to use us. Through the Spirit God works in His people "to will and to do of his good pleasure." But many will not submit to this. They want to manage themselves. This is why they do not receive the heavenly gift.

Only to those who wait humbly upon God, who watch for His guidance and grace, is the Spirit given. The power of God awaits their demand and reception. This promised blessing, claimed by faith, brings all other blessings in its train. It is given according to the riches of the grace of Christ, and He is ready to supply every soul according to the capacity to receive.

When the Spirit of God takes possession of the heart, He transforms the life. Sinful thoughts are put away, evil deeds are renounced; love, humility, and peace take the place of anger, envy, and strife. Joy takes the place of sadness, and the countenance reflects the joy of heaven. No one sees the hand that lifts the burden, or beholds the light descend from the courts above. The blessing comes when by faith the soul surrenders itself to God. Then that power which no human eye can see creates a new being in the image of God.

The Holy Spirit is the breath of spiritual life in the soul. The impartation of the Spirit is the impartation of the life of Christ. [The Spirit] imbues the receiver with the attributes of Christ.—*Review and Herald*, Nov. 19, 1908.

SELF SUBDUED

I counsel thee to buy of me gold tried in the fire, that thou mayest be rich; and white raiment, that thou mayest be clothed, and that the shame of thy nakedness do not appear; and anoint thine eyes with eyesalve, that thou mayest see. Rev. 3:18.

There is to be in the churches a wonderful manifestation of the power of God, but it will not move upon those who have not humbled themselves before the Lord, and opened the door of the heart by confession and repentance. In the manifestation of that power which lightens the earth with the glory of God, they will see only something which in their blindness they think dangerous, something which will arouse their fears, and they will brace themselves to resist it. Because the Lord does not work according to their ideas and expectations, they will oppose the work. "Why," they say, "should not we know the Spirit of God, when we have been in the work so many years?" Because they did not respond to the warnings, the entreaties of the messages of God, but persistently said, "I am rich, and increased with goods, and have need of nothing" (Rev. 3:17).

Talent, long experience, will not make men channels of light, unless they place themselves under the bright beams of the Sun of righteousness, and are called, and chosen, and prepared by the endowment of the Holy Spirit. When men who handle sacred things will humble themselves under the mighty hand of God, the Lord will lift them up. He will make them men of discernment—men rich in the grace of His Spirit. Their strong, selfish traits of character, their stubbornness, will be seen in the light shining from the Light of the world. "I will come unto thee quickly, and will remove thy candlestick out of his place, except thou repent" (Rev. 2:5). If you seek the Lord with all your heart, He will be found of you.

The end is near! We have not a moment to lose! Light is to shine forth from God's people in clear, distinct rays, bringing Jesus before the churches and before the world.—*Review and Herald*, Dec. 23, 1890.

A MIND SUBMISSIVE

That he would grant you, according to the riches of his glory, to be strengthened with might by his Spirit in the inner man. Eph. 3:16.

The gospel of Christ makes progress in every human agent that is consecrated to the Lord's service. The Holy Spirit takes possession of everyone who has a willing mind, not that that person may work the Holy Spirit, but that the Holy Spirit may work His miracle through the grace that is poured upon the human agency. The goodness of God becomes a working power through a consistent life, through fervent love for Jesus, and through heaven-inspired zeal. Those who are in association with Jesus will partake of His melting love, and manifest His overflowing sympathy for souls who are yielding to Satan's specious temptations. They will plan and study and exercise tact, in order that they may make a success of so presenting the unselfish love of Christ that sinful and impenitent hearts may be won to loyalty to Jesus, who gave His life for them. . . .

Lose no time; confess Christ without delay. It is the Holy Spirit, the Comforter, the Spirit of truth that testifies of Christ. Jesus said, "Ye shall receive power, after that the Holy Ghost is come upon you: and ye shall be witnesses unto me both in Jerusalem, and in all Judea, and in Samaria, and unto the uttermost part of the earth" (Acts 1:8).

To grieve the Holy Spirit which would make you a witness of Christ is a terrible thing. You know not when you may grieve the Spirit for the last time. The Holy Spirit does not work upon the human heart to compel you to give yourself to Christ, to force you to yield your conscience: but [the Spirit] shines into the chambers of the mind in a way to convict of sin, and to entice you unto righteousness. If you do not confess Christ now, the time will come when, overwhelmed with a sense of the great things that you have lost, you will make confession. But why not confess Christ now while mercy's voice invites you?—*Youth's Instructor*, Aug. 1, 1895.

REMOVING EVERY HINDRANCE

Now I beseech you, brethren, by the name of our Lord Jesus Christ, that ye all speak the same thing, and that there be no divisions among you; but that ye be perfectly joined together in the same mind and in the same judgment. 1 Cor. 1:10.

For the outpouring of the Spirit every lover of the cause of truth should pray. And as far as lies in our power, we are to remove every hindrance to His working. The Spirit can never be poured out while variance and bitterness toward one another are cherished by the members of the church. Envy, jealousy, evil surmising, and evil-speaking are of Satan, and they effectually bar the way against the Holy Spirit's working.

Nothing else in this world is so dear to God as His church. Nothing is guarded by Him with such jealous care. Nothing so offends God as an act that injures the influence of those who are doing His service. He will call to account all who aid Satan in his work of criticizing and discouraging.

Those who are destitute of sympathy, tenderness, and love cannot do Christ's work. Before the prophecy can be fulfilled, The weak shall be "as David," and the house of David "as the angel of the Lord" (Zech. 12:8), the children of God must put away every thought of suspicion in regard to their brethren. Heart must beat in unison with heart. Christian benevolence and brotherly love must be far more abundantly shown. The words are ringing in my ears: "Draw together, draw together." The solemn, sacred truth for this time is to unify the people of God. The desire for preeminence must die. One subject of emulation must swallow up all others—who will most nearly resemble Christ in character? who will most entirely hide self in Jesus?

"Herein is my Father glorified," Christ says, "that ye bear much fruit" (John 15:8). If there was ever a place where the believers should bear much fruit, it is at our camp meetings. At these meetings our acts, our words, our spirit, are marked, and our influence is as far-reaching as eternity.—*Testimonies*, vol. 6, p. 42.

ACCEPTING THE SPIRIT'S INFLUENCE

Having therefore these promises, dearly beloved, let us cleanse ourselves from all filthiness of the flesh and spirit, perfecting holiness in the fear of God. 2 Cor. 7:1.

The Lord sends us warning, counsel, and reproof, that we may have opportunity to correct our errors before they become second nature. But if we refuse to be corrected, God does not interfere to counteract the tendencies of our own course of action. He works no miracle that the seed sown may not spring up and bear fruit. That man who manifests an infidel hardihood or a stolid indifference to divine truth is but reaping the harvest which he has himself sown. Such has been the experience of many. They listen with stoical indifference to the truths which once stirred their very souls. They sowed neglect, indifference, and resistance to the truth; and such is the harvest which they reap.

The coldness of ice, the hardness of iron, the impenetrable, unimpressible nature of rock—all these find a counterpart in the character of many a professed Christian. It was thus that the Lord hardened the heart of Pharaoh. God spoke to the Egyptian king by the mouth of Moses, giving him the most striking evidences of divine power; but the monarch stubbornly refused the light which would have brought him to repentance. God did not send a supernatural power to harden the heart of the rebellious king, but as Pharaoh resisted the truth, the Holy Spirit was withdrawn, and he was left to the darkness and unbelief which he had chosen.

By persistent rejection of the Spirit's influence, men cut themselves off from God. He has in reserve no more potent agency to enlighten their minds. No revelation of His will can reach them in their unbelief.

Would that I could lead every professed follower of Christ to see this matter as it is. We are all sowing either to the flesh or to the Spirit, and we reap the harvest from the seed we sow. In choosing our pleasures or employments, we should seek only those things that are excellent. The trifling, the worldly, the debasing, should have no power to control the affections or the will.—*Review and Herald*, June 20, 1882.

EXPECTING GREAT THINGS

Now we have received, not the spirit of the world, but the spirit which is of God; that we might know the things that are freely given to us of God. 1 Cor. 2:12.

It is not because of any restriction on God's part that the riches of His grace do not flow to men. His gift is godlike. He gave with a liberality that men do not appreciate because they do not love to receive. If all were willing to receive, all would be filled with the Spirit. By resting content with small blessings, we disqualify ourselves for receiving the Spirit in . . . unlimited fullness. We are too easily satisfied with a ripple on the surface, when it is our privilege to expect the deep moving of the Spirit of God. Expecting little, we receive little.

The necessity of the Holy Spirit's working should be realized by all. Unless this Spirit is accepted and cherished as the representative of Christ, whose work it is to renew and sanctify the entire being, the momentous truths that have been entrusted to human beings will lose their power on the mind. It is not enough for us to have a knowledge of the truth. We are to walk and work in love, conforming our will to the will of God. Of those who do this the Lord declares, "I will put my laws into their mind, and write them in their hearts" (Heb. 8:10). God is the mighty, all-powerful agency in this work of transformation. By His Holy Spirit He writes His law in the heart.

Thus divine relationship is renewed between God and man. "I will be to them a God," He says, "and they shall be to Me a people" (see Ex. 6:7; Jer. 31:33). "There is no attribute of My nature that I will not freely give in order than man may reveal My image." When we allow God to work His will in us, we shall harbor no sin. In the refining furnace all dross will be consumed.

When the Holy Spirit came down on the day of Pentecost, it was like a rushing, mighty wind. [The Spirit] was given in no stinted measure; for He filled all the place where the disciples were sitting. So will He be given to us when our hearts are prepared to receive Him.—*Review and Herald*, June 10, 1902.

ASKING FOR HIS BLESSING

And shall not God avenge his own elect, which cry day and night unto him, though he bear long with them? Luke 18:7.

We may have long followed the narrow path, but it is not safe to take this as proof that we shall follow it to the end. If we have walked with God in fellowship of the Spirit, it is because we have sought Him daily by faith. From the two olive trees, the golden oil flowing through the golden pipes has been communicated to us. But those who do not cultivate the spirit and habit of prayer cannot expect to receive the golden oil of goodness, patience, long-suffering, gentleness, love.

Everyone is to keep himself separate from the world, which is full of iniquity. We are not to walk with God for a time, and then part from His company, and walk in the sparks of our own kindling. There must be a firm continuance, a perseverance in acts of faith. We are to praise God, to show forth His glory in a righteous character. No one of us will gain the victory without persevering, untiring effort, proportionate to the value of the object which we seek, even eternal life.

The dispensation in which we are now living is to be, to those that ask, the dispensation of the Holy Spirit. Ask for His blessing. It is time we were more intense in our devotion. To us is committed the arduous, but happy, glorious work of revealing Christ to those who are in darkness. We are called to proclaim the special truths for this time. For all this the outpouring of the Spirit is essential. We should pray for [the Spirit]. The Lord expects us to ask Him. We have not been wholehearted in this work.

What can I say to my brethren in the name of the Lord? What proportion of our efforts has been made in accordance with the light the Lord has been pleased to give? We cannot depend upon form or external machinery. What we need is the quickening influence of the Holy Spirit of God. "Not by might, nor by power, but by my Spirit, saith the Lord of hosts" (Zech. 4:6). Pray without ceasing, and watch by working in accordance with your prayers. As you pray, believe, trust in God. It is the time of the latter rain, when the Lord will give largely of His Spirit. Be fervent in prayer, and watch in the Spirit.—*Review and Herald*, Mar. 2, 1897.

TRUSTING HIS PROMISE

Let us therefore come boldly unto the throne of grace, that we may obtain mercy, and find grace to help in time of need. Heb. 4:16.

The Lord will not leave His afflicted, tried children to be the sport of Satan's temptations. It is our privilege to trust in Jesus. The heavens are full of rich blessings, and it is our privilege to have the joy of Christ in us that our joy may be full. We have not because we ask not, or because we do not pray in faith, believing that we shall be blessed with the special influence of the Holy Spirit. To the true seeker through the mediation of Christ the gracious influences of the Holy Spirit are imparted in order that the receiver may impart a knowledge of saving truth.

Why do we not believe the plain "Thus saith the Lord"? Do not cease to pray under any circumstances. The Spirit may be willing but the flesh may be weak, but Jesus knows all about that. In your weakness you are not to be anxious; for anxiety means doubt and distrust. You are simply to believe that Christ is able to save unto the uttermost all who come unto God by Him, seeing He ever liveth to make intercession for us.

What does intercession comprehend? It is the golden chain which binds finite man to the throne of the infinite God. The human agent whom Christ has died to save importunes the throne of God, and his petition is taken up by Jesus, who has purchased him with His own blood. Our great High Priest places His righteousness on the side of the sincere suppliant, and the prayer of Christ blends with that of the human petitioner.

Christ has urged that His people pray without ceasing. This does not mean that we should always be upon our knees, but that prayer is to be as the breath of the soul. Our silent requests, wherever we may be, are to be ascending unto God, and Jesus, our advocate, pleads in our behalf, bearing up with the incense of His righteousness our requests to the Father.

The Lord Jesus loves His people, and when they put their trust in Him, depending wholly upon Him, He strengthens them. He will live through them, giving them the inspiration of His sanctifying Spirit, imparting to the soul a vital transfusion of Himself.—*Sabbath School Worker*, Feb. 1, 1896.

A PERMANENT CONNECTION

And he spake a parable unto them to this end, that men ought always to pray, and not to faint. Luke 18:1.

At no point in our experience can we dispense with the assistance of that which enables us to make the first start. The blessings received under the former rain are needful to us to the end. Yet these alone will not suffice. While we cherish the blessing of the early rain, we must not, on the other hand, lose sight of the fact that without the latter rain, to fill out the ears and ripen the grain, the harvest will not be ready for the sickle, and the labor of the sower will have been in vain. Divine grace is needed at the beginning, divine grace at every step of advance, and divine grace alone can complete the work.

There is no place for us to rest in a careless attitude. We must never forget the warnings of Christ, "Watch unto prayer," "Watch . . . and pray always" (Luke 21:36). A connection with the divine agency every moment is essential to our progress. We may have had a measure of the Spirit of God, but by prayer and faith we are continually to seek more of the Spirit. It will never do to cease our efforts. If we do not progress, if we do not place ourselves in an attitude to receive both the former and the latter rain, we shall lose our souls, and the responsibility will lie at our own door.

"Ask ye of the Lord rain in the time of the latter rain" (Zech. 10:1). Do not rest satisfied that in the ordinary course of the season, rain will fall. Ask for it. The growth and perfection of the seed rests not with the husbandman. God alone can ripen the harvest. But man's cooperation is required. God's work for us demands the action of our mind, the exercise of our faith. We must seek His favors with the whole heart if the showers of grace are to come to us.

We should improve every opportunity of placing ourselves in the channel of blessing. Christ has said, "Where two or three are gathered together in my name, there am I in the midst" (Matt. 18:20). The convocations of the church, as in camp meetings, the assemblies of the home church, and all occasions where there is personal labor for souls, are God's appointed opportunities for giving the early and the latter rain.—*Review and Herald*, Mar. 2, 1897.

REAL APPRECIATION

And when they had prayed, the place was shaken where they were assembled together; and they were all filled with the Holy Ghost, and they spake the word of God with boldness. Acts 4:31.

The outpouring of the Spirit in the days of the apostles was the "former rain"; and glorious was the result. But the "latter rain" will be still more abundant. What is the promise to those living in these last days? "Turn you to the stronghold, ye prisoners of hope: even today do I declare that I will render double unto thee" (Zech. 9:12). "Ask ye of the Lord rain in the time of the latter rain; so the Lord shall make bright clouds, and give them showers of rain, to every one grass in the field" (Zech. 10:1).

Christ declares that the divine influence of the Spirit was to be with His followers unto the end. But by some this promise is not appreciated as it should be; its fulfillment is not realized as it might be. Learning, talents, eloquence, every natural or acquired endowment, may be possessed; but without the presence of the Spirit of God, no heart will be touched, no sinner won to Christ. When His disciples are connected with Christ, when the gifts of the Spirit are theirs, even the poorest and most ignorant of them will have a power that will tell upon hearts. God makes them the channel for the outworking of the highest influence in the universe.

As the divine endowment—the power of the Holy Spirit—was given to the disciples, so it will today be given to all who seek aright. This power alone is able to make us wise unto salvation, and to fit us for the courts above. Christ wants to give us a blessing that will make us holy. "These things have I spoken unto you," He says, "that my joy might remain in you, and that your joy might be full" (John 15:11). Joy in the Holy Spirit is health-giving, life-giving. In giving us His Spirit, God gives us Himself—a fountain of divine influences, to give health and life to the world.—*Signs of the Times*, Mar. 15, 1910.

MORE PREACHING

Which things also we speak, not in the words which man's wisdom teacheth, but which the Holy Ghost teacheth; comparing spiritual things with spiritual. 1 Cor. 2:13.

Just prior to His leaving His disciples for the heavenly courts, Jesus encouraged them with the promise of the Holy Spirit. This promise belongs as much to us as it did to them, and yet how rarely it is presented before the people, and its reception spoken of in the church.

In consequence of this silence upon this most important theme, what promise do we know less about by its practical fulfillment than this rich promise of the gift of the Holy Spirit, whereby efficiency is to be given to all our spiritual labor? The promise of the Holy Spirit is casually brought into our discourses, is incidentally touched upon, and that is all. Prophecies have been dwelt upon, doctrines have been expounded; but that which is essential to the church in order that they may grow in spiritual strength and efficiency, in order that the preaching may carry conviction with it, and souls be converted to God, has been largely left out of ministerial effort.

This subject has been set aside, as if some time in the future would be given to its consideration. Other blessings and privileges have been presented before the people until a desire has been awakened in the church for the attainment of the blessing promised of God; but the impression concerning the Holy Spirit has been that this gift is not for the church now, but that at some time in the future it would be necessary for the church to receive it.

This promised blessing, if claimed by faith, would bring all other blessings in its train, and it is to be given liberally to the people of God. Through the cunning devices of the enemy the minds of God's people seem to be incapable of comprehending and appropriating the promises of God. . . . A harvest of joy will be reaped by those who sow the holy seeds of truth. "He that goeth forth and weepeth, bearing precious seed, shall doubtless come again with rejoicing, bringing his sheaves with him" (Ps. 126:6).—*Testimonies to Ministers*, pp. 174, 175.

MORE COMMITMENT

Every man's work shall be made manifest: for the day shall declare it, because it shall be revealed by fire; and the fire shall try every man's work of what sort it is. 1 Cor. 3:13.

The end of all things is at hand. God is moving upon every mind that is open to receive the impressions of His Holy Spirit. He is sending out messengers that they may give the warning in every locality. God is testing the devotion of His churches and their willingness to render obedience to the Spirit's guidance. Knowledge is to be increased. The messengers of heaven are to be seen running to and fro, seeking in every possible way to warn the people of the coming judgments, and presenting the glad tidings of salvation through our Lord Jesus Christ. The standard of righteousness is to be exalted.

The Spirit of God is moving upon men's hearts, and those who respond to His influence will become lights in the world. Everywhere they are seen going forth to communicate to others the light they have received as they did after the descent of the Holy Spirit on the day of Pentecost. And as they let their light shine, they receive more and more of the Spirit's power. The earth is lighted with the glory of God.

But, oh, sad picture! Those who do not submit to the influence of the Holy Spirit soon lose the blessings received when they acknowledged the truth as from heaven. They fall into a cold, spiritless formality; they lose their interest in perishing souls: they have "left their first love." And Christ says unto them, "Remember therefore from whence thou art fallen, and repent, and do the first works; or else I will come unto thee quickly, and will remove thy candlestick out of his place, except thou repent" (Rev. 2:5). He will take His Holy Spirit from the church, and give [the Spirit] to others who will appreciate Him.

There is no greater evidence that those who have received great light do not appreciate that light, than is given by their refusal to let their light shine upon those who are in darkness, and devoting their time and energies in celebrating forms and ceremonies.—*Review and Herald*, July 16, 1895.

MORE CONSECRATED MEMBERS

And they, continuing daily with one accord in the temple, and breaking bread from house to house, did eat their meat with gladness and singleness of heart, praising God, and having favour with all the people. And the Lord added to the church daily such as should be saved. Acts 2:46, 47.

Every truly converted soul will be intensely desirous to bring others from the darkness of error into the marvelous light of the righteousness of Jesus Christ. The great outpouring of the Spirit of God, which lightens the whole earth with His glory, will not come until we have an enlightened people, that know by experience what it means to be laborers together with God. When we have entire, wholehearted consecration to the service of Christ, God will recognize the fact by an outpouring of His Spirit without measure; but this will not be while the largest portion of the church are not laborers together with God. God cannot pour out His Spirit when selfishness and self-indulgence are so manifest; when a spirit prevails that, if put into words, would express that answer of Cain—"Am I my brother's keeper?" (Gen. 4:9).

If the truth for this time, if the signs that are thickening on every hand, that testify that the end of all things is at hand, are not sufficient to arouse the sleeping energy of those who profess to know the truth, then darkness proportionate to the light which has been shining will overtake these souls. There is not the semblance of an excuse for their indifference that they will be able to present to God in the great day of final reckoning. There will be no reason to offer as to why they did not live and walk and work in the light of the sacred truth of the Word of God, and thus reveal to a sin-darkened world, through their conduct, their sympathy, and their zeal, that the power and reality of the gospel could not be controverted.

It is not the ministers alone, but the laymen, who are not contributing all that they can to persuade men, by precept and example, to accept the saving grace of Christ. With skill and tact, with wisdom received from above, they should persuade men to behold the Lamb of God, who taketh away the sin of the world.—*Review and Herald*, July 21, 1896.

MORE CHARITY

Then shalt thou call, and the Lord shall answer; thou shalt cry, and he shall say, Here I am. If thou take away from the midst of thee the yoke, the putting forth of the finger, and speaking vanity: and if thou draw out thy soul to the hungry, and satisfy the afflicted soul; then shall thy light rise in obscurity, and thy darkness be as the noonday. Isa. 58:9, 10.

Let all who claim to keep the commandments of God look well to this matter, and see if there are not reasons why they do not have more of the outpouring of the Holy Spirit. How many have lifted up their souls unto vanity! They think themselves exalted in the favor of God, but they neglect the needy, they turn a deaf ear to the calls of the oppressed, and speak sharp, cutting words to those who need altogether different treatment. Thus they offend God daily by their hardness of heart. These afflicted ones have claims upon the sympathies and the interest of their fellow men. They have a right to expect help, comfort, and Christlike love. But this is not what they receive.

Every neglect of God's suffering ones is written in the books of heaven as if shown to Christ Himself. Let every member of the church closely examine his heart, and investigate his course of action, to see if these are in harmony with the Spirit and work of Jesus; for if not, what can he say when he stands before the Judge of all the earth? Can the Lord say to him, "Come, ye blessed of my Father, inherit the kingdom prepared for you from the foundation of the world" (Matt. 25:34)?

Christ has identified His interest with that of suffering humanity; and while He is neglected in the person of His afflicted ones, all our assemblies, all our appointed meetings, all the machinery that is set in operation to advance the cause of God, will be of little avail. "These ought ye to have done, and not to leave the other undone" (Luke 11:42). "Thou art weighed in the balances, and art found wanting" (Dan. 5:27).

All who are to be saints in heaven will first be saints upon the earth. They will not follow the sparks of their own kindling, they will not work for praise, nor speak words of vanity, nor put forth the finger in condemnation and oppression; but they will follow the Light of life, diffuse light, comfort, hope, and courage to the very ones who need help, and not censure and reproach.—*Review and Herald*, Aug. 4, 1891.

MORE EARNEST PRAYING

We acknowledge, O Lord, our wickedness, and the iniquity of our fathers: for we have sinned against thee. Do not abhor us, for thy name's sake, do not disgrace the throne of thy glory: remember, break not thy covenant with us. Jer. 14:20, 21.

Let our prayers ascend to God for His converting, transforming grace. Meetings should be held in every church for solemn prayer and earnest searching of the Word to know what is truth. Take the promises of God, and ask God in living faith for the outpouring of His Holy Spirit. When the Holy Spirit is shed upon us, marrow and fatness will be drawn from the Word of God. . . .

When the churches become living, working churches, the Holy Spirit will be given in answer to their sincere request. Then the truth of God's Word will be regarded with new interest, and will be explored as if it were a revelation just from the courts above. Every declaration of inspiration concerning Christ will take hold of the inmost soul of those who love Him. Envy, jealousy, evil surmising, will cease. The Bible will be regarded as a charter from heaven. Its study will absorb the mind, and its truths will feast the soul. The promises of God now repeated as if the soul had never tasted of His love will then glow upon the altar of the heart, and fall in burning words from the lips of the messengers of God. They will then plead with souls with an earnestness that cannot be repulsed. Then the windows of heaven will be open for the showers of the latter rain. The followers of Christ will be united in love.

The only way the truth can be presented to the world, in its pure and holy character, is for those who claim to believe it to be exponents of its power. The Bible requires the sons and daughters of God to stand on an elevated platform; for God calls upon them to represent Christ to the world. As they represent Christ, they represent the Father. Unity of believers testifies of their oneness with Christ, and this unity is required by the accumulated light which now shines upon the pathway of the children of God.—*Review and Herald*, Feb. 25, 1890.

A PRAYER IN BEHALF OF GOD'S PEOPLE

O Lord, hear; O Lord, forgive; O Lord, hearken and do; defer not, for thine own sake, O my God: for thy city and thy people are called by thy name. Dan. 9:19.

Heavenly Father, Thou hast said, "Ask, and it shall be given you; seek, and ye shall find; knock, and it shall be opened unto you" (Matt. 7:7). Heavenly Father, we need Thy Holy Spirit. We do not want to work ourselves, only as we work in unity with God. We want to be in a position where the Holy Spirit of God shall be upon us with His reviving, sanctifying power. Wilt Thou manifest Thyself unto us this very morning! Wilt Thou sweep away every mist and every cloud of darkness!

We come to Thee, our compassionate Redeemer; and we ask Thee, for Christ's sake—for Thine own Son's sake, my Father, that Thou wilt manifest Thy power unto Thy people here. We want wisdom; we want righteousness; we want truth; we want the Holy Spirit to be with us.

Thou hast presented before us a great work that must be carried forward in behalf of those that are in the truth, and in behalf of those that are in ignorance of our faith; and oh, Lord, as Thou hast given to every man his work, we beseech of Thee that the Holy Spirit may impress the human mind in regard to the burden of work that shall rest upon every individual soul, according to Thine appointment. We want to be proved; we want to be sanctified through and through; we want to be fitted up for the work; and here, right here in this session of the conference, we want to see a revelation of the Holy Spirit of God. We want light, Lord—Thou art the Light. We want truth, Lord—Thou art the Truth. We want the right way—Thou art the Way.

Lord, I beseech of Thee that we may all be wise enough to discern that we must individually open the heart to Jesus Christ, that through the Holy Spirit He may come in to mold and fashion us anew, in accordance with the divine Image. Oh, my Father, my Father! melt and subdue our hearts.—*General Conference Bulletin*, Apr. 2, 1903.

REVIVAL AT PENTECOST

And by the hands of the apostles were many signs and wonders wrought among the people; and they were all with one accord in Solomon's porch. Acts 5:12.

Christ has made provision that His church shall be a transformed body, illumined with the light of heaven, possessing the glory of Immanuel. It is His purpose that every Christian shall be surrounded with a spiritual atmosphere of light and peace. There is no limit to the usefulness of the one who, putting self aside, makes room for the working of the Holy Spirit upon the heart, and lives a life wholly consecrated to God.

What was the result of the outpouring of the Spirit upon the day of Pentecost? The glad tidings of a risen Saviour were carried to the utmost bounds of the inhabited world. The hearts of the disciples were surcharged with the benevolence so full, so deep, so far-reaching, that it impelled them to go to the ends of the earth, testifying, "God forbid that I should glory, save in the cross of our Lord Jesus Christ" (Gal. 6:14). As they proclaimed the truth as it is in Jesus, hearts yielded to the power of the message. The church beheld converts flocking to her from all directions. Backsliders were reconverted. Sinners united with Christians in seeking the Pearl of great price.

Those who had been the bitterest opponents of the gospel became its champions. The prophecy was fulfilled, that the weak shall be "as David," and the house of David "as the angel of the Lord." Every Christian saw in his brother the divine similitude of love and benevolence. One interest prevailed. One subject of emulation swallowed up all others. The only ambition of the believers was to reveal the likeness of Christ's character and to labor for the enlargement of His kingdom.

Notice that it was after the disciples had come into perfect unity, when they were no longer striving for the highest place, that the Spirit was poured out. They were of one accord. All differences had been put away. And the testimony borne of them after the Spirit had been given was the same.—*Review and Herald*, Apr. 30, 1908.

UNLIMITED SUPPLIES
OF MISSIONARY SPIRIT

*And believers were the more added to the Lord, multitudes both of men
and women. Insomuch that they brought forth the sick into the streets, and
laid them on beds and couches, that at the least the shadow of Peter passing by might overshadow some of them. Acts 5:14, 15.*

The last words of Christ [to His disciples] were "Go ye into all
the world, and preach the gospel to every creature" (Mark
16:15). And spreading His hands above them in benediction,
He ascended to heaven, surrounded by hosts of heavenly angels who
had come to escort Him on His way to the portals of God. His last commission to His disciples made them the agents whereby His gospel of
glad tidings was to go to the nations. This was Christ's last will and testament to His followers who walked with Him during the years of His
earthly ministry, and to those who should believe on Him through their
word. His first work in heaven was in harmony with His last commission on earth; for He sent the promise of the Father upon them. On the
day of Pentecost the Holy Spirit was poured out upon the praying disciples, and they testified as to its source to all, wherever they went.

The missionary spirit was poured out in unlimited supplies, and the
disciples testified of a crucified and risen Saviour, and convinced the
world of sin, of righteousness, and of judgment to come. They did just
as their risen Lord had directed them to do, and began at Jerusalem to
publish the gospel, in the very place where the deepest prejudice existed,
and where the most confused ideas prevailed in regard to Him who had
been crucified as a malefactor. Three thousand received the message,
and were converted. They were not intimidated through persecution,
imprisonment, and death; but they continued to speak with all boldness
the words of truth, setting before the Jews the work and mission and
ministry of Christ, His crucifixion, resurrection, and ascension; and believers were added daily to the Lord, both of men and women.—*Review
and Herald*, Nov. 6, 1894.

A NEW PENTECOST

And the word of God increased; and the number of the disciples multiplied in Jerusalem greatly; and a great company of the priests were obedient to the faith. Acts 6:7.

As the disciples, filled with the power of the Spirit, went forth to proclaim the gospel, so God's servants are to go forth today. Filled with an unselfish desire to give the message of mercy to those who are in the darkness of error and unbelief, we are to take up the Lord's work. He gives us our part to do in cooperation with Him, and He will also move on the hearts of unbelievers to carry forward His work in the regions beyond. Already many are receiving the Holy Spirit, and no longer will the way be blocked by listless indifference.

Why has the history of the work of the disciples, as they labored with holy zeal, animated and vitalized by the Holy Spirit, been recorded, if it is not that from this record the Lord's people today are to gain an inspiration to work earnestly for Him? What the Lord did for His people in that time, it is just as essential, and more so, that He do for His people today. All that the apostles did, every church member today is to do. And we are to work with as much more fervor, to be accompanied by the Holy Spirit in as much greater measure, as the increase of wickedness demands a more decided call to repentance.

Everyone on whom is shining the light of present truth is to be stirred with compassion for those who are in darkness. From all believers light is to be reflected in clear, distinct rays. A work similar to that which the Lord did through His delegated messengers after the day of Pentecost He is waiting to do today. At this time, when the end of all things is at hand, should not the zeal of the church exceed even that of the early church? Zeal for the glory of God moved the disciples to bear witness to the truth with mighty power. Should not this zeal fire our hearts with a longing to tell the story of redeeming love, of Christ and Him crucified? Should not the power of God be even more mightily revealed today than in the time of the apostles?—*Review and Herald*, Jan. 13, 1903.

A SPECIAL
BESTOWAL OF SPIRITUAL GRACE

Then they that gladly received his word were baptized: and the same day there were added unto them about three thousand souls. And they continued stedfastly in the apostles' doctrine and fellowship, and in breaking of bread, and in prayers. Acts 2:41, 42.

It is true that in the time of the end, when God's work in the earth is closing, the earnest efforts put forth by consecrated believers under the guidance of the Holy Spirit are to be accompanied by special tokens of divine favor. Under the figure of the early and the latter rain, that falls in Eastern lands at seedtime and harvest, the Hebrew prophets foretold the bestowal of spiritual grace in extraordinary measure upon God's church. The outpouring of the Spirit in the days of the apostles was the beginning of the early, or former, rain, and glorious was the result. To the end of time the presence of the Spirit is to abide with the true church.

But near the close of earth's harvest, a special bestowal of spiritual grace is promised to prepare the church for the coming of the Son of man. This outpouring of the Spirit is likened to the falling of the latter rain; and it is for this added power that Christians are to send their petitions to the Lord of the harvest "in the time of the latter rain." In response, "the Lord shall make bright clouds, and give them showers of rain" (Zech. 10:1). "He will cause to come down . . . the rain, the former rain, and the latter rain" (Joel 2:23).

But unless the members of God's church today have a living connection with the Source of all spiritual growth, they will not be ready for the time of reaping. Unless they keep their lamps trimmed and burning, they will fail of receiving added grace in times of special need.—*The Acts of the Apostles*, pp. 54, 55.

FULL IMPARTATION OF THE SPIRIT

And suddenly there came a sound from heaven as of a rushing mighty wind, and it filled all the house where they were sitting. Acts 2:2.

When the Holy Spirit came down on the day of Pentecost, it was like a rushing, mighty wind. [The Spirit] was given in no stinted measure; for He filled all the place where the disciples were sitting. So will He be given to us when our hearts are prepared to receive Him.

Let every church member kneel before God, and pray earnestly for the impartation of the Spirit. Cry, "Lord, increase my faith. Make me to understand Thy Word; for the entrance of Thy Word giveth light. Refresh me by Thy presence. Fill my heart with Thy Spirit that I may love my brethren as Christ loves me."

God will bless those who thus prepare themselves for His service. They will understand what it means to have the assurance of the Spirit, because they have received Christ by faith. The religion of Christ means more than the forgiveness of sin; it means that sin is taken away, and that the vacuum is filled with the Spirit. It means that the mind is divinely illumined, that the heart is emptied of self, and filled with the presence of Christ. When this work is done for church members, the church will be a living, working church.

We are to seek most earnestly to be of one mind, of one purpose. The baptism of the Holy Spirit, and nothing less, can bring us to this place. Let us by self-renunciation prepare our hearts to receive the Holy Spirit that a great work may be done for us, so that we can say, not "See what I am doing," but "Behold the goodness and love of God!" . . .

We may talk of the blessings of the Holy Spirit, but unless we prepare ourselves for His reception, of what avail are our works? Are we striving with all our power to attain to the stature of men and women in Christ? Are we seeking for His fullness, ever pressing toward the mark set before us—the perfection of His character?—*Review and Herald*, June 10, 1902.

NO SPECIFIC TIME

Take ye heed, watch and pray: for ye know not when the time is. Mark 13:33.

God grant that His converting power may be felt throughout this large assembly. Oh, that the power of God may rest upon the people. What we need is daily piety. We need to search the Scriptures daily, to pray earnestly that by the power of the Holy Spirit God may fit every one of us up to work in our place in His vineyard. No one is prepared to educate and strengthen the church unless he has received the gift of the Holy Spirit. No minister is prepared to labor intelligently for the salvation of souls, unless he is endowed by the Holy Spirit, unless he is feeding on Christ, and has an intense hatred of sin. . . .

I have no specific time of which to speak when the outpouring of the Holy Spirit will take place—when the mighty angel will come down from heaven, and unite with the third angel in closing up the work for this world; my message is that our only safety is in being ready for the heavenly refreshing, having our lamps trimmed and burning. Christ has told us to watch; "for in such an hour as ye think not the Son of man cometh" (Matt. 24:44). "Watch and pray" is the charge that is given us by our Redeemer. Day by day we are to seek the enlightenment of the Spirit of God, that He may do its office work upon the soul and character. Oh, how much time has been wasted through giving attention to trifling things. Repent and be converted, that your sins may be blotted out when the times of refreshing shall come from the presence of the Lord.

We now call upon you to give yourselves to the service of God. Too long have you given your powers to the service of Satan, and have been slaves to his will. God calls upon you to behold the glory of His character, that by beholding, you may become changed into His image. . . . Jesus came to reveal to the world the love and goodness of God.— *Review and Herald*, Mar. 29, 1892.

WITHOUT EXCITEMENT

When they therefore were come together, they asked of him, saying, Lord, wilt thou at this time restore again the kingdom to Israel? And he said unto them, It is not for you to know the times or the seasons, which the Father hath put in his own power. Acts 1:6, 7.

The disciples were anxious to know the exact time for the revelation of the kingdom of God; but Jesus tells them that they may not know the times and the seasons; for the Father has not revealed them. To understand when the kingdom of God should be restored was not the thing of most importance for them to know. They were to be found following the Master, praying, waiting, watching, and working. They were to be representatives to the world of the character of Christ.

That which was essential for a successful Christian experience in the days of the disciples is essential in our day. "And he said unto them, It is not for you to know the times or the seasons, which the Father hath put in his own power. But ye shall receive power, after that the Holy Ghost is come upon you." And after the Holy Ghost was come upon them, what were they to do? "And ye shall be witnesses unto me both in Jerusalem, and in all Judea, and in Samaria, and unto the uttermost part of the earth" (Acts 1:7, 8).

This is the work in which we also are to be engaged. Instead of living in expectation of some special season of excitement, we are wisely to improve present opportunities, doing that which must be done in order that souls may be saved. Instead of exhausting the powers of our mind in speculations in regard to the times and seasons which the Lord has placed in His own power, and withheld from men, we are to yield ourselves to the control of the Holy Spirit, to do present duties, to give the bread of life, unadulterated with human opinions, to souls who are perishing for the truth.

Satan is ever ready to fill the mind with theories and calculations that will divert men from the present truth, and disqualify them for the giving of the third angel's message to the world.—*Review and Herald*, Mar. 22, 1892.

IN UNEXPECTED WAYS

And they were all amazed, and were in doubt, saying one to another, What meaneth this? Acts 2:12.

We are to pray for the impartation of the Spirit as the remedy for sin-sick souls. The church needs to be converted, and why should we not prostrate ourselves at the throne of grace, as representatives of the church, and from a broken heart and contrite spirit make earnest supplication that the Holy Spirit shall be poured out upon us from on high? Let us pray that when He shall be graciously bestowed, our cold hearts may be revived, and we may have discernment to understand that He is from God, and receive Him with joy.

Some have treated the Spirit as an unwelcome guest, refusing to receive the rich gift, refusing to acknowledge Him, turning from Him, and condemning Him as fanaticism. When the Holy Spirit works the human agent, He does not ask us in what way He shall operate. Often He moves in unexpected ways. Christ did not come as the Jews expected. He did not come in a manner to glorify them as a nation. His forerunner came to prepare the way for Him by calling upon the people to repent of their sins and be converted, and be baptized. Christ's message was "The kingdom of heaven is at hand: repent ye, and believe the gospel" (Mark 1:15).

The Jews refused to receive Christ, because He did not come in accordance with their expectations. The ideas of finite men were held as infallible, because [they were] hoary with age. This is the danger to which the church is now exposed—that the inventions of finite men shall mark out the precise way for the Holy Spirit to come. Though they would not care to acknowledge it, some have already done this. And because the Spirit is to come, not to praise men or to build up their erroneous theories, but to reprove the world of sin, and of righteousness, and of judgment, many turn away from Him. . . . The Holy Spirit flatters no man, neither does He work according to the devising of any man.

Finite, sinful men are not to work the Holy Spirit. When He shall come as a reprover, through any human agent whom God shall choose, it is man's place to hear and obey His voice.—*The Ellen G. White 1888 Materials*, vol. 4, pp. 1540, 1541.

To Unexpected People

But Peter, standing up with the eleven, lifted up his voice, and said unto them, Ye men of Judaea, and all ye that dwell at Jerusalem, be this known unto you, and hearken to my words: for these are not drunken, as ye suppose, seeing it is but the third hour of the day. But this is that which was spoken by the prophet Joel. Acts 2:14-16.

The baptism of the Holy Ghost as on the day of Pentecost will lead to a revival of true religion and to the performance of many wonderful works. Heavenly intelligences will come among us, and men will speak as they are moved upon by the Holy Spirit of God. But should the Lord work upon men as He did on and after the day of Pentecost, many who now claim to believe the truth would know so very little of the operation of the Holy Spirit that they would cry, "Beware of fanaticism." They would say of those who were filled with the Spirit, "These men are full of new wine" (Acts 2:13).

The time is not far off now when men will want a much closer relation to Christ, a much closer union with His Holy Spirit than ever they have had, or will have, unless they give up their will and their way, and submit to God's will and God's way. The great sin of those who profess to be Christians is that they do not open the heart to receive the Holy Spirit. When souls long after Christ, and seek to become one with Him, then those who are content with the form of godliness exclaim, "Be careful, do not go to extremes." When the angels of heaven come among us, and work through human agents, there will be solid, substantial conversions, after the order of the conversions after the day of Pentecost.

Now brethren, be careful and do not go into or try to create human excitement. But while we should be careful not to go into human excitement, we should not be among those who will raise inquiries and cherish doubts in reference to the work of the Spirit of God; for there will be those who will question and criticize when the Spirit of God takes possession of men and women, because their own hearts are not moved, but are cold and unimpressible.—*Selected Messages*, book 2, p. 57.

AS GOD PLEASES

Nicodemus answered and said unto him, How can these things be? Jesus answered and said unto him, Art thou a master of Israel, and knowest not these things? Verily, verily, I say unto thee, We speak that we do know, and testify that we have seen; and ye receive not our witness. If I have told you earthly things, and ye believe not, how shall ye believe, if I tell you of heavenly things? John 3:9-12.

At infinite cost provision has been made for men to reach perfection of Christian character. Those who have been impressed by the Holy Scriptures as the voice of God, and desire to follow its teachings, are to be daily learning, daily receiving spiritual fervor and power, which have been provided for every true believer in the gift of the Holy Spirit.

The Holy Spirit is a free, working, independent agency. The God of heaven uses His Spirit as it pleases Him: and human minds, human judgment, and human methods can no more set boundaries to His working, or prescribe the channel through which He shall operate, than they can say to the wind, "I bid you to blow in a certain direction, and to conduct yourself in such and such a manner." As the wind moves in its force, bending and breaking the lofty trees in its path, so the Holy Spirit influences human hearts, and no finite man can circumscribe His work. . . .

Nicodemus was not willing to admit the truth, because he could not understand all that was connected with the operation of the power of God; and yet he accepted the facts of nature, although he could not explain or even comprehend them. Like other men of all ages, he was looking to forms and precise ceremonies as more essential to religion than the deep movings of the Spirit of God. . . .

The fountain of the heart must be purified before the streams can become pure. There is no safety for one who has merely a legal religion, a form of godliness. The Christian's life is not a modification or improvement of the old life, but a transformation of the nature. There is a death to sin and self, and a new life altogether. This change can be brought about only by the effectual working of the Holy Spirit.—*Signs of the Times,* Mar. 8, 1910.

AT TIMES, HUMAN
MACHINERY SET ASIDE

Now when they saw the boldness of Peter and John, and perceived that they were unlearned and ignorant men, they marvelled; and they took knowledge of them, that they had been with Jesus. Acts 4:13.

I f we will open the door to Jesus, He will come in and abide with us. Our strength will always be reinforced by His actual representative, the Holy Spirit.

The truth is a living principle made to shine in precious clearness to the understanding, and then, oh, then, it is time to speak words from the living Christ. "We are labourers together with God" (1 Cor. 3:9).

Under the showers of the latter rain, the inventions of man, the human machinery, will at times be swept away, the boundary of man's authority will be as broken reeds, and the Holy Spirit will speak through the living, human agent with convincing power. No one will then watch to see if the sentences are well rounded off, if the grammar is faultless. The living water will flow in God's own channels. . . . I am sure that there is a heaven full of the richest, enduring treasures to be freely given to all who will appropriate them to themselves, and becoming enriched, thereby, will impart freely to others. I know this to be the truth.

We need to obtain a rich, daily experience in prayer; we should be like the importunate widow, who, in her conscious need, overcame the unjust judge by the bare force of her determined pleadings. God will be inquired of to do these things for us; for this is giving depth and solidity to our experience. The soul that seeks God will need to be in earnest. He is a rewarder of all those that seek Him diligently. . . .

We want the truth spoken to human hearts by men that have been baptized with holy love for Christ, and for the purchase of His blood, men who are themselves thoroughly impressed with the truth they are presenting to others; and who are practicing the same in their own life.—*General Conference Bulletin*, Feb. 15, 1895.

OFTEN REJECTED

And they called them, and commanded them not to speak at all nor teach in the name of Jesus. But Peter and John answered and said unto them, Whether it be right in the sight of God to hearken unto you more than unto God, judge ye. For we cannot but speak the things which we have seen and heard. Acts 4:18-20.

The promise of the Holy Spirit was the brightest hope and the strongest consolation that Christ could leave His disciples when He ascended to heaven. The truths of God's Word had been buried beneath the rubbish of misinterpretation; the maxims of men, the sayings of finite beings, had been exalted above the Word of the living God. Under the enlightening power of the Holy Spirit, the apostles separated truth from false theories, and gave to the people the word of life.

The Holy Spirit is often rejected because He comes in unexpected ways. Evidence upon evidence that the apostles were speaking and acting under divine inspiration had been given to the Jewish priests and rulers, but still they firmly resisted the message of truth. Christ had not come in the way they expected, and though at times they were convinced that He was the Son of God, yet they stifled conviction, and thus became blinder and more hardened than before. They crucified Christ, yet Christ in His mercy gave them additional evidence in the works wrought by the disciples. He sent His servants to tell them what they had done, and even in the terrible charge that they had killed the Prince of life, He gave them another call to repentance. But, feeling secure in their own righteousness, the Jewish teachers were not prepared to admit that the men who had reproved them for crucifying Christ were speaking by the direction of the Holy Spirit. . . .

The wrath of God is not declared against men merely because of the sin they have committed, but because they choose to continue in a state of resistance, because they repeat the sins of the past in spite of the light and evidence given them. If the Jewish leaders had submitted, they would have been pardoned; but they were determined not to yield. In the same way, the sinner, by continued resistance, places himself where he knows nothing but resistance.—*Signs of the Times*, Sept. 27, 1899.

BEWARE OF RESISTING

And to him they agreed: and when they had called the apostles, and beaten them, they commanded that they should not speak in the name of Jesus, and let them go. And they departed from the presence of the council, rejoicing that they were counted worthy to suffer shame for his name. Acts 5:40, 41.

When God moves upon the hearts of men to draw them to Christ, it seems that a compelling power comes over them, and they believe, and give themselves up to the influence of the Spirit of God. But if they do not maintain the precious victory that God has given; if they permit old practices and habits to revive, and indulge in amusement or worldly luxury; if they neglect prayer, and cease resisting evil, then Satan's temptations are accepted, and they are led to doubt the verity of their former experience. They find that they are weak in moral power, and Satan declares to them that it is of no use for them to try the experiment of living a Christian life. He says, "The experience you thought was of God was only the result of undue emotion and impulse."

As soon as the human agent entertains these suggestions of the evil one, they begin to appear plausible, and then those who ought to know better, who have had a longer experience in the work of God, second the suggestions of Satan, and the Holy Spirit is grieved from the soul. There are those who almost imperceptibly come to take this position, who will immediately recover themselves when they realize what they are doing; but there are others who will continue to resist the Holy Spirit, until resistance appears to them as a virtue.

It is a dangerous thing to doubt the manifestations of the Holy Spirit; for if this agency is doubted, there is no reserve power left by which to operate on the human heart. Those who attribute the work of the Holy Spirit to human agencies, saying that an undue influence was brought to bear upon them, are cutting their souls off from the fountain of blessing.—*Review and Herald*, Feb. 13, 1894.

NOT AN EMOTION OR RAPTURE

Therefore seeing we have this ministry, as we have received mercy, we faint not; but have renounced the hidden things of dishonesty, not walking in craftiness, nor handling the word of God deceitfully; but by manifestation of the truth commending ourselves to every man's conscience in the sight of God. 2 Cor. 4:1, 2.

My brother, there is danger of those in our ranks making a mistake in regard to receiving the Holy Ghost. Many suppose an emotion or a rapture of feeling to be an evidence of the presence of the Holy Spirit. There is danger that right sentiments will not be understood, and that Christ's words "Teaching them to observe all things whatsoever I have commanded you" (Matt. 28:20) will lose their significance. There is danger that original devisings and superstitious imaginings will take the place of the Scriptures. Tell our people, Be not anxious to bring in something not revealed in the Word. Keep close to Christ. Remember His words: "Teaching them to observe all things whatsoever I have commanded you: and, lo, I am with you alway, even unto the end of the world" (verse 20).

He is with us as we teach the words He spoke in the Old Testament as well as in the New. He who gave commandment in the New Testament is the One also who gave the instruction contained in the Old Testament. The Old and New Testaments are both sacred; for they both contain the words of Christ. All communication from heaven to earth since Adam's fall has come through Christ. He who believes the instruction contained in the New Testament and in the Old, doing those things which Christ has commanded therein, has the Saviour always with him.—*Kress Collection*, p. 126.

The apostles and prophets and holy men of old did not perfect their characters by miracles, by some wonderful and unusual demonstration; but they used the ability given them by God, trusting alone in the righteousness of Christ. And all who will use the same means may secure the same result.—*General Conference Bulletin*, July 1, 1900.

Satan is willing that every transgressor of God's law shall claim to be holy. This is what he himself is doing. He is satisfied when men rest their faith on spurious doctrines and religious enthusiasm; for he can use such persons to good purpose in deceiving souls.—*Evangelism*, p. 597.

NEITHER EXCITEMENT NOR SENSATIONALISM

In all things shewing thyself a pattern of good works: in doctrine shewing uncorruptness, gravity, sincerity, sound speech, that cannot be condemned; that he that is of the contrary part may be ashamed, having no evil thing to say of you. Titus 2:7, 8.

The Lord has a work for you to do, and if you listen to His voice, you will not be left in darkness. The Saviour says, "My sheep hear my voice, and I know them, and they follow me" (John 10:27). "And a stranger will they not follow, . . . for they know not the voice of strangers" (verse 5). I am sure that the Lord is revealing to you the perfection and fullness of the atoning work, that your whole heart may be filled with love and thanksgiving, and that you may reveal to others that which the Lord is revealing to you. The image of Christ engraved upon the heart is reflected in character, in practical life, day by day, because we represent a personal Saviour.

The Holy Spirit is promised to all who will ask for it. When you search the Scriptures, the Holy Spirit is by your side, personating Jesus Christ. The truth is a living principle made to shine in precious clearness to the understanding, and then, oh, then, it is time to speak words from the living Christ. "We are labourers together with God" (1 Cor. 3:9). Christ said to the woman of Samaria, "If thou knewest the gift of God, and who it is that saith to thee, Give me to drink; thou wouldest have asked of him, and he would have given thee living water. . . . A well of water springing up into everlasting life" (John 4:10-14).

Those who have the outpouring of the gospel of Christ which comes from the heart imbued by His Holy Spirit will give light and comfort and hope to hearts that are hungering and thirsting for righteousness. It is not excitement we wish to create, but deep, earnest consideration, that those who hear shall do solid work, real, sound, genuine work that will be enduring as eternity. We hunger not for excitement, for the sensational; the less we have of this, the better. The calm, earnest reasoning from the Scriptures is precious and fruitful. Here is the secret of success, in preaching a living, personal Saviour in so simple and earnest a manner that the people may be able to lay hold by faith of the power of the Word of Life.—*The Paulson Collection*, pp. 101, 102.

NOT LOOKING FOR ORIGINALITY

But speak thou the things which become sound doctrine. Titus 2:1.

We are in continual danger of getting above the simplicity of the gospel. There is an intense desire on the part of many to startle the world with something original, that shall lift the people into a state of spiritual ecstasy, and change the present order of experience. There is certainly great need of a change in the present order of experience; for the sacredness of present truth is not realized as it should be, but the change we need is a change of heart, and can only be obtained by seeking God individually for His blessing, by pleading with Him for His power, by fervently praying that His grace may come upon us, and that our characters may be transformed. This is the change we need today, and for the attainment of this experience we should exercise persevering energy and manifest heartfelt earnestness. We should ask with true sincerity, "What shall I do to be saved?" We should know just what steps we are taking heavenward.

Christ gave to His disciples truths whose breadth and depth and value they little appreciated, or even comprehended, and the same condition exists among the people of God today. We too have failed to take in the greatness, to perceive the beauty of the truth which God has entrusted to us today. Should we advance in spiritual knowledge, we would see the truth developing and expanding in lines of which we have little dreamed, but it will never develop in any line that will lead us to imagine that we may know the times and the seasons which the Father hath put in His own power.

Again and again have I been warned in regard to time-setting. There will never again be a message for the people of God that will be based on time. We are not to know the definite time either for the outpouring of the Holy Spirit or for the coming of Christ.—*Review and Herald*, Mar. 22, 1892.

NO DISORDER OR FANATICISM

Holding fast the faithful word as he hath been taught, that he may be able by sound doctrine both to exhort and to convince the gainsayers. Titus 1:9.

There is constant danger of allowing something to come into our midst that we may regard as the workings of the Holy Spirit, but that in reality is the fruit of a spirit of fanaticism. So long as we allow the enemy of truth to lead us into a wrong way, we cannot hope to reach the honest in heart with the third angel's message. We are to be sanctified through obedience to the truth. I am afraid of anything that would have a tendency to turn the mind away from the solid evidences of the truth as revealed in God's Word. I am afraid of it; I am afraid of it.

We must bring our minds within the bounds of reason, lest the enemy so come in as to set everything in a disorderly way. There are persons of an excitable temperament who are easily led into fanaticism; and should we allow anything to come into our churches that would lead such persons into error, we would soon see these errors carried to extreme lengths, and then because of the course of these disorderly elements, a stigma would rest upon the whole body of Seventh-day Adventists.

I have been studying how to get some of these early experiences into print again, so that more of our people may be informed, for I have long known that fanaticism will be manifest again, in different ways. We are to strengthen our position by dwelling on the Word, and by avoiding all oddities and strange exercisings that some would be very quick to catch up and practice. If we were to allow confusion to come into our ranks, we could not bind off our work as we should. . . .

How afraid I am to have anything of a fanatical nature brought in among our people. There are many, many who must be sanctified, but they are to be sanctified through obedience to the message of truth.—*Selected Messages*, book 2, pp. 43, 44.

GOD'S WORK CHARACTERIZED BY CALMNESS

Let all things be done decently and in order. 1 Cor. 14:40.

I . . . met a man and his wife who claim to follow the Word of God and to believe the Testimonies. They have had an unusual experience during the past two or three years. They seemed to be honest-hearted people. . . .

I told this brother and his wife that the experience through which I passed in my youth, shortly after the passing of the time in 1844, had led me to be very, very cautious about accepting anything similar to that which we then met and rebuked in the name of the Lord.

No greater harm could be done to the work of God at this time than for us to allow a spirit of fanaticism to come into our churches, accompanied by strange workings which are incorrectly supposed to be operations of the Spirit of God.

As this brother and his wife outlined their experiences, which they claim have come to them as the result of receiving the Holy Ghost with apostolic power, it seemed to be a facsimile of that which we were called to meet and correct in our early experience.

Toward the close of our interview Brother L proposed that we unite in prayer, with the thought that possibly while in prayer his wife would be exercised as they had described to me, and that then I might be able to discern whether this was of the Lord or not. To this I could not consent, because I have been instructed that when one offers to exhibit these peculiar manifestations, this is a decided evidence that it is not the work of God.

We must not permit these experiences to lead us to feel discouraged. Such experiences will come to us from time to time. Let us give no place to strange exercisings, which really take the mind away from the deep movings of the Holy Spirit. God's work is ever characterized by calmness and dignity. We cannot afford to sanction anything that would bring in confusion and weaken our zeal in regard to the great work that God has given us to do in the world to prepare for the second coming of Christ.—*Selected Messages*, book 2, pp. 41, 42.

A SPIRITUAL REVOLUTION

Yea, doubtless, and I count all things but loss for the excellency of the knowledge of Christ Jesus my Lord: for whom I have suffered the loss of all things, and do count them but dung, that I may win Christ. Phil. 3:8.

Through Christ, moral power is brought to man that will change the entire affections, and enable man to work with a will for the cause of God. Where all the power of mind and body was before concentrated to work the works of evil, by the Spirit of God a revolution is brought about. The Holy Spirit enlightens, renews, and sanctifies the soul. Angels behold with inexpressible rapture the results of the working of the Holy Spirit in man.

By the revelation of the attractive loveliness of Christ, by the knowledge of His love expressed to us while we were yet sinners, the stubborn heart is melted and subdued, and the sinner is transformed and becomes a child of God. Love is the agency which God uses to expel sin from the human soul. By it He changes pride into humility, enmity and unbelief into love and faith. He does not employ compulsory measures; Jesus is revealed to the soul, and if man will look in faith to the Lamb of God, he will live. . . .

Christ is presented to men that they may catch His temper, His perfection; and as the model is complete and perfect in every part, so, as man is conformed to the image of Christ, he is made complete in Him; for aside from Christ there never can be righteousness in the human heart.

When the Spirit was poured out from on high, the church was flooded with light, but Christ was that light; the church was filled with joy, but Christ was the subject of that joy. When the Spirit is poured upon His people in this day, Christ's name will be upon every tongue, His love will fill every soul; and when the heart embraces Jesus, it will embrace God; for all the fullness of God dwells in Christ. When the beams of Christ's righteousness shine upon the soul, joy, adoration, and glory will be woven with the experience.—*Signs of the Times*, June 9, 1890.

THE SPIRIT BRINGS PEACE AND JOY

Now the God of hope fill you with all joy and peace in believing, that ye may abound in hope, through the power of the Holy Ghost. Rom. 15:13.

Much is being said regarding the impartation of the Holy Spirit, and by some this is being so interpreted that it is an injury to the churches. Eternal life is the receiving of the living elements in the Scriptures and doing the will of God. This is eating the flesh and drinking the blood of the Son of God. To those who do this, life and immortality are brought to light through the gospel, for God's Word is verity and truth, spirit and life. It is the privilege of all who believe in Jesus Christ as their personal Saviour to feed on the Word of God. The Holy Spirit's influence renders that Word, the Bible, an immortal truth, which to the prayerful searcher gives spiritual sinew and muscle.

"Search the Scriptures," Christ declared, "for in them ye think ye have eternal life: and they are they which testify of me" (John 5:39). Those who dig beneath the surface discover the hidden gems of truth. The Holy Spirit is present with the earnest searcher. His illumination shines upon the Word, stamping the truth upon the mind with a new, fresh importance. The searcher is filled with a sense of peace and joy never before felt. The preciousness of truth is realized as never before. A new, heavenly light shines upon the Word, illuminating it as though every letter were tinged with gold. God Himself has spoken to the mind and heart, making the Word Spirit and life.

Every true searcher of the Word lifts his heart to God, imploring the aid of the Spirit. And he soon discovers that which carries him above all the fictitious statements of the would-be teacher, whose weak, tottering theories are not sustained by the Word of the living God.—*Manuscript Releases*, vol. 21, pp. 131, 132.

IT CALLS FOR A JOYFUL PRAISE

Rejoice in the Lord alway: and again I say, Rejoice. Phil. 4:4.

Pray, pray earnestly and without ceasing, but do not forget to praise. It becomes every child of God to vindicate His character. You can magnify the Lord; you can show the power of sustaining grace. There are multitudes who do not appreciate the great love of God nor the divine compassion of Jesus. Thousands even regard with disdain the matchless grace shown in the plan of redemption. All who are partakers of this great salvation are not clear in this matter. They do not cultivate grateful hearts. But the theme of redemption is one that the angels desire to look into; it will be the science and the song of the ransomed throughout the ceaseless ages of eternity. Is it not worthy of careful thought and study now? Should we not praise God with heart and soul and voice "for his wonderful works to the children of men" (Ps. 107:8)?

Praise the Lord in the congregation of His people. When the word of the Lord was spoken to the Hebrews anciently, the command was: "And let all the people say, Amen" (Ps. 106:48). When the ark of the covenant was brought into the city of David, and a psalm of joy and triumph was chanted, "all the people said, Amen, and praised the Lord" (1 Chron. 16:36). This fervent response was an evidence that they understood the word spoken and joined in the worship of God.

There is too much formality in our religious services. The Lord would have His ministers who preach the Word energized by His Holy Spirit; and the people who hear should not sit in drowsy indifference, or stare vacantly about, making no responses to what is said. The impression that is thus given to the unbeliever is anything but favorable for the religion of Christ. These dull, careless professed Christians are not destitute of ambition and zeal when engaged in worldly business; but things of eternal importance do not move them deeply. The voice of God through His messengers may be a pleasant song; but its sacred warnings, reproofs, and encouragements are all unheeded. The spirit of the world has paralyzed them. The truths of God's Word are spoken to leaden ears and hard, unimpressible hearts. There should be wide-awake, active churches to encourage and uphold the ministers of Christ and to aid them in the work of saving souls. Where the church is walking in the light, there will ever be cheerful, hearty responses and words of joyful praise.—*Testimonies*, vol. 5, pp. 317, 318.

FRATERNAL LOVE EXPRESSED

And the multitude of them that believed were of one heart and of one soul: neither said any of them that aught of the things which he possessed was his own; but they had all things common. Acts 4:32.

The record declares, "Neither was there any among them that lacked," and it tells how the need was filled. Those among the believers who had money and possessions cheerfully sacrificed them to meet the emergency. Selling their houses or their lands, they brought the money and laid it at the apostles' feet, "and distribution was made unto every man according as he had need" (Acts 4:34, 35).

This liberality on the part of the believers was the result of the outpouring of the Spirit. The converts to the gospel were "of one heart and of one soul." One common interest controlled them—the success of the mission entrusted to them; and covetousness had no place in their lives. Their love for their brethren and the cause they had espoused was greater than their love of money and possessions. Their works testified that they accounted the souls of men of higher value than earthly wealth.

Thus it will ever be when the Spirit of God takes possession of the life. Those whose hearts are filled with the love of Christ will follow the example of Him who for our sake became poor, that through His poverty we might be made rich. Money, time, influence—all the gifts they have received from God's hand, they will value only as a means of advancing the work of the gospel. Thus it was in the early church; and when in the church of today it is seen that by the power of the Spirit the members have taken their affections from the things of the world, and that they are willing to make sacrifices in order that their fellow men may hear the gospel, the truths proclaimed will have a powerful influence upon the hearers.—*The Acts of the Apostles*, pp. 70, 71.

LIBERALITY AND BENEVOLENCE SHOWN

For to their power, I bear record, yea, and beyond their power they were willing of themselves; praying us with much entreaty that we would receive the gift, and take upon us the fellowship of the ministering to the saints. 2 Cor. 8:3, 4.

The gospel, extending and widening, required greater provisions to sustain the warfare since the death of Christ, and this made the law of almsgiving a more urgent necessity than under the Hebrew government. Now God requires, not less gifts, but greater than at any other period of the world. The principle laid down by Christ is that the gifts and offerings should be in proportion to the light and blessings enjoyed. He has said, "For unto whomsoever much is given, of him shall be much required" (Luke 12:48).

The blessings of the Christian age were responded to by the first disciples in works of charity and benevolence. The outpouring of the Spirit of God, after Christ left His disciples and ascended to heaven, led to self-denial, and self-sacrifice for the salvation of others. When the poor saints at Jerusalem were in distress, Paul writes to the Gentile Christians in regard to works of benevolence, and says, "Therefore, as ye abound in everything, in faith, and utterance, and knowledge, and in all diligence, and in your love to us, see that ye abound in this grace also" (2 Cor. 8:7). Here benevolence is placed by the side of faith, love, and Christian diligence.

Those who think that they can be good Christians, and close their ears and hearts to the calls of God for their liberalities, are in a fearful deception. There are those who abound in a profession of great love for the truth, and as far as words are concerned, have an interest to see the truth advance, but do nothing for its advancement. The faith of such is dead, not being made perfect by works. The Lord never made such a mistake as to convert a soul, and leave [that soul] under the power of covetousness.—*Review and Herald*, Aug. 25, 1874.

PREJUDICE AND RACISM DESTROYED

For as many of you as have been baptized into Christ have put on Christ. There is neither Jew nor Greek, there is neither bond nor free, there is neither male nor female: for ye are all one in Christ Jesus. Gal. 3:27, 28.

No distinction on account of nationality, race, or caste, is recognized by God. He is the Maker of all mankind. All men are of one family by creation, and all are one through redemption. Christ came to demolish every wall of partition, to throw open every compartment of the temple, that every soul may have free access to God.—*Christ's Object Lessons*, p. 386.

The religion of the Bible recognizes no caste or color. It ignores rank, wealth, worldly honor. God estimates men as men. With Him, character decides their worth. And we are to recognize the Spirit of Christ in whomsoever He is revealed.—*Testimonies*, vol. 9, p. 223.

Thus Christ sought to teach the disciples the truth that in God's kingdom there are no territorial lines, no caste, no aristocracy; that they must go to all nations, bearing to them the message of a Saviour's love.—*The Acts of the Apostles*, p. 20.

The walls of sectarianism and caste and race will fall down when the true missionary spirit enters the hearts of men. Prejudice is melted away by the love of God.—*Review and Hearld*, Jan. 21, 1896.

Walls of separation have been built up between the whites and the blacks. These walls of prejudice will tumble down of themselves as did the walls of Jericho, when Christians obey the Word of God, which enjoins on them supreme love to their Maker and impartial love to their neighbors.—*Ibid.*, Dec. 17, 1895.

When the Holy Spirit is poured out, there will be a triumph of humanity over prejudice in seeking the salvation of the souls of human beings. God will control minds. Human hearts will love as Christ loved. And the color line will be regarded by many very differently from the way in which it is now regarded. To love as Christ loves lifts the mind into a pure, heavenly, unselfish atmosphere.—*Testimonies*, vol. 9, p. 209.

Selfishness and Dishonesty Swept Away

And fear came upon every soul: and many wonders and signs were done by the apostles. And all that believed were together, and had all things common; and sold their possessions and goods, and parted them to all men, as every man had need. Acts 2:43-45.

It is not because of niggardliness on the part of God that there is a dearth of the Holy Spirit in our churches. This dearth, the churches alone can change. God says to His people, "Arouse and create an interest in holy things." Where is our faith? Wherein do we sustain a proper relation to Jesus Christ? Do we follow Him in self-denial and stability? Do we talk the truth with the understanding? When God pours out His Spirit upon the churches, they will bear fruit to His glory. The sword of the Spirit, newly edged with power, will cut both ways.

In God's vineyard there is earnest work to be done. The third angel's message is to be proclaimed with a loud voice all over the land. Every vestige of business that breeds dishonesty, every thread of selfishness, is to be swept away by the latter rain. All idolatry is to be consumed. Let every altar be thrown down, save the one that sanctifies the gift and the giver—the cross of Calvary.

New territory is to be added to God's kingdom. New tracts of moral vineyard are to be cultivated as the garden of the Lord. The honor of the law of God is to be vindicated before the unfallen worlds, before the heavenly universe, and before the fallen world. The bitterest persecution will come, but when Zion arises, and puts on her beautiful garments, she will shine forth in the beauty of holiness. God designs us to have more life and more power, because the glory of God has risen upon the church. If the truth is received, unsightly barrenness will not continue to exist. Christ's Word is eternal life to the receiver.—*Bible Training School*, Dec. 1, 1903.

FEAR OF WITNESSING GONE

Saying, Did not we straitly command you that ye should not teach in this name? and, behold, ye have filled Jerusalem with your doctrine, and intend to bring this man's blood upon us. Then Peter and the other apostles answered and said, We ought to obey God rather than men. Acts 5:28, 29.

I heard those clothed with the armor speak forth the truth in great power. It had effect. I saw those who had been bound; some wives had been bound by their husbands, and some children had been bound by their parents. The honest who had been held or prevented from hearing the truth now eagerly laid hold of the truth spoken. All fear of their relatives was gone. The truth alone was exalted to them. It was dearer and more precious than life. They had been hungering and thirsting for truth. I asked what had made this great change. An angel answered, "It is the latter rain. The refreshing from the presence of the Lord. The loud cry of the third angel."

Great power was with these chosen ones. Said the angel, "Look ye!" My attention was turned to the wicked, or unbelievers. They were all astir. The zeal and power with the people of God had aroused and enraged them. Confusion, confusion was on every side. I saw measures taken against this company, who were having the power and light of God. Darkness thickened around them, yet there they stood, approved of God, and trusting in Him. I saw them perplexed.

Next I heard them crying unto God earnestly. Through the day and night their cry ceased not. I heard these words, "Thy will, O God, be done! If it can glorify Thy name, make a way of escape for Thy people! Deliver us from the heathen round about us! They have appointed us unto death; but Thine arm can bring salvation." These are all the words I can bring to mind. They seemed to have a deep sense of their unworthiness, and manifested entire submission to the will of God. Yet everyone, without an exception, was earnestly pleading, and wrestling like Jacob for deliverance.—*Review and Herald*, Dec. 31, 1857.

SATAN'S WRATH AWAKENED

Casting all your care upon him; for he careth for you. Be sober, be vigilant; because your adversary the devil, as a roaring lion, walketh about, seeking whom he may devour. 1 Peter 5:7, 8.

If the world is to be convinced of sin as transgressors of God's law, the agency must be the Holy Spirit working through human instrumentalities. The church needs now to shake off her deathlike slumber; for the Lord is waiting to bless His people who will recognize the blessing when it comes, and diffuse it in clear, strong rays of light. "Then will I sprinkle clean water upon you, and ye shall be clean. . . . And I will put my spirit within you, and cause you to walk in my statutes" (Eze. 36:25-27).

If the wilderness of the church is to become as a fruitful field, and the fruitful field to be as a forest, it is through the Holy Spirit of God poured out upon His people. The heavenly agencies have long been waiting for the human agents, the members of the church, to cooperate with them in the great work to be done. They are waiting for you. So vast is the field, so comprehensive the design, that every sanctified heart will be pressed into service as an agent of divine power.

At the same time there will be a power stirring everything from beneath. The working of evil angels will be manifest in deceptions, delusions, in calamities, and in casualties and crimes of no ordinary character. While God employs the angels of mercy to work through His human agents, Satan sets his agencies in operation, laying under tribute all the powers that submit to his control. There will be lords many and gods many. The cry will be heard, "Lo, here is Christ" and "Lo, He is there." The deep plotting of Satan will reveal its workings everywhere, for the purpose of distracting attention from present duty. The appearance of a false christ will awaken delusive hopes in the minds of those who will allow themselves to be deceived. The church members that are awake will arise to the emergency, and manifestations of satanic power are to be presented in their true light before the people.—*General Conference Bulletin*, Feb. 28, 1893.

TRUE AND COUNTERFEIT REVIVALS

And I heard another voice from heaven, saying, Come out of her, my people, that ye be not partakers of her sins, and that ye receive not of her plagues. Rev. 18:4.

Notwithstanding the widespread declension of faith and piety, there are true followers of Christ in these churches. Before the final visitation of God's judgments upon the earth there will be among the people of the Lord such a revival of primitive godliness as has not been witnessed since apostolic times. The Spirit and power of God will be poured out upon His children. At that time many will separate themselves from those churches in which the love of this world has supplanted love for God and His Word. Many, both of ministers and people, will gladly accept those great truths which God has caused to be proclaimed at this time to prepare a people for the Lord's second coming.

The enemy of souls desires to hinder this work; and before the time for such a movement shall come, he will endeavor to prevent it by introducing a counterfeit. In those churches which he can bring under his deceptive power he will make it appear that God's special blessing is poured out; there will be manifest what is thought to be great religious interest. Multitudes will exult that God is working marvelously for them, when the work is that of another spirit. Under a religious guise, Satan will seek to extend his influence over the Christian world.

In many of the revivals which have occurred during the last half century, the same influences have been at work, to a greater or less degree, that will be manifest in the more extensive movements of the future. There is an emotional excitement, a mingling of the true with the false, that is well adapted to mislead. Yet none need be deceived. In the light of God's Word it is not difficult to determine the nature of these movements.—*The Great Controversy*, p. 464.

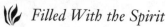

STRENGTH FOR THE TIME OF TROUBLE

And at that time shall Michael stand up, the great prince which standeth for the children of thy people: and there shall be a time of trouble, such as never was since there was a nation even to that same time: and at that time thy people shall be delivered, every one that shall be found written in the book. Dan. 12:1.

As the members of the body of Christ approach the period of their last conflict, "the time of Jacob's trouble," they will grow up into Christ, and will partake largely of His Spirit. As the third message swells to a loud cry, and as great power and glory attend the closing work, the faithful people of God will partake of that glory. It is the latter rain which revives and strengthens them to pass through the time of trouble. Their faces will shine with the glory of that light which attends the third angel.

I saw that God will in a wonderful manner preserve His people through the time of trouble. As Jesus poured out His soul in agony in the garden, they will earnestly cry and agonize day and night for deliverance. The decree will go forth that they must disregard the Sabbath of the fourth commandment, and honor the first day, or lose their lives; but they will not yield, and trample under their feet the Sabbath of the Lord, and honor an institution of papacy. Satan's host and wicked men will surround them, and exult over them, because there will seem to be no way of escape for them. But in the midst of their revelry and triumph, there is heard peal upon peal of the loudest thunder. The heavens have gathered blackness, and are only illuminated by the blazing light and terrible glory from heaven, as God utters His voice from His holy habitation.

The foundations of the earth shake; buildings totter and fall with a terrible crash. The sea boils like a pot, and the whole earth is in terrible commotion. The captivity of the righteous is turned, and with sweet and solemn whisperings they say to one another, "We are delivered. It is the voice of God." With solemn awe they listen to the words of the voice.— *Testimonies*, vol. 1, pp. 353, 354.

NOW IS THE TIME FOR PREPARATION

Watch ye therefore, and pray always, that ye may be accounted worthy to escape all these things that shall come to pass, and to stand before the Son of man. Luke 21:36.

Those professed believers who come up to the time of trouble unprepared, will, in their despair, confess their sins before the world in words of burning anguish, while the wicked exult over their distress. The case of all such is hopeless. When Christ stands up, and leaves the most holy place, the time of trouble commences, the case of every soul is decided, and there will be no atoning blood to cleanse from sin and pollution. As Jesus leaves the most holy, He speaks in tones of decision and kingly authority: "He that is unjust, let him be unjust still: and he which is filthy, let him be filthy still: and he that is righteous, let him be righteous still: and he that is holy, let him be holy still. And, behold, I come quickly; and my reward is with me, to give every man according as his work shall be" (Rev. 22:11, 12).

Those who have delayed a preparation for the day of God cannot obtain it in the time of trouble, or at any future period. The righteous will not cease their earnest, agonizing cries for deliverance. They cannot bring to mind any particular sins; but in their whole life they can see little good. Their sins have gone beforehand to judgment, and pardon has been written. Their sins have been borne away into the land of forgetfulness, and they cannot bring them to remembrance. Certain destruction threatens them, and, like Jacob, they will not suffer their faith to grow weak because their prayers are not immediately answered. Though suffering the pangs of hunger, they will not cease their intercessions. They lay hold of the strength of God, as Jacob laid hold of the angel; and the language of their soul is "I will not let thee go, except thou bless me" (Gen. 32:26).

That season of distress and anguish will require an effort of earnestness and determined faith that can endure delay and hunger, and will not fail under weakness, though severely tried. The period of probation is the time granted to all to prepare for the day of God.—*Signs of the Times*, Nov. 27, 1879.

A SPIRITUAL FIGHT

For we wrestle not against flesh and blood, but against principalities, against powers, against the rulers of the darkness of this world, against spiritual wickedness in high places. Eph. 6:12.

The Christian life is a warfare. But "we wrestle not against flesh and blood, but against principalities, against powers, against the rulers of the darkness of this world, against spiritual wickedness in high places." In this conflict of righteousness against unrighteousness we can be successful only by divine aid. Our finite will must be brought into submission to the will of the Infinite; the human will must be blended with the divine. This will bring the Holy Spirit to our aid; and every conquest will tend to the recovery of God's purchased possession, to the restoration of His image in the soul.

The Lord Jesus acts through the Holy Spirit; for He is His representative. Through Him He infuses spiritual life into the soul, quickening its energies for good, cleansing it from moral defilement, and giving it a fitness for His kingdom. Jesus has large blessings to bestow, rich gifts to distribute among men. He is the wonderful Counselor, infinite in wisdom and strength; and if we will acknowledge the power of His Spirit, and submit to be molded by it, we shall stand complete in Him. What a thought is this! In Christ "dwelleth all the fulness of the Godhead bodily. And ye are complete in him" (Col. 2:9, 10).

Never will the human heart know happiness until it is submitted to be molded by the Spirit of God. The Spirit conforms the renewed soul to the model, Jesus Christ. Through the influence of the Spirit, enmity against God is changed into faith and love, and pride into humility. The soul perceives the beauty of truth, and Christ is honored in excellence and perfection of character. As these changes are effected, angels break out in rapturous song, and God and Christ rejoice over souls fashioned after the divine similitude.—*Review and Herald*, Feb. 10, 1903.

SOLDIERS FOR CHRIST

Wherefore take unto you the whole armour of God, that ye may be able to withstand in the evil day, and having done all, to stand. Stand therefore, having your loins girt about with truth, and having on the breastplate of righteousness; and your feet shod with the preparation of the gospel of peace; above all, taking the shield of faith, wherewith ye shall be able to quench all the fiery darts of the wicked. And take the helmet of salvation, and the sword of the Spirit, which is the word of God. Eph. 6:13-17.

Soldiers engaged in battle have to meet difficulties and hardships. Coarse food is given them, and that often in limited quantities. They have long marches, day by day, over rough roads and under burning suns, camping out at night, sleeping on the bare ground, with only the canopy of heaven for a covering, exposed to drenching rains and chilling frosts, hungry, faint, exhausted, now standing as a target for the foe, now in deadly encounter. Thus they learn what hardship means. Those who enlist in Christ's army are also expected to do difficult work, and to bear painful trials patiently for Christ's sake. But those who suffer with Him shall also reign with Him.

Then who of us have entered the service to expect the conveniences of life, to be off duty when we please, laying aside the soldier's armor and putting on the civilian's dress, sleeping at the post of duty, and so exposing the cause of God to reproach? The ease-loving ones will not practice self-denial and patient endurance; and when men are wanted to make mighty strokes for God, these are not ready to answer, "Here am I; send me." Hard and trying work has to be done, but blessed are those who are ready to do it when their names are called. God will not reward men and women in the next world for seeking to be comfortable in this.

We are now on the battlefield. There is no time for resting, no time for ease, no time for selfish indulgence. After gaining one advantage, you must do battle again; you must go on conquering and to conquer, gathering fresh strength for fresh struggles. Every victory gained gives an increase of courage, faith, and determination. Through divine strength you will prove more than a match for your enemies.—*Signs of the Times*, Sept. 7, 1891.

HAPPINESS IN SERVING OUR CAPTAIN

Fight the good fight of faith, lay hold on eternal life, whereunto thou art also called, and hast professed a good profession before many witnesses. 1 Tim. 6:12.

In earnest, determined exercise as faithful soldiers, obeying the orders of the Captain of our salvation, there is genuine enjoyment such as can be obtained in no other employment. The peace of Christ will be in the heart of the faithful soldier. There is rest for the soul in wearing Christ's yoke, in lifting Christ's burdens. It seems a contradiction to say that there is no rest for the soul except that which is found in continuous and devoted service. But this is true. Happiness comes in willing, obedient service, where all the powers of our being are moving in happy, healthy, harmonious action in obeying our Captain's orders. The more responsible the task assigned to Christ's soldiers, the more the soul exults in the Saviour's love and approval. The soul realizes a freedom in the performance of the weightiest and most taxing duties.

But this doing the duty of a soldier means work. It is not always just such work as we would choose. Outward inconveniences, difficulties, and trials have to be borne by the soldiers of Jesus. There is a constant warfare to be maintained against the evils and inclinations of our own natural hearts. We must not pick and choose the work most agreeable to us; for we are Christ's soldiers, under His discipline, and we are not to study our own pleasure. We must fight the battles of the Lord manfully. We have enemies to conquer that would gain the control of all our powers.

Self-will in us must die; Christ's will alone must be obeyed. The soldier in Christ's army must learn to endure hardness, deny self, take up the cross, and follow where his Captain leads the way. There are many things to do which are trying to human nature, and painful to flesh and blood. This work of self-subduing requires determined, continuous effort. In fighting the good fight of faith, obtaining precious victories, we are laying hold of eternal life.—*Youth's Instructor*, Dec. 22, 1886.

TRIALS AND OPPOSITION BRING BENEFIT

Beloved, think it not strange concerning the fiery trial which is to try you, as though some strange thing happened unto you: but rejoice, inasmuch as ye are partakers of Christ's sufferings; that, when his glory shall be revealed, ye may be glad also with exceeding joy. 1 Peter 4:12, 13.

The opposition we meet may prove a benefit to us in many ways. If it is well borne, it will develop virtues which would never have appeared if the Christian had nothing to endure. And faith, patience, forbearance, heavenly mindedness, trust in Providence, and genuine sympathy with the erring, are the results of trial well borne. These are the graces of the Spirit, which bud, blossom, and bear fruit amid trials and adversity. Meekness, humility, and love always grow on the Christian tree. If the word is received into good and honest hearts, the obdurate soul will be subdued, and faith, grasping the promises, and relying upon Jesus, will prove triumphant. "This is the victory that overcometh the world, even our faith" (1 John 5:4).

He who opens the Scriptures, and feeds upon the heavenly manna, becomes a partaker of the divine nature. He has no life or experience apart from Christ. He hears the voice of God speaking from heaven, "This is my beloved Son, in whom I am well pleased" (Matt. 3:17). That voice is assurance to him that he is accepted in the Beloved. And he knows that in character he must be like Him with whom God is well pleased. God has fully accepted Christ as our substitute, our surety; then let everyone who names the name of Christ depart from all iniquity, and be one with Christ in character, that Jesus may not be ashamed to call us brethren.

He in whom we trust has proved Himself a present help in every time of need; and as we dwell with Him, we grow more and more into His image. "We all, with open face beholding as in a glass the glory of the Lord, are changed into the same image from glory to glory [which means from character to character] even as by the Spirit of the Lord" (2 Cor. 3:18). "For God, who commanded the light to shine out of darkness, hath shined in our hearts, to give the light of the knowledge of the glory of God in the face of Jesus Christ" (2 Cor. 4:6).—*Review and Herald*, June 28, 1892.

THE ENEMY DOES NOT GIVE UP EASILY

Therefore rejoice, ye heavens, and ye that dwell in them. Woe to the inhabiters of the earth and of the sea! for the devil is come down unto you, having great wrath, because he knoweth that he hath but a short time. Rev. 12:12.

Those who consecrate their all to God will not be left unmolested by the enemy of souls. Satan will come to them with his specious temptations, designing to allure them from their loyalty to God. He will present to them his bribe, as he did to Christ in the wilderness of temptation, saying, "All these things will I give thee, if thou wilt fall down and worship me" (Matt. 4:9).

But what should be the answer of the Christian to all the temptations of the evil one? He should say, "I will not lend my influence in any way to the advancement of anything save the cause of Christ. I am not my own; I have been bought with a price. I am not to live to please myself; for I have been purchased, ransomed by the blood of Christ. It is not possible for me to give to Christ more than that which belongs to Him; for every moment of my life belongs to Him. I am His possession, a servant employed to do the will of my Master."

This is the only position that is safe for us to occupy; and if the individual members of the church felt in this way, what a power would the church exert to draw and win souls to Christ. It is this halfhearted work, the effort to serve God and the devil at the same time, that leaves the church so destitute of the Spirit of God.

Were the members of the church consecrated to God, were they in the unity of the Spirit, in the bond of peace, were they organized for the purpose of imparting to others an influence of good, the church would be indeed the light of the world. Should the individual members seek to represent Christ to the world in character and life, thousands would be attracted to the Saviour, who now have reason to criticize the words and works of those who profess the name of Christ.

"For God, who commanded the light to shine out of darkness, hath shined in our hearts, to give the light of the knowledge of the glory of God in the face of Jesus Christ. But we have this treasure in earthen vessels, that the excellency of the power may be of God, and not of us" (2 Cor. 4:6, 7).—*Home Missionary*, Oct. 1, 1892.

UNCOVERING THE ENEMY'S DEVICES

Finally, my brethren, be strong in the Lord, and in the power of his might. Eph. 6:10.

As a people, we are looking for the coming of the Lord in the clouds of heaven; and how carefully should we examine our hearts that we may know whether or not we are in the faith. There seems to be a mist before the eyes of many, for they fail to discern spiritual things, and do not recognize the workings of Satan to entrap their souls. Christians are not to be the slaves of passion; they are to be controlled by the Spirit of God. But many become the sport of the enemy, because when temptation comes, they do not rest in Jesus, but worry themselves out of His arms, and in perplexity lose all their faith and courage. They do not remember that Jesus has helped them out of difficulties in the past, that His grace is sufficient for the daily trials, and that He can help in the present trouble.

We make failures in our little, daily difficulties, and allow them to irritate and vex us; we fall under them, and so make stumbling blocks for ourselves and others. But blessings of the greatest importance are to result from the patient endurance of these daily vexations; for we are to gain strength to bear greater difficulties. Satan will press upon us the most severe temptations, and we must learn to come to God in any and every emergency. . . .

We profess to be Bible Christians, and we are not left in the dark to take step after step in uncertainty. We are to know where we are going. We cannot be in darkness if we are following Christ as our leader; for He says, "He that followeth me shall not walk in darkness, but shall have the light of life" (John 8:12). When the way seems beset with difficulty, and clouded with darkness, we must believe that there is light ahead, and not turn to the right or left, but press forward, notwithstanding all our trials and temptations.—*Review and Herald*, May 19, 1891.

NOT IN "MY OWN WAY"

For ye have not received the spirit of bondage again to fear; but ye have received the Spirit of adoption, whereby we cry, Abba, Father. Rom. 8:15.

The work of sanctification begins in the heart, and we must come into such a relation with God, that Jesus can put His divine mold upon us. We must be emptied of self in order to give room to Jesus, but how many have their hearts so filled with idols that they have no room for the Redeemer of the world. The world holds the hearts of men in captivity. They center their thoughts and affections upon their business, their position, their family. They hold to their opinions and ways, and cherish them as idols in the soul; but we cannot afford to yield ourselves to the service of self, holding to our own ways and ideas, and excluding the truth of God.

We must be emptied of self. But this is not all that is required; for when we have renounced our idols, the vacuum must be supplied. If the heart is left desolate, and the vacuum not supplied, it will be in the condition of him whose house was "empty, swept, and garnished" (Matt. 12:44), but without a guest to occupy it. The evil spirit took unto himself seven other spirits more wicked than himself, and they entered in and dwelt there; and the last state of that man was worse than the first. . . .

You may feel that you cannot meet the approval of heaven. You may say, "I was born with a natural tendency toward this evil, and I cannot overcome." But every provision has been made by our heavenly Father whereby you may be able to overcome every unholy tendency. You are to overcome even as Christ overcame in your behalf. He says, "To him that overcometh will I grant to sit with me in my throne, even as I also overcame, and am set down with my Father in his throne" (Rev. 3:21). It was sin that imperiled the human family; and before man was created the provision was made that if man failed to bear the test, Jesus would become His sacrifice and surety, that through faith in Him, man might be reconciled to God, for Christ was the Lamb "slain from the foundation of the world" (Rev. 13:8). Christ died on Calvary that man might have power to overcome his natural tendencies to sin.

But one says, "Can I not have my own way, and act myself?" No, you cannot have your way, and enter the kingdom of heaven. No "my way" will be there. No human ways will find place in the kingdom of heaven. Our ways must be lost in God's ways.—*Review and Herald*, Feb. 23, 1892.

PRAYER BRINGS STRENGTH

For whatsoever is born of God overcometh the world: and this is the victory that overcometh the world, even our faith. 1 John 5:4.

While Jesus, our Intercessor, pleads for us in heaven, the Holy Spirit works in us, to will and to do of His good pleasure. All heaven is interested in the salvation of the soul. Then what reason have we to doubt that the Lord will and does help us? We who teach the people must ourselves have a vital connection with God. In Spirit and Word we should be to the people as a wellspring, because Christ is in us a well of water springing up unto everlasting life. Sorrow and pain may test our patience and our faith; but the brightness of the presence of the Unseen is with us, and we must hide self behind Jesus.

Talk courage to the church; lift them up to God in prayer. Tell them that when they feel that they have sinned, and cannot pray, it is then the time to pray. Many feel humiliated at their failures, that they have been overcome by the enemy in the place of overcoming. Worldliness, selfishness, and carnality have weakened them, and they think it is no use to approach unto God; but this thought is one of the enemy's suggestions. Ashamed they may be, and deeply humbled; but they must pray and believe. As they confess their sins, He who is faithful and just will forgive them their sins, and cleanse them from all unrighteousness (see 1 John 1:9). Though the mind may wander in prayer, be not discouraged, bring it back to the throne, and do not leave the mercy seat until you have the victory.

Are you to think your victory will be testified by strong emotion? No; "this is the victory that overcometh the world, even our faith." The Lord knows your desire; by faith keep close to Him, and expect to receive the Holy Spirit.

The office of the Holy Spirit is to control all our spiritual exercises. The Father has given His Son for us that through the Son the Holy Spirit might come to us, and lead us unto the Father. Through divine agency, we have the spirit of intercession, whereby we may plead with God, as a man pleadeth with his friend.—*Signs of the Times*, Oct. 3, 1892.

THERE IS ALWAYS AN OPEN DOOR

I know thy works: behold, I have set before thee an open door, and no man can shut it: for thou hast a little strength, and hast kept my word, and hast not denied my name. Rev. 3:8.

Those who shall be overcomers are to be highly exalted before God and before His angels. Christ has promised that He will confess their names before His Father and before the holy angels of heaven. He has given us abundant promises to encourage us to be overcomers. The True Witness has given us the assurance that He has set before us an open door, which no man can shut.

Those who are seeking to be faithful to God may be denied many of the privileges of the world; their way may be hedged up and their work hindered by the enemies of truth; but there is no power that can close the door of communication between God and their souls. The Christian himself may close this door by indulgence in sin, or by rejection of heaven's light. He may turn away his ears from hearing the message of truth, and in this way sever the connection between God and his soul.

You may have ears, and not hear. You may have eyes, and not see the light, nor receive the illumination that God has provided for you. You may close the door to light as effectually as the Pharisees closed the door to Christ when He taught among them. They would not receive the light and knowledge He brought, because it did not come in the way they had expected it to come. Christ was the Light of the world, and if they had received the light He graciously brought to them, it would have resulted in their salvation, but they rejected the Holy One of Israel.

Christ said of them that they "loved darkness rather than light, because their deeds were evil. For every one that doeth evil hateth the light, neither cometh to the light, lest his deeds should be reproved" (John 3:19, 20). He said, "Ye will not come to me, that ye might have life" (John 5:40). The way was open; but by their own course of action they closed the door, and severed their connection with Christ. We may do the same by rejecting light and truth.—*Review and Herald*, Mar. 26, 1889.

LOOKING FOR A DAILY VICTORY

Know ye not that they which run in a race run all, but one receiveth the prize? So run, that ye may obtain. And every man that striveth for the mastery is temperate in all things. Now they do it to obtain a corruptible crown; but we an incorruptible. 1 Cor. 9:24, 25.

How many years have we been in the Lord's garden? And what profit have we brought to the Master? How are we meeting the inspecting eye of God? Are we increasing in reverence, love, humility, confidence in God? Do we cherish gratitude for all His mercies? Are we seeking to bless those around us? Do we manifest the spirit of Jesus in our families? Are we teaching His Word to our children, and making known to them the wonderful works of God? The Christian must represent Jesus by both being good and doing good. Then there will be a fragrance about the life, a loveliness of character, which will reveal the fact that he is a child of God, an heir of heaven.

Brethren, be no longer slothful servants. Every soul must battle against inclination. Christ came not to save men in their sins, but from their sins. He has made it possible for us to possess a holy character; do not, then, be content with defects and deformities. But while we are to seek earnestly for perfection of character, we must remember that sanctification is not the work of a moment, but of a lifetime. Said Paul, "I die daily" (1 Cor. 15:31). Day by day the work of overcoming must go forward. Every day we are to resist temptation, and gain the victory over selfishness in all its forms.

Day by day we should cherish love and humility, and cultivate in ourselves all those excellencies of character which will please God and fit us for the blessed society of heaven. To all who are seeking to accomplish this work, the promise is very precious, "He that overcometh, the same shall be clothed in white raiment; and I will not blot out his name out of the book of life, but I will confess his name before my Father, and before his angels" (Rev. 3:5).—*Historical Sketches*, p. 181.

EACH VICTORY MAKES THE FOLLOWING EASIER

Nay, in all these things we are more than conquerors through him that loved us. Rom. 8:37.

The work is before you to improve the remnant of your life in reforming and elevating the character. A new life begins in the renewed soul. Christ is the indwelling Saviour. That which may be regarded as hard to give up must be yielded. The overbearing, dictatorial word must be left unspoken; then a precious victory will be gained.

True happiness will be the result of every self-denial, every crucifixion of self. One victory won, the next is more easily gained. Had Moses neglected the opportunities and privileges granted him of God, he would have neglected the light from heaven and would have been a disappointed, miserable man. Sin is from beneath; and when it is indulged, Satan is enshrined in the soul, there to kindle the very fires of hell. God has not given His law to prevent the salvation of souls, but He wants all to be saved. Man has light and opportunities, and if he will improve them he may overcome. You may show by your life the power of the grace of God in overcoming.

Satan is trying to set up his throne in the soul-temple. When he reigns he makes himself heard and felt in angry passions, in words of bitterness that grieve and wound; but as light has no communion with darkness, and Christ no union with Belial, the man must be wholly for one or the other. In yielding to self-indulgence, avarice, deception, fraud, or sin of any kind, he encourages the principles of Satan in his soul and closes the door of heaven to himself. Because of sin, Satan was thrust out of heaven; and no man indulging and fostering sin can go to heaven, for then Satan would again have a foothold there.

When a man is earnestly engaged day by day in overcoming the defects in his character, he is cherishing Christ in his soul-temple; the light of Christ is in him. Under the bright beams of the light of Christ's countenance his entire being becomes elevated and ennobled.—*Testimonies*, vol. 4, pp. 345, 346.

SUPERNATURAL STRENGTH PROMISED

There is therefore now no condemnation to them which are in Christ Jesus, who walk not after the flesh, but after the Spirit. Rom. 8:1.

The Holy Spirit was promised to be with those who were wrestling for victory, demonstrating the power of might by endowing the human agent with supernatural strength, and instructing the ignorant in the mysteries of the kingdom of God. The Holy Spirit is to be our helper. Of what avail would it have been to us that the only-begotten Son of God had humbled Himself, endured the temptations of the wily foe, and wrestled with him during His entire life on earth, and died, the just for the unjust, that humanity might not perish, if the Spirit had not been given as a constant working, regenerating agent to make effectual in our cases what had been wrought by the world's Redeemer?

The Holy Spirit implanted in the disciples enabled them to stand firmly against idolatry, and to exalt the Lord alone.

The Holy Spirit guided the pens of the sacred historians that the record of the precious words and works of Christ might be presented to the world. The Holy Spirit is constantly at work seeking to draw the attention of men to the great sacrifice made upon the cross of Calvary, to unfold to the world the love of God to man, and to open to the convicted soul the precious promises in the Scriptures.

It is the Holy Spirit that brings to the darkened minds the bright beams of the Sun of righteousness. It is the Holy Spirit that makes men's hearts burn within them with an awakened intelligence of the truths of eternity. It is the Holy Spirit that presents before the mind the moral standard of rightousness and convinces of sin. It is the Holy Spirit that produces godly sorrow which worketh repentance that needeth not to be repented of, and inspires faith in Him who alone can save from all sin. It is the Holy Spirit that works to transform character by withdrawing the affections of men from those things which are temporal and perishable, and fixing them upon the immortal inheritance, the eternal substance which is imperishable. The Holy Spirit re-creates, refines, and sanctifies the human agents, that they may become members of the royal family, children of the heavenly King.—*Signs of the Times*, Apr. 17, 1893.

CLOSER TO JESUS

Submit yourselves therefore to God. Resist the devil, and he will flee from you. Draw nigh to God, and he will draw nigh to you. Cleanse your hands, ye sinners; and purify your hearts, ye double minded. James 4:7, 8.

Whence temptation comes upon us, we need spiritual discernment, that we may detect Satan's agency, and draw close to Jesus. Draw nigh to God, and He will draw nigh to you. Resist the devil, and he will flee from you. Every moment it is necessary to fight the good fight of faith; for doubt must be resisted, and faith must be encouraged. In temptation, inclination must be overruled by reason. Self will clamor for indulgence, but inclination must be resisted, and temptation overcome.

The Lord has given warnings, He has presented principles that it is necessary for every Christian to heed, and bring into his practical life. Those who pass on in indifference to the light and warning which God has been pleased to give will grow more and more egotistical and self-sufficient. Those who do not place their dependence upon God will certainly be overthrown by the enemy. Satan is working by every conceivable device to keep in his own ranks those who claim to be on the Lord's side. He can blind their eyes until they will call light darkness, and darkness light. . . .

Though the light of God is shining in more distinct rays than ever before, and will shine more and more clearly as we near the close of earth's history, those who will be able to discern truth from error will be men who are often upon their knees, seeking wisdom from God. The bright beams of the Sun of righteousness can alone reveal the numerous and varied plottings of the enemy. The wicked one is at work with all deceivableness of unrighteousness; and while we are not to keep our eyes upon the powers of darkness, we cannot be ignorant of their devices.

But our faith must center in Jesus Christ. Looking unto Him, clinging to His strength as sufficient for every emergency, our heart joins His heart, our life is knit by hidden links to His life, and because He lives, we shall live also. This is practical religion; for we are to be kept by the power of God through faith unto salvation. No one of us can be safe save as we join the Lord in a perpetual covenant, that shall not be forgotten by us.—*Review and Herald*, Mar. 14, 1893.

VICTORY BRINGS JOY TO HEAVEN

I say unto you, that likewise joy shall be in heaven over one sinner that repenteth, more than over ninety and nine just persons, which need no repentance. Luke 15:7.

Satanic agencies are always warring for the mastery over the human mind, but the angels of God are constantly at work, strengthening the weak hands and confirming the feeble knees of all who call upon God for help. The promise to every child of God is "Ask, and it shall be given you; seek, and ye shall find; knock, and it shall be opened unto you: for every one that asketh receiveth; and he that seeketh findeth; and to him that knocketh it shall be opened" (Matt. 7:7, 8). . . .

The Lord has had true-hearted men and women, those who have made a covenant with Him by sacrifice. They have not swerved from their integrity. They have kept themselves unspotted from the world, and they have been led by the Light of life to defeat the purposes of the wily foe. Will human beings now act their part in resisting the devil? If they will do this, he will surely flee from them. Angels, who will do for you what you cannot do for yourselves, are waiting for your cooperation. They are waiting for you to respond to the drawing of Christ. Draw nigh to God and to one another. By desire, by silent prayer, by resistance of satanic agencies, put your will on the side of God's will. While you have one desire to resist the devil, and sincerely pray, Deliver me from temptation, you will have strength for your day.

It is the work of the heavenly angels to come close to the tried, the tempted, the suffering ones. They labor long and untiringly to save the souls for whom Christ has died. And when souls appreciate their advantages, appreciate the heavenly assistance sent them, respond to the Holy Spirit's working on their behalf; when they put their will on the side of Christ's will, angels bear the tidings heavenward. Returning to the heavenly courts, they report their success with the souls for whom they have ministered, and there is rejoicing among the heavenly host.—*Review and Herald*, July 4, 1899.

NOTHING MORE INVINCIBLE

But thanks be to God, which giveth us the victory through our Lord Jesus Christ. 1 Cor. 15:57.

The Christian life is a life of constant conflict. It is a battle and a march. Every act of obedience, every deed of self-denial, every trial bravely endured, every temptation resisted, every victory gained, is a step forward in the march to eternal triumph.

There is hope for man. Christ says, "To him that overcometh will I grant to sit with me in my throne, even as I also overcame, and am set down with my Father in his throne" (Rev. 3:21). But let us never forget that the efforts we make in our own strength are utterly worthless. Our strength is weakness; our judgment foolishness. Only in the name and strength of the Conqueror can we conquer. When we are pressed with temptation, when un-christlike desires clamor for the mastery, let us offer fervent, importunate prayer to the heavenly Father, in the name of Christ. This will bring divine aid. In the Redeemer's name we may gain the victory.

As, seeing the sinfulness of sin, we fall helpless before the cross, asking forgiveness and strength, our prayer is heard and answered. Those who present their petitions to God in Christ's name will never be turned away. The Lord says, "Him that cometh to me I will in no wise cast out" (John 6:37). "He will regard the prayer of the destitute" (Ps. 102:17). Our help comes from Him who holds all things in His hands. The peace that He sends is the assurance of His love to us.

Nothing can be more helpless and yet more invincible than the soul that feel its nothingness, and relies wholly upon the merits of a crucified and risen Saviour. God would send every angel in heaven to the aid of the one who places his whole dependence on Christ, rather than allow him to be overcome.

If we accept Christ as our guide, He will lead us safely along the narrow way. The road may be rough and thorny, and the ascent steep and dangerous; there may be pitfalls on the right hand and on the left. When weary and longing for rest, we may have to toil on; when faint, we may have to fight; but with Christ as our guide, we shall not fail of reaching heaven.—*Signs of the Times*, Oct. 29, 1902.

A BRAND PLUCKED OUT OF THE FIRE

And the Lord said unto Satan, The Lord rebuke thee, O Satan; even the Lord that hath chosen Jerusalem rebuke thee: is not this a brand plucked out of the fire? Zech. 3:2.

Jesus speaks of His people as a brand plucked out of the fire, and Satan understands what this means. The infinite sufferings of the Son of God in Gethsemane and on Calvary were endured that He might rescue His people from the power of the evil one. The work of Jesus for the salvation of perishing souls is as if He thrust His hand into the fire to save them. Joshua, who represents God's people, is clothed in filthy garments, and stands before the angel; but as the people repent before God for the transgression of His law, and reach up by the hand of faith to lay hold on the righteousness of Christ, Jesus says, "Take away the filthy garments from them, and clothe them with change of raiment" (see Zech. 3:4).

It is through Christ's righteousness alone that we are enabled to keep the law. Those who worship God in sincerity and truth, and afflict their souls before Him as in the great day of atonement, will wash their robes of character and make them white in the blood of the Lamb. Satan seeks to bind about the human mind with deception, so that men will not repent and believe, that they may have their filthy garments removed. Why will you cling to your miserable defects of character, and by so doing bar the way, that Jesus may not work in your behalf?

During the time of trouble, the position of God's people will be similar to the position of Joshua. They will not be ignorant of the work going on in heaven in their behalf. They will realize that sin is recorded against their names, but they will also know that the sins of all who repent and lay hold of the merits of Christ will be canceled. . . . Those who have manifested true repentance for sin, and by living faith in Christ are obedient to God's commandments, will have their names retained in the book of life, and they will be confessed before the Father and before the holy angels. Jesus will say, "They are Mine; I have purchased them with My own blood."—*Signs of the Times*, June 2, 1890.

VICTORY ON THE BATTLEFIELD

I have given them thy word; and the world hath hated them, because they are not of the world, even as I am not of the world. I pray not that thou shouldest take them out of the world, but that thou shouldest keep them from the evil. John 17:14, 15.

The Christian has duties to do in the world, and God holds him responsible for their faithful performance. He is not to confine himself in monastic walls, nor to avoid all association with worldlings. It is true that his principles will be put to the severest test, and he will be pained by what his eyes see and his ears hear. But he must not, by becoming familiar with these sights and sounds, learn to love them. By association with the world, we incline to catch the spirit of the world, and to adopt their customs, tastes, and preferences. But we are commanded, "Come out from among them, and be ye separate, saith the Lord, and touch not the unclean thing; and I will receive you, and will be a Father unto you, and ye shall be my sons and daughters" (2 Cor. 6:17, 18).

Never let the world say that worldlings and Christ's followers are alike in their tastes and pursuits; for God has drawn a line between His people and the world. This line of demarcation is broad and deep and clear; it is not so blended with the world that it is not discernible. "The Lord knoweth them that are his" (2 Tim. 2:19). "By their fruits ye shall know them" (Matt. 7:20).

It is only by watching unto prayer, and the exercise of living faith, that the Christian can preserve his integrity in the midst of the temptations that Satan brings to bear upon him. But "whatsoever is born of God overcometh the world: and this is the victory that overcometh the world, even our faith" (1 John 5:4). Talk to your heart constantly the language of faith: "Jesus said He would receive me, and I believe His word. I will praise Him; I will glorify His name." Satan will be close by your side to suggest that you do not feel any joy. Answer him, "'This is the victory that overcometh the world, even our faith.' I have everything to be glad of; for I am a child of God. I am trusting in Jesus. The law of God is in my heart; none of my steps shall slide."—*Signs of the Times*, May 15, 1884.

EATING OF THE TREE OF LIFE

He that hath an ear, let him hear what the Spirit saith unto the churches;
To him that overcometh will I give to eat of the tree of life, which is in the
midst of the paradise of God. Rev. 2:7.

This message concerns all our churches. You can never employ your faculty of hearing better than in hearkening to hear what the voice of God speaks to you in His Word. There is a rich and abundant promise to those who overcome. It is not enough to enter upon this warfare, we must pursue it to the end. We must know nothing of yielding. We must fight the good fight of faith to the very end. To the overcomer is promised the triumphal victory. "To him that overcometh will I give to eat of the tree of life, which is in the midst of the paradise of God." Whatever was lost in the fall of Adam is more than restored in redemption. He that sitteth on the throne saith, "Behold, I make all things new" (Rev. 21:5).

Let us look closely and critically to ourselves. Are not the vows we entered into at our baptism violated? Are we dead to the world and alive unto Christ? Are we seeking those things which are above, where Christ sitteth at the right hand of God? Is the cable cut which anchored us to the eternal Rock? Are we drifting with the current to perdition? Shall we make no effort to press and urge our passage upstream? Let us not hesitate longer, but vigorously apply the oars; and let us do our first works ere we make hopeless shipwreck.

It is our work to know our special failings and sins, which cause darkness and spiritual feebleness, and quenched our first love. Is it worldliness? Is it selfishness? Is it the love of self-esteem? Is it striving to be first? Is it the sin of sensuality that is intensely active? Is it the sin of the Nicolaitans, turning the grace of God into lasciviousness? Is it the misuse and abuse of great light and opportunities and privileges, marking boasted claims to wisdom and religious knowledge, while the life and character are inconsistent and immoral? Whatever it is that has been petted and cultivated until it has become strong and overmastering, make determined efforts to overcome, else you will be lost.—*Review and Herald*, June 7, 1887.

WEARING THE VICTOR'S CROWN

He that hath an ear, let him hear what the Spirit saith unto the churches;
He that overcometh shall not be hurt of the second death. Rev. 2:11.

The words "He that hath an ear, let him hear what the Spirit saith unto the churches" are repeated after these promises, weighty with importance to the children of God. It is for our eternal interest to know and understand what the Spirit saith unto the churches, and we should search carefully for light and knowledge that we may not be in ignorance of what God has commanded and promised in His precious Word. We have souls to be saved or lost, and with the greatest earnestness we should inquire, "What shall I do in order to obtain eternal life?" At the best, life is but short, and it is necessary that we should live this short life in harmony with the law of God, which is the law of the universe. We must have ears to hear, and hearts to understand, what the Spirit saith unto the churches.

The angels of God attain unto no higher knowledge than to know the will of God; and it is their greatest delight to accomplish the perfect will of the heavenly Father. Fallen man has the privilege of becoming intelligent in regard to the will of God. While probationary time is granted us, we should put our faculties to the very highest use, that we may make of ourselves all that it is possible; and while we endeavor to reach a high standard of intelligence, we should feel our dependence upon God, for without His grace, our efforts cannot bring lasting benefit. It is through the grace of Christ that we are to be overcomers; through the merits of His blood we are to be of that number whose names will not be blotted out of the book of life.

Those who are final overcomers will have the life that runs parallel with the life of God, and wear the crown of the victor. When such great and eternal reward awaits us, we should run the race with patience, looking unto Jesus, the author and finisher of our faith.—*Signs of the Times*, June 15, 1891.

WALKING WITH HIM IN WHITE

Thou hast a few names even in Sardis which have not defiled their garments; and they shall walk with me in white: for they are worthy. Rev. 3:4.

Thank God, He can keep His people in a place where they shall not defile their garments. If we submit to Christ, we shall be kept unspotted from the world. "Then shall we know, if we follow on to know the Lord: his going forth is prepared as the morning" (Hosea 6:3). We are to follow on. We are not to rest content with the capabilities and the knowledge of today. All the inhabitants of the universe are watching, as in these last days God is preparing a people to stand in the judgment. Let us ask God to clothe us with the robe of Christ's righteousness, that we may be prepared for the coming of the Son of man.

Of those who have not defiled their garments, Christ says, "They shall walk with me in white: for they are worthy." Through infinite sacrifice made in our behalf, we may have an abundance of grace. God has a whole heaven full for us. All He asks is that by living faith we receive His promises, saying: "I do believe. I do accept the blessings which Thou hast for those who love Thee."

"He that overcometh, the same shall be clothed in white raiment; and I will not"—oh, how precious is that "not"!—"I will not blot out his name out of the book of life, but I will confess his name before my Father, and before his angels" (Rev. 3:5). When the gates of the city of God swing back on their glittering hinges, and the nations who have kept the truth shall enter in, Christ will be there to welcome us, to call us the blessed of the Father, because we have overcome. He will welcome us before the Father, and before His angels. As we enter the kingdom of God, there to spend eternity, the trials and the difficulties and the perplexities that we have had here will sink into insignificance. Our life will measure with the life of God.—*General Conference Bulletin*, Apr. 6, 1903.

HAVING OUR NAMES
IN THE BOOK OF LIFE

He that overcometh, the same shall be clothed in white raiment; and I will not blot out his name out of the book of life, but I will confess his name before my Father, and before his angels. Rev. 3:5.

The expression "he that overcometh" indicates that there is something for every one of us to overcome. The overcomer is to be clothed in the white raiment of Christ's righteousness, and of Him it is written: "I will not blot out his name out of the book of life, but I will confess his name before my Father, and before his angels." Oh, what a privilege it is to be an overcomer, and to have our names presented before the Father by the Saviour Himself! And when, as overcomers, we shall be "clothed in white raiment," the Lord will acknowledge our faithfulness as verily as in the days of the early Christian church. He acknowledged the "few names even in Sardis" who had "not defiled their garments"(Rev. 3:4); and we shall walk with Him in white, for through His atoning sacrifice we shall be accounted worthy.

My dear friends, in view of these encouraging promises, how earnestly should we strive to perfect a character that will enable us to stand before the Son of God! Only those who are clothed in the garments of His righteousness will be able to endure the glory of His presence when He shall appear with "power and great glory."

It means much to be an overcomer. The besetments of the enemy and all his evil agencies must be firmly resisted. Every moment we must be on guard. Not for one instant are we to lose sight of Christ, and of His power to save in the hour of trial. Our hand must be placed in His, that we may be upheld by the power of His might. . . .

The True Witness declares: "Behold, I have set before thee an open door" (verse 8). Let us thank God with heart and soul and voice; and let us learn to approach unto Him as through an open door, believing that we may come freely with our petitions, and that He will hear and answer. It is by a living faith in His power to help, that we shall receive strength to fight the battles of the Lord with the confident assurance of victory.—*Review and Herald*, July 9, 1908.

KEPT SAFE IN THE HOUR OF TEMPTATION

Because thou hast kept the word of my patience, I also will keep thee from the hour of temptation, which shall come upon all the world, to try them that dwell upon the earth. Rev. 3:10.

A battle is continually going on between the forces for good and the forces for evil, between the angels of God and the fallen angels. We are beset before and behind, on the right hand and on the left. The conflict that we are passing through is the last we shall have in this world. We are now in the midst of it. Two parties are striving for the supremacy. In this conflict we cannot be neutral. We must stand either on one side or on the other. If we take our position on the side of Christ, if we acknowledge Him before the world in word and work, we are bearing a living testimony as to whom we have chosen to serve and honor. In this important period of earth's history, we cannot afford to leave anyone in uncertainty as to whose side we are on. . . .

"Because thou hast kept the word of my patience, I also will keep thee from the hour of temptation, which shall come upon all the world, to try them that dwell upon the earth." In this scripture is brought to view the hour of temptation that is to try them that dwell upon the earth. We are now living in this trying hour. There is no escape for any from this conflict. If in your life there are defective traits of character that you are not striving to overcome, you may be assured that the enemy will endeavor to take advantage of them; for he is watching vigilantly, seeking to spoil the faith of everyone.

In order to gain the victory over every besetment of the enemy, we must lay hold on a power that is out of and beyond ourselves. We must maintain a constant, living connection with Christ, who has power to give victory to every soul that will maintain an attitude of faith and humility. If we are self-sufficient, and think that we may go on just as we please, and yet hope to come out on the right side finally, we shall find that we have made a terrible mistake. As those who hope to receive the overcomer's reward, we must press forward in the Christian warfare, though at every advance we meet with opposition.—*Review and Herald,* July 9, 1908.

A PILLAR IN GOD'S TEMPLE

Him that overcometh will I make a pillar in the temple of my God, and he shall go no more out: and I will write upon him the name of my God, and the name of the city of my God, which is new Jerusalem, which cometh down out of heaven from my God: and I will write upon him my new name. Rev. 3:12.

It may seem wonderful to us that Christ should reveal Himself to John as He is, strange that He should thus address Himself to the churches. But we should remember that the church, enfeebled and defective though it is, is the object of Christ's supreme regard. Constantly He watches over it with tender solicitude, and strengthens it by His Holy Spirit. Will we, as members of His church, allow Him to impress our minds and to work through us to His glory? Will we heed the messages He addresses to the church? Let us determine to be among the number who shall meet Him with joy at His coming, and not among those who "shall wail because of him" (Rev. 1:7). Let us make certain our redemption by obeying the messages that He gives to His church.

Christ bears to the church the words of consolation: "Because thou hast kept the word of my patience, I also will keep thee from the hour of temptation, which shall come upon all the world, to try them that dwell upon the earth. Behold, I come quickly: hold that fast which thou hast, that no man take thy crown. Him that overcometh will I make a pillar in the temple of my God, and he shall go no more out: and I will write upon him the name of my God, and the name of the city of my God, which is new Jerusalem, which cometh down out of heaven from my God: and I will write upon him my new name" (Rev. 3:10-12).

Let us strive to obtain an abundant entrance into the kingdom of our Lord. Let us diligently study the gospel that Christ came in person to present to John on the Isle of Patmos—the gospel that is termed "The Revelation of Jesus Christ, which God gave unto him, to shew unto his servants things which must shortly come to pass" (Rev. 1:1). Let us remember always that "blessed is he that readeth, and they that hear the words of this prophecy, and keep those things which are written therein: for the time is at hand" (verse 3).—*Signs of the Times*, Feb. 4, 1903.

A SEAT UPON HIS THRONE

To him that overcometh will I grant to sit with me in my throne, even as I also overcame, and am set down with my Father in his throne. Rev. 3:21.

We can overcome. Yes; fully, entirely. Jesus died to make a way of escape for us, that we might overcome every fault, resist every temptation, and sit down at last with Him in His throne. It is our privilege to have faith and salvation. The power of God has not decreased. It would be just as freely bestowed now as formerly; but the church have lost their faith to claim, their energy to wrestle, as did Jacob, crying, "I will not let thee go, except thou bless me" (Gen. 32:26). Enduring faith has been dying away. It must be revived in the hearts of God's people. They must claim the blessing. Faith, living faith, always leads upward to God and glory; unbelief, downward to darkness and death.

Many are so absorbed in their worldly cares and perplexities that they have little time to pray, and feel but little interest in prayer. They may observe the form of worship, but the spirit of true supplication is lacking. Such have departed widely from the Pattern. Jesus our example was much in prayer; and oh, how earnest, how fervent were His petitions! If He, the beloved Son of God, was moved to such earnestness, such agony, in our behalf, how much more need that we, who are dependent upon Heaven for all our strength, have our whole souls stirred to wrestle with God.

We should not be satisfied until every known sin is confessed, then it is our privilege and duty to believe that God accepts us. We must not wait for others to press through the darkness and obtain the victory for us to enjoy. Such enjoyment will not be lasting. God must be served from principle instead of from feeling. Morning and evening we should obtain the victory for ourselves, in our own families. Our daily labor should not keep us from this. We must take time to pray, and as we pray, believe that God hears us. We may not at all times feel the immediate answer, but then it is that faith is tried. We are proved to see whether we will trust in God, whether we have living, abiding faith.—
Review and Herald, Sept. 4, 1883.

VICTORY THROUGH CHRIST

Forasmuch then as the children are partakers of flesh and blood, he also himself likewise took part of the same; that through death he might destroy him that had the power of death, that is, the devil; and deliver them who through fear of death were all their lifetime subject to bondage. Heb. 2:14, 15.

The fall of man filled all heaven with sorrow, and the heart of Jesus was moved with infinite compassion for the lost world, the ruined race. He beheld man plunged in sin and misery, and knew that he had not moral power to overcome in his own behalf the power of his unsleeping enemy. In divine love and pity He came to earth to fight our battles for us; for He alone could conquer the adversary. He came to unite man with God, to impart divine strength to the repenting soul, and from the manger to Calvary to pass over the path which man would travel, at every step giving man a perfect example of what he should do, presenting in His character what humanity might become when united with divinity.

But many say that Jesus was not like us, that He was not as we are in the world, that He was divine, and therefore we cannot overcome as He overcame. But this is not true; "for verily he took not on him the nature of angels; but he took on him the seed of Abraham. . . . For in that he himself hath suffered being tempted, he is able to succour them that are tempted" (Heb. 2:16-18). Christ knows the sinner's trials; He knows his temptations. He took upon Himself our nature; He was tempted in all points like as we are. He has wept, He was a man of sorrows, and acquainted with grief.

As a man He lived upon earth. As a man He ascended to heaven. As a man He is the substitute of humanity. As a man He liveth to make intercession for us. As a man He will come again with kingly power and glory to receive those who love Him, and for whom He is now preparing a place. We should rejoice and give thanks that God "hath appointed a day, in the which he will judge the world in righteousness by that man whom he hath ordained" (Acts 17:31).—*Bible Echo*, Nov. 1, 1892.

BY THE BLOOD OF THE LAMB

And they overcame him by the blood of the Lamb, and by the word of their testimony; and they loved not their lives unto the death. Rev. 12:11.

Let us consider the life and suffering of our precious Saviour in our behalf, and remember that if we are not willing to endure trial, toil, and conflict, if we are not willing to be partakers with Christ of His sufferings, we shall be found unworthy of a seat upon His throne.

We have everything to gain in the conflict with our mighty foe, and we dare not for a moment yield to his temptations. We know that in our own strength it is not possible for us to succeed; but as Christ humbled Himself, and took upon Himself our nature, He is acquainted with our necessities, and has Himself borne the heaviest temptations that man will have to bear, has conquered the enemy in resisting his suggestions, in order that man may learn how to be conqueror. He was clothed with a body like ours, and in every respect suffered what man will suffer, and very much more. We shall never be called upon to suffer as Christ suffered; for the sins not of one, but the sins of the whole world were laid upon Christ. He endured humiliation, reproach, suffering, and death, that we by following His example might inherit all things.

Christ is our pattern, the perfect and holy example that has been given us to follow. We can never equal the pattern; but we may imitate and resemble it according to our ability. When we fall, all helpless, suffering in consequence of our realization of the sinfulness of sin; when we humble ourselves before God, afflicting our souls by true repentance and contrition; when we offer our fervent prayers to God in the name of Christ, we shall as surely be received by the Father, as we sincerely make a complete surrender of our all to God. We should realize in our inmost soul that all our efforts in and of ourselves will be utterly worthless; for it is only in the name and strength of the Conqueror that we shall be overcomers.—*Review and Herald*, Feb. 5, 1895.

FOLLOWING THE PATTERN

For even hereunto were ye called: because Christ also suffered for us, leaving us an example, that ye should follow his steps: who did no sin, neither was guile found in his mouth: who, when he was reviled, reviled not again; when he suffered, he threatened not; but committed himself to him that judgeth righteously: who his own self bare our sins in his own body on the tree, that we, being dead to sins, should live unto righteousness: by whose stripes ye were healed. 1 Peter 2:21-24.

In all our afflictions Jesus was afflicted, and the Captain of our salvation was made perfect through suffering. In this life we shall be proved to see whether or not we shall be able to bear the test of God. Satan's temptations will come upon us, and we shall be tried, but the question of most importance to us is Shall we be overcome? or shall we be overcomers? . . . Like our great Example, we may be able to meet Satan with the weapon of God's Word, saying to him as he tempts us to do evil, "It is written" (Matt. 4:4).

Satan knows better than many professed Christians what is written, for he is a diligent student of the Bible, and he works to pervert the truth, and lead men into the paths of disobedience. He leads men to neglect the searching of the Word of God; for he knows that it testifies against him, that his works are evil. It describes him as the apostate angel who fell from heaven, and drew many of the hosts of heaven after him in a course of rebellion against their Creator.

Satan is seeking continually to draw away the minds of men from God and His Word. He knows that if he can cause men to neglect the Word of God, he can soon cause them to depart from its precepts, and finally to forget their Maker. They will then take the suggestions and instructions of the adversary of God and man, and evil men and evil angels will form a confederacy against the God of heaven.

Those who would be loyal to God will be subject to trials and temptations; but if they are truly alive unto God, and have their life hid with Christ in God, they will also know what it is to have the blessings which God bestows upon the faithful and obedient.—*Signs of the Times*, Aug. 28, 1893.

VICTORY ASSURED

These things I have spoken unto you, that in me ye might have peace. In the world ye shall have tribulation: but be of good cheer; I have overcome the world. John 16:33.

While on earth there will be no escape from conflicts and temptations; but in every storm we have a sure refuge. Jesus has told us, "In the world ye shall have tribulation: but be of good cheer; I have overcome the world." The forces of Satan are marshaled against us, and we have to meet a diligent foe; but if we take heed to the admonition of Christ, we shall be safe. "Watch and pray, that ye enter not into temptation" (Matt. 26:41). There are foes to be resisted and overcome, but Jesus is by our side, ready to strengthen us for every attack. "This is the victory that overcometh the world, even our faith" (1 John 5:4).

Faith sees Jesus standing as our mediator at the right hand of God. Faith beholds the mansions that Jesus has gone to prepare for those who love Him. Faith sees the robe and the crown all prepared for the overcomer. Faith hears the song of the redeemed, and brings eternal glories near. We must come close to Jesus in loving obedience if we would see the King in His beauty.

There is peace in believing, and joy in the Holy Ghost. Believe! Believe! My soul cries, Believe! Rest in God. He is able to keep that which you have committed to Him, and will bring you off more than conqueror through Him that has loved you.

But remember that everyone who shall be found with the wedding garment on will have come out of great tribulation. The mighty surges of temptation will beat upon all. But the long night of watching, of toil, of hardship, is nearly past. Christ is soon to come. Get ready! The angels of God are seeking to attract you from yourself and from earthly things. Let them not labor in vain. Faith, living faith, is what you need; the faith that works by love and purifies the soul. Remember Calvary and the awful, the infinite sacrifice there made for man. Jesus now invites you to come to Him, just as you are, and make Him your strength and your everlasting friend.—*Review and Herald*, Apr. 17, 1894.

THE CHURCH TRIUMPHANT

Behold, he cometh with clouds; and every eye shall see him, and they also which pierced him: and all kindreds of the earth shall wail because of him. Even so, Amen. I am Alpha and Omega, the beginning and the ending, saith the Lord, which is, and which was, and which is to come, the Almighty. Rev. 1:7, 8.

God's way is to make the day of small things the beginning of the triumph of truth and righteousness. For this reason none need be elated by a prosperous beginning, nor cast down by apparent feebleness. God is to His people riches, fullness, and power. His purposes for His chosen people are, like the eternal hills, firm and immovable.

Remember that human might did not establish the church of God, neither can human might destroy it. From age to age the Holy Spirit is an overflowing fountain of life. . . . There is victory for all who strive lawfully, in perfect harmony with the law of God. They will triumph over all opposition. As they carry forward God's work in the face of all foes, they will be given the guardianship of holy angels.

Christ has pledged Himself to help all who join His army, to cooperate with Him in fighting against visible and invisible foes. He has promised that they shall be joint heirs with Him to an immortal inheritance, that they shall reign as kings and priests before God. Those who are willing to share in this life the humiliation of the Saviour will share with Him in His glory. Those who choose to suffer affliction with the people of God rather than to enjoy the pleasures of sin for a season will be given a place with Christ on His throne.

Hold fast the Word of life. The tempest of opposition will spend itself by its own fury. The clamor will die away. Carry forward the Master's work bravely and cheerfully. The Father above, who watches over His chosen ones with the tenderest solicitude, will bless the efforts made in His name. His work will never cease until its completion amid the triumphant shout, "Grace, grace unto it."—*Signs of the Times*, Nov. 14, 1900.

HEIRS OF THE KING

He that overcometh shall inherit all things; and I will be his God, and he shall be my son. Rev. 21:7.

Be not discouraged; be not fainthearted. Although you may have temptations; although you may be beset by the wily foe; yet, if you have the fear of God before you, angels that excel in strength will be sent to your help, and you can be more than a match for the powers of darkness. Jesus lives. He has died to make a way of escape for the fallen race; and He lives today to make intercession for us, that we may be exalted to His own right hand. Have hope in God. The world is traveling the broad way; and as you travel in the narrow way, and have principalities and powers to contend with, and the opposition of foes to meet, remember that there is provision made for you. Help has been laid upon One that is mighty; and through Him you can conquer.

Come out from among them and be separate, says God, and I will receive you, and ye shall be sons and daughters of the Lord Almighty. What a promise is this! It is a pledge to you that you shall become members of the royal family, heirs of the heavenly kingdom. If a person is honored by, or becomes connected with, any of the monarchs of earth, how it goes the rounds of the periodicals of the day, and excites the envy of those who do not think themselves so fortunate. But here is One who is king over all, the monarch of the universe, the originator of every good thing; and He says to us, I will make you My sons and daughters; I will unite you to Myself; you shall become members of the royal family, and children of the heavenly King.

And then says Paul, "Having therefore these promises, dearly beloved, let us cleanse ourselves from all filthiness of the flesh and spirit, perfecting holiness in the fear of God" (2 Cor. 7:1). Why should we not do this, when we have such an inducement, the privilege of becoming children of the Most High God, the privilege of calling the God of heaven our Father?—*Review and Herald*, May 31, 1870.

VICTORIOUS AT LAST

For yet a little while, and he that shall come will come, and will not tarry. Now the just shall live by faith: but if any man draw back, my soul shall have no pleasure in him. Heb. 10:37, 38.

Fellow pilgrim, we are still amid the shadows and turmoil of earthly activities; but soon our Saviour is to appear to bring deliverance and rest. Let us by faith behold the blessed hereafter, as pictured by the hand of God. He who died for the sins of the world, is opening wide the gates of Paradise to all who believe on Him. Soon the battle will have been fought, the victory won. Soon we shall see Him in whom our hopes of eternal life are centered. And in His presence the trials and sufferings of this life will seem as nothingness. The former things "shall not be remembered, nor come into mind" (Isa. 65:17). "Cast not away therefore your confidence, which hath great recompense of reward. For ye have need of patience, that, after ye have done the will of God, ye might receive the promise. For yet a little while, and he that shall come will come, and will not tarry" (Heb. 10:35-37). . . .

Look up, look up, and let your faith continually increase. Let this faith guide you along the narrow path that leads through the gates of the city into the great beyond, the wide, unbounded future of glory that is for the redeemed. "Be patient therefore, brethren, unto the coming of the Lord. Behold, the husbandman waiteth for the precious fruit of the earth, and hath long patience for it, until he receive the early and latter rain. Be ye also patient; stablish your hearts: for the coming of the Lord draweth nigh" (James 5:7, 8).

The nations of the saved will know no other law than the law of heaven. All will be a happy, united family, clothed with the garments of praise and thanksgiving. Over the scene the morning stars will sing together, and the sons of God will shout for joy, while God and Christ will unite in proclaiming, There shall be no more sin, neither shall there be any more death.—*Review and Herald*, July 1, 1915.

SCRIPTURE INDEX